THE ALHAMBRA

BY

WASHINGTON IRVING

WITH AN INTRODUCTION BY ANDREW B. MYERS

ILLUSTRATED BY F.O.C. DARLEY

SLEEPY HOLLOW PRESS

A FACSIMILE EDITION

Library of Congress Cataloguing in Publication Data

Irving, Washington, 1783-1859.
  The Alhambra.

  Reprint. Originally published: Author's rev. ed.
New York: G.P. Putnam, 1851. With new introd.
  I. Title
PS2056.A1 1982   813.2   82-5644
ISBN 0-912882-48-4   AACR2

Introduction Copyright © 1982 by Sleepy Hollow
Restorations, Inc.

For information, address the publisher:

SLEEPY HOLLOW PRESS
Sleepy Hollow Restorations, Inc.
150 White Plains Road
Tarrytown, New York 10591

ISBN 0-912882-48-4

Library of Congress Catalogue Card Number: 82-5644

First Printing

Manufactured in the United States of America

INTRODUCTION

When Washington Irving (1783-1859) wrote "dreams" as the very last word in his *Alhambra* of 1832 he let a genie out of this Andalusian literary bottle. The magic of his storyteller's pen had created a real, if modest, force for the good, the beautiful and, granting him a Romantic author's poetic license, for the true as well. For not only had he given the world's readers a treasure of exotic sketches and tales, the finest of which in timeless fashion still hold interest, but the actual Alhambra that inspired them may well have been saved from further official disinterest, and thus decay, by the sympathetic attentions his little book almost at once attracted to it.

Daydreams of "castles in Spain" have beguiled the English-speaking world for centuries. None of these often ruinous relics of a bygone age has been more spectacular in its past than the great Alhambra, crowning the city of Granada in the far south. And in its busy present this genuinely storied palace-cum-fortress, restored by the state as a historic monument and splendid showcase, continues as one of the wonders of modern Iberia. Indeed it was just such a prize and more, earlier during the long medieval centuries of impassioned conflict on the peninsula between Christian and Moslem.

Ironically, without that prolonged and destructive clash of crusaders and would-be conquerors, from either side, almost certainly the Alhambra and its extraordinary precincts would never have been constructed, damaged and rebuilt, until in its pre-Renaissance glory it was all but unique in the vast and varied Mediterranean world. In our time it has rightly been said this "apogee of Moorish architecture" survives as "the only large scale domestic complex preserved from the first thousand years of Islam."[1] This is the textbook side of things. But also, the Alhambra's interior decorations, and its fountains and gardens, and its beflowered Generalife retreat, are sensuously comely. It is this striking aspect too Irving had in mind when he wrote, "Here then I am, nestled in one of the most remarkable, romantic and delicious spots in the world."[2]

The highwater mark for the already ancient pile, as stately pleasure dome but even more as potentate's seat of government was, at least as far as the West was concerned, its capture in 1483 by the husband and wife team of Spanish monarchs, Ferdinand and Isabella. Then the huge interlocking structure was surrendered to them by Boabdil, last Moorish king of the longtime impregnable Islamic stronghold of Granada. After tight siege during 1492, that fertile province, mountainous but stretching down to the sea opposite North Africa, once fallen completed for continental Hispania a reunion of severed parts in the triumph of La Reconquista, the reconquest of all once Christian territories from the entrenched Infidel, who had been a peaceable or hostile neighbor in turn.

This successful conclusion to a widely proclaimed holy war was, as Irving musingly notes in the pages that follow, celebrated in Te Deum style throughout Europe. Almost simultaneously that turbulent family of nations found itself an Old World, adjusting with excitement (and greed) to the return the previous autumn of Columbus with news of a *novus mundus*, a whole New World, discovered but yet to be conquered. Whether Iberian vintages were good or not these early 1490's proved immaterial as toasts followed toasts to the beckoning new horizons for Castile and the Cross.

It was these fabulous moments for Christendom that Irving had, just before turning to his *Alhambra*, which is by contrast essentially a belletristic endeavor, narrated as serious chronicler in *The Life and Voyages of Christopher Columbus* (1828) and *The Conquest of Granada* (1829). Unmistakably, before he moved on to capture the sights, sounds and stories of the once royal Alhambra, now all but abandoned to chance sightseers and to squatters, Washington Irving had become a dedicated Hispanophile. The end result would be a career within a career that one authority has described thus:

> Altogether on Spain Irving wrote some three thousand pages and approximately one million words, amounting to about one third of his total writings. Although he is still known as the traditional interpreter in American literature of old England, he devoted far more space and effort to his books on Spain. Nor are these inferior. The *Columbus* and the *Granada* are the equals of *Bracebridge Hall* and *Tales of a Trdveller*, and except for one or two classic tales, such as "Rip Van Winkle" or "The Legend of Sleepy Hollow," they include some of his best writing. Apart from these, the *Alhambra* is the peer of *The Sketch Book*. To understand Irving we must recognize the importance of his writings on Spain.[3]

Symbolic of this importance is the Daniel Chester French monument put up a long generation ago at the head of Sunnyside Lane in Irvington, New York, the gate road to Irving's "Sunnyside" itself. Flanking a bronze bust of Irving, on the marble facade are two full-length figures in bas-relief, obviously chosen to represent the most famous aspects of his work. The immortal and local Rip is one. The other is the ill-fated Boabdil, last master of far-off Granada and its incomparable Alhambra.

Washington Irving's own road to Granada began as a happenstance though most welcome opportunity. As a fortyish expatriate in Paris in the mid-1820's, with the encouraging fame of "Geoffrey Crayon's" *Sketch Book* (1819-1820) behind him and the comedic notoriety of "Diedrich Knickerbocker's" *History of New-York* (1809) even further back, he had come to a professional crossroads. As a storyteller he was beginning to repeat himself. Publishers on both sides of the Atlantic were getting edgy. Critics were raising eyebrows. Just at this trying juncture a letter arrived from Alexander Everett, United States Minister to Spain, inviting his accomplished countryman to Madrid, hopefully to translate a Spanish scholar's ongoing series documenting the epic life of Columbus. Advantageous cover as an attaché was promised.

Irving pondered. Matters Spanish had long intrigued him in readings from chivalric romances to *Don Quixote*. He knew the musical language already. And strangely, no full-length description had even yet been put together in English on the heroic admiral's exploits. In short order Irving headed for the border, caught by the idea and the circumstances. For the next years, indeed for most of the rest of his life, he would be a biographer and historian before anything else. And as the quotation above attests, in all this the impact made on him by Spain was enormous and lasting.

Once rooted in Iberia, Irving came to know the inspiring Alhambra from two happy sojourns in Granada, as part of longer trips. In the spring of 1928 he spent leisurely weeks in the city, most of the time scrambling about the walled and towered "Palacio Arabe" part of the massive hilltop construct. He was less curious about the broken down fortress which was contiguous. And by author's instinct he took hurried notes, especially after the luck of meeting "Mateo Ximénes," self-proclaimed *hijo* of the Alhambra, who poured into his ears piquant gossip and regional folktales. Irving's travelling companion after leaving Granada was David Wilkie, a renowned Scottish painter who shared with him also the experience of appreciating great Spanish canvases visited on the way. A year later, in the early summer of 1829 after the rugged trip he describes graphically in "The Journey" that follows, Irving returned but with a new companion, Prince Dolgorouki, a minor Russian diplomat in Madrid. This time Irving would remain for several months lodged by courtesy of the absentee governor in rooms above the pretty, inside garden of Lindaraxa. Today normally this suite is closed to the touring public but one can see above the door a plaque remembering Irving's fruitful stay. It reads:

WASHINGTON IRVING
Escribo En Estas Habitaciones Sus
CUENTOS DE LA ALHAMBRA
En El Año De 1829

Strictly speaking Irving did not sit down to fashion

his Crayonesque local color and folklorist pages until settled in London later as a real diplomat, Secretary at the embassy. It is clear however that beforehand he had with profit absorbed the charged atmosphere of his once regal surroundings, and been teased into jotting down fragments of sketches and stories, his and others, in ready notebooks. Published finally in 1832, the first *Alhambra* (for there are two versions, with the later edition in 1851 substantially reworked, as Irving says in his "Preface") was, in the workaday fashion of much publishing then, rather plainly put together. It came out, in the United States and in Britain, in two volumes, in boards with paper labels, and without illustrations. Included was a dedication to friend Wilkie which would, after his death, be replaced in 1851. Much of that original salute is quoted next for its clues to the catalysts that helped the 1832 collection quickly become a hit. William Hickling Prescott, the historian, would dub accurately this return to impressionistic prose Irving's "beautiful Spanish Sketch-book."

You may remember that, in the course of the rambles we once took together about some of the old cities of Spain, particularly Toledo and Seville, we frequently remarked the mixture of the Saracenic with the Gothic, remaining from the time of the Moors, and were more than once struck with incidents and scenes in the streets, that brought to mind passages in the "Arabian Nights." You then urged me to write something illustrative of these peculiarities; "something in the Haroun Alraschid style," that should have a dash of that Arabian spice which pervades every thing in Spain. I call this to mind to show you that you are, in some degree, responsible for the present work; in which I have given a few "Arabesque" sketches and tales, taken from the life, or founded on local traditions, and mostly struck off during a residence in one of the most legendary and Morisco-Spanish places of the Peninsula.[4]

There is room next for only brief mention of two pertinent facts. The international popularity of the *Alhambra*, in English or in translation, gradually forced the hand of laggard officialdom and the palace was put more to rights than it long had been. Also, the realistic passages of description proved valuable as a well-written guide, a fact visible still today in the omnipresence of copies, many replete with color plates, wherever in Spain the world's tourists throng.

Irving himself in Spain is a longer story than need be retold step by step. It must suffice to say his return at last, and to an applauding America, in 1832, as *The Alhambra* was just off the press, argued the end of European adventures. And settling into his cherished "Sunnyside" provided an anchor alongside the Hudson. But in 1842, to Irving's astonishment, President Tyler appointed him Envoy Extraordinary and Minister Plenipotentiary to the Court of Isabella II of Spain. Back he went, conscious of the honor, conscientious about his duties, but unlikely to write much except dispatches, and letters home. It would be pleasant to add that "His Excellency" did make a triumphal return to Granada, but official responsibilities and intermittent illness kept Irving tied to the capital and the troubled court. The year 1846 found Irving home again, grateful to leave all pressures behind but those of his own quiet choice. Alas, it soon proved that return could not mean retirement, for his chief income had to be from books, and his inactive years of late, at least as author, had cost him reader interest to such an extent that his shelf of past works was in serious disarray.

At this low point in a long career (who could have guessed the busy, successful dozen years ahead?) there came another fateful offer, one as pregnant for Irving's future as Everett's unexpected invitation to Madrid some twenty years before. Maine-born George Palmer Putnam (1814-1872), newly the founder in New York City of the publishing house that still bears his honorable name, came up with a workable arrangement for an idea already in part in Irving's head but in full one novel in American publishing history. Why not combine Irving-Putnam forces on an ambitious Author's Revised Edition (ARE), a multi-volumed, uniform collection of reconsidered texts, each with the valuable addition, where thought fitting, of a prefatory essay addressed to the author's faithful "Worthy Reader"? Such freshening up could even, the shrewd Putnam argued, mean promising new interest among a younger audience too. And he was prepared, cautious Yankee though he had to be in his uncertain business, to put his money where his mouth was.

The financial arrangements he worked out gradually with the elderly and anxious writer, and with nephew Pierre Munro Irving who bargained hard for royalties, were for that era (and ours) most generous. And they included on Putnam's side the right to publish *illustrated* single volumes without sharing the extra profits —if any. The end result of the whole extended project, especially given the capital investment and the chancy market, could have been not only a literary embarrassment but a publishing disaster. Happily instead, this Putnam-sponsored ARE proved an idea that had found its time. Completed in fifteen volumes over 1848-1851, with a revised *Alhambra* as its final flourish, Irving's Author's Revised Edition was a resounding success with bookbuyer and bookkeeper, the first of its kind in our cultural annals. Putnam as enterprising publisher enhanced his reputation as a sound if visionary businessman. Irving as author won a new lease on life with critics and readers, among these grandchildren of men and women he had first charmed in youth. Irving the man could smile discreetly on his way to the bank.[5]

GPP's gamble on an "old" author, just as the American Renaissance was about to peak in the golden decade of the 1850's—with the appearance of major works by younger writers like Hawthorne and Melville, Emerson and Thoreau, Longfellow and Whitman, among others—was a measure of the spirit of daring that was making New York City a great magnet which drew in the multiple skills, in pressroom and editorial offices, that increasingly made it the major publishing center of the country. These divers competitors, from every point of the compass, across mid-century filled the book, magazine and newspaper worlds in the city to the bursting.

There is place here for a look at only one special aspect of all this motion and progress—book illustration. Without its special contribution then the present handsome facsimile volume today's reader holds could never have existed, for it had to have an equally elegant original. And that, an illustrated *Alhambra* that first in 1851 followed the conclusion of the parent ARE, added to the gifts of Irving and of Putnam those of Felix Octavius Carr Darley, the greatest American book illustrator of the age.

The third side on the equilateral triangle of talents that stand under that apex of the Author's Revised Edition of Irving, its illustrated volumes, was the young F.O.C. Darley (1822-1888). In his precocious prime, he was the premier American artist devoted to that challenging aspect of the making of impressive books, *qua* books, textual illustration. His extensive career as native craftsman and creative artist is a success story in the classic tradition of the American Dream. Born in Philadelphia to an immigrant family with a prehistory in the theatre, like the young Irving forty years before, he early showed, though he too would be only simply educated, a spontaneous gift of magnitude, in his case for drawing. Unlike the less decisive Irving he made the most of it in a hurry.

Darley's native city, a force in publishing since Franklin's time, gave him ample opportunity to practice his inborn skills with pencil and brush, engraver's and etcher's tools. In but little time his superlative abilities called attention to themselves, especially since his mastery in designing lively, detailed drawings, perfect for transferral into printed form in newspapers, periodicals and bound volumes, coincided in the United States with a revolution in mechanical improvements in printing processes. These last in turn supported a maturing of book illustration, particularly via woodcuts, that rivalled Europe's contemporary best.[6]

Recognized by early manhood for his touch of genius, Darley was soon summoned to New York. His arrival in 1848 coincided with the completion of ARE contractual details between the two Irvings and George Palmer Putnam. These included, remember, the publisher's right to any extra profit from any illustrated volumes. Surely the optimistic GPP saw to the inclusion of that balancing clause. And when he looked about for a surefire illustrator there was Darley, already working in Manhattan, on Printers Row near City Hall or in his own digs. By now his signature or sign on a cartoon or design was welcomed as a hallmark of quality. The publisher's choice was easy.

Regrettably not enough documentation survives to supply details of inevitable three-way conferences that had to follow among author, artist, and manager of business details. These meetings had to have included not only trips to downtown offices but upriver visits to Sunnyside, since Sleepy Hollow Restorations carefully preserves there a pencil sketch by Darley, dated 1848, showing Irving, drawn from life, as Squire *in situ*, relaxed and convivial in gentleman farmer's rig. This genial mood is a point to pause on. For whatever the reason for calling him Felix to begin with, the name proved prophetic of a rich sense of humor in the man and artist. In this priceless regard, as in technical skills, Darley could not have been better equipped to illustrate Irving's tales.

Both had a natural vein of merriment, one essentially warm and kindly, even if on occasion a wholesome satiric purpose called for more bite—if only to be true to truant human nature. Overall it is clear, in Irving's full canon, and in manifold commissions Darley undertook beyond the ARE, neither chose to sit in inquisitional judgment on fellow men or women. Good-natured laughter and forgiving smiles came easily to the narrator of *Alhambra*. Darley's numerous drawings for this volume, as for *Sketch Book*, *Knickerbocker's History*, and *Tales of a Traveller*, the four ARE's Putnam opted for, were bound to be a mirror image of the whimsical "Don" Washington Irving's mixed bag of colorful Alhambran materials.

This success is the more interesting because Darley's keen eyes never saw Spain. The one trip he made to Europe, in 1866-1867, included southward only the French Riviera and most of Italy. Nevertheless his fifteen *Alhambra* illustrations, including the frontispiece, hold our eyes with their truly Hispanic vivacity, or languor, plus authentic detail. He must have had good models to guide his romantic imagination, found both in Irving's conversation (as well as text) or in such widely popular engravings by contemporary Hispanophile artists as the British academicians John F. Lewis and David Roberts. It would seem impossible otherwise to have gotten so correct, even as shadowy background, many intricacies of the figured marble, ornamental plaster (atauriques), carved wooden lattices, tile in geometric patterns, and "mocárabes" (arch-shaped designs) so characteristic of the ageless Moorish fashions in the Alhambra's vaulting halls, long corridors and hideaway chambers. But above all, Darley's people, be they peasant or prince, maiden, monk or mailed warrior, are convincingly lifelike and appealing. Heightened dramatic touches were to be expected then.

The one disappointment worth mentioning is that congratulatory messages do not survive to attest to Irving's delight in having his "oriental" pages so well captured in equally picturesque or fittingly robust illustrations, large or small. Surely Putnam's vanished files, or Darley's elusive private papers, must once have held such. Thus far not even a hurried but explicit note has come to light. Even so, another form of honest flattery has, and is very much there to see at Sunnyside. For Irving kept Darley's work sketches on his walls.

On the first floor, in the little alcove beyond the Mid-Victorian parlor, a kind of simple picture gallery contains a score of Darley sketches for ARE illustrations. Among these are seven for *Alhambra*, wash drawings on paper, which when fully executed by engravers showed a few more details added. The viewer, with the present clear facsimile in hand, can compare for example the Spanish dancers (f. p. 25) in final form with the almost-finished earlier stage, to see the deftness of composition, ease of line and warmth of spirit with which FOCD finally transferred Irving's *posada* revellers to paper in another medium. How well met were these two aspiring native American artists—and their supportive Yankee publisher!

In the 1851 *Alhambra*, the author's last word so to speak on a favorite subject, the essentially autobiographical "Journey" was, like its shorter predecessor of 1832, designed to ease the distant and perhaps untravelled reader into a brilliant, and for the typical *norteamericano* strikingly foreign—if compellingly attractive—Andalusian setting. It takes care not to drive but leads invitingly, in a polished essay-sketch that is still sometimes separately printed. The initial pieces that follow, with Irving's familiar picturesque touches, and with the right panoramic views interwoven with veracious history (even if here and there like twentieth-century travel posters) hold the willing imagination as the spellweaving storyteller prepares to share his "Morisco-Spanish" *cuentes* and *leyendas*.

These, the heart of the book, are led into by usually graceful transitions, though given the *olla podrida* miscellany the *Alhambra* really is, the sharp-eyed reader may pick out a few imperfect but forgivable elements in construction along the way. The chief of Irving's tales—their exact origin(s) still much of a mystery—show him off as a masterful entertainer. He is stirring here, with tales of buried treasure or martial valor, sentimental there, with tender love stories. Don Geoffrey Crayon must have enjoyed immensely (printer's deadlines aside) working out the conjugate pieces of this definitively Romantic literary mosaic.

As his full-hearted last lines show, in the concluding "Farewell" to Granada-And-All-That specially put to the Author's Revised Edition of the *Alhambra*, Washington Irving left behind his actual Alhambra with sincere regret. Sleepy Hollow Press, and your occasionally daydreaming editor, just as sincerely hope that after finishing this gold-stamped, gold-tooled and carefully crafted Irving-Darley-Putnam facsimile, you will feel the same about your *Alhambra* too.

Andrew Breen Myers

1. *The Columbia Encyclopedia*, 3rd Ed. (New York: Columbia University Press, 1963), p. 1416.
2. Washington Irving to Henry Brevoort, May 23, 1829, in George S. Hellman, ed., *Letters of Washington Irving to Henry Brevoort* (New York: G.P. Putnam's Sons, 1918), pp. 425-426.
3. Stanley T. Williams, ed., *The Spanish Background of American Literature*, 2 vols. (New Haven: Yale University Press, 1955), II: 38.
4. Quoted from Washington Irving, *The Alhambra* (Philadelphia: Carey & Lea, 1832). The London (Colburn and Paris (Baudry) editions vary slightly. In Spain, pocket editions of *The Alhambra* abound, either of the 1832 or 1851 versions.
5. For a history of these negotiations see Wayne R. Kime, *Pierre M. Irving and Washington Irving: A Collaboration in Life and Letters* (Waterloo, Ontario: Wilfrid Laurier University Press, 1977), p. 101 ff.
6. On Darley's prowess see Theodore Bolton, "The Book Illustrations of Felix Octavius Carr Darley," *Publications of The American Antiquarian Society* (April, 1951), p. 137 ff. See also, Delaware Art Museum, *Illus-*

INTRODUCTION

*trated by Darley: An Exhibition of Original Drawings
by the American Book Illustrator Felix Octavius Carr
Darley, 1822-1888, May 4 - June 18, 1978* (Wilmington:
Delaware Art Museum, 1978). On the mastery of Darley
woodcuts, see Sinclair Hamilton, *Early American Book
Illustrators and Wood Engravers, 1670-1870,* 2 vols.
(Princeton: Princeton University Press, 1968), I:xxxii,
19n, 100 ff; II: vii, 67 ff.

PUBLISHER'S NOTE

In his Introduction to the present volume, Dr. Andrew B. Myers speaks of the collaboration of talents which resulted in the 1851 illustrated edition of *The Alhambra*. The Editors of Sleepy Hollow Press owe a debt of gratitude to Washington Irving, whose rich evocations of the Moorish tradition in Spain inspired this edition; to Felix O.C. Darley, whose perceptive hand provided the suitable graphic counterpoint to the narrative; and to George P. Putnam, who joined together these creative forces. Beyond the originators of this volume, however, the time and talents of many scholars, researchers, printers, and designers were called upon to prepare this facsimile edition.

This contemporary collaboration was necessary due to the difficulties encountered in obtaining a copy of *The Alhambra* suitable for reproduction. Although the 1851 edition chosen for reproduction was in excellent condition given its age, some pages were not acceptable for the intricate camera work involved. Another edition, published in 1852 by G. P. Putnam, which varies only slightly from the 1851 impression in the location of illustrations and the color of the cloth binding, was utilized to create a pristine "shooting" copy. *The Alhambra* is therefore a composite facsimile which, like its companion volumes *The Sketch Book* and *A History of New-York*, is the product of a page-by-page examination for clarity of type, reproductive value, and completeness.

During the selection process, a number of peculiarities were observed in the 1851 edition. The current publishers were forced to survey all known copies of this impression, to determine if the peculiarities were standard or unique features. In the course of this examination, an analysis of nineteenth-century book manufacturing techniques revealed that the idiosyncracies noted in the 1851 impression were typical of the revised, illustrated *Alhambra*, and lend an intrinsic and authentic value to the facsimile edition. As a result, the original impression has been left untouched, and is here reproduced in its great beauty and subtle defects.

The reader will detect some broken letters and numbers throughout the text, as well as uneven baselines and irregular borders. These are features of the 1851 impression; no presumption of editorial oversight should be made. Equal notice will be taken of bindery guides, printed on certain pages in progressions of 8 and 16. (Eight-page signatures, or printing forms, follow a numeral; 16-page signatures follow a numeral*.) This practice, designed to ensure the correct sequence of pages at the bindery, continues today, although in less obvious fashion.

Two liberties have been taken by the editors in preparing this facsimile. The first involves the illustrations which are contained throughout *The Alhambra*. A number of these were printed separately from text pages and tipped-in in the 1851 edition. The editors have chosen to print these as part of the text proper in the present volume.

The second liberty was taken with the intention of conforming the 1851 edition to other impressions exam-

PUBLISHER'S NOTE

ined during the research stage. The original 1851 edition selected for reproduction contained a page out of sequence in the front matter. Another copy from the 1851 impression which was surveyed contained the contents page in its proper position—between the copyright page and the illustrations page. An explanation of this error is a matter of conjecture at this time; none may be attainable. The editors decided to correct the error in order to eliminate potential confusion on the part of the reader.

The present facsimile edition of *The Alhambra* was reproduced and printed by Aristographics, Inc., of New York City, and bound by A. Horowitz & Sons, Bookbinders, of Fairfield, New Jersey. The cover die was prepared by Truart Engraving, also of New York. *The Alhambra* was printed on an acid-free paper manufactured especially for this edition by Mohawk Paper Mills, Inc., of Cohoes, New York. The front matter new to this edition was set in Century Schoolbook, a typeface selected because of its resemblance to the 1851 type used by G. P. Putnam.

Finally, special thanks go to Marvin Galanty and Ellen Galanty for their expert advice on the reproduction and printing of this volume; Edward J. McLaughlin, who designed the introductory matter and the jacket (which is not a facsimile but an original creation for this edition); and Professor Edwin Bowden of the University of Texas at Austin for sharing with us his knowledge of Irving editions. Publication of *The Alhambra*, as well as its companion volumes *The Sketch Book* and *A History of New-York*, was made possible in part by a grant from The Vincent Astor Foundation.

The Editors
Sleepy Hollow Press

THE ALHAMBRA.

BY

WASHINGTON IRVING

AUTHOR'S REVISED EDITION.

With Illustrations

BY FELIX O. C. DARLEY,

ENGRAVED BY THE MOST EMINENT ARTISTS.

NEW-YORK:

GEORGE P. PUTNAM, 155 BROADWAY.

M.DCCC.LI.

JOHN. F. TROW,
Printer and Stereotyper,
49 ANN-STREET.

CONTENTS

———•••———

	PAGE
THE JOURNEY,	13
PALACE OF THE ALHAMBRA,	47
IMPORTANT NEGOTIATIONS.—THE AUTHOR SUCCEEDS TO THE THRONE OF BOABDIL,	62
INHABITANTS OF THE ALHAMBRA,	70
THE HALL OF AMBASSADORS,	75
THE JESUITS' LIBRARY,	81
ALHAMAR, THE FOUNDER OF THE ALHAMBRA,	82
YUSEF ABUL HAGIG, THE FINISHER OF THE ALHAMBRA,	90
THE MYSTERIOUS CHAMBERS,	95
PANORAMA FROM THE TOWER OF COMARES,	105
THE TRUANT,	113
THE BALCONY,	117
THE ADVENTURE OF THE MASON,	124
THE COURT OF LIONS,	128
THE ABENCERRAGES,	136
MEMENTOS OF BOABDIL,	149
PUBLIC FETES OF GRANADA,	154
LOCAL TRADITIONS,	163
THE HOUSE OF THE WEATHERCOCK,	166
LEGEND OF THE ARABIAN ASTROLOGER,	169

	PAGE
VISITORS TO THE ALHAMBRA,	191
RELICS AND GENEALOGIES,	196
THE GENERALIFE,	200
LEGEND OF PRINCE AHMED AL KAMEL; OR THE PILGRIM OF LOVE,	202
A RAMBLE AMONG THE HILLS,	237
LEGEND OF THE MOOR'S LEGACY,	247
THE TOWER OF LAS INFANTAS,	270
LEGEND OF THE THREE BEAUTIFUL PRINCESSES,	272
LEGEND OF THE ROSE OF THE ALHAMBRA,	299
THE VETERAN,	317
THE GOVERNOR AND THE NOTARY,	320
GOVERNOR MANCO AND THE SOLDIER,	328
A FETE IN THE ALHAMBRA,	348
LEGEND OF THE TWO DISCREET STATUES,	354
THE CRUSADE OF THE GRAND MASTER OF ALCÁNTARA,	374
SPANISH ROMANCE,	383
LEGEND OF DON MUNIO SANCHO DE HINOJOSA,	386
POETS AND POETRY OF MOSLEM AUDALUS,	394
AN EXPEDITION IN QUEST OF A DIPLOMA,	402
THE LEGEND OF THE ENCHANTED SOLDIER,	406
THE AUTHOR'S FAREWELL TO GRANADA,	422

ILLUSTRATIONS.

PAGE.

FRONTISPIECE—The Alhambra.

TITLE PAGE,

THE WATER-CARRIER, (See page 250.) VIII

THE GATE, (See page 50.) 10

THE JOURNEY, ... 25

THE HERDSMAN, ... 46

THE LEVEE OF TIA ANTONIA, ... 69

MYSTERIOUS CHAMBERS, ... 104

THE ADVENTURE OF THE MASON, ... 125

THE SPELL-BOUND GATEWAY, ... 187

ENCHANTED ARMOR, ... 229

LEGEND OF THE MOOR'S LEGACY, ... 261

THE MULETEER, ... 298

THE CAPITULATION, ... 316

THE RUSTY CORPORAL. 323

PREFACE TO THE REVISED EDITION.

⎯⎯•◦•⎯⎯

Rough draughts of some of the following tales and essays, were actually written during a residence in the Alhambra; others were subsequently added, founded on notes and observations made there. Care was taken to maintain local coloring and verisimilitude; so that the whole might present a faithful and living picture of that microcosm, that singular little world into which I had been fortuitously thrown; and about which the external world had a very imperfect idea. It was my endeavor scrupulously to depict its half Spanish half Oriental character; its mixture of the heroic, the poetic, and the grotesque; to revive the traces of grace and beauty fast fading from its walls; to record the regal and chivalrous traditions concerning those who once trod its courts; and the whimsical and superstitious legends of the motley race now burrowing among its ruins.

The papers thus roughly sketched out lay for three or four years in my portfolio, until I found myself in London, in 1832, on the eve of returning to the United States. I then endeavored to arrange them for the press, but the preparations for departure did not allow sufficient leisure. Several were thrown aside as incomplete; the rest were put together somewhat hastily and in rather a crude and chaotic manner.

In the present edition I have revised and re-arranged the whole work, enlarged some parts, and added others, including the papers originally omitted; and have thus endeavored to render it more complete and more worthy of the indulgent reception with which it has been favored.

W. I.

Sunnyside, 1851.

THE JOURNEY.

In the spring of 1829, the author of this work, whom curiosity had brought into Spain, made a rambling expedition from Seville to Granada in company with a friend, a member of the Russian Embassy at Madrid. Accident had thrown us together from distant regions of the globe, and a similarity of taste led us to wander together among the romantic mountains of Andalusia. Should these pages meet his eye, wherever thrown by the duties of his station, whether mingling in the pageantry of courts, or meditating on the truer glories of nature, may they recall the scenes of our adventurous companionship, and with them the recollection of one, in whom neither time nor distance will obliterate the remembrance of his gentleness and worth.*

And here, before setting forth, let me indulge in a few previous remarks on Spanish scenery and Spanish travelling. Many are apt to picture Spain to their imaginations as a soft southern region, decked out with the luxuriant charms of voluptuous Italy. On the contrary, though there are exceptions in some of the maritime provinces, yet, for the greater part, it is a stern,

* *Note to the Revised Edition.*—The Author feels at liberty to mention that his travelling companion was the Prince Dolgorouki, at present Russian minister at the Court of Persia.

melancholy country, with rugged mountains, and long sweeping plains, destitute of trees, and indescribably silent and lonesome, partaking of the savage and solitary character of Africa. What adds to this silence and loneliness, is the absence of singing-birds, a natural consequence of the want of groves and hedges. The vulture and the eagle are seen wheeling about the mountain-cliffs, and soaring over the plains, and groups of shy bustards stalk about the heaths; but the myriads of smaller birds, which animate the whole face of other countries, are met with in but few provinces in Spain, and in those chiefly among the orchards and gardens which surround the habitations of man.

In the interior provinces the traveller occasionally traverses great tracts cultivated with grain as far as the eye can reach, waving at times with verdure, at other times naked and sun-burnt, but he looks round in vain for the hand that has tilled the soil. At length, he perceives some village on a steep hill, or rugged crag, with mouldering battlements and ruined watch-tower; a strong-hold, in old times, against civil war, or Moorish inroad; for the custom among the peasantry of congregating together for mutual protection is still kept up in most parts of Spain, in consequence of the maraudings of roving freebooters.

But though a great part of Spain is deficient in the garniture of groves and forests, and the softer charms of ornamental cultivation, yet its scenery is noble in its severity, and in unison with the attributes of its people; and I think that I better understand the proud, hardy, frugal and abstemious Spaniard, his manly defiance of hardships, and contempt of effeminate indulgences, since I have seen the country he inhabits.

There is something too, in the sternly simple features of the Spanish landscape, that impresses on the soul a feeling of sublimity. The immense plains of the Castiles and of La Mancha, extending as far as the eye can reach, derive an interest from their very nakedness and immensity, and possess, in some degree, the solemn grandeur of the ocean. In ranging over these boundless wastes, the eye catches sight here and there of a straggling herd of cattle attended by a lonely herdsman, motionless as a statue, with his long slender pike tapering up like a lance into the air ; or, beholds a long train of mules slowly moving along the waste like a train of camels in the desert ; or, a single horseman, armed with blunderbuss and stiletto, and prowling over the plain. Thus the country, the habits, the very looks of the people, have something of the Arabian character. The general insecurity of the country is evinced in the universal use of weapons. The herdsman in the field, the shepherd in the plain, has his musket and his knife. The wealthy villager rarely ventures to the market-town without his trabuco, and, perhaps, a servant on foot with a blunderbuss on his shoulder; and the most petty journey is undertaken with the preparation of a warlike enterprise.

The dangers of the road produce also a mode of travelling, resembling, on a diminutive scale, the caravans of the east. The arrieros, or carriers, congregate in convoys, and set off in large and well-armed trains on appointed days ; while additional travellers swell their number, and contribute to their strength. In this primitive way is the commerce of the country carried on. The muleteer is the general medium of traffic, and the legitimate traverser of the land, crossing the peninsula from the Pyrenees and the Asturias to the Alpuxarras, the Serrania de Ronda, and even to the gates of Gibraltar. He lives frugally and hardily: his alforjas of coarse cloth hold his scanty stock of provisions; a leathern bottle, hanging at his saddle-bow, contains wine or water, for a supply across barren mountains and thirsty plains; a mule-cloth spread upon the ground is his bed at night, and his pack-saddle his pillow. His low, but clean-limbed and sinewy form betokens strength; his complexion is dark and sun-burnt; his eye resolute, but quiet in its expression, except when kindled by sudden emotion; his demeanor is frank, manly, and courteous, and he never passes you without a grave salutation: "Dios guarde à usted!" "Va usted con Dios, Caballero!" "God guard you!" "God be with you, Cavalier!"

As these men have often their whole fortune at stake upon the burden of their mules, they have their weapons at hand, slung to their saddles, and ready to be snatched out for desperate defence; but their united numbers render them secure against petty bands of marauders, and the solitary bandolero, armed to the teeth, and mounted on his Andalusian steed, hovers about them, like a pirate about a merchant convoy, without daring to assault.

The Spanish muleteer has an inexhaustible stock of songs and ballads, with which to beguile his incessant wayfaring. The airs are rude and simple, consisting of but few inflections. These he chants forth with a loud voice, and long, drawling cadence, seated sideways on his mule, who seems to listen with infinite. gravity, and to keep time, with his paces, to the tune. The couplets thus chanted, are often old traditional romances about the Moors, or some legend of a saint, or some love-ditty; or, what is still more frequent, some ballad about a bold contrabandista, or hardy bandolero, for the smuggler and the robber are po-etical heroes among the common people of Spain. Often, the song of the muleteer is composed at the instant, and relates to some local scene, or some incident of the journey. This talent of singing and improvising is frequent in Spain, and is said to have been inherited from the Moors. There is something wildly pleasing in listening to these ditties among the rude and lonely scenes they illustrate; accompanied, as they are, by the occasional jingle of the mule-bell.

It has a most picturesque effect also to meet a train of muleteers in some mountain-pass. First you hear the bells of the leading mules, breaking with their simple melody the stillness of the airy height; or, perhaps, the voice of the muleteer admonishing some tardy or wandering animal, or chanting, at the full stretch of his lungs, some traditionary ballad. At length you see the mules slowly winding along the cragged defile, sometimes descending precipitous cliffs, so as to present themselves in full relief against the sky, sometimes toiling up the deep arid chasms below you. As they approach, you descry their gay decorations of worsted stuffs, tassels, and saddle-cloths, while, as they pass by, the ever-ready trabuco, slung behind the packs and saddles, gives a hint of the insecurity of the road.

The ancient kingdom of Granada, into which we were about to penetrate, is one of the most mountainous regions of Spain. Vast sierras, or chains of mountains, destitute of shrub or tree, and mottled with variegated marbles and granites, elevate their sunburnt summits against a deep-blue sky; yet in their rugged bosoms lie ingulfed verdant and fertile valleys, where the desert and the garden strive for mastery, and the very rock is, as it were, compelled to yield the fig, the orange, and the citron, and to blossom with the myrtle and the rose.

In the wild passes of these mountains the sight of walled towns and villages, built like eagles' nests among the cliffs, and surrounded by Moorish battlements, or of ruined watchtowers perched on lofty peaks, carries the mind back to the chivalric days of Christian and Moslem warfare, and to the romantic struggle for the conquest of Granada. In traversing these lofty sierras the traveller is often obliged to alight, and lead his horse up and down the steep and jagged ascents and descents, resembling the broken steps of a staircase. Sometimes the road winds along dizzy precipices, without parapet to guard him from the gulfs below, and then will plunge down steep, and dark, and dangerous declivities. Sometimes it struggles through rugged barrancos, or ravines, worn by winter torrents, the obscure path of the contrabandista; while, ever and anon, the ominous cross, the monument of robbery and murder, erected on a mound of stones at some lonely part of the road, admonishes the traveller that he is among the haunts of banditti, perhaps at that very moment under the eye of some lurking bandolero. Sometimes, in winding through the narrow valleys, he is startled by a hoarse bellowing, and beholds above him on some green fold of the mountain a herd of fierce Andalusian bulls, destined for the combat of the arena. I have felt, if I may so express it, an agreeable horror in thus contemplating, near at hand, these terrific animals, clothed with tremendous strength, and ranging their native pastures in untamed wildness, strangers almost to the face of man: they know no one but the solitary herdsman who attends upon them, and even he at times dares not venture to approach them. The low bellowing of these bulls, and their menacing aspect as they look down from their rocky height, give additional wildness to the savage scenery.

I have been betrayed unconsciously into a longer disquisition than I intended on the general features of Spanish travelling;

but there is a romance about all the recollections of the Peninsula dear to the imagination.

As our proposed route to Granada lay through mountainous
regions, where the roads are little better than mule paths, and
said to be frequently beset by robbers, we took due travelling
precautions. Forwarding the most valuable part of our luggage
a day or two in advance by the arrieros, we retained merely
clothing and necessaries for the journey and money for the expenses of the road; with a little surplus of hard dollars by way
of *robber purse,* to satisfy the gentlemen of the road should we be
assailed. Unlucky is the too wary traveller who, having.grudged
this precaution, falls into their clutches empty handed : they are
apt to give him a sound ribroasting for cheating them out of
their dues. "Caballeros like them cannot afford to scour the
roads and risk the gallows for nothing."

A couple of stout steeds were provided for our own mounting,
and a third for our scanty luggage and the conveyance of a sturdy
Biscayan lad, about twenty years of age, who was to be our guide,
our groom, our valet, and at all times our guard. For the latter
office he was provided with a formidable trabucho or carbine,
with which he promised to defend us against rateros or solitary
footpads; but as to powerful bands, like that of the "sons of
Ecija," he confessed they were quite beyond his prowess. He
made much vainglorious boast about his weapon at the outset of
the journey; though, to the discredit of his generalship, it was
suffered to hang unloaded behind his saddle.

According to our stipulations, the man from whom we hired
the horses was to be at the expense of their feed and stabling on
the journey, as well as of the maintenance of our Biscayan squire,
who of course was provided with funds for the purpose; we took

care, however, to give the latter a private hint, that, though we made a close bargain with his master, it was all in his favor, as, if he proved a good man and true, both he and the horses should live at our cost, and the money provided for their maintenance remain in his pocket. This unexpected largess, with the occasional present of a cigar, won his heart completely. He was, in truth, a faithful, cheery, kind-hearted creature, as full of saws and proverbs as that miracle of squires, the renowned Sancho himself, whose name, by the by, we bestowed upon him, and like a true Spaniard, though treated by us with companionable familiarity, he never for a moment, in his utmost hilarity, overstepped the bounds of respectful decorum.

Such were our minor preparations for the journey, but above all we laid in an ample stock of good humor, and a genuine disposition to be pleased; determining to travel in true contrabandista style; taking things as we found them, rough or smooth, and mingling with all classes and conditions in a kind of vagabond companionship. It is the true way to travel in Spain. With such disposition and determination, what a country is it for a traveller, where the most miserable inn is as full of adventure as an enchanted castle, and every meal is in itself an achievement! Let others repine at the lack of turnpike roads and sumptuous hotels, and all the elaborate comforts of a country cultivated and civilized into tameness and commonplace; but give me the rude mountain scramble; the roving, haphazard, wayfaring; the half wild, yet frank and hospitable manners, which impart such a true game flavor to dear old romantic Spain!

Thus equipped and attended, we cantered out of " Fair Seville city" at half-past six in the morning of a bright May day, in company with a lady and gentleman of our acquaintance, who rode a few miles with us, in the Spanish mode of taking leave. Our route lay through old Alcala de Guadaira (Alcala on the river Aira), the benefactress of Seville, that supplies it with bread and water. Here live the bakers who furnish Seville with that delicious bread for which it is renowned; here are fabricated those roscas well known by the well-merited appellation of *pan de Dios* (bread of God); with which, by the way, we ordered our man, Sancho, to stock his alforjas for the journey. Well has this beneficent little city been denominated the "Oven of Seville;" well has it been called Alcala de los Panaderos (Alcala of the bakers), for a great part of its inhabitants are of that handicraft, and the highway hence to Seville is constantly traversed by lines of mules and donkeys laden with great panniers of loaves and roscas.

I have said Alcala supplies Seville with water. Here are great tanks or reservoirs, of Roman and Moorish construction, whence water is conveyed to Seville by noble aqueducts. The springs of Alcala are almost as much vaunted as its ovens; and to the lightness, sweetness, and purity of its water is attributed in some measure the delicacy of its bread.

Here we halted for a time, at the ruins of the old Moorish castle, a favorite resort for pic-nic parties from Seville, where we had passed many a pleasant hour. The walls are of great extent, pierced with loopholes; inclosing a huge square tower or keep, with the remains of masmoras, or subterranean granaries. The Guadaira winds its stream round the hill, at the foot of these ruins, whimpering among reeds, rushes, and pond-lilies, and over-hung with rhododendron, eglantine, yellow myrtle, and a profusion of wild flowers and aromatic shrubs; while along its banks are groves of oranges, citrons, and pomegranates, among which we heard the early note of the nightingale.

A picturesque bridge was thrown across the little river, at one end of which was the ancient Moorish mill of the castle, defended by a tower of yellow stone; a fisherman's net hung against the wall to dry, and hard by in the river was his boat; a group of peasant women in bright-colored dresses, crossing the arched bridge, were reflected in the placid stream. Altogether it was an admirable scene for a landscape painter.

The old Moorish mills, so often found on secluded streams, are characteristic objects in Spanish landscape, and suggestive of the perilous times of old. They are of stone, and often in the form of towers with loopholes and battlements, capable of defence in those warlike days when the country on both sides of the border was subject to sudden inroad and hasty ravage, and when men had to labor with their weapons at hand, and some place of temporary refuge.

Our next halting place was at Gandul, where were the remains of another Moorish castle, with its ruined tower, a nestling place for storks, and commanding a view over a vast campiña or fertile plain, with the mountains of Ronda in the distance. These castles were strong-holds to protect the plains from the talas or forays to which they were subject, when the fields of corn would be laid waste, the flocks and herds swept from the vast pastures, and, together with captive peasantry, hurried off in long cavalgadas across the borders.

At Gandul we found a tolerable posada; the good folks could not tell us what time of day it was, the clock only struck once in the day, two hours after noon; until that time it was guess work. We guessed it was full time to eat; so, alighting, we ordered a repast. While that was in preparation, we visited the palace once the residence of the Marquis of Gandul. All was gone to decay; there were but two or three rooms habitable, and very poorly furnished. Yet here were the remains of grandeur; a terrace, where fair dames and gentle cavaliers may once have walked; a fish-pond and ruined garden, with grape-vines and date-bearing palm-trees. Here we were joined by a fat curate, who gathered a bouquet of roses and presented it, very gallantly, to the lady who accompanied us.

Below the palace was the mill, with orange-trees and aloes in front, and a pretty stream of pure water. We took a seat in the shade, and the millers, all leaving their work, sat down and smoked with us; for the Andalusians are always ready for a gossip. They were waiting for the regular visit of the barber, who came once a week to put all their chins in order. He arrived shortly afterwards; a lad of seventeen, mounted on a donkey, eager to display his new alforjas or saddle-bags, just bought at a fair; price one dollar, to be paid on St. John's day (in June), by which time he trusted to have mown beards enough to put him in funds.

By the time the laconic clock of the castle had struck two we had finished our dinner. So, taking leave of our Seville friends, and leaving the millers still under the hands of the barber, we set off on our ride across the campiña. It was one of those vast plains, common in Spain, where for miles and miles there is neither house nor tree. Unlucky the traveller who has to traverse it, exposed as we were to heavy and repeated showers of rain. There is no escape nor shelter. Our only protection was our Spanish cloaks, which nearly covered man and horse, but grew heavier every mile. By the time we had lived through one shower we would see another slowly but inevitably approaching; fortunately in the interval there would be an outbreak of bright, warm, Andalusian sunshine, which would make our cloaks send up wreaths of steam, but which partially dried them before the next drenching.

Shortly after sunset we arrived at Arahal, a little town among the hills. We found it in a bustle with a party of miquelets, who were patrolling the country to ferret out robbers. The appearance of foreigners like ourselves was an unusual circumstance in an interior country town; and little Spanish towns of the kind are easily put in a state of gossip and wonderment by such an occurrence. Mine host, with two or three old wiseacre comrades in brown cloaks, studied our passports in a corner of the posada, while an Alguazil took notes by the dim light of a lamp. The passports were in foreign languages and perplexed them, but our Squire Sancho assisted them in their studies, and magnified our importance with the grandiloquence of a Spaniard. In the mean time the magnificent distribution of a few cigars had won the hearts of all around us; in a little while the whole community seemed put in agitation to make us welcome. The corregidor himself waited upon us, and a great rush-bottomed arm-chair was ostentatiously bolstered into our room by our landlady, for the accommodation of that important personage. The commander of the patrol took supper with us; a lively, talking, laughing Andaluz, who had made a campaign in South America, and recounted his exploits in love and war with much pomp of phrase, vehemence of gesticulation, and mysterious rolling of the eye. He told us that he had a list of all the robbers in the country, and meant to ferret out every mother's son of them; he offered us at the same time some of his soldiers as an escort. "One is enough to protect you, señors; the robbers know me, and know my men; the sight of one is enough to spread terror through a whole sierra." We thanked him for his offer, but assured him, in his own strain, that

with the protection of our redoubtable squire, Sancho, we were not afraid of all the ladrones of Andalusia.

While we were supping with our drawcansir friend, we heard the notes of a guitar, and the click of castañets, and presently a chorus of voices singing a popular air. In fact mine host had gathered together the amateur singers and musicians, and the rustic belles of the neighborhood, and, on going forth, the court-yard or patio of the inn presented a scene of true Spanish festi-vity. We took our seats with mine host and hostess and the commander of the patrol, under an archway opening into the court; the guitar passed from hand to hand, but a jovial shoe-maker was the Orpheus of the place. He was a pleasant-looking fellow, with huge black whiskers; his sleeves were rolled up to his elbows. He touched the guitar with masterly skill, and sang a little amorous ditty with an expressive leer at the women, with whom he was evidently a favorite. He afterwards danced a fan-dango with a buxom Andalusian damsel, to the great delight of the spectators. But none of the females present could compare with mine host's pretty daughter, Pepita, who had slipped away and made her toilette for the occasion, and had covered her head with roses; and who distinguished herself in a bolero with a handsome young dragoon. We ordered our host to let wine and refreshment circulate freely among the company, yet, though there was a motley assembly of soldiers, muleteers, and villagers, no one exceeded the bounds of sober enjoyment. The scene was a study for a painter: the picturesque group of dancers, the troopers in their half military dresses, the peasantry wrapped in their brown cloaks; nor must I omit to mention the old meagre Alguazil, in a short black cloak, who took no notice of any thing going on, but sat in a corner diligently writing by the dim light

2

of a huge copper lamp, that might have figured in the days of Don Quixote.

The following morning was bright and balmy, as a May morning ought to be, according to the poets. Leaving Arahal at seven o'clock, with all the posada at the door to cheer us off we pursued our way through a fertile country, covered with grain and beautifully verdant; but which in summer, when the harvest is over and the fields parched and brown, must be monotonous and lonely; for, as in our ride of yesterday, there were neither houses nor people to be seen. The latter all congregate in villages and strong-holds among the hills, as if these fertile plains were still subject to the ravages of the Moor.

At noon we came to where there was a group of trees, beside a brook in a rich meadow. Here we alighted to make our midday meal. It was really a luxurious spot, among wild flowers and aromatic herbs, with birds singing around us. Knowing the scanty larders of Spanish inns, and the houseless tracts we might have to traverse, we had taken care to have the alforjas of our squire well stocked with cold provisions, and his bota, or leathern bottle, which might hold a gallon, filled to the neck with choice Valdepeñas wine.* As we depended more upon these for our well-being than even his trabucho, we exhorted him to be more attentive in keeping them well charged; and I must do him the justice to say that his namesake, the trencher-loving Sancho

---

* It may be as well to note here, that the alforjas are square pockets at each end of a long cloth about a foot and a half wide, formed by turning up its extremities. The cloth is then thrown over the saddle, and the pockets hang on each side like saddle-bags. It is an Arab invention. The bota is a leathern bag or bottle, of portly dimensions, with a narrow neck. It is also oriental. Hence the scriptural caution, which perplexed me in my boyhood, not to put new wine into old bottles.

Panza, was never a more provident purveyor. Though the alforjas and the bota were frequently and vigorously assailed throughout the journey, they had a wonderful power of repletion, our
vigilant squire sacking every thing that remained from our
repasts at the inns, to supply these junketings by the road-side,
which were his delight.

On the present occasion he spread quite a sumptuous variety
of remnants on the green-sward before us, graced with an excellent ham brought from Seville; then, taking his seat at a little
distance, he solaced himself with what remained in the alforjas.
A visit or two to the bota made him as merry and chirruping as
a grasshopper filled with dew. On my comparing his contents
of the alforjas to Sancho's skimming of the flesh-pots at the
wedding of Cammacho, I found he was well versed in the history
of Don Quixote, but, like many of the common people of Spain,
firmly believed it to be a true history.

" All that happened a long time ago, señor," said he, with an
inquiring look.

" A very long time," I replied.

" I dare say more than a thousand years"—still looking
dubiously.

" I dare say not less."

The squire was satisfied. Nothing pleased the simple-hearted
varlet more than my comparing him to the renowned Sancho for
devotion to the trencher; and he called himself by no other name
throughout the journey.

Our repast being finished, we spread our cloaks on the green-
sward under the tree, and took a luxurious siesta in the Spanish
fashion. The clouding up of the weather, however, warned us to
depart, and a harsh wind sprang up from the southeast. Towards

five o'clock we arrived at Osuna, a town of fifteen thousand inhabitants, situated on the side of a hill, with a church and a ruined
castle.   The posada was outside of the walls; it had a cheerless
look.   The evening being cold, the inhabitants were crowded
round a brasero in a chimney corner; and the hostess was a dry
old woman, who looked like a mummy.   Every one eyed us
askance as we entered, as Spaniards are apt to regard strangers;
a cheery, respectful salutation on our part, caballeroing them and
touching our sombreros, set Spanish pride at ease; and when we
took our seat among them, lit our cigars, and passed the cigar-
box round among them, our victory was complete.   I have never
known a Spaniard, whatever his rank or condition, who would
suffer himself to be outdone in courtesy; and to the common
Spaniard the present of a cigar (puro) is irresistible.   Care, however, must be taken never to offer him a present with an air of
superiority and condescension; he is too much of a caballero to
receive favors at the cost of his dignity.

Leaving Osuna at an early hour the next morning, we entered
the sierra or range of mountains.   The road wound through
picturesque scenery, but lonely; and a cross here and there by
the road side, the sign of a murder, showed that we were now
coming among the "robber haunts."   This wild and intricate
country, with its silent plains and valleys intersected by mountains,
has ever been famous for banditti.   It was here that Omar Ibn
Hassan, a robber-chief among the Moslems, held ruthless sway in
the ninth century, disputing dominion even with the caliphs of
Cordova.   This too was a part of the regions so often ravaged
during the reign of Ferdinand and Isabella by Ali Atar, the old
Moorish alcayde of Loxa, father-in-law of Boabdil, so that it was
called Ali Atar's garden, and here "Jose Maria," famous in
Spanish brigand story, had his favorite lurking places.

In the course of the day we passed through Fuente la Piedra near a little salt lake of the same name, a beautiful sheet of water, reflecting like a mirror the distant mountains. We now came in sight of Antiquera, that old city of warlike reputation, lying in the lap of the great sierra which runs through Andalusia. A noble vega spread out before it, a picture of mild fertility set in a frame of rocky mountains. Crossing a gentle river we approached the city between hedges and gardens, in which nightingales were pouring forth their evening song. About nightfall we arrived at the gates. Every thing in this venerable city has a decidedly Spanish stamp. It lies too much out of the frequented track of foreign travel to have its old usages trampled out. Here I observed old men still wearing the montero, or ancient hunting cap, once common throughout Spain; while the young men wore the little round-crowned hat, with brim turned up all round, like a cup turned down in its saucer; while the brim was set off with little black tufts like cockades. The women, too, were all in mantillas and basquinas. The fashions of Paris had not reached Antiquera.

Pursuing our course through a spacious street, we put up at the posada of San Fernando. As Antiquera, though a considerable city, is, as I observed, somewhat out of the track of travel, I had anticipated bad quarters and poor fare at the inn. I was agreeably disappointed, therefore, by a supper table amply supplied, and what were still more acceptable, good clean rooms and comfortable beds. Our man, Sancho, felt himself as well off as his namesake, when he had the run of the duke's kitchen, and let me know, as I retired for the night, that it had been a proud time for the alforjas.

Early in the morning (May 4th) I strolled to the ruins of the

old Moorish castle, which itself had been reared on the ruins of a
Roman fortress. Here, taking my seat on the remains of a
crumbling tower, I enjoyed a grand and varied landscape, beautiful in itself, and full of storied and romantic associations; for I
was now in the very heart of the country famous for the chivalrous contests between Moor and Christian. Below me, in its
lap of hills, lay the old warrior city so often mentioned in
chronicle and ballad. Out of yon gate and down yon hill paraded the band of Spanish cavaliers, of highest rank and bravest
bearing, to make that foray during the war and conquest of
Granada, which ended in the lamentable massacre among the
mountains of Malaga, and laid all Andalusia in mourning.
Beyond spread out the vega, covered with gardens and orchards
and fields of grain and enamelled meadows, inferior only to the
famous vega of Granada. To the right the Rock of the Lovers
stretched like a cragged promontory into the plain, whence the
daughter of the Moorish alcayde and her lover, when closely
pursued, threw themselves in despair.

The matin peal from church and convent below me rang
sweetly in the morning air, as I descended. The market place
was beginning to throng with the populace, who traffic in the
abundant produce of the vega; for this is the mart of an agricul-
tural region. In the market-place were abundance of freshly
plucked roses for sale; for not a dame or damsel of Andalusia
thinks her gala dress complete without a rose shining like a gem
among her raven tresses.

On returning to the inn I found our man Sancho, in high
gossip with the landlord and two or three of his hangers-on. He
had just been telling some marvellous story about Seville, which
mine host seemed piqued to match with one equally marvellous

about Antiquera. There was once a fountain, he said, in one of the public squares called *Il fuente del toro*, the fountain of the bull, because the water gushed from the mouth of a bull's head, carved of stone. Underneath the head was inscribed :

> En frente del toro
> Se hallen tesoro.

(In front of the bull there is treasure.) Many digged in front of the fountain, but lost their labor and found no money. At last one knowing fellow construed the motto a different way. It is in the forehead (frente) of the bull that the treasure is to be found, said he to himself, and I am the man to find it. Accordingly he came late at night, with a mallet, and knocked the head to pieces ; and what do you think he found ?

" Plenty of gold and diamonds !" cried Sancho eagerly.

" He found nothing," rejoined mine host dryly ; " and he ruined the fountain."

Here a great laugh was set up by the landlord's hangers-on ; who considered Sancho completely taken in by what I presume was one of mine host's standing jokes.

Leaving Antiquera at eight o'clock, we had a delightful ride along the little river, and by gardens and orchards, fragrant with the odors of spring and vocal with the nightingale. Our road passed round the Rock of the Lovers (el peñon de los enamorados), which rose in a precipice above us. In the course of the morning we passed through Archidona, situated in the breast of a high hill, with a three-pointed mountain towering above it, and the ruins of a Moorish fortress. It was a great toil to ascend a steep stony street leading up into the city, although it bore the encouraging name of Calle Real del Llano (the royal street of the plain), but it was still a greater toil to descend from this mountain city on the other side.

At noon we halted in sight of Archidona, in a pleasant little meadow among hills covered with olive-trees. Our cloaks were spread on the grass, under an elm by the side of a bubbling rivulet ; our horses were tethered where they might crop the herbage, and Sancho was told to produce his alforjas. He had been unusually silent this morning ever since the laugh raised at his expense, but now his countenance brightened, and he produced his alforjas with an air of triumph. They contained the contributions of four days' journeying, but had been signally enriched by the foraging of the previous evening in the plenteous inn at Antiquera ; and this seemed to furnish him with a set-off to the banter of mine host.

> En frente del toro
> Se hallen tesoro

would he exclaim, with a chuckling laugh, as he drew forth the heterogeneous contents one by one, in a series which seemed to have no end. First came forth a shoulder of roasted kid, very little the worse for wear ; then an entire partridge ; then a great morsel of salted codfish wrapped in paper ; then the residue of a ham ; then the half of a pullet, together with several rolls of bread, and a rabble rout of oranges, figs, raisins, and walnuts. His bota also had been recruited with some excellent wine of Malaga. At every fresh apparition from his larder, he would enjoy our ludicrous surprise, throwing himself back on the grass, shouting with laughter, and exclaiming " Frente del toro !—frente del toro ! Ah, señors, they thought Sancho a simpleton at Antiquera; but Sancho knew where to find the *tesoro* "

While we were diverting ourselves with his simple drollery, a solitary beggar approached, who had almost the look of a pilgrim. He had a venerable gray beard, and was evidently very old, supporting himself on a staff, yet age had not bowed him down ; he was tall and erect, and had the wreck of a fine form. He wore a round Andalusian hat, a sheep-skin jacket, and leathern breeches, gaiters, and sandals. His dress, though old and patched, was decent, his demeanor manly, and he addressed us with the grave courtesy that is to be remarked in the lowest Spaniard. We were in a favorable mood for such a visitor ; and in a freak of capricious charity gave him some silver, a loaf of fine wheaten bread, and a goblet of our choice wine of Malaga. He received them thankfully, but without any grovelling tribute of gratitude. Tasting the wine, he held it up to the light, with a slight beam of surprise in his eye, then quaffing it off at a draught ; " It is many years," said he, " since I have tasted such wine. It is a cordial to an old man's heart." Then, looking at the beautiful wheaten loaf, " *bendito sea tal pan !*" " blessed be such bread !" So saying, he put it in his wallet. We urged him to eat it on the spot. " No, señors," replied he, " the wine I had either to drink or leave ; but the bread I may take home to share with my family."

Our man Sancho sought our eye, and reading permission there, gave the old man some of the ample fragments of our repast, on condition, however, that he should sit down and make a meal.

He accordingly took his seat at some little distance from us, and began to eat slowly, and with a sobriety and decorum that would have become a hidalgo. There was altogether a measured manner and a quiet self-possession about the old man, that made me think that he had seen better days : his language too, though

2*

simple, had occasionally something picturesque and almost poetical in the phraseology. I set him down for some broken-down cavalier. I was mistaken; it was nothing but the innate courtesy of a Spaniard, and the poetical turn of thought and language often to be found in the lowest classes of this clear-witted people. For fifty years, he told us, he had been a shepherd, but now he was out of employ and destitute. " When I was a young man," said he, " nothing could harm or trouble me ; I was always well, always gay ; but now I am seventy-nine years of age, and a beggar, and my heart begins to fail me."

Still he was not a regular mendicant : it was not until recently that want had driven him to this degradation ; and he gave a touching picture of the struggle between hunger and pride, when abject destitution first came upon him. He was returning from Malaga without money ; he had not tasted food for some time, and was crossing one of the great plains of Spain, where there were but few habitations. When almost dead with hunger, he applied at the door of a venta or country inn. " *Perdon usted por Dios hermano !*" (Excuse us, brother, for God's sake !) was the reply—the usual mode in Spain of refusing a beggar. " I turned away," said he, " with shame greater than my hunger, for my heart was yet too proud. I came to a river with high banks, and deep, rapid current, and felt tempted to throw myself in : ' What should such an old, worthless, wretched man as I live for?' But when I was on the brink of the current, I thought on the blessed Virgin, and turned away. I travelled on until I saw a country-seat at a little distance from the road, and entered the outer gate of the court-yard. The door was shut, but there were two young señoras at a window. I approached and begged :— *Perdon usted por Dios hermano !*—and the window closed. I crept out of the court-yard, but hunger overcame me, and my heart gave way : I thought my hour at hand, so I laid myself down at the gate, commended myself to the Holy Virgin, and covered my head to die. In a little while afterwards the master of the house came home : seeing me lying at his gate, he uncovered my head, had pity on my gray hairs, took me into his house, and gave me food. So, señors, you see that one should always put confidence in the protection of the Virgin."

The old man was on his way to his native place, Archidona, which was in full view on its steep and rugged mountain. He pointed to the ruins of its castle : " That castle," he said, " was inhabited by a Moorish king at the time of the wars of Granada. Queen Isabella invaded it with a great army ; but the king looked down from his castle among the clouds, and laughed her to scorn ! Upon this the Virgin appeared to the queen, and guided her and her army up a mysterious path in the mountains, which had never before been known. When the Moor saw her coming, he was astonished, and springing with his horse from a precipice, was dashed to pieces ! The marks of his horse's hoofs," said the old man, " are to be seen in the margin of the rock to this day. And see, señors, yonder is the road by which the queen and her army mounted : you see it like a ribbon up the mountain's side ; but the miracle is, that, though it can be seen at a distance, when you come near it disappears !"

The ideal road to which he pointed was undoubtedly a sandy ravine of the mountain, which looked narrow and defined at a distance, but became broad and indistinct on an approach.

As the old man's heart warmed with wine and wassail, he went on to tell us a story of the buried treasure left under the castle by the Moorish king. His own house was next to the foundations of the castle. The curate and notary dreamed three times of the treasure, and went to work at the place pointed out in their dreams. His own son-in-law heard the sound of their pickaxes and spades at night. What they found nobody knows; they became suddenly rich, but kept their own secret. Thus the old man had once been next door to fortune, but was doomed never to get under the same roof.

I have remarked that the stories of treasure buried by the Moors, so popular throughout Spain, are most current among the poorest people. Kind nature consoles with shadows for the lack of substantials. The thirsty man dreams of fountains and running streams; the hungry man of banquets; and the poor man of heaps of hidden gold: nothing certainly is more opulent than the imagination of a beggar.

Our afternoon's ride took us through a steep and rugged defile of the mountains, called Puerte del Rey, the Pass of the King; being one of the great passes into the territories of Granada, and the one by which king Ferdinand conducted his army. Towards sunset the road, winding round a hill, brought us in sight of the famous little frontier city of Loxa, which repulsed Ferdinand from its walls. Its Arabic name implies guardian, and such it was to the vega of Granada; being one of its advanced guards. It was the strong-hold of that fiery veteran, old Ali Atar, father-in-law of Boabdil; and here it was that the latter collected his troops, and sallied forth on that disastrous foray which ended in the death of the old alcayde and his own captivity. From its commanding position at the gate. as it were, of this mountain pass, Loxa has not unaptly been termed the key of Granada. It is wildly picturesque; built along the face of an arid mountain. The ruins of a Moorish alcazar or citadel crown a rocky mound which rises out of the centre of the town. The river Xenil washes its base, winding among rocks, and groves, and gardens, and meadows, and crossed by a Moorish bridge. Above the city all is savage and sterile, below is the richest vegetation and the freshest verdure. A similar contrast is presented by the river; above the bridge it is placid and grassy, reflecting groves and gardens; below it is rapid, noisy and tumultuous. The Sierra Nevada, the royal mountains of Granada, crowned with perpetual snow, form the distant boundary to this varied landscape; one of the most characteristic of romantic Spain.

Alighting at the entrance of the city, we gave our horses to Sancho to lead them to the inn, while we strolled about to enjoy the singular beauty of the environs. As we crossed the bridge to a fine alameda, or public walk, the bells tolled the hour of oration. At the sound the wayfarers, whether on business or pleasure, paused, took off their hats, crossed themselves, and repeated their evening prayer; a pious custom still rigidly observed in retired parts of Spain. Altogether it was a solemn and beautiful evening scene, and we wandered on as the evening gradually closed, and the new moon began to glitter between the high elms of the alameda. We were roused from this quiet state of enjoyment by the voice of our trusty squire hailing us from a distance. He came up to us, out of breath. "Ah, señores," cried he, "el pobre Sancho no es nada sin Don Quixote." (Ah, señors, poor Sancho is nothing without Don Quixote.) He had been alarmed at our not coming to the inn; Loxa was such a wild mountain place, full of contrabandistas, enchanters and infiernos; he did not well know what might have happened, and set out to seek us, inquiring after us of every person he met, until he traced us across the bridge, and, to his great joy, caught sight of us strolling in the alameda.

The inn to which he conducted us was called the Corona, or Crown, and we found it quite in keeping with the character of the place, the inhabitants of which seem still to retain the bold, fiery spirit of the olden time. The hostess was a young and handsome Andalusian widow, whose trim basquiña of black silk, fringed with bugles, set off the play of a graceful form and round pliant limbs. Her step was firm and elastic; her dark eye was full of fire, and the coquetry of her air, and varied ornaments of her person, showed that she was accustomed to be admired.

She was well matched by a brother, nearly about her own age; they were perfect models of the Andalusian Majo and Maja. He was tall, vigorous, and well-formed, with a clear olive complexion, a dark beaming eye, and curling chesnut whiskers that met under his chin. He was gallantly dressed in a short green velvet jacket, fitted to his shape, profusely decorated with silver buttons, with a white handkerchief in each pocket. He had breeches of the same, with rows of buttons from the hips to the knees; a pink silk handkerchief round his neck, gathered through a ring, on the bosom of a neatly-plaited shirt; a sash round the waist to match; bottinas, or spatterdashes, of the finest russet leather, elegantly worked, and open at the calf to show his stocking and russet shoes, setting off a well-shaped foot.

As he was standing at the door, a horseman rode up and entered into low and earnest conversation with him. He was dressed in a similar style, and almost with equal finery; a man about thirty, square-built, with strong Roman features, handsome, though slightly pitted with the small-pox; with a free, bold, and somewhat daring air. His powerful black horse was decorated with tassels and fanciful trappings, and a couple of broad-mouthed blunderbusses hung behind the saddle. He had the air of one of those contrabandistas I have seen in the mountains of Ronda, and evidently had a good understanding with the brother of mine hostess; nay, if I mistake not, he was a favored admirer of the widow. In fact, the whole inn and its inmates had something of a contrabandista aspect, and a blunderbuss stood in a corner beside the guitar. The horseman I have mentioned passed his evening in the posada, and sang several bold mountain romances with great spirit. As we were at supper, two poor Asturians put in in distress, begging food and a night's lodging. They had been waylaid by robbers as they came from a fair among the mountains, robbed of a horse, which carried all their stock in trade, stripped of their money, and most of their apparel, beaten for having offered resistance, and left almost naked in the road. My companion, with a prompt generosity natural to him, ordered them a supper and a bed, and gave them a sum of money to help them forward towards their home.

As the evening advanced, the dramatis personæ thickened. A large man, about sixty years of age, of powerful frame, came strolling in, to gossip with mine hostess. He was dressed in the ordinary Andalusian costume, but had a huge sabre tucked under his arm; wore large moustaches, and had something of a lofty swaggering air. Every one seemed to regard him with great deference

Our man Sancho whispered to us that he was Don Ventura Rodriguez, the hero and champion of Loxa, famous for his prowess and the strength of his arm. In the time of the French invasion he surprised six troopers who were asleep: he first secured their horses, then attacked them with his sabre, killed some, and took the rest prisoners. For this exploit the king allows him a peseta (the fifth of a duro, or dollar) per day, and has dignified him with the title of Don.

I was amused to behold his swelling language and demeanor. He was evidently a thorough Andalusian, boastful as brave. His sabre was always in his hand or under his arm. He carries it always about with him as a child does her doll, calls it his Santa Teresa, and says, "When I draw it, the earth trembles" (tiembla la tierra).

I sat until a late hour listening to the varied themes of this motley group, who mingled together with the unreserve of a Spanish posada. We had contrabandista songs, stories of robbers, guerilla exploits, and Moorish legends. The last were from our handsome landlady, who gave a poetical account of the Infiernos, or infernal regions of Loxa, dark caverns, in which subterranean streams and waterfalls make a mysterious sound. The common people say that there are money-coiners shut up there from the time of the Moors; and that the Moorish kings kept their treasures in those caverns.

I retired to bed with my imagination excited by all that I had seen and heard in this old warrior city. Scarce had I fallen asleep when I was aroused by a horrid din and uproar, that might have confounded the hero of La Mancha himself whose experience of Spanish inns was a continual uproar. It seemed for a moment as if the Moors were once more breaking into the town, or the infiernos of which mine hostess talked had broken loose. I sallied forth half dressed to reconnoiter. It was nothing more nor less than a charivari to celebrate the nuptials of an old man with a buxom damsel. Wishing him joy of his bride and his serenade, I returned to my more quiet bed, and slept soundly until morning.

While dressing, I amused myself in reconnoitering the populace from my window. There were groups of fine-looking young men in the trim fanciful Andalusian costume, with brown cloaks, thrown about them in true Spanish style, which cannot be imitated, and little round majo hats stuck on with a peculiar knowing air They had the same galliard look which I have remarked among the dandy mountaineers of Ronda. Indeed, all this part of Andalusia abounds with such game-looking characters. They loiter about the towns and villages; seem to have plenty of time and plenty of money; "horse to ride and weapon to wear." Great gossips; great smokers; apt at touching the guitar, singing couplets to their maja belles, and famous dancers of the bolero. Throughout all Spain the men, however poor, have a gentleman-like abundance of leisure ; seeming to consider it the attribute of a true cavaliero never to be in a hurry; but the Andalusians are gay as well as leisurely, and have none of the squalid accompaniments of idleness. The adventurous contraband trade which prevails throughout these mountain regions, and along the maritime borders of Andalusia, is doubtless at the bottom of this galliard character.

In contrast to the costume of these groups was that of two long-legged Valencians conducting a donkey, laden with articles of merchandise ; their musket slung crosswise over his back ready for action. They wore round jackets (jalecos), wide linen bragas or drawers scarce reaching to the knees and looking like kilts, red fajas or sashes swathed tightly round their waists, sandals of espartal or bass weed, colored kerchiefs round their heads somewhat in the style of turbans but leaving the top of the head uncovered ; in short, their whole appearance having much of the traditional Moorish stamp.

On leaving Loxa we were joined by a cavalier, well mounted and well armed. and followed on foot by an escopetero or musketeer

He saluted us courteously, and soon let us into his quality. He was chief of the customs, or rather, I should suppose, chief of an armed company whose business it is to patrol the roads and look out for contrabandistas. The escopetero was one of his guards. In the course of our morning's ride I drew from him some particulars concerning the smugglers, who have risen to be a kind of mongrel chivalry in Spain. They come into Andalusia, he said, from various parts, but especially from La Mancha; sometimes to receive goods, to be smuggled on an appointed night across the line at the plaza or strand of Gibraltar; sometimes to meet a vessel, which is to hover on a given night off a certain part of the coast. They keep together and travel in the night. In the daytime they lie quiet in barrancos, gullies of the mountains or lonely farm-houses; where they are generally well received, as they make the family liberal presents of their smuggled wares. Indeed, much of the finery and trinkets worn by the wives and daughters of the mountain hamlets and farm-houses are presents from the gay and open-handed contrabandistas.

Arrived at the part of the coast where a vessel is to meet them, they look out at night from some rocky point or headland. If they descry a sail near the shore they make a concerted signal; sometimes it consists in suddenly displaying a lantern three times from beneath the folds of a cloak. If the signal is answered, they descend to the shore and prepare for quick work. The vessel runs close in, all her boats are busy landing the smuggled goods, made up into snug packages for transportation on horseback. These are hastily thrown on the beach, as hastily gathered up and packed on the horses, and then the contrabandistas clatter off to the mountains. They travel by the roughest, wildest, and most solitary roads, where it is almost fruitless to pursu₂ them. The custom-house guards do not attempt it: they take a different course. When they hear of one of these bands returning full freighted through the mountains, they go out in force, sometimes twelve infantry and eight horsemen, and take their station where the mountain defile opens into the plain. The infantry, who lie in ambush some distance within the defile, suffer the band to pass, then rise and fire upon them. The contrabandistas dash forward, but are met in front by the horsemen. A wild skirmish ensues. The contrabandistas, if hard pressed, become desperate. Some dismount, use their horses as breast-works, and fire over their backs; others cut the cords, let the packs fall off to delay the enemy, and endeavor to escape with their steeds. Some get off in this way with the loss of their packages; some are taken, horses, packages, and all; others abandon every thing, and make their escape by scrambling up the mountains. "And then," cried Sancho, who had been listening with a greedy ear, "*se hacen ladrones legitimos,*"—and then they become legitimate robbers.

I could not help laughing at Sancho's idea of a legitimate calling of the kind; but the chief of customs told me it was really the case that the smugglers, when thus reduced to extremity, thought they had a kind of right to take the road, and lay travellers under contribution, until they had collected funds enough to mount and equip themselves in contrabandista style.

Towards noon our wayfaring companion took leave of us and turned up a steep defile, followed by his escopetero; and shortly afterwards we emerged from the mountains, and entered upon the far famed Vega of Granada.

Our last mid-day's repast was taken under a grove of olive-trees on the border of a rivulet. We were in a classical neighborhood; for not far off were the groves and orchards of the Soto de Roma. This, according to fabulous tradition, was a retreat founded by Count Julian to console his daughter Florinda. It was a rural resort of the Moorish kings of Granada; and has in modern times been granted to the Duke of Wellington.

Our worthy squire made a half melancholy face as he drew forth, for the last time, the contents of his alforjas, lamenting that our expedition was drawing to a close, for, with such cavaliers, he said, he could travel to the world's end. Our repast, however, was a gay one; made under such delightful auspices. The day was without a cloud. The heat of the sun was tempered by cool breezes from the mountains. Before us extended the glorious Vega. In the distance was romantic Granada surmounted by the ruddy towers of the Alhambra, while far above it the snowy summits of the Sierra Nevada shone like silver.

Our repast finished, we spread our cloaks and took our last siesta *al fresco*, lulled by the humming of bees among the flowers and the notes of doves among the olive-trees. When the sultry hours were passed we resumed our journey. After a time we overtook a pursy little man, shaped not unlike a toad and mounted on a mule. He fell into conversation with Sancho, and finding we were strangers, undertook to guide us to a good posada. He was an escribano (notary), he said, and knew the city as thoroughly as his own pocket. "Ah Dios Señores! what a city you are going to see. Such streets! such squares! such palaces! and then the women—ah Santa Maria purisima—what women!" "But the posada you talk of," said I, "are you sure it is a good one?"

"Good! Santa Maria! the best in Granada. Salones grandes —camas de luxo—colchones de pluma (grand saloons—luxurious sleeping rooms—beds of down). Ah, señores, you will fare like king Chico in the Alhambra."

"And how will my horses fare?" cried Sancho.

" Like king Chico's horses. *Chocolate con leche y bollos para almuerza*" (chocolate and milk with sugar cakes for breakfast), giving the squire a knowing wink and a leer.

After such satisfactory accounts nothing more was to be desired on that head. So we rode quietly on, the squab little notary taking the lead, and turning to us every moment with some fresh exclamation about the grandeurs of Granada and the famous times we were to have at the posada.

Thus escorted, we passed between hedges of aloes and Indian figs, and through that wilderness of gardens with which the vega is embroidered, and arrived about sunset at the gates of the city. Our officious little conductor conveyed us up one street and down another, until he rode into the court-yard of an inn where he appeared to be perfectly at home. Summoning the landlord by his Christian name, he committed us to his care as two cavalleros de mucho valor, worthy of his best apartments and most sumptuous fare. We were instantly reminded of the patronizing stranger who introduced Gil Blas with such a flourish of trumpets to the host and hostess of the inn at Pennaflor, ordering trouts for his supper, and eating voraciously at his expense. " You " know not what you possess," cried he to the innkeeper and his wife. " You have a treasure in your house. Behold in this young gentleman the eighth wonder of the world—nothing in this house is too good for Señor Gil Blas of Santillane, who deserves to be entertained like a prince."

Determined that the little notary should not eat trouts at our expense, like his prototype of Pennaflor, we forbore to ask him

to supper; nor had we reason to reproach ourselves with ingrati-
tude; for we found before morning the little varlet, who was no
doubt a good friend of the landlord, had decoyed us into one of
the shabbiest posadas in Granada.

PALACE OF THE ALHAMBRA.

To the traveller imbued with a feeling for the historical and poetical, so inseparably intertwined in the annals of romantic Spain, the Alhambra is as much an object of devotion as is the Caaba to all true Moslems. How many legends and traditions, true and fabulous; how many songs and ballads, Arabian and Spanish, of love and war and chivalry, are associated with this oriental pile! It was the royal abode of the Moorish kings, where, surrounded with the splendors and refinements of Asiatic luxury, they held dominion over what they vaunted as a terrestrial paradise, and made their last stand for empire in Spain. The royal palace forms but a part of a fortress, the walls of which, studded with towers, stretch irregularly round the whole crest of a hill, a spur of the Sierra Nevada or Snowy Mountains, and overlook the city; externally it is a rude congregation of towers and battlements, with no regularity of plan nor grace of architecture, and giving little promise of the grace and beauty which prevail within.

In the time of the Moors the fortress was capable of containing within in its outward precincts an army of forty thousand men, and served occasionally as a strong-hold of the sovereigns against their rebellious subjects. After the kingdom had passed into the hands of the Christians, the Alhambra continued to be a royal demesne, and was occasionally inhabited by the Castilian monarchs. The emperor Charles V. commenced a sumptuous palace within its walls, but was deterred from completing it by repeated shocks of earthquakes. The last royal residents were Philip V. and his beautiful queen, Elizabetta of Parma, early in the eighteenth century. Great preparations were made for their reception. The palace and gardens were placed in a state of repair, and a new suite of apartments erected, and decorated by artists brought from Italy. The sojourn of the sovereigns was transient, and after their departure the palace once more became desolate. Still the place was maintained with some military state. The governor held it immediately from the crown, its jurisdiction extended down into the suburbs of the city, and was independent of the captain-general of Granada. A considerable garrison was kept up, the governor had his apartments in the front of the old Moorish palace, and never descended into Granada without some military parade. The fortress, in fact, was a little town of itself, having several streets of houses within its walls, together with a Franciscan convent and a parochial church.

The desertion of the court, however, was a fatal blow to the Alhambra. Its beautiful halls became desolate, and some of them fell to ruin; the gardens were destroyed, and the fountains ceased to play. By degrees the dwellings became filled with a loose and lawless population; contrabandistas, who availed themselves of its independent jurisdiction to carry on a wide and daring course of smuggling, and thieves and rogues of all sorts, who made this their place of refuge whence they might depredate upon Granada and its vicinity. The strong arm of government at length interfered; the whole community was thoroughly sifted; none were suffered to remain but such as were of honest character, and had legitimate right to a residence; the greater part of the houses were demolished and a mere hamlet left, with the parochial church and the Franciscan convent. During the recent troubles in Spain, when Granada was in the hands of the French, the Alhambra was garrisoned by their troops, and the palace was occasionally inhabited by the French commander. With that enlightened taste which has ever distinguished the French nation in their conquests, this monument of Moorish elegance and grandeur was rescued from the absolute ruin and desolation that were overwhelming it. The roofs were repaired, the saloons and galleries protected from the weather, the gardens cultivated, the watercourses restored, the fountains once more made to throw up their sparkling showers; and Spain may thank her invaders for having preserved to her the most beautiful and interesting of her historical monuments.

On the departure of the French they blew up several towers of the outer wall, and left the fortifications scarcely tenable. Since that time the military importance of the post is at an end. The garrison is a handful of invalid soldiers, whose principal duty is to guard some of the outer towers, which serve occasionally as a prison of state; and the governor, abandoning the lofty hill of the Alhambra, resides in the centre of Granada, for the more convenient dispatch of his official duties. I cannot conclude this brief notice of the state of the fortress without bearing testimony to the honorable exertions of its present commander, Don Francisco de Serna, who is tasking all the limited resources at his command to put the palace in a state of repair, and by his judicious precautions, has for some time arrested its too certain decay. Had his predecessors discharged the duties of their station with equal fidelity, the Alhambra might yet have remained in almost its pristine beauty: were government to second him with means equal to his zeal, this relic of it might still be preserved for many generations to adorn the land, and attract the curious and enlightened of every clime.

Our first object of course, on the morning after our arrival, was a visit to this time-honored edifice; it has been so often, however, and so minutely described by travellers, that I shall not undertake to give a comprehensive and elaborate account of it, but merely occasional sketches of parts with the incidents and associations connected with them.

Leaving our posada, and traversing the renowned square of the Vivarrambla, once the scene of Moorish jousts and tournaments, now a crowded market-place, we proceeded along the Zacatin, the main street of what, in the time of the Moors, was the Great Bazaar, and where small shops and narrow alleys still retain the oriental character. Crossing an open place in front of the palace of the captain-general, we ascended a confined and winding street, the name of which reminded us of the chivalric days of Granada. It is called the Calle, or street of the Gomeres, from a Moorish family famous in chronicle and song. This street led up to the Puerta de las Granadas, a massive gateway of Grecian architecture, built by Charles V., forming the entrance to the domains of the Alhambra.

At the gate were two or three ragged superannuated soldiers, dozing on a stone bench, the successors of the Zegris and the Abencerrages; while a tall, meagre varlet, whose rusty-brown cloak was evidently intended to conceal the ragged state of his nether garments, was lounging in the sunshine and gossiping with

an ancient sentinel on duty. He joined us as we entered the
gate, and offered his services to show us the fortress.

I have a traveller's dislike to officious ciceroni, and did not
altogether like the garb of the applicant.

"You are well acquainted with the place, I presume?"

"Ninguno mas; pues señor, soy hijo de la Alhambra."—(Nobody better; in fact, sir, I am a son of the Alhambra!)

The common Spaniards have certainly a most poetical way of
expressing themselves. "A son of the Alhambra!" the appellation caught me at once; the very tattered garb of my new acquaintance assumed a dignity in my eyes. It was emblematic of
the fortunes of the place, and befitted the progeny of a ruin.

I put some farther questions to him, and found that his title
was legitimate. His family had lived in the fortress from generation to generation ever since the time of the conquest. His name
was Mateo Ximenes. "Then, perhaps," said I, "you may be a
descendant from the great Cardinal Ximenes?"—"Dios Sabe!
God knows, Señor! It may be so. We are the oldest family in
the Alhambra,—*Christianos Viejos*, old Christians, without any
taint of Moor or Jew. I know we belong to some great family
or other, but I forget whom. My father knows all about it: he
has the coat-of-arms hanging up in his cottage, up in the fortress."
—There is not any Spaniard, however poor, but has some claim
to high pedigree. The first title of this ragged worthy, however,
had completely captivated me, so I gladly accepted the services
of the "son of the Alhambra."

We now found ourselves in a deep narrow ravine, filled with
beautiful groves, with a steep avenue, and various footpaths winding through it, bordered with stone seats, and ornamented with
fountains. To our left, we beheld the towers of the Alhambra

beetling above us; to our right, on the opposite side of the ravine, we were equally dominated by rival towers on a rocky eminence. These, we were told, were the Torres Vermejos, or vermilion towers, so called from their ruddy hue. No one knows their origin. They are of a date much anterior to the Alhambra: some suppose them to have been built by the Romans; others, by some wandering colony of Phœnicians. Ascending the steep and shady avenue, we arrived at the foot of a huge square Moorish tower, forming a kind of barbican, through which passed the main entrance to the fortress. Within the barbican was another group of veteran invalids, one mounting guard at the portal, while the rest, wrapped in their tattered cloaks, slept on the stone benches. This portal is called the Gate of Justice, from the tribunal held within its porch during the Moslem domination, for the immediate trial of petty causes: a custom common to the oriental nations, and occasionally alluded to in the Sacred Scriptures. " Judges and officers shalt thou make thee *in all thy gates*, and they shall judge the people with just judgment."

The great vestibule, or porch of the gate, is formed by an immense Arabian arch, of the horseshoe form, which springs to half the height of the tower. On the keystone of this arch is engraven a gigantic hand. Within the vestibule, on the keystone of the portal, is sculptured, in like manner, a gigantic key. Those who pretend to some knowledge of Mohammedan symbols, affirm that the hand is the emblem of doctrine; the five fingers designating the five principal commandments of the creed of Islam, fasting, pilgrimage, alms-giving, ablution, and war againt infidels. The key, say they, is the emblem of the faith or of power; the key of Daoud or David, transmitted to the prophet. " And the key of the house of David will I lay upon his shoulder; so he shall open

and none shall shut, and he shall shut and none shall open."
(Isaiah xxii. 22.) The key we are told was emblazoned on the
standard of the Moslems in opposition to the Christian emblem
of the cross, when they subdued Spain or Andalusia. It betokened
the conquering power invested in the prophet. "He that hath
the key of David, he that openeth and no man shutteth; and
shutteth and no man openeth. (Rev. iii. 7.)

A different explanation of these emblems, however, was given
by the legitimate son of the Alhambra, and one more in unison
with the notions of the common people, who attach something of
mystery and magic to every thing Moorish, and have all kind of
superstitions connected with this old Moslem fortress. According to Mateo, it was a tradition handed down from the oldest inhabitants, and which he had from his father and grandfather, that
the hand and key were magical devices on which the fate of the
Alhambra depended. The Moorish king who built it was a great
magician, or, as some believed, had sold himself to the devil, and
had laid the whole fortress under a magic spell. By this means
it had remained standing for several hundred years, in defiance
of storms and earthquakes, while almost all other buildings of the
Moors had fallen to ruin, and disappeared. This spell, the tradition went on to say, would last until the hand on the outer arch
should reach down and grasp the key, when the whole pile would
tumble to pieces, and all the treasures buried beneath it by the
Moors would be revealed.

Notwithstanding this ominous prediction, we ventured to pass
through the spell-bound gateway, feeling some little assurance
against magic art in the protection of the Virgin, a statue of
whom we observed above the portal.

After passing through the barbican, we ascended a narrow

lane, winding between walls, and came on an open esplanade within the fortress, called the Plaza de los Algibes, or Place of the Cisterns, from great reservoirs which undermine it, cut in the living rock by the Moors to receive the water brought by conduits from the Darro, for the supply of the fortress. Here, also, is a well of immense depth, furnishing the purest and coldest of water; another monument of the delicate taste of the Moors, who were indefatigable in their exertions to obtain that element in its crystal purity.

In front of this esplanade is the splendid pile commenced by Charles V., and intended, it is said, to eclipse the residence of the Moorish kings. Much of the oriental edifice intended for the winter season was demolished to make way for this massive pile. The grand entrance was blocked up; so that the present entrance to the Moorish palace is through a simple and almost humble portal in a corner. With all the massive grandeur and architectural merit of the palace of Charles V., we regarded it as an arrogant intruder, and passing by it with a feeling almost of scorn, rang at the Moslem portal.

While waiting for admittance, our self-imposed cicerone, Mateo Ximenes, informed us that the royal palace was intrusted to the care of a worthy old maiden dame called Doña Antonia-Molina, but who, according to Spanish custom, went by the more neighborly appellation of Tia Antonia (Aunt Antonia), who maintained the Moorish halls and gardens in order and showed them to strangers. While we were talking, the door was opened by a plump little black-eyed Andalusian damsel, whom Mateo addressed as Dolores, but who from her bright looks and cheerful disposition evidently merited a merrier name. Mateo informed me in a whisper that she was the niece of Tia Antonia, and I found she was the good fairy who was to conduct us through the enchanted palace. Under her guidance we crossed the threshold, and were at once transported, as if by magic wand, into other times and an oriental realm, and were treading the scenes of Arabian story. Nothing could be in greater contrast than the unpromising exterior of the pile with the scene now before us. We found ourselves in a vast patio or court one hundred and fifty feet in length, and upwards of eighty feet in breadth, paved with white marble, and decorated at each end with light Moorish peristyles, one of which supported an elegant gallery of fretted architecture. Along the mouldings of the cornices and on various parts of the walls were escutcheons and ciphers, and cufic and Arabic characters in high relief, repeating the pious mottoes of the Moslem monarchs, the builders of the Alhambra, or extolling their grandeur and munificence. Along the centre of the court extended an immense basin or tank (estanque) a hundred and twenty-four feet in length, twenty-seven in breadth, and five in depth, receiving its water from two marble vases. Hence it is called the Court of the Alberca (from al Beerkah, the Arabic for a pond or tank). Great numbers of gold-fish were to be seen gleaming through the waters of the basin, and it was bordered by hedges of roses.

Passing from the court of the Alberca under a Moorish archway, we entered the renowned court of Lions. No part of the edifice gives a more complete idea of its original beauty than this, for none has suffered so little from the ravages of time. In the centre stands the fountain famous in song and story. The alabaster basins still shed their diamond drops; the twelve lions which support them, and give the court its name, still cast forth crystal streams as in the days of Boabdil. The lions, however are unworthy of their fame, being of miserable sculpture, the work probably of some Christian captive. The court is laid out in flower-beds, instead of its ancient and appropriate pavement of tiles or marble; the alteration, an instance of bad taste, was made by the French when in possession of Granada. Round the four sides of the court are light Arabian arcades of open filigree work supported by slender pillars of white marble, which it is supposed were originally gilded. The architecture, like that in most parts of the interior of the palace, is characterized by elegance, rather than grandeur; bespeaking a delicate and graceful taste, and a disposition to indolent enjoyment. When one looks upon the fairy traces of the peristyles, and the apparently fragile fretwork of the walls, it is difficult to believe that so much has survived the wear and tear of centuries, the shocks of earthquakes, the violence of war, and the quiet, though no less baneful, pilferings of the tasteful traveller: it is almost sufficient to excuse the popular tradition, that the whole is protected by a magic charm.

On one side of the court a rich portal opens into the hall of the Abencerrages; so called from the gallant cavaliers of that illustrious line who were here perfidiously massacred. There are some who doubt the whole story, but our humble cicerone Mateo pointed out the very wicket of the portal through which they were introduced one by one into the court of Lions, and the white marble fountain in the centre of the hall beside which they were beheaded He showed us also certain broad ruddy stains on the pavement, traces of their blood, which, according to popular belief, can never be effaced.

Finding we listened to him apparently with easy faith, he added, that there was often heard at night, in the court of Lions.

a low confused sound, resembling the murmuring of a multitude; and now and then a faint tinkling, like the distant clank of chains. These sounds were made by the spirits of the murdered Abencerrages; who nightly haunt the scene of their suffering and invoke the vengeance of Heaven on their destroyer.

The sounds in question had no doubt been produced, as I had afterwards an opportunity of ascertaining, by the bubbling currents and tinkling falls of water conducted under the pavement through pipes and channels to supply the fountains; but I was too considerate to intimate such an idea to the humble chronicler of the Alhambra.

Encouraged by my easy credulity, Mateo gave me the following as an undoubted fact, which he had from his grandfather:

There was once an invalid soldier, who had charge of the Alhambra to show it to strangers: as he was one evening, about twilight, passing through the court of Lions, he heard footsteps on the hall of the Abencerrages; supposing some strangers to be lingering there, he advanced to attend upon them, when to his astonishment he beheld four Moors richly dressed, with gilded cuirasses and cimeters, and poniards glittering with precious stones. They were walking to and fro, with solemn pace; but paused and beckoned to him. The old soldier, however, took to flight, and could never afterwards be prevailed upon to enter the Alhambra. Thus it is that men sometimes turn their backs upon fortune; for it is the firm opinion of Mateo, that the Moors intended to reveal the place where their treasures lay buried. A successor to the invalid soldier was more knowing; he came to the Alhambra poor; but at the end of a year went off to Malaga, bought houses, set up a carriage, and still lives there one of the richest as well as oldest men of the place; all which, Mateo

3*

sagely surmised, was in consequence of his finding out the golden
secret of these phantom Moors.

I now perceived I had made an invaluable acquaintance in
this son of the Alhambra, one who knew all the apocryphal history of the place, and firmly believed in it, and whose memory
was stuffed with a kind of knowledge for which I have a lurking
fancy, but which is too apt to be considered rubbish by less indulgent philosophers. I determined to cultivate the acquaintance of this learned Theban.

Immediately opposite the hall of the Abencerrages a portal,
richly adorned, leads into a hall of less tragical associations. It
is light and lofty, exquisitely graceful in its architecture,
paved with white marble, and bears the suggestive name of the
Hall of the Two Sisters. Some destroy the romance of the
name by attributing it to two enormous slabs of alabaster which
lie side by side, and form a great part of the pavement; an
opinion strongly supported by Mateo Ximenes. Others are disposed to give the name a more poetical significance, as the vague
memorial of Moorish beauties who once graced this hall, which
was evidently a part of the royal harem. This opinion I was
happy to find entertained by our little bright-eyed guide, Dolores,
who pointed to a balcony over an inner porch; which gallery, she
had been told, belonged to the women's apartment. "You see,
señor," said she, "it is all grated and latticed, like the gallery
in a convent chapel where the nuns hear mass; for the Moorish
kings," added she, indignantly, "shut up their wives just like
nuns."

The latticed "jalousies," in fact, still remain, whence the
dark-eyed beauties of the harem might gaze unseen upon the
zambras and other dances and entertainments of the hall below.

On each side of this hall are recesses or alcoves for ottomans and couches, on which the voluptuous lords of the Alhambra indulged in that dreamy repose so dear to the Orientalists. A cupola or lantern admits a tempered light from above and a free circulation of air; while on one side is heard the refreshing sound of waters from the fountain of the lions, and on the other side the soft plash from the basin in the garden of Lindaraxa.

It is impossible to contemplate this scene so perfectly Oriental without feeling the early associations of Arabian romance, and almost expecting to see the white arm of some mysterious princess beckoning from the gallery, or some dark eye sparkling through the lattice. The abode of beauty is here, as if it had been inhabited but yesterday; but where are the two sisters; where the Zoraydas and Lindaraxas!

An abundant supply of water, brought from the mountains by old Moorish aqueducts, circulates throughout the palace, supplying its baths and fishpools, sparkling in jets within its halls, or murmuring in channels along the marble pavements. When it has paid its tribute to the royal pile, and visited its gardens and parterres, it flows down the long avenue leading to the city, tinkling in rills, gushing in fountains, and maintaining a perpetual verdure in those groves that embower and beautify the whole hill of the Alhambra.

Those only who have sojourned in the ardent climates of the South, can appreciate the delights of an abode, combining the breezy coolness of the mountain with the freshness and verdure of the valley. While the city below pants with the noontide heat, and the parched Vega trembles to the eye, the delicate airs from the Sierra Nevada play through these lofty halls, bringing with them the sweetness of the surrounding gardens. Every thing invites to that indolent repose, the bliss of southern climes; and while the half-shut eye looks out from shaded balconies upon the glittering landscape, the ear is lulled by the rustling of groves, and the murmur of running streams.

I forbear for the present, however, to describe the other delightful apartments of the palace. My object is merely to give the reader a general introduction into an abode where, if so disposed, he may linger and loiter with me day by day until we gradually become familiar with all its localities.

NOTE ON MORISCO ARCHITECTURE.

To an unpractised eye the light relievos and fanciful arabesques which cover the walls of the Alhambra appear to have been sculptured by the hand, with a minute and patient labor, an inexhaustible variety of detail, yet a general uniformity and harmony of design truly astonishing; and this may especially be said of the vaults and cupolas, which are wrought like honey-combs, or frostwork, with stalactites and pendants which confound the beholder with the seeming intricacy of their patterns. The astonishment ceases, however, when it is discovered that this is all stucco-work; plates of plaster of Paris, cast in moulds and skilfully joined so as to form patterns of every size and form. This mode of diapering walls with arabesques and stuccoing the vaults with grotto-work, was invented in Damascus; but highly improved by the Moors in Morocco, to whom Saracenic architecture owes its most graceful and fanciful details. The process by which all this fairy tracery was produced was ingeniously simple. The wall in its naked state was divided off by lines crossing at right angles, such as artists use in copying a picture; over these were drawn a succession of intersecting segments of circles. By the aid of these the artists could work with celerity and certainty, and from the mere intersection of the plain and curved lines arose the interminable variety of patterns and the general uniformity of their character.*

* See Urquhart's Pillars of Hercules, B. iii. C. 8.

Much gilding was used in the stucco-work, especially of the cupolas: and the interstices were delicately pencilled with brilliant colors, such as vermilion and lapis lazuli, laid on with the whites of eggs. The primitive colors alone were used, says Ford, by the Egyptians, Greeks, and Arabs, in the early period of art; and they prevail in the Alhambra whenever the artist has been Arabic or Moorish. It is remarkable how much of their original brilliancy remains after the lapse of several centuries.

The lower part of the walls in the saloons, to the height of several feet, is incrusted with glazed tiles, joined like the plates of stucco-work, so as to form various patterns. On some of them are emblazoned the escutcheons of the Moslem kings, traversed with a band and motto. These glazed tiles (azulejos in Spanish, az-zulaj in Arabic) are of Oriental origin; their coolness, cleanliness, and freedom from vermin, render them admirably fitted in sultry climates for paving halls and fountains; incrusting bathing rooms and lining the walls of chambers. Ford is inclined to give them great antiquity. From their prevailing colors, sapphire and blue, he deduces that they may have formed the kind of pavements alluded to in the sacred Scriptures—"There was under his feet as it were a paved work of a sapphire stone" (Exod. xxiv. 10); and again, "Behold I will lay thy stones with fair colors, and lay thy foundations with sapphires" (Isaiah liv. 11).

These glazed or porcelain tiles were introduced into Spain at an early date by the Moslems. Some are to be seen among the Moorish ruins which have been there upwards of eight centuries. Manufactures of them still exist in the peninsula, and they are much used in the best Spanish houses, especially in the southern provinces, for paving and lining the summer apartments.

The Spaniards introduced them into the Netherlands when they had possession of that country. The people of Holland adopted them with avidity, as wonderfully suited to their passion for household cleanliness; and thus these Oriental inventions, the azulejos of the Spanish, the az-zulaj of the Arabs, have come to be commonly known as Dutch tiles.

IMPORTANT NEGOTIATIONS.—THE AUTHOR SUCCEEDS TO THE THRONE OF BOABDIL.

THE day was nearly spent before we could tear ourself from this region of poetry and romance to descend to the city and return to the forlorn realities of a Spanish posada. In a visit of ceremony to the Governor of the Alhambra, to whom we had brought letters, we dwelt with enthusiasm on the scenes we had witnessed, and could not but express surprise that he should reside in the city when he had such a paradise at his command. He pleaded the inconvenience of a residence in the palace from its situation on the crest of a hill, distant from the seat of business and the resorts of social intercourse. It did very well for monarchs, who often had need of castle walls to defend them from their own subjects. "But señors," added he, smiling, "if you think a residence there so desirable, my apartments in the Alhambra are at your service."

It is a common and almost indispensable point of politeness in a Spaniard, to tell you his house is yours.—" Esta casa es siempre à la disposicion de Vm." " This house is always at the command of your Grace." In fact, any thing of his which you admire, is immediately offered to you. It is equally a mark of good breeding in you not to accept it; so we merely bowed our acknowledgments of the courtesy of the Governor in offering us a royal palace. We were mistaken, however. The Governor was in earnest. "You will find a rambling set of empty, unfurnished rooms," said he; "but Tia Antonia, who has charge of the palace, may be able to put them in some kind of order; and to take care of you while you are there. If you can make any arrangement with her for your accommodation, and are content with scanty fare in a royal abode, the palace of King Chico is at your service."

We took the Governor at his word, and hastened up the steep Calle de los Gomeres, and through the Great Gate of Justice, to negotiate with Dame Antonia; doubting at times if this were not a dream, and fearing at times that the sage Dueña of the fortress might be slow to capitulate. We knew we had one friend at least in the garrison, who would be in our favor, the bright-eyed little Dolores, whose good graces we had propitiated on our first visit; and who hailed our return to the palace with her brightest looks.

All, however, went smoothly. The good Tia Antonia had a little furniture to put in the rooms, but it was of the commonest kind. We assured her we could bivouac on the floor. She could supply our table; but only in her own simple way—we wanted nothing better. Her niece, Dolores, would wait upon us—and at the word we threw up our hats and the bargain was complete.

The very next day we took up our abode in the palace, and never did sovereigns share a divided throne with more perfect harmony. Several days passed by like a dream, when my worthy associate, being summoned to Madrid on diplomatic duties, was compelled to abdicate, leaving me sole monarch of this shadowy realm. For myself, being in a manner a hap-hazard loiterer

about the world and prone to linger in its pleasant places, here
have I been suffering day by day to steal away unheeded, spell-
bound, for aught I know, in this old enchanted pile. Having
always a companionable feeling for my reader, and being prone
to live with him on confidential terms, I shall make it a point to
communicate to him my reveries and researches during this state
of delicious thraldom. If they have the power of imparting to
his imagination any of the witching charms of the place, he will
not repine at lingering with me for a season in the legendary
halls of the Alhambra.

And first it is proper to give him some idea of my domestic
arrangements; they are rather of a simple kind for the occupant
of a regal palace; but I trust they will be less liable to disastrous reverses than those of my royal predecessors.

My quarters are at one end of the Governor's apartment, a
suite of empty chambers, in front of the palace, looking out
upon the great esplanade called *la plaza de los algibes* (the place
of the cisterns); the apartment is modern, but the end opposite
to my sleeping-room communicates with a cluster of little chambers, partly Moorish, partly Spanish, allotted to the *châtelaine*
Doña Antonia and her family. In consideration of keeping the
palace in order, the good dame is allowed all the perquisites received from visitors, and all the produce of the gardens; excepting that she is expected to pay an occasional tribute of fruits and
flowers to the Governor. Her family consists of a nephew and
niece, the children of two different brothers. The nephew, Manuel Molina, is a young man of sterling worth and Spanish gravity. He had served in the army, both in Spain and the West
Indies; but is now studying medicine in the hope of one day or
other becoming physician to the fortress, a post worth at least

one hundred and forty dollars a year. The niece is the plump little black-eyed Dolores already mentioned ; and who, it is said, will one day inherit all her aunt's possessions, consisting of certain petty tenements in the fortress, in a somewhat ruinous condition it is true, but which, I am privately assured by Mateo Ximenes, yield a revenue of nearly one hundred and fifty dollars ; so that she is quite an heiress in the eyes of the ragged son of the Alhambra. I am also informed by the same observant and authentic personage, that a quiet courtship is going on between the discreet Manuel and his bright-eyed cousin, and that nothing is wanting to enable them to join their hands and expectations but his doctor's diploma, and a dispensation from the Pope on account of their consanguinity.

The good dame Antonia fulfils faithfully her contract in regard to my board and lodging ; and as I am easily pleased, I find my fare excellent ; while the merry-hearted little Dolores keeps my apartment in order, and officiates as handmaid at meal-times. I have also at my command a tall, stuttering, yellow-haired lad, named Pépe, who works in the gardens, and would fain have acted as valet ; but, in this, he was forestalled by Mateo Ximenes, " the son of the Alhambra." This alert and officious wight has managed, somehow or other, to stick by me ever since I first encountered him at the outer gate of the fortress, and to weave himself into all my plans, until he has fairly appointed and installed himself my valet, cicerone, guide, guard, and historiographic squire ; and I have been obliged to improve the state of his wardrobe, that he may not disgrace his various functions ; so that he has cast his old brown mantle, as a snake does his skin, and now appears about the fortress with a smart Andalusian hat and jacket, to his infinite satisfaction, and the great astonishment of

his comrades.   The chief fault of honest Mateo is an over anxiety
to be useful.   Conscious of having foisted himself into my employ, and that my simple and quiet habits render his situation a
sinecure, he is at his wit's ends to devise modes of making himself important to my welfare.   I am, in a manner, the victim of
his officiousness; I cannot put my foot over the threshold of the
palace, to stroll about the fortress, but he is at my elbow, to explain every thing I see ; and if I venture to ramble among the
surrounding hills, he insists upon attending me as a guard, though
I vehemently suspect he would be more apt to trust to the length
of his legs than the strength of his arms, in case of attack.   After
all, however, the poor fellow is at times an amusing companion ;
he is simple-minded, and of infinite good humor, with the loqua-
city and gossip of a village barber, and knows all the small-talk
of the place and its environs ; but what he chiefly values himself
on, is his stock of local information, having the most marvellous
stories to relate of every tower, and vault, and gateway of the
fortress, in all of which he places the most implicit faith.

Most of these he has derived, according to his own account,
from his grandfather, a little legendary tailor, who lived to the
age of nearly a hundred years, during which he made but two
migrations beyond the precincts of the fortress.   His shop, for
the greater part of a century, was the resort of a knot of venerable gossips, where they would pass half the night talking about
old times, and the wonderful events and hidden secrets of the
place.   The whole living, moving, thinking, and acting, of this
historical little tailor, had thus been bounded by the walls of the
Alhambra ; within them he had been born, within them he lived,
breathed, and had his being ; within them he died, and was buried.   Fortunately for posterity, his traditionary lore died not

with him. The authentic Mateo, when an urchin, used to be an attentive listener to the narratives of his grandfather, and of the gossip group assembled round the shopboard ; and is thus possessed of a stock of valuable knowledge concerning the Alhambra, not to be found in books, and well worthy the attention of every curious traveller.

Such are the personages that constitute my regal household ; and I question whether any of the potentates, Moslem or Christian, who have preceded me in the palace, have been waited upon with greater fidelity, or enjoyed a serener sway.

When I rise in the morning, Pépe, the stuttering lad from the gardens, brings me a tribute of fresh culled flowers, which are afterwards arranged in vases, by the skilful hand of Dolores, who takes a female pride in the decorations of my chamber. My meals are made wherever caprice dictates ; sometimes in one of the Moorish halls, sometimes under the arcades of the court of Lions, surrounded by flowers and fountains : and when I walk out, I am conducted by the assiduous Mateo, to the most romantic retreats of the mountains, and delicious haunts of the adjacent valleys, not one of which but is the scene of some wonderful tale.

Though fond of passing the greater part of my day alone, yet I occasionally repair in the evenings to the little domestic circle of Doña Antonia. This is generally held in an old Moorish chamber, which serves the good dame for parlor, kitchen and hall of audience, and which must have boasted of some splendor in the time of the Moors, if we may judge from the traces yet remaining ; but a rude fireplace has been made in modern times in one corner, the smoke from which has discolored the walls, and almost obliterated the ancient arabesques. A window, with a bal-

cony overhanging the valley of the Darro, lets in the cool evening breeze ; and here I take my frugal supper of fruit and milk,
and mingle with the conversation of the family.   There is a
natural talent or mother wit, as it is called, about the Spaniards,
which renders them intellectual and agreeable companions, whatever may be their condition in life, or however imperfect may
have been their education : add to this, they are never vulgar ;
nature has endowed them with an inherent dignity of spirit.
The good Tia Antonia is a woman of strong and intelligent,
though uncultivated mind ; and the bright-eyed Dolores, though
she has read but three or four books in the whole course of her
life, has an engaging mixture of naïveté and good sense, and
often surprises me by the pungency of her artless sallies.   Sometimes the nephew entertains us by reading some old comedy of
Calderon or Lope de Vega, to which he is evidently prompted
by a desire to improve, as well as amuse his cousin Dolores ;
though, to his great mortification, the little damsel generally falls
asleep before the first act is completed.   Sometimes Tia Antonia
has a little levee of humble friends and dependents, the inhabitants of the adjacent hamlet, or the wives of the invalid soldiers.
These look up to her with great deference, as the custodian of
the palace, and pay their court to her by bringing the news of the
place, or the rumors that may have straggled up from Granada.
In listening to these evening gossipings I have picked up many
curious facts, illustrative of the manners of the people and the
peculiarities of the neighborhood.

 These are simple details of simple pleasures ; it is the nature
of the place alone that gives them interest and importance.   I
tread haunted ground, and am surrounded by romantic associations.   From earliest boyhood, when, on the banks of the Hud-

son, I first pored over the pages of old Gines Perez de Hytas's apocryphal but chivalresque history of the civil wars of Granada, and the feuds of its gallant cavaliers, the Zegries and Abencerrages, that city has ever been a subject of my waking dreams; and often have I trod in fancy the romantic halls of the Alhambra. Behold for once a day-dream realized; yet I can scarce credit my senses, or believe that I do indeed inhabit the palace of Boabdil, and look down from its balconies upon chivalric Granada. As I loiter through these Oriental chambers, and hear the murmur of fountains and the song of the nightingale; as I inhale the odor of the rose, and feel the influence of the balmy climate, I am almost tempted to fancy myself in the paradise of Mahomet, and that the plump little Dolores is one of the bright-eyed houris, destined to administer to the happiness of true believers.

INHABITANTS OF THE ALHAMBRA.

I HAVE often observed that the more proudly a mansion has been tenanted in the day of its prosperity, the humbler are its inhabitants in the day of its decline, and that the palace of a king commonly ends in being the nestling-place of the beggar.

The Alhambra is in a rapid state of similar transition. Whenever a tower falls to decay, it is seized upon by some tatter-demalion family, who become joint-tenants, with the bats and owls, of its gilded halls ; and hang their rags, those standards of poverty, out of its windows and loopholes.

I have amused myself with remarking some of the motley characters that have thus usurped the ancient abode of royalty, and who seem as if placed here to give a farcical termination to the drama of human pride. One of these even bears the mockery of a regal title. It is a little old woman named Maria Antonia Sabonea, but who goes by the appellation of la Reyna Coquina, or the Cockle-queen. She is small enough to be a fairy, and a fairy she may be for aught I can find out, for no one seems to know her origin. Her habitation is in a kind of closet under the outer staircase of the palace, and she sits in the cool stone corridor, plying her needle and singing from morning till night, with a ready joke for every one that passes ; for though one of the poorest, she is one of the merriest little women breathing. Her great merit is a gift for story-telling, having, I verily believe, as many stories at her command, as the inexhaustible Scheherezade of the thousand and one nights. Some of these I have heard her relate in the evening tertulias of Dame Antonia, at which she is occasionally a humble attendant.

That there must be some fairy gift about this mysterious little old woman, would appear from her extraordinary luck, since, notwithstanding her being very little, very ugly, and very poor, she has had, according to her own account, five husbands and a half, reckoning as a half one a young dragoon, who died during courtship. A rival personage to this little fairy queen is a portly old fellow with a bottle-nose, who goes about in a rusty garb with a cocked hat of oil-skin and a red cockade. He is one of the legitimate sons of the Alhambra, and has lived here all his life, filling various offices, such as deputy alguazil, sexton of the parochial church, and marker of a fives-court established at the foot of one of the towers. He is as poor as a rat, but as proud as he is ragged, boasting of his descent from the illustrious house of Aguilar, from which sprang Gonzalvo of Cordova, the grand captain. Nay, he actually bears the name of Alonzo de Aguilar, so renowned in the history of the conquest; though the graceless wags of the fortress have given him the title of *el padre santo*, or the holy father, the usual appellation of the Pope, which I had thought too sacred in the eyes of true Catholics to be thus ludicrously applied. It is a whimsical caprice of fortune to present, in the grotesque person of this tatterdemalion, a namesake and descendant of the proud Alonzo de Aguilar, the mirror of Andalusian chivalry, leading an almost mendicant existence about this once haughty fortress, which his ancestor

aided to reduce; yet, such might have been the lot of the
descendants of Agamemnon and Achilles, had they lingered
about the ruins of Troy!

Of this motley community, I find the family of my gossiping
squire, Mateo Ximenes, to form, from their numbers at least, a
very important part. His boast of being a son of the Alhambra,
is not unfounded. His family has inhabited the fortress ever
since the time of the conquest, handing down an hereditary
poverty from father to son; not one of them having ever been
known to be worth a maravedi. His father, by trade a ribbon-
weaver, and who succeeded the historical tailor as the head of
the family, is now near seventy years of age, and lives in a hovel
of reeds and plaster, built by his own hands, just above the iron
gate. The furniture consists of a crazy bed, a table, and two or
three chairs; a wooden chest, containing, besides his scanty
clothing, the " archives of the family." These are nothing more
nor less than the papers of various lawsuits sustained by
different generations; by which it would seem that, with all their
apparent carelessness and good humor, they are a litigious brood.
Most of the suits have been brought against gossiping neighbors for questioning the purity of their blood, and denying their
being *Christianos viejos*, i. e. old Christians, without Jewish or
Moorish taint. In fact, I doubt whether this jealousy about
their blood has not kept them so poor in purse: spending all
their earnings on escribanos and alguazils. The pride of the
hovel is an escutcheon suspended against the wall, in which are
emblazoned quarterings of the arms of the Marquis of Caiesedo,
and of various other noble houses, with which this poverty-
stricken brood claim affinity.

As to Mateo himself, who is now about thirty-five years of age, he has done his utmost to perpetuate his line and continue the poverty of the family, having a wife and a numerous progeny, who inhabit an almost dismantled hovel in the hamlet. How they manage to subsist, he only who sees into all mysteries can tell; the subsistence of a Spanish family of the kind, is always a riddle to me; yet they do subsist, and what is more, appear to enjoy their existence. The wife takes her holiday stroll on the Paseo of Granada, with a child in her arms and half a dozen at her heels; and the eldest daughter, now verging into womanhood, dresses her hair with flowers, and dances gayly to the castañets.

There are two classes of people to whom life seems one long holiday, the very rich, and the very poor; one because they need do nothing, the other because they have nothing to do; but there are none who understand the art of doing nothing and living upon nothing, better than the poor classes of Spain. Climate does one half, and temperament the rest. Give a Spaniard the shade in summer, and the sun in winter; a little bread, garlic, oil, and garbances, an old brown cloak and a guitar, and let the world roll on as it pleases. Talk of poverty! with him it has no disgrace. It sits upon him with a grandiose style, like his ragged cloak. He is a hidalgo, even when in rags.

The "sons of the Alhambra" are an eminent illustration of this practical philosophy. As the Moors imagined that the celestial paradise hung over this favored spot, so I am inclined at times to fancy, that a gleam of the golden age still lingers about this ragged community. They possess nothing, they do nothing, they care for nothing. Yet, though apparently idle all the week, they are as observant of all holy days and saints' days as the most laborious artisan. They attend all fêtes and dancings in Gran-

4

ada and its vicinity, light bonfires on the hills on St. John's eve, and dance away the moonlight nights on the harvest-home of a small field within the precincts of the fortress, which yield a few bushels of wheat.

Before concluding these remarks, I must mention one of the amusements of the place which has particularly struck me. I had repeatedly observed a long lean fellow perched on the top of one of the towers, manœuvring two or three fishing-rods, as though he were angling for the stars. I was for some time perplexed by the evolutions of this aerial fisherman, and my perplexity increased on observing others employed in like manner on different parts of the battlements and bastions; it was not until I consulted Mateo Ximenes, that I solved the mystery.

It seems that the pure and airy situation of this fortress has rendered it, like the castle of Macbeth, a prolific breeding-place far swallows and martlets, who sport about its towers in myriads, with the holiday glee of urchins just let loose from school. To entrap these birds in their giddy circlings, with hooks baited with flies, is one of the favorite amusements of the ragged "sons of the Alhambra," who, with the good-for-nothing ingenuity of arrant idlers, have thus invented the art of angling in the sky.

THE HALL OF AMBASSADORS.

IN one of my visits to the old Moorish chamber, where the good Tia Antonia cooks her dinner and receives her company, I observed a mysterious door in one corner, leading apparently into the ancient part of the edifice. My curiosity being aroused, I opened it, and found myself in a narrow, blind corridor, groping along which I came to the head of a dark winding staircase, leading down an angle of the tower of Comares. Down this staircase I descended darkling, guiding myself by the wall until I came to a small door at the bottom, throwing which open, I was suddenly dazzled by emerging into the brilliant antechamber of the Hall of Ambassadors; with the fountain of the court of the Alberca sparkling before me. The antechamber is separated from the court by an elegant gallery, supported by slender columns with spandrels of open work in the Morisco style. At each end of the antechamber are alcoves, and its ceiling is richly stuccoed and painted. Passing through a magnificent portal I found myself in the far-famed Hall of Ambassadors, the audience chamber of the Moslem monarchs. It is said to be thirty-seven feet square, and sixty feet high; occupies the whole interior of the Tower of Comares; and still bears the traces of past magnificence. The walls are beautifully stuccoed and decorated with

Morisco fancifulness; the lofty ceiling was originally of the same favorite material, with the usual frostwork and pensile ornaments or stalactites; which, with the embellishments of vivid coloring and gilding, must have been gorgeous in the extreme. Unfortunately it gave way during an earthquake, and brought down with it an immense arch which traversed the hall. It was replaced by the present vault or dome of larch or cedar, with intersecting ribs, the whole curiously wrought and richly colored; still Oriental in its character, reminding one of "those ceilings of cedar and vermilion that we read of in the prophets and the Arabian Nights."*

From the great height of the vault above the windows the upper part of the hall is almost lost in obscurity; yet there is a magnificence as well as solemnity in the gloom, as through it we have gleams of rich gilding and the brilliant tints of the Moorish pencil.

The royal throne was placed opposite the entrance in a recess, which still bears an inscription intimating that Yusef I. (the monarch who completed the Alhambra) made this the throne of his empire. Every thing in this noble hall seems to have been calculated to surround the throne with impressive dignity and splendor; there was none of the elegant voluptuousness which reigns in other parts of the palace. The tower is of massive strength, domineering over the whole edifice and overhanging the steep hillside. On three sides of the Hall of Ambassadors are windows cut through the immense thickness of the walls, and commanding extensive prospects. The balcony of the central window especially looks down upon the verdant valley of the

* Urquhart's Pillars of Hercules.

Darro, with its walks, its groves, and gardens. To the left it enjoys a distant prospect of the Vega, while directly in front rises the rival height of the Albaycin, with its medley of streets, and terraces, and gardens, and once crowned by a fortress that vied in power with the Alhambra. "Ill fated the man who lost all this!" exclaimed Charles V., as he looked forth from this window upon the enchanting scenery it commands.

The balcony of the window where this royal exclamation was made, has of late become one of my favorite resorts. I have just been seated there, enjoying the close of a long brilliant day. The sun, as he sank behind the purple mountains of Alhama, sent a stream of effulgence up the valley of the Darro, that spread a melancholy pomp over the ruddy towers of the Alhambra; while the Vega, covered with a slight sultry vapor that caught the setting ray, seemed spread out in the distance like a golden sea. Not a breath of air disturbed the stillness of the hour, and though the faint sound of music and merriment now and then rose from the gardens of the Darro, it but rendered more impressive the monumental silence of the pile which overshadowed me. It was one of those hours and scenes in which memory asserts an almost magical power; and, like the evening sun beaming on these mouldering towers, sends back her retrospective rays to light up the glories of the past.

As I sat watching the effect of the declining daylight upon this Moorish pile, I was led into a consideration of the light, elegant, and voluptuous character, prevalent throughout its internal architecture; and to contrast it with the grand but gloomy solemnity of the Gothic edifices reared by the Spanish conquerors. The very architecture thus bespeaks the opposite and irreconcilable natures of the two warlike people who so long battled here for the mastery of the peninsula. By degrees, I fell into a course of musing upon the singular fortunes of the Arabian or Morisco-Spaniards, whose whole existence is as a tale that is told, and certainly forms one of the most anomalous yet splendid episodes in history. Potent and durable as was their dominion, we scarcely know how to call them. They were a nation without a legitimate country or name. A remote wave of the great Arabian inundation, cast upon the shores of Europe, they seem to have all the impetus of the first rush of the torrent. Their career of conquest, from the rock of Gibraltar to the cliffs of the Pyrenees, was as rapid and brilliant as the Moslem victories of Syria and Egypt. Nay, had they not been checked on the plains of Tours, all France, all Europe, might have been overrun with the same facility as the empires of the East, and the crescent at this day have glittered on the fanes of Paris and London.

Repelled within the limits of the Pyrenees, the mixed hordes of Asia and Africa, that formed this great irruption, gave up the Moslem principle of conquest, and sought to establish in Spain a peaceful and permanent dominion. As conquerors, their heroism was only equalled by their moderation; and in both, for a time, they excelled the nations with whom they contended. Severed from their native homes, they loved the land given them as they supposed by Allah, and strove to embellish it with every thing that could administer to the happiness of man. Laying the foundations of their power in a system of wise and equitable laws, diligently cultivating the arts and sciences, and promoting agriculture, manufactures, and commerce; they gradually formed an empire unrivalled for its prosperity by any of the empires of Christendom; and diligently drawing round them the graces and refinements which marked the Arabian empire in the East, at the time of its greatest civilization, they diffused the light of Oriental knowledge, through the Western regions of benighted Europe.

The cities of Arabian Spain became the resort of Christian artisans, to instruct themselves in the useful arts. The universities of Toledo, Cordova, Seville, and Granada, were sought by the pale student from other lands to acquaint himself with the sciences of the Arabs, and the treasured lore of antiquity; the lovers of the gay science, resorted to Cordova and Granada, to imbibe the poetry and music of the East; and the steel-clad warriors of the North hastened thither to accomplish themselves in the graceful exercises and courteous usages of chivalry.

If the Moslem monuments in Spain, if the Mosque of Cordova, the Alcazar of Seville, and the Alhambra of Granada, still bear inscriptions fondly boasting of the power and permanency of their dominion: can the boast be derided as arrogant and vain? Generation after generation, century after century, passed away, and still they maintained possession of the land. A period elapsed longer than that which has passed since England was subjugated by the Norman Conqueror, and the descendants of Musa and Taric might as little anticipate being driven into exile across the same straits, traversed by their triumphant ancestors, as the descendants of Rollo and William, and their veteran peers, may dream of being driven back to the shores of Normandy.

With all this, however, the Moslem empire in Spain was but a brilliant exotic, that took no permanent root in the soil it embellished. Severed from all their neighbors in the West, by impassable barriers of faith and manners, and separated by seas and deserts from their kindred of the East, the Morisco Spaniards were an isolated people. Their whole existence was a prolonged, though gallant and chivalric struggle, for a foothold in a usurped land.

They were the outposts and frontiers of Islamism.   The peninsula was the great battle-ground where the Gothic conquerors of the North and the Moslem conquerors of the East, met and strove for mastery ; and the fiery courage of the Arab was at length subdued by the obstinate and persevering valor of the Goth.

Never was the annihilation of a people more complete than that of the Morisco-Spaniards.   Where are they?   Ask the shores of Barbary and its desert places.   The exiled remnant of their once powerful empire disappeared among the barbarians of Africa, and ceased to be a nation.   They have not even left a distinct name behind them, though for nearly eight centuries they were a distinct people.   The home of their adoption, and of their occupation for ages, refuses to acknowledge them, except as invaders and usurpers.   A few broken monuments are all that remain to bear witness to their power and dominion, as solitary rocks, left far in the interior, bear testimony to the extent of some vast inundation.   Such is the Alhambra.   A Moslem pile in the midst of a Christian land ; an Oriental palace amidst the Gothic edifices of the West ; an elegant memento of a brave, intelligent, and graceful people, who conquered, ruled, flourished, and passed away.

THE JESUITS' LIBRARY.

Since indulging in the foregoing reverie, my curiosity has been aroused to know something of the princes, who left behind them this monument of Oriental taste and magnificence; and whose names still appear among the inscriptions on its walls. To gratify this curiosity, I have descended from this region of fancy and fable, where every thing is liable to take an imaginary tint, and have carried my researches among the dusty tomes of the old Jesuits' Library, in the University. This once boasted repository of erudition is now a mere shadow of its former self, having been stripped of its manuscripts and rarest works by the French, when masters of Granada; still it contains among many ponderous tomes of the Jesuit fathers, which the French were careful to leave behind, several curious tracts of Spanish literature; and above all, a number of those antiquated parchment-bound chronicles for which I have a particular veneration.

In this old library, I have passed many delightful hours of quiet, undisturbed, literary foraging; for the keys of the doors and bookcases were kindly intrusted to me, and I was left alone, to rummage at my pleasure—a rare indulgence in these sanctuaries of learning, which too often tantalize the thirsty student with the sight of sealed fountains of knowledge.

In the course of these visits I gleaned a variety of facts concerning historical characters connected with the Alhambra, some of which I here subjoin, trusting they may prove acceptable to the reader.

4*

ALHAMAR, THE FOUNDER OF THE ALHAMBRA.

THE Moors of Granada regarded the Alhambra as a miracle of art, and had a tradition that the king who founded it dealt in magic, or at least in alchemy, by means whereof he procured the immense sums of gold expended in its erection. A brief view of his reign will show the secret of his wealth. He is known in Arabian history as Muhamed Ibn-l-Ahmar; but his name in general is written simply Alhamar, and was given to him, we are told, on account of his ruddy complexion.*

He was of the noble and opulent line of the Beni Nasar, or tribe of Nasar, and was born in Arjona, in the year of the Hegira 592 (A. D. 1195). At his birth the astrologers, we are told, cast his horoscope according to Oriental custom, and pronounced it highly auspicious; and a santon predicted for him a glorious career. No expense was spared in fitting him for the high destinies prognosticated. Before he attained the full years of manhood, the famous battle of the Navas (or plains) of Tolosa shattered the Moorish empire, and eventually severed the Mos-

---

* Et porque era muy rubio llamaban lo los Moros Abenalhamar, que quiere decir bermejo . . . . et porque los Moros lo llamaban Benalhamar que quiere decir bermejo tomo los señales bermejos, segun que los ovieron despues los Reyes de Granada.—BLEDA, *Cronica de Alfonso XI.*, P. i. C. 44.

lems of Spain from the Moslems of Africa. Factions soon
arose among the former, headed by warlike chiefs, ambitious of
grasping the sovereignty of the Peninsula. Alhamar became engaged in these wars; he was the general and leader of the Beni
Nasar, and, as such, he opposed and thwarted the ambition of
Aben Hud, who had raised his standard among the warlike
mountains of the Alpuxaras, and been proclaimed king of Murcia and Granada. Many conflicts took place between these warring
chieftains; Alhamar dispossessed his rival of several important
places, and was proclaimed king of Jaen by his soldiery; but he
aspired to the sovereignty of the whole of Andalusia, for he was
of a sanguine spirit and lofty ambition. His valor and generosity
went hand in hand; what he gained by the one he secured by
the other; and at the death of Aben Hud (A. D. 1238), he became sovereign of all the territories which owned allegiance to
that powerful chief. He made his formal entry into Granada
in the same year, amid the enthusiastic shouts of the multitude,
who hailed him as the only one capable of uniting the various
factions which prevailed, and which threatened to lay the empire
at the mercy of the Christian princes.

Alhamar established his court in Granada; he was the first
of the illustrious line of Nasar that sat upon a throne. He took
immediate measures to put his little kingdom in a posture of
defence against the assaults to be expected from his Christian neighbors, repairing and strengthening the frontier posts and fortifying
the capital. Not content with the provisions of the Moslem law, by
which every man is made a soldier, he raised a regular army to garrison his strong-holds, allowing every soldier stationed on the frontier a portion of land for the support of himself, his horse, and his
family; thus interesting him in the defence of the soil in which

he had a property. These wise precautions were justified by events. The Christians, profiting by the dismemberment of the Moslem power, were rapidly regaining their ancient territories. James the Conqueror had subjected all Valencia, and Ferdinand the Saint sat down in person before Jaen, the bulwark of Granada. Alhamar ventured to oppose him in open field, but met with a signal defeat, and retired discomfited to his capital. Jaen still held out, and kept the enemy at bay during an entire winter, but Ferdinand swore not to raise his camp until he had gained possession of the place. Alhamar found it impossible to throw reinforcements into the besieged city ; he saw that its fall must be followed by the investment of his capital, and was conscious of the insufficiency of his means to cope with the potent sovereign of Castile. Taking a sudden resolution, therefore, he repaired privately to the Christian camp, made his unexpected appearance in the presence of King Ferdinand, and frankly announced himself as the king of Granada. " I come," said he, " confiding in your good faith, to put myself under your protection. Take all I possess and receive me as your vassal ;" so saying, he knelt and kissed the king's hand in token of allegiance.

Ferdinand was won by this instance of confiding faith, and determined not to be outdone in generosity. He raised his late enemy from the earth, embraced him as a friend, and, refusing the wealth he offered, left him sovereign of his dominions, under the feudal tenure of a yearly tribute, attendance at the Cortes as one of the nobles of the empire, and service in war with a certain number of horsemen. He moreover conferred on him the honor of knighthood, and armed him with his own hands.

It was not long after this that Alhamar was called upon, for his military services, to aid King Ferdinand in his famous siege of Seville. The Moorish king sallied forth with five hundred chosen horsemen of Granada, than whom none in the world knew better how to manage the steed or wield the lance. It was a humiliating service, however, for they had to draw the sword against their brethren of the faith.

Alhamar gained a melancholy distinction by his prowess in this renowned conquest, but more true honor by the humanity which he prevailed upon Ferdinand to introduce into the usages of war. When in 1248 the famous city of Seville surrendered to the Castilian monarch, Alhamar returned sad and full of care to his dominions. He saw the gathering ills that menaced the Moslem cause ; and uttered an ejaculation often used by him in moments of anxiety and trouble—" How straitened and wretched would be our life, if our hope were not so spacious and extensive." " Que angoste y miserabile seria nuestra vida, sino fuera tan dilatada y espaciosa nuestra esperanza !"

As he approached Granada on his return he beheld arches of triumph which had been erected in honor of his martial exploits. The people thronged forth to see him with impatient joy, for his benignant rule had won all hearts. Wherever he passed he was hailed with acclamations as " El Ghalib !" (the conqueror). Alhamar gave a melancholy shake of the head on hearing the appellation. "Wa le ghalib ile Aláh !" (there is no conqueror but God) exclaimed he. From that time forward this exclamation became his motto, and the motto of his descendants, and appears to this day emblazoned on his escutcheons in the halls of the Alhambra.

Alhamar had purchased peace by submission to the Christian yoke ; but he was conscious that, with elements so discordant and motives for hostility so deep and ancient, it could not be per-

manent. Acting, therefore, upon the old maxim, " arm thyself
in peace and clothe thyself in summer," he improved the present
interval of tranquillity by fortifying his dominions, replenishing
his arsenals, and promoting those useful arts which give wealth
and real power. He confided the command of his various cities
to such as had distinguished themselves by valor and prudence,
and who seemed most acceptable to the people. He organized a
vigilant police, and established rigid rules for the administration
of justice. The poor and the distressed always found ready ad-
mission to his presence, and he attended personally to their
assistance and redress. He erected hospitals for the blind, the
aged, and infirm, and all those incapable of labor, and visited
them frequently; not on set days with pomp and form, so as to
give time for every thing to be put in order, and every abuse
concealed; but suddenly, and unexpectedly, informing himself, by
actual observation and close inquiry, of the treatment of the
sick, and the conduct of those appointed to administer to their
relief. He founded schools and colleges, which he visited in the
same manner, inspecting personally the instruction of the youth.
He established butcheries and public ovens, that the people
might be furnished with wholesome provisions at just and regular prices. He introduced abundant streams of water into the
city, erecting baths and fountains, and constructing aqueducts
and canals to irrigate and fertilize the Vega. By these means
prosperity and abundance prevailed in this beautiful city, its
gates were thronged with commerce, and its warehouses filled
with luxuries and merchandise of every clime and country.

He moreover gave premiums and privileges to the best artisans; improved the breed of horses and other domestic animals;
encouraged husbandry; and increased the natural fertility of the

soil twofold by his protection, making the lovely valleys of his kingdom to bloom like gardens. He fostered also the growth and fabrication of silk, until the looms of Granada surpassed even those of Syria in the fineness and beauty of their productions. He moreover caused the mines of gold and silver and other metals, found in the mountainous regions of his dominions, to be diligently worked, and was the first king of Granada who struck money of gold and silver with his name, taking great care that the coins should be skilfully executed

It was towards the middle of the thirteenth century, and just after his return from the siege of Seville, that he commenced the splendid palace of the Alhambra; superintending the building of it in person; mingling frequently among the artists and workmen, and directing their labors.

Though thus magnificent in his works and great in his enterprises, he was simple in his person and moderate in his enjoyments. His dress was not merely void of splendor, but so plain as not to distinguish him from his subjects. His harem boasted but few beauties, and these he visited but seldom, though they were entertained with great magnificence. His wives were daughters of the principal nobles, and were treated by him as friends and rational companions. What is more, he managed to make them live in friendship with one another. He passed much of his time in his gardens; especially in those of the Alhambra, which he had stored with the rarest plants and the most beautiful and aromatic flowers. Here he delighted himself in reading histories, or in causing them to be read and related to him, and sometimes, in intervals of leisure, employed himself in the instruction of his three sons, for whom he had provided the most learned and virtuous masters.

As he had frankly and voluntarily offered himself a tributary vassal to Ferdinand, so he always remained loyal to his word, giving him repeated proofs of fidelity and attachment. When that renowned monarch died in Seville in 1254, Alhamar sent ambassadors to condole with his successor, Alonzo X., and with them a gallant train of a hundred Moorish cavaliers of distinguished rank, who were to attend round the royal bier during the funeral ceremonies, each bearing a lighted taper. This grand testimonial of respect was repeated by the Moslem monarch during the remainder of his life on each anniversary of the death of King Ferdinand el Santo, when the hundred Moorish knights repaired from Granada to Seville, and took their stations with lighted tapers in the centre of the sumptuous cathedral round the cenotaph of the illustrious deceased.

Alhamar retained his faculties and vigor to an advanced age. In his seventy-ninth year (A. D. 1272) he took the field on horseback, accompanied by the flower of his chivalry, to resist an invasion of his territories. As the army sallied forth from Granada, one of the principal adalides, or guides, who rode in the advance, accidentally broke his lance against the arch of the gate. The councillors of the king, alarmed by this circumstance, which was considered an evil omen, entreated him to return. Their supplications were in vain. The king persisted, and at noontide the omen, say the Moorish chroniclers, was fatally fulfilled. Alhamar was suddenly struck with illness, and had nearly fallen from his horse. He was placed on a litter, and borne back towards Granada, but his illness increased to such a degree that they were obliged to pitch his tent in the Vega. His physicians were filled with consternation, not knowing what remedy to prescribe. In a few hours he died, vomiting blood and in violent

convulsions. The Castilian prince, Don Philip, brother of Alonzo
X., was by his side when he expired. His body was embalmed,
enclosed in a silver coffin, and buried in the Alhambra in a sepulchre of precious marble, amidst the unfeigned lamentations of
his subjects, who bewailed him as a parent.

I have said that he was the first of the illustrious line of
Nasar that sat upon a throne. I may add that he was the founder
of a brilliant kingdom, which will ever be famous in history and
romance, as the last rallying place of Moslem power and splendor
in the peninsula. Though his undertakings were vast, and his
expenditures immense, yet his treasury was always full; and this
seeming contradiction gave rise to the story that he was versed
in magic art, and possessed of the secret for transmuting baser
metals into gold. Those who have attended to his domestic policy, as here set forth, will easily understand the natural magic
and simple alchemy which made his ample treasury to overflow.

YUSEF ABUL HAGIG,

THE FINISHER OF THE ALHAMBRA.

To the foregoing particulars, concerning the Moslem princes who once reigned in these halls, I shall add a brief notice of the monarch who completed and embellished the Alhambra. Yusef Abul Hagig (or as it is sometimes written, Haxis) was another prince of the noble line of Nasar. He ascended the throne of Granada in the year of grace 1333, and is described by Moslem writers as having a noble presence, great bodily strength, and a fair complexion, and the majesty of his countenance increased, say they, by suffering his beard to grow to a dignified length and dying it black. His manners were gentle, affable, and urbane; he carried the benignity of his nature into warfare, prohibiting all wanton cruelty, and enjoining mercy and protection towards women and children, the aged and infirm, and all friars and other persons of holy and recluse life. But though he possessed the courage common to generous spirits, the bent of his genius was more for peace than war, and though repeatedly obliged by circumstances to take up arms, he was generally unfortunate.

Among other ill-starred enterprises, he undertook a great campaign, in conjunction with the king of Morocco, against the

kings of Castile and Portugal, but was defeated in the memorable
battle of Salado, which had nearly proved a death-blow to the
Moslem power in Spain.

Yusef obtained a long truce after this defeat, and now his
character shone forth in its true lustre. He had an excellent
memory, and had stored his mind with science and erudition; his
taste was altogether elegant and refined, and he was accounted
the best poet of his time. Devoting himself to the instruction of
his people and the improvement of their morals and manners, he
established schools in all the villages, with simple and uniform
systems of education; he obliged every hamlet of more than
twelve houses to have a mosque, and purified the ceremonies of
religion, and the festivals and popular amusements, from various
abuses and indecorums which had crept into them. He attended
vigilantly to the police of the city, establishing nocturnal guards
and patrols, and superintending all municipal concerns. His
attention was also directed towards finishing the great architectural works commenced by his predecessors, and erecting others
on his own plans. The Alhambra, which had been founded by
the good Alhamar, was now completed. Yusef constructed the
beautiful Gate of Justice, forming the grand entrance to the fortress, which he finished in 1348. He likewise adorned many of
the courts and halls of the palace, as may be seen by the inscriptions on the walls, in which his name repeatedly occurs. He
built also the noble Alcazar or citadel of Malaga, now unfortunately a mere mass of crumbling ruins, but which most probably
exhibited in its interior, similar elegance and magnificence with
the Alhambra.

The genius of a sovereign stamps a character upon his time.
The nobles of Granada, imitating the elegant and graceful taste

of Yusef, soon filled the city of Granada with magnificent palaces;
the halls of which were paved with Mosaic, the walls and ceilings
wrought in fretwork, and delicately gilded and painted with
azure, vermilion, and other brilliant colors, or minutely inlaid
with cedar and other precious woods; specimens of which have
survived, in all their lustre, the lapse of several centuries. Many
of the houses had fountains, which threw up jets of water to refresh and cool the air. They had lofty towers also, of wood or
stone, curiously carved and ornamented, and covered with plates
of metal that glittered in the sun. Such was the refined and
delicate taste in architecture that prevailed among this elegant
people; insomuch that to use the beautiful simile of an Arabian
writer, "Granada, in the days of Yusef, was as a silver vase filled
with emeralds and jacinths."

One anecdote will be sufficient to show the magnanimity of
this generous prince. The long truce which had succeeded the
battle of Salado was at an end, and every effort of Yusef to renew
it was in vain. His deadly foe, Alfonzo XI. of Castile, took the
field with great force, and laid siege to Gibraltar. Yusef reluc-
tantly took up arms, and sent troops to the relief of the place.
In the midst of his anxiety, he received tidings that his
dreaded foe had suddenly fallen a victim to the plague. Instead
of manifesting exultation on the occasion, Yusef called to mind
the great qualities of the deceased, and was touched with a noble
sorrow. " Alas !" cried he, " the world has lost one of its most
excellent princes; a sovereign who knew how to honor merit,
whether in friend or foe !"

The Spanish chroniclers themselves bear witness to this magnanimity. According to their accounts, the Moorish cavaliers
partook of the sentiment of their king, and put on mourning for

the death of Alfonzo. Even those of Gibraltar, who had been so closely invested, when they knew that the hostile monarch lay dead in his camp, determined among themselves that no hostile movement should be made against the Christians. The day on which the camp was broken up, and the army departed bearing the corpse of Alfonzo, the Moors issued in multitudes from Gibraltar, and stood mute and melancholy, watching the mournful pageant. The same reverence for the deceased was observed by all the Moorish commanders on the frontiers, who suffered the funeral train to pass in safety, bearing the corpse of the Christian sovereign from Gibraltar to Seville.*

Yusef did not long survive the enemy he had so generously deplored. In the year 1354, as he was one day praying in the royal mosque of the Alhambra, a maniac rushed suddenly from behind and plunged a dagger in his side. The cries of the king brought his guards and courtiers to his assistance. They found him weltering in his blood. He made some signs as if to speak, but his words were unintelligible. They bore him senseless to the royal apartments, where he expired almost immediately. The murderer was cut to pieces, and his limbs burnt in public to gratify the fury of the populace.

The body of the king was interred in a superb sepulchre of white marble; a long epitaph, in letters of gold upon an azure ground, recorded his virtues. " Here lies a king and martyr, of an illustrious line, gentle, learned, and virtuous; renowned for

---

* " Y los moros que estaban en la villa y Castillo de Gibraltar despues que sopieron que el Rey Don Alonzo era muerto, ordenaron entresi que ninguno non fuesse osado de fazer ningun movimiento contra los Christianos, ni mover pelear contra ellos, estovieron todos quedos y dezian entre ellos qui aquel dia muriera un noble rey y Gran principe del mundo."

the graces of his person and his manners ; whose clemency, piety
and benevolence, were extolled throughout the kingdom of Granada.   He was a great prince; an illustrious captain; a sharp
sword of the Moslems; a valiant standard-bearer among the most
potent monarchs," &c.

The mosque still exists which once resounded with the dying
cries of Yusef, but the monument which recorded his virtues has
long since disappeared.   His name, however, remains inscribed
among the delicate and graceful ornaments of the Alhambra, and
will be perpetuated in connection with this renowned pile, which
it was his pride and delight to beautify.

THE MYSTERIOUS CHAMBERS.

As I was rambling one day about the Moorish halls, my attention was, for the first time, attracted to a door in a remote gallery, communicating apparently with some part of the Alhambra which I had not yet explored. I attempted to open it, but it was locked. I knocked, but no one answered, and the sound seemed to reverberate through empty chambers. Here then was a mystery. Here was the haunted wing of the castle. How was I to get at the dark secrets here shut up from the public eye? Should I come privately at night with lamp and sword, according to the prying custom of heroes of romance; or should I endeavor to draw the secret from Pepe the stuttering gardener; or the ingenuous Dolores, or the loquacious Mateo? Or should I go frankly and openly to Dame Antonia the chatelaine, and ask her all about it? I chose the latter course, as being the simplest though the least romantic; and found, somewhat to my disappointment, that there was no mystery in the case. I was welcome to explore the apartment, and there was the key.

Thus provided, I returned forthwith to the door. It opened, as I had surmised, to a range of vacant chambers; but they were quite different from the rest of the palace. The architecture, though rich and antiquated, was European. There was nothing Moorish about it. The first two rooms were lofty; the ceilings, broken in many places, were of cedar, deeply panelled and skilfully carved with fruits and flowers, intermingled with grotesque masks or faces.

The walls had evidently in ancient times been hung with damask; but now were naked, and scrawled over by that class of aspiring travellers who defile noble monuments with their worthless names. The windows, dismantled and open to wind and weather, looked out into a charming little secluded garden, where an alabaster fountain sparkled among roses and myrtles, and was surrounded by orange and citron trees, some of which flung their branches into the chambers. Beyond these rooms were two saloons, longer but less lofty, looking also into the garden. In the compartments of the panelled ceilings were baskets of fruit and garlands of flowers, painted by no mean hand, and in tolerable preservation. The walls also had been painted in fresco in the Italian style, but the paintings were nearly obliterated; the windows were in the same shattered state with those of the other chambers. This fanciful suite of rooms terminated in an open gallery with balustrades, running at right angles along another side of the garden. The whole apartment, so delicate and elegant in its decorations, so choice and sequestered in its situation along this retired little garden. and so different in architecture from the neighboring halls, awakened an interest in its history. I found on inquiry that it was an apartment fitted up by Italian artists in the early part of the last century, at the time when Philip V. and his second wife, the beautiful Elizabetta of Farnese, daughter of the Duke of Parma, were expected at the Alhambra. It was destined for the queen and the ladies of her train. One of the loftiest chambers had been her sleeping room. A narrow staircase, now walled up, led up to a delightful belvidere, originally a mirador of the Moorish sultanas, communicating with the harem ; but which was fitted up as a boudoir for the fair Elizabetta, and still retains the name of *el tocador de la Reyna*, or the queen's toilette.

One window of the royal sleeping-room commanded a prospect of the Generalife and its embowered terraces, another looked out into the little secluded garden I have mentioned, which was decidedly Moorish in its character, and also had its history. It was in fact the garden of Lindaraxa, so often mentioned in descriptions of the Alhambra ; but who this Lindaraxa was I had never heard explained. A little research gave me the few particulars known about her. She was a Moorish beauty who flourished in the court of Muhamed the Left-Handed, and was the daughter of his loyal adherent, the alcayde of Malaga, who sheltered him in his city when driven from the throne. On regaining his crown, the alcayde was rewarded for his fidelity. His daughter had her apartment in the Alhambra, and was given by the king in marriage to Nasar, a young Cetimerien prince descended from Aben Hud the Just. Their espousals were doubtless celebrated in the royal palace, and their honey-moon may have passed among these very bowers.*

Four centuries had elapsed since the fair Lindaraxa passed

---

* Una de las cosas en que tienen precisa intervencion los Reyes Moros s en el matrimonio de sus grandes: de aqui nace que todos los señores llegadas à la persona real si casan en palacio, y siempre huvo su quarto destinado para esta ceremonia.

One of the things in which the Moorish kings interfered was in the marriage of their nobles : hence it came that all the señors attached to the royal person were married in the palace ; and there was always a chamber destined for the ceremony.—*Paseos por Granada*, Paseo XXI.

5

away, yet how much of the fragile beauty of the scenes she inhabited remained! The garden still bloomed in which she delighted; the fountain still presented the crystal mirror in which her charms may once have been reflected; the alabaster, it is true, had lost its whiteness; the basin beneath, overrun with weeds, had become the lurking-place of the lizard, but there was something in the very decay that enhanced the interest of the scene, speaking as it did of that mutability, the irrevocable lot of man and all his works.

The desolation too of these chambers, oncce the abode of the proud and elegant Elizabetta, had a more touching charm for me than if I had beheld them in their pristine splendor, glittering with the pageantry of a court.

When I returned to my quarters, in the governor's apartment, every thing seemed tame and common-place after the poetic region I had left. The thought suggested itself: Why could I not change my quarters to these vacant chambers? that would indeed be living in the Alhambra, surrounded by its gardens and fountains, as in the time of the Moorish sovereigns. I proposed the change to Dame Antonia and her family, and it occasioned vast surprise. They could not conceive any rational inducement for the choice of an apartment so forlorn, remote and solitary. Dolores exclaimed at its frightful loneliness; nothing but bats and owls flitting about—and then a fox and wild-cat kept in the vaults of the neighboring baths, and roamed about at night. The good Tia had more reasonable objections. The neighborhood was infested by vagrants; gipsies swarmed in the caverns of the adjacent hills; the palace was ruinous and easy to be entered in many places; the rumor of a stranger quartered alone in one of the remote and ruined apartments, out of the hearing of the rest of the inhabitants, might tempt unwelcome visitors in the night, especially as foreigners were always supposed to be well stocked with money. I was not to be diverted from my humor, however, and my will was law with these good people. So, calling in the assistance of a carpenter, and the ever officious Mateo Xemenes, the doors and windows were soon placed in a state of tolerable security, and the sleeping-room of the stately Elizabetta prepared for my reception. Mateo kindly volunteered as a body-guard to sleep in my antechamber; but I did not think it worth while to put his valor to the proof.

With all the hardihood I had assumed and all the precautions I had taken, I must confess the first night passed in these quarters was inexpressibly dreary. I do not think it was so much the apprehension of dangers from without that affected me, as the character of the place itself, with all its strange associations: the deeds of violence committed there; the tragical ends of many of those who had once reigned there in splendor. As I passed beneath the fated halls of the tower of Comares on the way to my chamber, I called to mind a quotation, that used to thrill me in the days of boyhood:

> Fate sits on these dark battlements and frowns;
> And, as the portal opens to receive me,
> A voice in sullen echoes through the courts
> Tells of a nameless deed!

The whole family escorted me to my chamber, and took leave of me as of one engaged on a perilous enterprise; and when I heard their retreating steps die away along the waste antechambers and echoing galleries; and turned the key of my door, I was reminded of those hobgoblin stories, where the hero is left to accomplish the adventure of an enchanted house.

Even the thoughts of the fair Elizabetta and the beauties of her court, who had once graced these chambers, now, by a perversion of fancy, added to the gloom. Here was the scene of their transient gayety and loveliness; here were the very traces of their elegance and enjoyment; but what and where were they? —Dust and ashes! tenants of the tomb! phantoms of the memory!

A vague and indescribable awe was creeping over me. I would fain have ascribed it to the thoughts of robbers awakened by the evening's conversation, but I felt it was something more unreal and absurd. The long-buried superstitions of the nursery were reviving, and asserting their power over my imagination. Every thing began to be affected by the working of my mind. The whispering of the wind, among the citron-trees beneath my window, had something sinister. I cast my eyes into the garden of Lindaraxa; the groves presented a gulf of shadows; the thickets, indistinct and ghastly shapes. I was glad to close the window, but my chamber itself became infected. There was a slight rustling noise overhead; a bat suddenly emerged from a broken panel of the ceiling, flitting about the room and athwart my solitary lamp; and as the fateful bird almost flouted my face with his noiseless wing, the grotesque faces carved in high relief in the cedar ceiling, whence he had emerged, seemed to mope and mow at me.

Rousing myself, and half smiling at this temporary weakness, I resolved to brave it out in the true spirit of the hero of the enchanted house; so, taking lamp in hand, I sallied forth to make a tour of the palace. Notwithstanding every mental exertion the task was a severe one. I had to traverse waste halls and mysterious galleries, where the rays of the lamp extended but a short distance around me. I walked, as it were, in a mere

halo of light, walled in by impenetrable darkness. The vaulted
corridors were as caverns; the ceilings of the halls were lost in
gloom. I recalled all that had been said of the danger from
interlopers in these remote and ruined apartments. Might not
some vagrant foe be lurking before or behind me, in the outer
darkness? My own shadow, cast upon the wall, began to disturb
me. The echoes of my own footsteps along the corridors made
me pause and look round. I was traversing scenes fraught with
dismal recollections. One dark passage led down to the mosque
where Yusef, the Moorish monarch, the finisher of the Alhambra,
had been basely murdered. In another place, I trod the gallery
where another monarch had been struck down by the poniard of a
relative whom he had thwarted in his love.

A low murmuring sound, as of stifled voices and clanking
chains, now reached me. It seemed to come from the Hall of
the Abencerrages. I knew it to be the rush of water through
subterranean channels, but it sounded strangely in the night,
and reminded me of the dismal stories to which it had given
rise.

Soon, however, my ear was assailed by sounds too fearfully
real to be the work of fancy. As I was crossing the Hall of
Ambassadors, low moans and broken ejaculations rose, as it were,
from beneath my feet. I paused and listened. They then appeared to be outside of the tower—then again within. Then
broke forth howlings as of an animal—then stifled shrieks and
inarticulate ravings. Heard in that dead hour and singular
place, the effect was thrilling. I had no desire for further per-
ambulation; but returned to my chamber with infinitely more
alacrity than I had sallied forth, and drew my breath more freely
when once more within its walls and the door bolted behind me.

When I awoke in the morning, with the sun shining in at my window and lighting up every part of the building with his cheerful and truth-telling beams, I could scarcely recall the shadows and fancies conjured up by the gloom of the preceding night ; or believe that the scenes around me, so naked and apparent, could have been clothed with such imaginary horrors.

Still, the dismal howlings and ejaculations I had heard were not ideal; they were soon accounted for, however, by my handmaid Dolores : being the ravings of a poor maniac, a brother of her aunt, who was subject to violent paroxysms, during which he was confined in a vaulted room beneath the Hall of Ambassadors.

In the course of a few evenings a thorough change took place in the scene and its associations. The moon, which when I took possession of my new apartments was invisible, gradually gained each evening upon the darkness of the night, and at length rolled in full splendor above the towers, pouring a flood of tempered light into every court and hall. The garden beneath my window, before wrapped in gloom, was gently lighted up, the orange and citron trees were tipped with silver ; the fountain sparkled in the moonbeams, and even the blush of the rose was faintly visible.

I now felt the poetic merit of the Arabic inscription on the walls : " How beauteous is this garden ; where the flowers of the earth vie with the stars of heaven. What can compare with the vase of yon alabaster fountain filled with crystal water ? nothing but the moon in her fulness, shining in the midst of an unclouded sky !"

On such heavenly nights I would sit for hours at my window inhaling the sweetness of the garden, and musing on the checkered fortunes of those whose history was dimly shadowed

out in the elegant memorials around   Sometimes, when all was
quiet, and the clock from the distant cathedral of Granada struck
the midnight hour, I have sallied out on another tour and wandered over the whole building; but how different from my first
tour! No longer dark and mysterious; no longer peopled with
shadowy foes; no longer recalling scenes of violence and murder; all was open, spacious, beautiful; every thing called up
pleasing and romantic fancies; Lindaraxa once more walked in
her garden; the gay chivalry of Moslem Granada once more
glittered about the Court of Lions! Who can do justice to a
moonlight night in such a climate and such a place? The tem-
perature of a summer midnight in Andalusia is perfectly
ethereal. We seem lifted up into a purer atmosphere; we feel
a serenity of soul, a buoyancy of spirits, an elasticity of frame,
which render mere existence happiness. But when moonlight is
added to all this, the effect is like enchantment. Under its
plastic sway the Alhambra seems to regain its pristine glories.
Every rent and chasm of time; every mouldering tint and
weather-stain is gone; the marble resumes its original white
ness; the long colonnades brighten in the moonbeams; the halls
are illuminated with a softened radiance,—we tread the enchanted palace of an Arabian tale!

What a delight, at such a time, to ascend to the little airy
pavilion of the queen's toilet (el tocador de la reyna), which,
like a bird-cage, overhangs the valley of the Darro, and gaze
from its light arcades upon the moonlight prospect! To the
right, the swelling mountains of the Sierra Nevada, robbed of
their ruggedness and softened into a fairy land, with their
snowy summits gleaming like silver clouds against the deep
blue sky. And then to lean over the parapet of the Tocador and

gaze down upon Granada and the Albaycin spread out like a map below; all buried in deep repose; the white palaces and convents sleeping in the moonshine, and beyond all these the vapory Vega fading away like a dream-land in the distance.

Sometimes the faint click of castanets rise from the Alameda, where some gay Andalusians are dancing away the summer night. Sometimes the dubious tones of a guitar and the notes of an amorous voice, tell perchance the whereabout of some moon-struck lover serenading his lady's window.

Such is a faint picture of the moonlight nights I have passed loitering about the courts and halls and balconies of this most suggestive pile; " feeding my fancy with sugared suppositions," and enjoying that mixture of reverie and sensation which steal away existence in a southern climate; so that it has been almost morning before I have retired to bed, and been lulled to sleep by the falling waters of the fountain of Lindaraxa.

PANORAMA FROM THE TOWER OF COMARES.

IT is a serene and beautiful morning: the sun has not gained sufficient power to destroy the freshness of the night. What a morning to mount to the summit of the Tower of Comares, and take a bird's-eye view of Granada and its environs!

Come then, worthy reader and comrade, follow my steps into this vestibule, ornamented with rich tracery, which opens into the Hall of Ambassadors. We will not enter the hall, however, but turn to this small door opening into the wall. Have a care! here are steep winding steps and but scanty light; yet up this narrow, obscure, and spiral staircase, the proud monarchs of Granada and their queens have often ascended to the battlements to watch the approach of invading armies, or gaze with anxious hearts on the battles in the Vega.

At length we have reached the terraced roof, and may take breath for a moment, while we cast a general eye over the splendid panorama of city and country; of rocky mountain, verdant valley, and fertile plain; of castle, cathedral, Moorish towers, and Gothic domes, crumbling ruins, and blooming groves. Let us approach the battlements, and cast our eyes immediately below. See, on this side we have the whole plain of the Alhambra laid open to us, and can look down into its courts and gardens. At the foot of the tower is the Court of the Alberca, with its great tank or fishpool, bordered with flowers; and yonder is the Court of Lions, with its famous fountain, and its light Moorish arcades; and in the centre of the pile is the little garden of Lindaraxa, buried in the heart of the building, with its roses and citrons, and shrubbery of emerald green.

That belt of battlements, studded with square towers, straggling round the whole brow of the hill, is the outer boundary of the fortress. Some of the towers, you may perceive, are in ruins, and their massive fragments buried among vines, fig-trees and aloes.

Let us look on this northern side of the tower. It is a giddy height; the very foundations of the tower rise above the groves of the steep hill-side. And see! a long fissure in the massive walls, shows that the tower has been rent by some of the earth-quakes, which from time to time have thrown Granada into consternation; and which, sooner or later, must reduce this crumbling pile to a mere mass of ruin. The deep narrow glen below us, which gradually widens as it opens from the mountains, is the valley of the Darro; you see the little river winding its way under imbowered terraces, and among orchards and flower-gardens. It is a stream famous in old times for yielding gold, and its sands are still sifted occasionally, in search of the precious ore. Some of those white pavilions, which here and there gleam from among groves and vineyards, were rustic retreats of the Moors, to enjoy the refreshment of their gardens. Well have they been compared by one of their poets to so many pearls set in a bed of emeralds.

The airy palace, with its tall white towers and long arcades, which breasts yon mountain, among pompous groves and hanging gardens, is the Generalife, a summer palace of the Moorish kings, to which they resorted during the sultry months to enjoy a still more breezy region than that of the Alhambra. The naked summit of the height above it, where you behold some shapeless ruins, is the Silla del Moro, or Seat of the Moor, so called from having been a retreat of the unfortunate Boabdil during the time of an insurrection, where he seated himself, and looked down mournfully upon his rebellious city.

A murmuring sound of water now and then rises from the valley. It is from the aqueduct of yon Moorish mill, nearly at the foot of the hill. The avenue of trees beyond is the Alameda, along the bank of the Darro, a favorite resort in evenings, and a rendezvous of lovers in the summer nights, when the guitar may be heard at a late hour from the benches along its walks. At present you see none but a few loitering monks there, and a group of water-carriers. The latter are burdened with water jars of ancient Oriental construction, such as were used by the Moors. They have been filled at the cold and limpid spring called the fountain of Avellanos. Yon mountain path leads to the fountain, a favorite resort of Moslems as well as Christians; for this is said to be the Adinamar (Aynu-l-adamar), the "Fountain of Tears," mentioned by Ibn Batuta the traveller, and celebrated in the histories and romances of the Moors.

You start! 'tis nothing but a hawk that we have frightened from his nest. This old tower is a complete breeding-place for vagrant birds; the swallow and martlet abound in every chink and cranny, and circle about it the whole day long; while at night, when all other birds have gone to rest, the moping owl comes out of its lurking-place, and utters its boding cry from the battlements. See how the hawk we have dislodged sweeps away below us, skimming over the tops of the trees, and sailing up to the ruins above the Generalife !

I see you raise your eyes to the snowy summit of yon pile of mountains, shining like a white summer cloud in the blue sky. It is the Sierra Nevada, the pride and delight of Granada ; the source of her cooling breezes and perpetual verdure; of her gushing fountains and perennial streams. It is this glorious pile of mountains which gives to Granada that combination of delights so rare in a southern city : the fresh vegetation and temperate airs of a northern climate, with the vivifying ardor of a tropical sun, and the cloudless azure of a southern sky. It is this aerial treasury of snow, which, melting in proportion to the increase of the summer heat, sends down rivulets and streams through every glen and gorge of the Alpuxarras, diffusing emerald verdure and fertility throughout a chain of happy and sequestered valleys.

Those mountains may be well called the glory of Granada. They dominate the whole extent of Andalusia, and may be seen from its most distant parts. The muleteer hails them, as he views their frosty peaks from the sultry level of the plain ; and the Spanish mariner on the deck of his bark, far, far off on the bosom of the blue Mediterranean, watches them with a pensive eye, thinks of delightful Granada, and chants, in low voice, some old romance about the Moors.

See to the south at the foot of those mountains a line of arid hills, down which a long train of mules is slowly moving. Here was the closing scene of Moslem domination. From the summit of one of those hills the unfortunate Boabdil cast back his last look upon Granada, and gave vent to the agony of his soul. It is the spot famous in song and story, " The last sigh of the Moor."

Further this way these arid hills slope down into the luxurious Vega, from which he had just emerged : a blooming wilderness of grove and garden, and teeming orchard, with the Xenil
winding through it in silver links, and feeding innumerable rills ;
which, conducted through ancient Moorish channels, maintain the
landscape in perpetual verdure. Here were the beloved bowers
and gardens, and rural pavilions, for which the unfortunate Moors
fought with such desperate valor. The very hovels and rude
granges, now inhabited by boors, show, by the remains of arabesques and other tasteful decoration, that they were elegant resi-
dences in the days of the Moslems. Behold, in the very centre
of this eventful plain, a place which in a manner links the history
of the Old World with that of the New. Yon line of walls and
towers gleaming in the morning sun, is the city of Santa Fe,
built by the Catholic sovereigns during the siege of Granada,
after a conflagration had destroyed their camp. It was to these
walls Columbus was called back by the heroic queen, and within
them the treaty was concluded which led to the discovery of the
Western World. Behind yon promontory to the west is the
bridge of Pinos, renowned for many a bloody fight between Moors
and Christians. At this bridge the messenger overtook Columbus when, despairing of success with the Spanish sovereigns, he
was departing to carry his project of discovery to the court of
France.

Above the bridge a range of mountains bounds the Vega to
the west: the ancient barrier between Granada and the Christian territories. Among their heights you may still discern
warrior towns ; their gray walls and battlements seeming of a
piece with the rocks on which they are built. Here and there a
solitary atalaya, or watchtower, perched on a mountain peak,

looks down as it were from the sky into the valley on either side.
How often have these atalayas given notice, by fire at night or
smoke by day, of an approaching foe! It was down a cragged
defile of these mountains, called the Pass of Lope, that the
Christian armies descended into the Vega. Round the base of
yon gray and naked mountain (the mountain of Elvira), stretching its bold rocky promontory into the bosom of the plain, the
invading squadrons would come bursting into view, with flaunting
banners and clangor of drum and trumpet.

Five hundred years have elapsed since Ismael ben Ferrag, a
Moorish king of Granada, beheld from this very tower an invasion of the kind, and an insulting ravage of the Vega; on which
occasion he displayed an instance of chivalrous magnanimity,
often witnessed in the Moslem princes; "whose history," says
an Arabian writer, "abounds in generous actions and noble
deeds that will last through all succeeding ages, and live for ever
in the memory of man."—But let us sit down on this parapet
and I will relate the anecdote.

It was in the year of Grace 1319, that Ismael ben Ferrag
beheld from this tower a Christian camp whitening the skirts of
yon mountain of Elvira. The royal princes, Don Juan and Don
Pedro, regents of Castile during the minority of Alfonso XI.,
had already laid waste the country from Alcaudete to Alcalá la
Real, capturing the castle of Illora and setting fire to its suburbs,
and they now carried their insulting ravages to the very gates of
Granada, defying the king to sally forth and give them battle.

Ismael, though a young and intrepid prince, hesitated to
accept the challenge. He had not sufficient force at hand, and
awaited the arrival of troops summoned from the neighboring
towns. The Christian princes, mistaking his motives, gave up

all hope of drawing him forth, and having glutted themselves
with ravage, struck their tents and began their homeward march.
Don Pedro led the van, and Don Juan brought up the rear, but
their march was confused and irregular, the army being greatly
encumbered by the spoils and captives they had taken.

By this time King Ismael had received his expected resources, and putting them under the command of Osmyn, one of
the bravest of his generals, sent them forth in hot pursuit of
the enemy. The Christians were overtaken in the defiles of the
mountains. A panic seized them; they were completely routed,
and driven with great slaughter across the borders. Both of the
princes lost their lives. The body of Don Pedro was carried off
by his soldiers, but that of Don Juan was lost in the darkness of
the night. His son wrote to the Moorish king, entreating that
the body of his father might be sought and honorably treated.
Ismael forgot in a moment that Don Juan was an enemy, who
had carried ravage and insult to the very gate of his capital; he
only thought of him as a gallant cavalier and a royal prince. By
his command diligent search was made for the body. It was
found in a barranco and brought to Granada. There Ismael
caused it to be laid out in state on a lofty bier, surrounded by
torches and tapers, in one of these halls of the Alhambra. Osmyn
and other of the noblest cavaliers were appointed as a guard
of honor, and the Christian captives were assembled to pray
around it.

In the mean time, Ismael wrote to the son of Prince Juan to
send a convoy for the body, assuring him it should be faithfully
delivered up. In due time, a band of Christian cavaliers arrived
for the purpose. They were honorably received and entertained
by Ismael, and, on their departure with the body, the guard of

honor of Moslem cavaliers escorted the funeral train to the frontier.

But enough—the sun is high above the mountains, and pours his full fervor on our heads. Already the terraced roof is hot beneath our feet; let us abandon it, and refresh ourselves under the Arcades by the Fountain of the Lions.

THE TRUANT.

WE have had a scene of a petty tribulation in the Alhambra, which has thrown a cloud over the sunny countenance of Dolores. This little damsel has a female passion for pets of all kinds, and from the superabundant kindness of her disposition one of the ruined courts of the Alhambra is thronged with her favorites. A stately peacock and his hen seem to hold regal sway here, over pompous turkeys, querulous guinea-fowls, and a rabble rout of common cocks and hens. The great delight of Dolores, however, has for some time past been centred in a youthful pair of pigeons, who have lately entered into the holy state of wedlock, and even supplanted a tortoise-shell cat and kittens in her affections.

As a tenement for them wherein to commence housekeeping, she had fitted up a small chamber adjacent to the kitchen, the window of which looked into one of the quiet Moorish courts. Here they lived in happy ignorance of any world beyond the court and its sunny roofs. Never had they aspired to soar above the battlements, or to mount to the summit of the towers. Their virtuous union was at length crowned by two spotless and milk-white eggs, to the great joy of their cherishing little mistress. Nothing could be more praiseworthy than the conduct of the young married folks on this interesting occasion. They took turns to sit upon the nest until the eggs were hatched, and while their callow progeny required warmth and shelter; while one thus stayed at home, the other foraged abroad for food, and brought home abundant supplies.

This scene of conjugal felicity has suddenly met with a reverse. Early this morning, as Dolores was feeding the male pigeon, she took a fancy to give him a peep at the great world Opening a window, therefore, which looks down upon the valley of the Darro, she launched him at once beyond the walls of the Alhambra. For the first time in his life the astonished bird had to try the full vigor of his wings. He swept down into the valley, and then rising upwards with a surge, soared almost to the clouds. Never before had he risen to such a height, or experienced such delight in flying; and, like a young spendthrift just come to his estate, he seemed giddy with excess of liberty, and with the boundless field of action suddenly opened to him. For the whole day he has been circling about in capricious flights, from tower to tower, and tree to tree. Every attempt has been vain to lure him back by scattering grain upon the roofs; he seems to have lost all thought of home, of his tender helpmate, and his callow young. To add to the anxiety of Dolores, he has been joined by two *palomas ladrones*, or robber pigeons, whose instinct it is to entice wandering pigeons to their own dovecotes. The fugitive, like many other thoughtless youths on their first launching upon the world, seems quite fascinated with these knowing but graceless companions, who have undertaken to show him life, and introduce him to society. He has been soaring with them over all the roofs and steeples of Granada. A thunder-storm has passed over the city, but he has not sought his home; night has closed in, and still he comes not. To deepen the pathos of the affair, the female pigeon, after remaining several hours on the nest without being relieved, at length went forth to seek her recreant mate; but stayed away so long that the young ones perished for want of the warmth and shelter of the parent bosom. At a late hour in the evening, word was brought to Dolores, that the truant bird had been seen upon the towers of the Generalife. Now it happens that the *Administrador* of that ancient palace has likewise a dove-cote, among the inmates of which are said to be two or three of these inveigling birds, the terror of all neighboring pigeon-fanciers. Dolores immediately concluded, that the two feathered sharpers who had been seen with her fugitive, were these bloods of the Generalife. A council of war was forthwith held in the chamber of Tia Antonia The Generalife is a distinct jurisdiction from the Alhambra, and of course some punctilio, if not jealousy, exists between their custodians. It was determined, therefore, to send Pèpe, the stuttering lad of the gardens, as ambassador to the Administrador, requesting that if such fugitive should be found in his dominions, he might be given up as a subject of the Alhambra. Pèpe departed accordingly, on his diplomatic expedition, through the moonlit groves and avenues, but returned in an hour with the afflicting intelligence that no such bird was to be found in the dovecote of the Generalife. The Administrador, however, pledged his sovereign word that if such vagrant should appear there, even at midnight, he should instantly be arrested, and sent back prisoner to his little black-eyed mistress.

Thus stands the melancholy affair, which has occasioned much distress throughout the palace, and has sent the inconsolable Dolores to a sleepless pillow.

——— "Sorrow endureth for a night," says the proverb, "but joy cometh in the morning." The first object that met my eyes, on leaving my room this morning, was Dolores, with the truant pigeon in her hands, and her eyes sparkling with joy. He had appeared at an early hour on the battlements, hovering shyly about from roof to roof, but at length entered the window, and surrendered himself prisoner. He gained little credit, however, by his return; for the ravenous manner in which he devoured the food set before him showed that, like the prodigal son, he had been driven home by sheer famine. Dolores upbraided him for his faithless conduct, calling him all manner of vagrant names, though, woman-like, she fondled him at the same time to her bosom, and covered him with kisses. I observed, however, that she had taken care to clip his wings to prevent all future soarings; a precaution which I mention for the benefit of all those who have truant lovers or wandering husbands. More than one valuable moral might be drawn from the story of Dolores and her pigeon.

THE BALCONY.

I HAVE spoken of a balcony of the central window of the Hall of Ambassadors. It served as a kind of observatory, where I used often to take my seat, and consider not merely the heaven above but the earth beneath. Besides the magnificent prospect which it commanded of mountain, valley, and vega, there was a little busy scene of human life laid open to inspection immediately below. At the foot of the hill was an alameda, or public walk, which, though not so fashionable as the more modern and splendid paseo of the Xenil, still boasted a varied and picturesque concourse. Hither resorted the small gentry of the suburbs, together with priests and friars, who walked for appetite and digestion; majos and majas, the beaux and belles of the lower classes, in their Andalusian dresses; swaggering contrabandistas, and sometimes half-muffled and mysterious loungers of the higher ranks, on some secret assignation.

It was a moving picture of Spanish life and character, which I delighted to study; and as the astronomer has his grand telescope with which to sweep the skies, and, as it were, bring the stars nearer for his inspection, so I had a smaller one, of pocket size, for the use of my observatory, with which I could sweep the regions below, and bring the countenances of the motley groups so close as almost, at times, to make me think I could divine their conversation by the play and expression of their features. I was thus, in a manner, an invisible observer, and, without quit ting my solitude, could throw myself in an instant into the midst of society,—a rare advantage to one of somewhat shy and quiet habits, and fond, like myself, of observing the drama of life without becoming an actor in the scene.

There was a considerable suburb lying below the Alhambra, filling the narrow gorge of the valley, and extending up the oppo- site hill of the Albaycin. Many of the houses were built in the Moorish style, round patios, or courts, cooled by fountains and open to the sky; and as the inhabitants passed much of their time in these courts, and on the terraced roofs during the sum- mer season, it follows that many a glance at their domestic life might be obtained by an aerial spectator like myself, who could look down on them from the clouds.

I enjoyed, in some degree, the advantages of the student in the famous old Spanish story, who beheld all Madrid unroofed for his inspection; and my gossiping squire, Mateo Ximenes, officiated occasionally as my Asmodeus, to give me anecdotes of the different mansions and their inhabitants.

I preferred, however, to form conjectural histories for myself, and thus would sit for hours, weaving, from casual incidents and indications passing under my eye, a whole tissue of schemes, intrigues, and occupations of the busy mortals below. There was scarce a pretty face or a striking figure that I daily saw, about which I had not thus gradually framed a dramatic story, though some of my characters would occasionally act in direct opposition to the

part assigned them, and disconcert the whole drama. Reconnoi
tring one day with my glass the streets of the Albaycin, I beheld
the procession of a novice about to take the veil; and remarked
several circumstances which excited the strongest sympathy in the
fate of the youthful being thus about to be consigned to a living
tomb. I ascertained to my satisfaction that she was beautiful;
and, from the paleness of her cheek, that she was a victim, rather
than a votary. She was arrayed in bridal garments, and decked
with a chaplet of white flowers, but her heart evidently revolted
at this mockery of a spiritual union, and yearned after its earthly
loves. A tall stern-looking man walked near her in the procession; it was, of course, the tyrannical father, who, from some
bigoted or sordid motive, had compelled this sacrifice. Amid the
crowd was a dark handsome youth, in Andalusian garb, who
seemed to fix on her an eye of agony. It was doubtless the
secret lover from whom she was for ever to be separated. My
indignation rose as I noted the malignant expression painted on
the countenances of the attendant monks and friars. The procession arrived at the chapel of the convent; the sun gleamed for
the last time upon the chaplet of the poor novice, as she crossed
the fatal threshold, and disappeared within the building. The
throng poured in with cowl, and cross, and minstrelsy; the lover
paused for a moment at the door. I could divine the tumult
of his feelings; but he mastered them, and entered. There was
a long interval—I pictured to myself the scene passing within;
the poor novice despoiled of her transient finery, and clothed in
the conventual garb; the bridal chaplet taken from her brow, and
her beautiful head shorn of its long silken tresses. I heard her
murmur the irrevocable vow. I saw her extended on a bier; the
death-pall spread over her; the funeral service performed that

proclaimed her dead to the world; her sighs were drowned in the deep tones of the organ, and the plaintive requiem of the nuns; the father looked on, unmoved, without a tear; the lover— no—my imagination refused to portray the anguish of the lover —there the picture remained a blank.

After a time the throng again poured forth, and dispersed various ways, to enjoy the light of the sun and mingle with the stirring scenes of life; but the victim, with her bridal chaplet, was no longer there. The door of the convent closed that severed her from the world for ever. I saw the father and the lover issue forth; they were in earnest conversation. The latter was vehement in his gesticulations; I expected some violent termination to my drama; but an angle of a building interfered and closed the scene. My eye afterwards was frequently turned to that convent with painful interest. I remarked late at night a solitary light twinkling from a remote lattice of one of its towers. " There," said I, " the unhappy nun sits weeping in her cell, while perhaps her lover paces the street below in unavailing anguish."

—The officious Mateo interrupted my meditations and destroyed in an instant the cobweb tissue of my fancy. With his usual zeal he had gathered facts concerning the scene, which put my fictions all to flight. The heroine of my romance was neither young nor handsome; she had no lover; she had entered the convent of her own free will, as a respectable asylum, and was one of the most cheerful residents within its walls.

It was some little while before I could forgive the wrong done me by the nun in being thus happy in her cell, in contradiction to all the rules of romance; I diverted my spleen, however, by watching, for a day or two, the pretty coquetries of a

dark-eyed brunette, who, from the covert of a balcony shrouded
with flowering shrubs and a silken awning, was carrying on a
mysterious correspondence with a handsome, dark, well-whiskered
cavalier, who lurked frequently in the street beneath her window.
Sometimes I saw him at an early hour, stealing forth wrapped
to the eyes in a mantle. Sometimes he loitered at a corner, in
various disguises, apparently waiting for a private signal to slip
into the house. Then there was the tinkling of a guitar at
night, and a lantern shifted from place to place in the balcony.
I imagined another intrigue like that of Almaviva; but was again
disconcerted in all my suppositions.—The supposed lover turned
out to be the husband of the lady, and a noted contrabandista ;
and all his mysterious signs and movements had doubtless some
smuggling scheme in view.

—I occasionally amused myself with noting from this balcony the gradual changes of the scenes below, according to the
different stages of the day.

Scarce has the gray dawn streaked the sky, and the earliest
cock crowed from the cottages of the hill-side, when the suburbs
give sign of reviving animation ; for the fresh hours of dawning
are precious in the summer season in a sultry climate. All are
anxious to get the start of the sun, in the business of the day.
The muleteer drives forth his loaded train for the journey ; the
traveller slings his carbine behind his saddle, and mounts his steed
at the gate of the hostel ; the brown peasant from the country
urges forward his loitering beasts, laden with panniers of sunny
fruit and fresh dewy vegetables : for already the thrifty housewives are hastening to the market.

The sun is up and sparkles along the valley, tipping the transparent foliage of the groves. The matin bells resound melodiously

6

through the pure bright air, announcing the hour of devotion. The muleteer halts his burdened animals before the chapel, thrusts his staff through his belt behind, and enters with hat in hand, smoothing his coal-black hair, to hear a mass, and put up a prayer for a prosperous wayfaring across the sierra. And now steals forth on fairy foot the gentle Señora, in trim basquiña, with restless fan in hand, and dark eye flashing from beneath the gracefully folded mantilla; she seeks some well-frequented church to offer up her morning orisons; but the nicely-adjusted dress, the dainty shoe and cobweb stocking, the raven tresses exquisitely braided, the fresh plucked rose, gleaming among them like a gem, show that earth divides with Heaven the empire of her thoughts. Keep an eye upon her, careful mother, or virgin aunt, or vigilant duenna, whichever you be, that walk behind!

As the morning advances, the din of labor augments on every side; the streets are thronged with man, and steed, and beast of burden, and there is a hum and murmur, like the surges of the ocean. As the sun ascends to his meridian the hum and bustle gradually decline; at the height of noon there is a pause. The panting city sinks into lassitude, and for several hours there is a general repose. The windows are closed, the curtains drawn; the inhabitants retired into the coolest recesses of their mansions; the full-fed monk snores in his dormitory; the brawny porter lies stretched on the pavement beside his burden; the peasant and the laborer sleep beneath the trees of the Alameda, lulled by the sultry chirping of the locust. The streets are deserted, except by the water-carrier, who refreshes the ear by proclaiming the merits of his sparkling beverage, "colder than the mountain snow (*mas fria que la nieve*)."

As the sun declines, there is again a gradual reviving, and

when the vesper bell rings out his sinking knell, all nature seems to rejoice that the tyrant of the day has fallen. Now begins the bustle of enjoyment, when the citizens pour forth to breathe the evening air, and revel away the brief twilight in the walks and gardens of the Darro and Xenil.

As night closes, the capricious scene assumes new features Light after light gradually twinkles forth ; here a taper from a balconied window ; there a votive lamp before the image of a Saint. Thus, by degrees, the city emerges from the pervading gloom, and sparkles with scattered lights, like the starry firmament. Now break forth from court and garden, and street and lane, the tinkling of innumerable guitars, and the clicking of castañets ; blending, at this lofty height, in a faint but general concert. " Enjoy the moment," is the creed of the gay and amorous Andalusian, and at no time does he practise it more zealously than in the balmy nights of summer, wooing his mistress with the dance, the love ditty, and the passionate serenade.

I was one evening seated in the balcony, enjoying the light breeze that came rustling along the side of the hill, among the tree-tops, when my humble historiographer Mateo, who was at my elbow, pointed out a spacious house, in an obscure street of the Albaycin, about which he related, as nearly as I can recollect, the following anecdote.

THE ADVENTURE OF THE MASON.

"There was once upon a time a poor mason, or bricklayer, in Granada, who kept all the saints' days and holidays, and Saint Monday into the bargain, and yet, with all his devotion, he grew poorer and poorer, and could scarcely earn bread for his numerous family. One night he was roused from his first sleep by a knocking at his door. He opened it, and beheld before him a tall, meagre, cadaverous-looking priest.

"'Hark ye, honest friend!' said the stranger; 'I have observed that you are a good Christian, and one to be trusted; will you undertake a job this very night?'

"'With all my heart, Señor Padre, on condition that I am paid accordingly.'

"'That you shall be; but you must suffer yourself to be blindfolded.'

"To this the mason made no objection; so, being hoodwinked, he was led by the priest through various rough lanes and winding passages, until they stopped before the portal of a house. The priest then applied a key, turned a creaking lock, and opened what sounded like a ponderous door. They entered, the door was closed and bolted, and the mason was conducted through an echoing corridor, and a spacious hall, to an interior part of the

building. Here the bandage was removed from his eyes, and he found himself in a patio, or court, dimly lighted by a single lamp. In the centre was the dry basin of an old Moorish fountain, under which the priest requested him to form a small vault, bricks and mortar being at hand for the purpose. He accordingly worked all night, but without finishing the job. Just before daybreak the priest put a piece of gold into his hand, and having again blindfolded him, conducted him back to his dwelling.

"'Are you willing,' said he, 'to return and complete your work?'

"'Gladly, Señor Padre, provided I am so well paid.'

"'Well, then, to-morrow at midnight I will call again.'

"He did so, and the vault was completed.

"'Now,' said the priest, 'you must help me to bring forth the bodies that are to be buried in this vault.'

"The poor mason's hair rose on his head at these words: he followed the priest, with trembling steps, into a retired chamber of the mansion, expecting to behold some ghastly spectacle of death, but was relieved on perceiving three or four portly jars standing in one corner. They were evidently full of money, and it was with great labor that he and the priest carried them forth and consigned them to their tomb. The vault was then closed, the pavement replaced, and all traces of the work were obliterated. The mason was again hoodwinked and led forth by a route different from that by which he had come. After they had wandered for a long time through a perplexed maze of lanes and alleys, they halted. The priest then put two pieces of gold into his hand : 'Wait here,' said he, 'until you hear the cathedral bell toll for matins. If you presume to uncover your eyes before that time, evil will befall you :' so saying, he departed. The mason waited faithfully, amusing himself by weighing the gold pieces in his hand, and clinking them against each other. The moment the cathedral bell rang its matin peal, he uncovered his eyes, and found himself on the banks of the Xenil; whence he made the best of his way home, and revelled with his family for a whole fortnight on the profits of his two nights' work; after which, he was as poor as ever.

" He continued to work a little, and pray a good deal, and keep saints' days and holidays, from year to year, while his family grew up as gaunt and ragged as a crew of gipsies. As he was seated one evening at the door of his hovel, he was accosted by a rich old curmudgeon, who was noted for owning many houses, and being a griping landlord. The man of money eyed him for a moment from beneath a pair of anxious shagged eyebrows.

" ' I am told, friend, that you are very poor.'

" ' There is no denying the fact, señor—it speaks for itself.'

" ' I presume then, that you will be glad of a job, and will work cheap.'

" ' As cheap, my master, as any mason in Granada.'

" ' That's what I want. I have an old house fallen into decay, which costs me more money than it is worth to keep it in repair, for nobody will live in it; so I must contrive to patch it up and keep it together at as small expense as possible.'

" The mason was accordingly conducted to a large deserted house that seemed going to ruin. Passing through several empty halls and chambers, he entered an inner court, where his eye was caught by an old Moorish fountain. He paused for a moment, for a dreaming recollection of the place came over him.

" ' Pray," said he, ' who occupied this house formerly ?'

" ' A pest upon him !' cried the landlord, ' it was an old miserly priest, who cared for nobody but himself. He was said to be immensely rich, and, having no relations, it was thought he would leave all his treasures to the church. He died suddenly, and the priests and friars thronged to take possession of his wealth; but nothing could they find but a few ducats in a leathern purse. The worst luck has fallen on me, for, since his death, the old fellow continues to occupy my house without paying rent, and there is no taking the law of a dead man. The people pretend to hear the clinking of gold all night in the chamber where the old priest slept, as if he were counting over his money, and sometimes a groaning and moaning about the court. Whether true or false, these stories have brought a bad name on my house, and not a tenant will remain in it.'

"'Enough,' said the mason sturdily: 'let me live in your house rent-free until some better tenant present, and I will engage to put it in repair, and to quiet the troubled spirit that disturbs it I am a good Christian and a poor man, and am not to be daunted by the Devil himself, even though he should come in the shape of a big bag of money!'

"The offer of the honest mason was gladly accepted; he moved with his family into the house, and fulfilled all his engagements. By little and little he restored it to its former state; the clinking of gold was no more heard at night in the chamber of the defunct priest, but began to be heard by day in the pocket of the living mason. In a word, he increased rapidly in wealth, to the admiration of all his neighbors, and became one of the richest men in Granada: he gave large sums to the church, by way, no doubt, of satisfying his conscience, and never revealed the secret of the vault until on his deathbed to his son and heir."

THE COURT OF LIONS.

THE peculiar charm of this old dreamy palace, is its power of calling up vague reveries and picturings of the past, and thus clothing naked realities with the illusions of the memory and the imagination. As I delight to walk in these " vain shadows," I am prone to seek those parts of the Alhambra which are most favorable to this phantasmagoria of the mind ; and none are more so than the Court of Lions, and its surrounding halls. Here the hand of time has fallen the lightest, and the traces of Moorish elegance and splendor exist in almost their original brilliancy. Earthquakes have shaken the foundations of this pile, and rent its rudest towers; yet see ! not one of those slender columns has been displaced, not an arch of that light and fragile colonnade given way, and all the fairy fretwork of these domes, apparently as unsubstantial as the crystal fabrics of a morning's frost, exist after the lapse of centuries, almost as fresh as if from the hand of the Moslem artist. I write in the midst of these mementos of the past, in the fresh hour of early morning, in the fated Hall of the Abencerrages. The blood-stained fountain, the legendary monument of their massacre, is before me ; the lofty jet almost casts its dew upon my paper. How difficult to reconcile the ancient tale of violence and blood with the gentle and peaceful scene around ! Every thing here appears calculated to inspire kind and happy feelings, for every thing is delicate and beautiful. The very light falls tenderly from above, through the lantern of a dome tinted and wrought as if by fairy hands. Through the ample and fretted arch of the portal I behold the Court of Lions, with brilliant sunshine gleaming along its colonnades, and sparkling in its fountains. The lively swallow dives into the court, and, rising with a surge, darts away twittering over the roofs; the busy bee toils humming among the flower beds, and painted butterflies hover from plant to plant, and flutter up and sport with each other in the sunny air. It needs but a slight exertion of the fancy to picture some pensive beauty of the harem, loitering in these secluded haunts of Oriental luxury.

He, however, who would behold this scene under an aspect more in unison with its fortunes, let him come when the shadows of evening temper the brightness of the court, and throw a gloom into the surrounding. halls. Then nothing can be more serenely melancholy, or more in harmony with the tale of departed grandeur.

At such times I am apt to seek the Hall of Justice, whose deep shadowy arcades extend across the upper end of the court. Here was performed, in presence of Ferdinand and Isabella, and their triumphant court, the pompous ceremonial of high mass, on taking possession of the Alhambra. The very cross is still to be seen upon the wall, where the altar was erected, and where officited the Grand Cardinal of Spain, and others of the highest religious dignitaries of the land. I picture to myself the scene when this place was filled with the conquering host, that mixture of mitred prelate and shaven monk, and steel-clad knight and silken courtier; when crosses and crosiers and religious stand-

6*

ards were mingled with proud armorial ensigns and the banners
of the haughty chiefs of Spain, and flaunted in triumph through
these Moslem halls. I picture to myself Columbus, the future
discoverer of a world, taking his modest stand in a remote corner, the humble and neglected spectator of the pageant. I see
in imagination the Catholic sovereigns prostrating themselves
before the altar, and pouring forth thanks for their victory;
while the vaults resound with sacred minstrelsy, and the deep-
toned Te Deum.

The transient illusion is over—the pageant melts from the
fancy—monarch, priest, and warrior. return into oblivion, with
the poor Moslems over whom they exulted. The hall of their
triumph is waste and desolate. The bat flits about its twilight
vault, and the owl hoots from the neighboring tower of Comares.

Entering the Court of the Lions a few evenings since, I was
almost startled at beholding a turbaned Moor quietly seated near
the fountain. For a moment one of the fictions of the place
seemed realized: an enchanted Moor had broken the spell of centuries, and become visible. He proved, however, to be a mere
ordinary mortal; a native of Tetuan in Barbary, who had a shop
in the Zacatin of Granada, where he sold rhubarb, trinkets, and
perfumes. As he spoke Spanish fluently, I was enabled to hold
conversation with him, and found him shrewd and intelligent.
He told me that he came up the hill occasionally in the summer,
to pass a part of the day in the Alhambra, which reminded him
of the old palaces in Barbary, being built and adorned in similar
style, though with more magnificence.

As we walked about the palace, he pointed out several of the
Arabic inscriptions, as possessing much poetic beauty.

Ah, señor, said he, when the Moors held Granada, they were

a gayer people than they are now-a-days. They thought only of love, music, and poetry. They made stanzas upon every occasion, and set them all to music. He who could make the best verses, and she who had the most tuneful voice, might be sure of favor and preferment. In those days, if any one asked for bread, the reply was, make me a couplet; and the poorest beggar, if he begged in rhyme, would often be rewarded with a piece of gold.

"And is the popular feeling for poetry," said I, "entirely lost among you?"

"By no means, señor; the people of Barbary, even those of the lower classes, still make couplets, and good ones too, as in old times; but talent is not rewarded as it was then; the rich prefer the jingle of their gold to the sound of poetry or music."

As he was talking, his eye caught one of the inscriptions which foretold perpetuity to the power and glory of the Moslem monarchs, the masters of this pile. He shook his head, and shrugged his shoulders, as he interpreted it. "Such might have been the case," said he; "the Moslems might still have been reigning in the Alhambra, had not Boabdil been a traitor, and given up his capital to the Christians. The Spanish monarchs would never have been able to conquer it by open force."

I endeavored to vindicate the memory of the unlucky Boabdil from this aspersion, and to show that the dissensions which led to the downfall of the Moorish throne, originated in the cruelty of his tiger-hearted father; but the Moor would admit of no palliation.

"Muley Abul Hassan," said he, "might have been cruel; but he was brave, vigilant, and patriotic. Had he been properly seconded, Granada would still have been ours; but his son Boabdil thwarted his plans, crippled his power, sowed treason in his palace, and dissension in his camp. May the curse of God light upon him for his treachery!" With these words the Moor left the Alhambra.

The indignation of my turbaned companion agrees with an anecdote related by a friend, who, in the course of a tour in Barbary, had an interview with the Pacha of Tetuan. The Moorish governor was particular in his inquiries about Spain and especially concerning the favored region of Andalusia, the delights of Granada, and the remains of its royal palace. The replies awakened all those fond recollections, so deeply cherished by the Moors, of the power and splendor of their ancient empire in Spain. Turning to his Moslem attendants, the Pacha stroked his beard, and broke forth in passionate lamentations, that such a sceptre should have fallen from the sway of true believers. He consoled himself, however, with the persuasion, that the power and prosperity of the Spanish nation were on the decline; that a time would come when the Moors would reconquer their rightful domains; and that the day was perhaps not far distant, when Mohammedan worship would again be offered up in the Mosque of Cordova, and a Mohammedan prince sit on his throne in the Alhambra.

Such is the general aspiration and belief among the Moors of Barbary; who consider Spain, or Andaluz, as it was anciently called, their rightful heritage, of which they have been despoiled by treachery and violence. These ideas are fostered and perpetuated by the descendants of the exiled Moors of Granada, scattered among the cities of Barbary. Several of these reside in Tetuan, preserving their ancient names, such as Paez and Medina, and refraining from intermarriage with any families who cannot claim the same high origin. Their vaunted lineage is regarded with a degree of popular deference, rarely shown in Mohammedan communities to any hereditary distinction, excepting in the royal line.

These families, it is said, continue to sigh after the terrestrial paradise of their ancestors, and to put up prayers in their mosques on Fridays, imploring Allah to hasten the time when Granada shall be restored to the faithful: an event to which they look forward as fondly and confidently as did the Christian crusaders to the recovery of the Holy Sepulchre. Nay, it is added, that some of them retain the ancient maps and deeds of the estates and gardens of their ancestors at Granada, and even the keys of the houses; holding them as evidences of their hereditary claims, to be produced at the anticipated day of restoration.

My conversation with the Moor set me to musing on the fate of Boabdil. Never was surname more applicable than that bestowed upon him by his subjects of el Zogoybi, or the Unlucky. His misfortunes began almost in his cradle, and ceased not even with his death. If ever he cherished the desire of leaving an honorable name on the historic page, how cruelly has he been defrauded of his hopes! Who is there that has turned the least attention to the romantic history of the Moorish domination in Spain, without kindling with indignation at the alleged atrocities of Boabdil? Who has not been touched with the woes of his lovely and gentle queen, subjected by him to a trial of life and death, on a false charge of infidelity? Who has not been shocked by his alleged murder of his sister and her two children, in a transport of passion? Who has not felt his blood boil at the inhuman massacre of the gallant

Abencerrages, thirty-six of whom, it is affirmed, he ordered to
be beheaded in the Court of Lions? All these charges have
been reiterated in various forms; they have passed into ballads,
dramas, and romances, until they have taken too thorough possession of the public mind to be eradicated There is not a
foreigner of education that visits the Alhambra, but asks for the
fountain where the Abencerrages were beheaded; and gazes
with horror at the grated gallery where the queen is said to have
been confined; not a peasant of the Vega or the Sierra, but sings
the story in rude couplets, to the accompaniment of his guitar,
while his hearers learn to execrate the very name of Boabdil.

Never, however, was name more foully and unjustly slandered.
I have examined all the authentic chronicles and letters written
by Spanish authors, contemporary with Boabdil; some of whom
were in the confidence of the Catholic sovereigns, and actually
present in the camp throughout the war. I have examined all
the Arabian authorities I could get access to, through the medium of translation, and have found nothing to justify these dark
and hateful accusations. The most of these tales may be traced
to a work commonly called " The Civil Wars of Granada," containing a pretended history of the feuds of the Zegries and
Abencerrages, during the last struggle of the Moorish empire.
The work appeared originally in Spanish, and professed be trans-
lated from the Arabic by one Gines Perez de Hita, an inhabitant
of Murcia. It has since passed into various languages, and
Florian has taken from it much of the fable of his Gonsalvo of
Cordova; it has thus, in a great measure, usurped the authority
of real history, and is currently believed by the people, and
especially the peasantry of Granada. The whole of it, however,
is a mass of fiction, mingled with a few disfigured truths, which

give it an air of veracity. It bears internal evidence of its falsity ; the manners and customs of the Moors being extravagantly misrepresented in it, and scenes depicted totally incompatible with their habits and their faith, and which never could have been recorded by a Mahometan writer.

I confess there seems to me something almost criminal, in the wilful perversions of this work : great latitude is undoubtedly to be allowed to romantic fiction, but there are limits which it must not pass ; and the names of the distinguished dead, which belong to history, are no more to be calumniated than those of the illustrious living. One would have thought, too, that the unfortunate Boabdil had suffered enough for his justifiable hostility to the Spaniards, by being stripped of his kingdom, without having his name thus wantonly traduced, and rendered a by-word and a theme of infamy in his native land, and in the very mansion of his fathers !

If the reader is sufficiently interested in these questions to tolerate a little historical detail, the following facts, gleaned from what appear to be authentic sources, and tracing the fortunes of the Abencerrages, may serve to exculpate the unfortunate Boabdil from the perfidious massacre of that illustrious line so shamelessly charged to him. It will also serve to throw a proper light upon the alleged accusation and imprisonment of his queen.

THE ABENCERRAGES.

A GRAND line of distinction existed among the Moslems of Spain, between those of Oriental origin and those from Western Africa. Among the former the Arabs considered themselves the purest race, as being descended from the countrymen of the Prophet, who first raised the standard of Islam; among the latter, the most warlike and powerful were the Berber tribes from Mount Atlas and the deserts of Sahara, commonly known as Moors, who subdued the tribes of the sea-coast, founded the city of Morocco, and for a long time desputed with the oriental races the control of Moslem Spain.

Among the oriental races the Abencerrages held a distinguished rank, priding themselves on a pure Arab descent from the Beni Seraj, one of the tribes who were Ansares or Companions of the Prophet. The Abencerrages flourished for a time at Cordova; but probably repaired to Granada after the downfall of the Western Caliphat; it was there they attained their historical and romantic celebrity, being foremost among the splendid chivalry which graced the court of the Alhambra.

Their highest and most dangerous prosperity was during the precarious reign of Muhamed Nasar, surnamed El Hayzari, or the Left-handed. That ill-starred monarch, when he ascended the throne in 1423, lavished his favors upon this gallant line, making the head of the tribe, Jusef Aben Zeragh, his vizier, or prime minister, and advancing his relatives and friends to the most distinguished posts about the court. This gave great offence to other tribes, and caused intrigues among their chiefs. Muhamed lost popularity also by his manners. He was vain, inconsiderate and haughty; disdained to mingle among his subjects; forbade those jousts and tournaments, the delight of high and low, and passed his time in the luxurious retirement of the Alhambra. The consequence was a popular insurrection; the palace was stormed; the king escaped through the gardens; fled to the sea-coast, crossed in disguise to Africa, and took refuge with his kinsman, the sovereign of Tunis.

Muhamed el Zaguer, cousin of the fugitive monarch, took possession of the vacant throne. He pursued a different course from his predecessor. He not only gave fêtes and tourneys, but entered the lists himself, in grand and sumptuous array; he distinguished himself in managing his horse, in tilting, riding at the ring, and other chivalrous exercises; feasted with his cavaliers, and made them magnificent presents.

Those who had been in favor with his predecessor, now experienced a reverse; he manifested such hostility to them that more than five hundred of the principal cavaliers left the city. Jusef Aben Zeragh, with forty of the Abencerrages, abandoned Granada in the night, and sought the court of Juan the king of Castile. Moved by their representations, that young and generous monarch wrote letters to the sovereign of Tunis, inviting him to assist in punishing the usurper and restoring the exiled king to his throne. The faithful and indefatigable vizier accompanied the bearer of these letters to Tunis, where he re-

joined his exiled sovereign. The letters were successful. Muhamed el Hayzari landed in Andalusia with five hundred African
horse, and was joined by the Abencerrages and others of
his adherents and by his Christian allies; wherever he appeared the people submitted to him; troops sent against him deserted to his standard ; Granada was recovered without a blow :
the usurper retreated to the Alhambra, but was beheaded by
his own soldiers (1428), after reigning between two and three
years.

El Hayzari, once more on the throne, heaped honors on the
loyal vizier, *through* whose faithful services he had been restored,
and once more the line of the Abencerrages basked in the sunshine of royal favor. El Hayzari sent ambassadors to King Juan,
thanking him for his aid, and proposing a perpetual league of
amity. The king of Castile required homage and yearly tribute
These the left-handed monarch refused, supposing the youthful king too much engaged in civil war to enforce his claims.
Again the kingdom of Granada was harassed by invasions, and
its Vega laid waste. Various battles took place with various
success. But El Hayzari's greatest danger was near at home.
There was at that time in Granada a cavalier, Don Pedro Venegas by name, a Moslem by faith, but Christian by descent, whose
early history borders on romance. He was of the noble house of
Luque, but captured when a child, eight years of age, by Cid Yahia
Alnayar, prince of Almeria,* who adopted him as his son, educated
him in the Moslem faith, and brought him up among his children,
the Celtimerian princes, a proud family, descended in direct line
from Aben Hud, one of the early Granadian kings. A mutual

* ALCANTARA, *Hist. Granad.*, O. 3, p. 226, note.

attachment sprang up between Don Pedro and the princess Ceti-merien, a daughter of Cid Yahia, famous for her beauty, and whose name is perpetuated by the ruins of her palace in Granada; still bearing traces of Moorish elegance and luxury. In process of time they were married; and thus a scion of the Spanish house of Luque became engrafted on the royal stock of Aben Hud.

Such is the early story of Don Pedro Venegas, who at the time of which we treat was a man mature in years, and of an active, ambitious spirit. He appears to have been the soul of a conspiracy set on foot about this time, to topple Muhamed the Left-handed from his unsteady throne, and elevate in his place Yusef Aben Alhamar, the eldest of the Celtimerian princes. The aid of the king of Castile was to be secured, and Don Pedro proceeded on a secret embassy to Cordova for the purpose. He informed King Juan of the extent of the conspiracy ; that Yusef Aben Alhamar could bring a large force to his standard as soon as he should appear in the Vega, and would acknowledge himself his vassal, if with his aid he should attain the crown. The aid was promised, and Don Pedro hastened back to Granada with the tidings. The conspirators now left the city, a few at a time, under various pretexts ; and when King Juan passed the frontier, Yusef Aben Alhamar brought eight thousand men to his standard and kissed his hand in token of allegiance.

It is needless to recount the various battles by which the kingdom was desolated, and the various intrigues by which one half of it was roused to rebellion. The Abencerrages stood by the failing fortunes of Muhamed throughout the struggle ; their last stand was at Loxa, where their chief, the vizier Yusef Aben Zeragh, fell bravely fighting, and many of their noblest cavaliers were slain: in fact, in that disastrous war the fortunes of the family were nearly wrecked.

Again, the ill-starred Muhamed was driven from his throne, and took refuge in Malaga, the alcayde of which still remained true to him.

Yusef Aben Alhamar, commonly known as Yusef II., entered Granada in triumph on the first of January, 1432, but he found it a melancholy city, where half of the inhabitants were in mourning. Not a noble family but had lost some member; and in the slaughter of the Abencerrages at Loxa, had fallen some of the brightest of the chivalry.

The royal pageant passed through silent streets, and the barren homage of a court in the halls of the Alhambra ill supplied the want of sincere and popular devotion. Yusef Aben Alhamar felt the insecurity of his position. The deposed monarch was at hand in Malaga; the sovereign of Tunis espoused his cause, and pleaded with the Christian monarchs in his favor; above all, Yusef felt his own unpopularity in Granada; previous fatigues had impaired his health, a profound melancholy settled upon him, and in the course of six months he sank into the grave.

At the news of his death, Muhamed the Left-handed hastened from Malaga, and again was placed on the throne. From the wrecks of the Abencerrages he chose as vizier Abdelbar, one of the worthiest of that magnanimous line. Through his advice he restrained his vindictive feelings and adopted a conciliatory policy. He pardoned most of his enemies. Yusef, the defunct usurper, had left three children. His estates were apportioned among them. Aben Celim, the oldest son, was confirmed in the title of Prince of Almeria and Lord of Marchena in the Alpux-

arras. Ahmed, the youngest, was made Señor of Luchar ; and
Equivila, the daughter, received rich patrimonial lands in the
fertile Vega, and various houses and shops in the Zacatin of
Granada. The vizier Abdelbar counselled the king, moreover, to
secure the adherence of the family by matrimonial connections.
An aunt of Muhamed was accordingly given in marriage to Aben
Celim, while the prince Nasar, younger brother of the deceased
usurper, received the hand of the beautiful Lindaraxa, daughter
of Muhamed's faithful adherent, the alcayde of Malaga. This
was the Lindaraxa whose name still designates one of the gardens
of the Alhambra.

Don Pedro de Venegas alone, the husband of the princess
Cetimerien, received no favor.   He was considered as having produced the late troubles by his intrigues. The Abencerrages
charged him with the reverses of their family and the deaths of
so many of their bravest cavaliers. The king never spoke of
him but by the opprobrious appellation of the Tornadizo, or
Renegade. Finding himself in danger of arrest and punishment, he took leave of his wife, the princess, his two sons, Abul
Cacem and Reduan, and his daughter, Cetimerien, and fled to
Jaen   There, like his brother-in-law, the usurper, he expiated
his intrigues and irregular ambition by profound humiliation and
melancholy, and died in 1434 a penitent, because a disappointed
man.*

Muhamed el Hayzari was doomed to further reverses. He
had two nephews, Aben Osmyn, surnamed el Anaf, or the Lame,
and Aben Ismael. The former, who was of an ambitious spirit,
resided in Almeria ; the latter in Granada, where he had many

---

* SALAZAR Y CASTRO, *Hist. Genealog. de la Casa de Lara*, lib. v., c. 12, cited
by Alcantara in his *Hist. Granad.*

friends. He was on the point of espousing a beautiful girl, when
his royal uncle interfered and gave her to one of his favorites.
Enraged at this despotic act, the prince Aben Ismael took horse
and weapons and sallied from Granada for the frontier, followed
by numerous cavaliers. The affair gave general disgust, especially to the Abencerrages who were attached to the prince. No
sooner did tidings reach Aben Osmyn of the public discontent
than his ambition was aroused. Throwing himself suddenly into
Granada, he raised a popular tumult, surprised his uncle in the
Alhambra, compelled him to abdicate, and proclaimed himself
king. This occurred in September, 1445. The Abencerrages
now gave up the fortunes of the left-handed king as hopeless, and
himself as incompetent to rule. Led by their kinsman, the vizier
Abdelbar, and accompanied by many other cavaliers, they abandoned the court and took post in Montefrio Thence Abdelbar
wrote to Prince Aben Ismael, who had taken refuge in Castile,
inviting him to the camp, offering to support his pretensions to
the throne, and advising him to leave Castile secretly, lest his
departure should be opposed by King Juan II. The prince,
however, confiding in the generosity of the Castilian monarch,
told him frankly the whole matter. He was not mistaken.
King Juan not merely gave him permission to depart, but promised him aid, and gave him letters to that effect to his commanders on the frontiers. Aben Ismael departed with a brilliant
escort, arrived in safety at Montefrio, and was proclaimed king of
Granada by Abdelbar and his partisans, the most important of
whom were the Abencerrages. A long course of civil wars ensued
between the two cousins, rivals for the throne. Aben Osmyn
was aided by the kings of Navarre and Aragon, while Juan II,
at war with his rebellious subjects, could give little assistance to
Aben Ismael.

Thus for several years the country was torn by internal strife and desolated by foreign inroads, so that scarce a field but was stained with blood. Aben Osmyn was brave, and often signalized himself in arms; but he was cruel and despotic, and ruled with an iron hand. He offended the nobles by his caprices, and the populace by his tyranny, while his rival cousin conciliated all hearts by his benignity. Hence there were continual desertions from Granada to the fortified camp at Montefrio, and the party of Aben Ismael was constantly gaining strength. At length the king of Castile, having made peace with the kings of Aragon and Navarre, was enabled to send a choice body of troops to the assistance of Aben Ismael. The latter now left his trenches in Montefrio, and took the field. The combined forces marched upon Granada. Aben Osmyn sallied forth to the encounter. A bloody battle ensued, in which both of the rival cousins fought with heroic valor. Aben Osmyn was defeated and driven back to his gates. He summoned the inhabitants to arms, but few answered to his call; his cruelty had alienated all hearts. Seeing his fortunes at an end, he determined to close his career by a signal act of vengeance. Shutting himself up in the Alhambra, he summoned thither a number of the principal cavaliers whom he suspected of disloyalty. As they entered, they were one by one put to death. This is supposed by some to be the massacre which gave its fatal name to the hall of the Abencerrages. Having perpetrated this atrocious act of vengeance, and hearing by the shouts of the populace that Aben Ismael was already proclaimed king in the city, he escaped with his satellites by the Cerro del Sol and the valley of the Darro to the Alpuxarra mountains; where he and his followers led a kind of robber life, laying villages and roads under contribution.

Aben Ismael II, who thus attained the throne in 1454, secured the friendship of King Juan II by acts of homage and
magnificent presents.   He gave liberal rewards to those who had
been faithful to him, and consoled the families of those who had
fallen in his cause.   During his reign, the Abencerrages were
again among the most favored of the brilliant chivalry that
graced his court.   Aben Ismael, however, was not of a warlike
spirit; his reign was distinguished rather by works of public
utility, the ruins of some of which are still to be seen on the
Cerro del Sol.

In the same year of 1454 Juan II died, and was succeeded by
Henry IV of Castile, surnamed the Impotent.   Aben Ismael
neglected to renew the league of amity with him which had
existed with his predecessor, as he found it to be unpopular with
the people of Granada.   King Henry resented the omission, and,
under pretext of arrears of tribute, made repeated forays into
the kingdom of Granada.   He gave countenance also to Aben
Osmyn and his robber hordes, and took some of them into pay;
but his proud cavaliers refused to associate with infidel outlaws,
and determined to seize Aben Osmyn; who, however, made his
escape, first to Seville, and thence to Castile.

In the year 1456, on the occasion of a great foray into the
Vega by the Christians, Aben Ismael, to secure a peace, agreed
to pay the king of Castile a certain tribute annually, and at the
same time to liberate six hundred Christian captives; or, should
the number of captives fall short, to make it up in Moorish
hostages.   Aben Ismael fulfilled the rigorous terms of the treaty,
and reigned for a number of years with more tranquillity than
usually fell to the lot of the monarchs of that belligerent kingdom.   Granada enjoyed a great state of prosperity during his

reign, and was the seat of festivity and splendor. His sultana was a daughter of Cid Hiaya Abraham Alnayar, prince of Almeria ; and he had by her two sons, Abul Hassan, and Abi Abdallah, surnamed El Zagal, the father and uncle of Boabdil. We approach now the eventful period signalized by the conquest of Granada.

Muley Abul Hassan succeeded to the throne on the death of his father in 1465.   One of his first acts was to refuse payment of the degrading tribute exacted by the Castilian monarch. His refusal was one of the causes of the subsequent disastrous war. I confine myself, however, to facts connected with the fortunes of the Abencerrages and the charges advanced against Boabdil.

The reader will recollect that Don Pedro Venegas, surnamed El Tornadizo, when he fled from Granada in 1433, left behind him two sons, Abul Cacim and Reduan, and a daughter, Cetimerien.   They always enjoyed a distinguished rank in Granada, from their royal descent by the mother's side ; and from being connected, through the princes of Almeria, with the last and the present king.   The sons had distinguished themselves by their talents and bravery, and the daughter Cetimerien was married to Cid Hiaya, grandson of King Jusef and brother-in-law of El Zagal.   Thus powerfully connected, it is not surprising to find Abul Cacim Venegas advanced to the post of vizier of Muley Abul Hassan, and Reduan Venegas one of his most favored generals.   Their rise was regarded with an evil eye by the Abencerrages, who remembered the disasters brought upon their family, and the deaths of so many of their line, in the war fomented by the intrigues of Don Pedro, in the days of Jusef Aben Alhamar.   A feud had existed ever since between the Abencerrages and the house of Venegas. It was soon to be aggravated by a formidable schism which took place in the royal harem.

Muley Abul Hassan, in his youthful days, had married his cousin, the princess Ayxa la Horra, daughter of his uncle, the ill-starred sultan, Muhamed the Left-handed;[*] by her he had two sons, the eldest of whom was Boabdil, heir presumptive to the throne. Unfortunately at an advanced age he took another wife, Isabella de Solis, a young and beautiful Christian captive ; better known by her Moorish appellation of Zoraya; by her he had also two sons. Two factions were produced in the palace by the rivalry of the sultanas, who were each anxious to secure for their children the succession to the throne. Zoraya was supported by the vizier Abul Cacim Venegas, his brother Reduan Venegas, and their numerous connections, partly through sympathy with her as being, like themselves, of Christian lineage, and partly because they saw she was the favorite of the doting monarch.

The Abencerrages, on the contrary, rallied round the sultana Ayxa; partly through hereditary opposition to the family of Venegas, but chiefly, no doubt, through a strong feeling of loyalty to her as daughter of Muhamed Alhayzari, the ancient benefactor of their line.

The dissensions of the palace went on increasing. Intrigues of all kinds took place, as is usual in royal palaces. Suspicions were artfully instilled in the mind of Muley Abul Hassan that Ayxa was engaged in a plot to depose him and put her son Boabdil on the throne. In his first transports of rage he confined them both in the tower of Comares, threatening the life of Boabdil. At dead of night the anxious mother lowered her son from a window of the tower by the scarfs of herself and her

* AL MAKKARI, B. viii. c. 7.

female attendants; and some of her adherents, who were in waiting with swift horses, bore him away to the Alpuxarras. It is this imprisonment of the sultana Ayxa which possibly gave rise to the fable of the queen of Boabdil being confined by him in a tower to be tried for her life. No other shadow of a ground exists for it, and here we find the tyrant jailer was his father, and the captive sultana, his mother.

The massacre of the Abencerrages in the halls of the Alhambra, is placed by some about this time, and attributed also to Muley Abul Hassan, on suspicion of their being concerned in the conspiracy. The sacrifice of a number of the cavaliers of that line is said to have been suggested by the vizier Abul Cacim Venegas, as a means of striking terror into the rest.* If such were really the case, the barbarous measure proved abortive. The Abencerrages continued intrepid, as they were loyal, in their adherence to the cause of Ayxa and her son Boabdil, throughout the war which ensued, while the Venegas were ever foremost in the ranks of Muley Abul Hassan and El Zagal. The ultimate fortunes of these rival families is worthy of note. The Venegas, in the last struggle of Granada, were among those who submitted to the conquerors, renounced the Moslem creed, returned to the faith from which their ancestor had apostatized, were rewarded with offices and estates, intermarried with Spanish families, and have left posterity among the nobles of the land. The Abencerrages remained true to their faith, true to their king, true to their desperate cause, and went down with the foundering wreck of Moslem domination, leaving nothing behind them but a gallant and romantic name in history.

* ALCANTARA, *Hist. Granad.*, c. 17. See also AL MAKKARI, *Hist. Mohamd. Dynasties*, B. viii. c. 7, with the Commentaries of Don Pascual de Guyangos.

In this historical outline, I trust I have shown enough to put the fable concerning Boabdil and the Abencerrages in a true light. The story of the accusation of his queen, and his cruelty to his sister, are equally void of foundation. In his domestic relations he appears to have been kind and affectionate. History gives him but one wife, Morayma, the daughter of the veteran alcayde of Loxa, old Aliatar, famous in song and story for his exploits in border warfare; and who fell in that disastrous foray into the Christian lands in which Boabdil was taken prisoner. Morayma was true to Boabdil throughout all his vicissitudes. When he was dethroned by the Castilian monarchs, she retired with him to the petty domain allotted him in the valleys of the Alpuxarras. It was only when (dispossessed of this by the jealous precautions and subtle chicanery of Ferdinand, and elbowed, as it were, out of his native land,) he was preparing to embark for Africa, that her health and spirits, exhausted by anxiety and long suffering, gave way, and she fell into a lingering illness, aggravated by corroding melancholy. Boabdil was constant and affectionate to her to the last; the sailing of the ships was delayed for several weeks, to the great annoyance of the suspicious Ferdinand. At length Morayma sank into the grave, evidently the victim of a broken heart, and the event was reported to Ferdinand by his agent, as one propitious to his purposes, removing the only obstacle to the embarkation of Boabdil.*

---

* For authorities for these latter facts, see the Appendix to the author's revised edition of the Conquest of Granada.

MEMENTOS OF BOABDIL.

WHILE my mind was still warm with the subject of the un fortunate Boabdil, I set forth to trace the mementos of him still existing in this scene of his sovereignty and misfortunes. In the Tower of Comares, immediately under the Hall of Ambas sadors, are two vaulted rooms, separated by a narrow passage; these are said to have been the prisons of himself and his mother, the virtuous Ayxa la Horra, indeed, no other part of the tower would have served for the purpose. The external walls of these chambers are of prodigious thickness, pierced with small windows secured by iron bars. A narrow stone gallery, with a low para- pet, extends along three sides of the tower just below the win- dows, but at a considerable height from the ground. From this gallery, it is presumed, the queen lowered her son with the scarfs of herself and her female attendants during the darkness of the night to the hill-side, where some of his faithful adherents waited with fleet steeds to bear him to the mountains.

Between three and four hundred years have elapsed, yet this scene of the drama remains almost unchanged. As I paced the gallery, my imagination pictured the anxious queen leaning over the parapet; listening, with the throbbings of a mother's heart, to the last echoes of the horses' hoofs as her son scoured along the narrow valley of the Darro.

I next sought the gate by which Boabdil made his last exit from the Alhambra, when about to surrender his capital and kingdom. With the melancholy caprice of a broken spirit, or perhaps with some superstitious feeling, he requested of the Catholic monarchs that no one afterwards might be permitted to pass through it. His prayer, according to ancient chronicles, was complied with, through the sympathy of Isabella, and the gate was walled up.*

I inquired for some time in vain for such a portal; at length my humble attendant, Mateo Ximenes, said it must be one closed up with stones, which, according to what he had heard from his father and grandfather, was the gateway by which King Chico had left the fortress. There was a mystery about it, and it had never been opened within the memory of the oldest inhabitant.

He conducted me to the spot. The gateway is in the centre of what was once an immense pile, called the Tower of the Seven Floors (*la Torre de los siete suelos*). It is famous in the neighborhood as the scene of strange apparitions and Moorish enchantments. According to Swinburne the traveller, it was originally the great gate of entrance. The antiquaries of Granada pronounce it the entrance to that quarter of the royal residence where the king's body-guards were stationed. It therefore might well form an immediate entrance and exit to the palace; while the grand Gate of Justice served as the entrance

---

* Ay una puerta en la Alhambra por la qual salio Chico Rey de los Moros, quando si riudio prisionero al Rey de España D. Fernando, y le entregó la ciudad con el castillo. Pidio esta principe como por merced, y en memoria de tan importante conquista, al que quedasse siempre cerrada esta puerta. Consintio en allo el Rey Fernando, y des de aquel tiempo no sola· mente no se abrio la puerta sino tambien se construyo junto à ella fuerte bastion.—MORERI's *Historical Dictionary*, Spanish Edition, Vol. i. p. 372.

of state to the fortress. When Boabdil sallied by this gate to descend to the Vega, where he was to surrender the keys of the city to the Spanish sovereigns, he left his vizier Aben Comixa to receive, at the Gate of Justice, the detachment from the Christian army and the officers to whom the fortress was to be given up.[*]

The once redoubtable Tower of the Seven Floors is now a mere wreck, having been blown up with gunpowder by the French, when they abandoned the fortress. Great masses of the wall lie scattered about, buried in luxuriant herbage, or overshadowed by vines and fig-trees. The arch of the gateway, though rent by the shock, still remains ; but the last wish of poor Boabdil has again, though unintentionally, been fulfilled, for the portal has been closed up by loose stones gathered from the ruins, and remains impassable.

Mounting my horse, I followed up the route of the Moslem monarch from this place of his exit. Crossing the hill of Los Martyros, and keeping along the garden wall of a convent bearing the same name, I descended a rugged ravine beset by thickets of aloes and Indian figs, and lined with caves and hovels swarming with gipsies. The descent was so steep and broken that I was fain to alight and lead my horse. By this *via dolorosa* poor Boabdil took his sad departure to avoid passing through the city; partly, perhaps, through unwillingness that its inhabitants should behold his humiliation : but chiefly, in all probability, lest it might cause some popular agitation. For the last reason, undoubtedly, the detachment sent to take possession of the fortress ascended by the same route.

[*] The minor details of the surrender of Granada have been stated in different ways even by eye-witnesses. The author, in his revised edition of the Conquest, has endeavored to adjust them according to the latest and apparently best authorities.

Emerging from this rough ravine, so full of melancholy asso ciations, and passing by the *puerta de los molinos* (the gate of the mills), I issued forth upon the public promenade called the Prado; and pursuing the course of the Xenil, arrived at a small chapel, once a mosque, now the Hermitage of San Sebastian Here, according to tradition, Boabdil surrendered the keys of Granada to King Ferdinand. I rode slowly thence across the Vega to a village where the family and household of the unhappy king awaited him, for he had sent them forward on the preceding night from the Alhambra, that his mother and wife might not participate in his personal humiliation, or be exposed to the gaze of the conquerors. Following on in the route of the melancholy band of royal exiles, I arrived at the foot of a chain of barren and dreary heights, forming the skirt of the Alpuxarra mountains. From the summit of one of these the unfortunate Boabdil took his last look at Granada; it bears a name expressive of his sorrows, *La Cuesta de las Lagrimas* (the hill of tears). Beyond it, a sandy road winds across a rugged cheerless waste, doubly dismal to the unhappy monarch, as it led to exile.

I spurred my horse to the summit of a rock, where Boabdil uttered his last sorrowful exclamation, as he turned his eyes from taking their farewell gaze: it is still denominated *el ultimo suspiro del Moro* (the last sigh of the Moor). Who can wonder at his anguish at being expelled from such a kingdom and such an abode? With the Alhambra he seemed to be yielding up all the honors of his line, and all the glories and delights of life.

It was here, too, that his affliction was embittered by the reproach of his mother, Ayxa, who had so often assisted him in times of peril, and had vainly sought to instil into him her own resolute spirit. "You do well," said she, "to weep as a woman over what you could not defend as a man;" a speech savoring more of the pride of the princess than the tenderness of the mother.

When this anecdote was related to Charles V, by bishop Guevara, the emperor joined in the expression of scorn at the weakness of the wavering Boabdil. "Had I been he, or he been I," said the haughty potentate, "I would rather have made this Alhambra my sepulchre than have lived without a kingdom in the Alpuxarra." How easy it is for those in power and prosperity to preach heroism to the vanquished! how little can they understand that life itself may rise in value with the unfortunate, when nought but life remains!

Slowly descending the "Hill of Tears;" I let my horse take his own loitering gait back to Granada, while I turned the story of the unfortunate Boabdil over in my mind. In summing up the particulars I found the balance inclining in his favor. Throughout the whole of his brief, turbulent, and disastrous reign, he gives evidence of a mild and amiable character. He, in the first instance, won the hearts of his people by his affable and gracious manners; he was always placable, and never inflicted any severity of punishment upon those who occasionally rebelled against him. He was personally brave; but wanted moral courage; and, in times of difficulty and perplexity, was wavering and irresolute. This feebleness of spirit hastened his downfall, while it deprived him of that heroic grace which would have given grandeur and dignity to his fate, and rendered him worthy of closing the splendid drama of the Moslem domination in Spain.

PUBLIC FETES OF GRANADA.

My devoted squire and whilom ragged cicerone Mateo Ximenes, had a poor-devil passion for fêtes and holidays, and was never so eloquent as when detailing the civil and religious festivals of Granada. During the preparations for the annual Catholic fête of Corpus Christi, he was in a state of incessant transition between the Alhambra and the subjacent city, bringing me daily accounts of the magnificent arrangements that were in progress, and endeavoring, but in vain, to lure me down from my cool and airy retreat to witness them. At length, on the eve of the eventful day I yielded to his solicitations and descended from the regal halls of the Alhambra under his escort, as did of yore the adventure-seeking Haroun Alraschid, under that of his Grand Vizier Giaffar. Though it was yet scarce sunset, the city gates were already thronged with the picturesque villagers of the mountains, and the brown peasantry of the Vega. Granada has ever been the rallying place of a great mountainous region, studded with towns and villages. Hither, during the Moorish domination, the chivalry of this region repaired, to join in the splendid and semi-warlike fêtes of the Vivarrambla, and hither the élite of its population still resort to join in the pompous ceremonials of the church. Indeed, many of the mountaineers from the Alpuxarras and the Sierra de Ronda, who now bow to the cross as zealous Catholics, bear the stamp of their Moorish origin, and are indubitable descendants of the fickle subjects of Boabdil.

Under the guidance of Mateo, I made my way through streets already teeming with a holiday population, to the square of the Vivarrambla, that great place for tilts and tourneys, so often sung in the Moorish ballads of love and chivalry. A gallery or arcade of wood had been erected along the sides of the square, for the grand religious procession of the following day. This was brilliantly illuminated for the evening as a promenade; and bands of music were stationed on balconies on each of the four façades of the square. All the fashion and beauty of Granada, all of its population of either sex that had good looks or fine clothes to display, thronged this arcade, promenading round and round the Vivarrambla. Here, too, were the *Majos* and *Majas*, the rural beaux and belles, with fine forms, flashing eyes, and gay Andalusian costumes; some of them from Ronda itself, that strong-hold of the mountains, famous for contrabandistas, bull-fighters, and beautiful women.

While this gay but motley throng kept up a constant circulation in the gallery, the centre of the square was occupied by the peasantry from the surrounding country; who made no pretensions to display, but came for simple, hearty enjoyment. The whole square was covered with them; forming separate groups of families and neighborhoods, like gipsy encampments, some were listening to the traditional ballad drawled out to the tinkling of the guitar; some were engaged in gay conversation; some were dancing to the click of the castanet. As I threaded my way through this teeming region with Mateo at my heels, I passed occasionally some rustic party, seated on the ground, making a merry though frugal repast. If they caught my eye as I loitered by, they almost invariably invited me to partake of their simple fare. This hospitable usage, inherited from their Moslem invaders, and originating in the tent of the Arab, is universal throughout the land, and observed by the poorest Spaniard.

As the night advanced, the gayety gradually died away in the arcades; the bands of music ceased to play, and the brilliant crowd dispersed to their homes. The centre of the square still remained well peopled, and Mateo assured me that the greater part of the peasantry, men, women, and children, would pass the night there, sleeping on the bare earth beneath the open canopy of heaven. Indeed, a summer night requires no shelter in this favored climate; and a bed is a superfluity, which many of the hardy peasantry of Spain never enjoy, and which some of them affect to despise. The common Spaniard wraps himself in his brown cloak, stretches himself on his manta or mule-cloth, and sleeps soundly, luxuriously accommodated if he can have a saddle for a pillow. In a little while the words of Mateo were made good; the peasant multitude nestled down on the ground to their night's repose, and by midnight, the scene on the Vivarrambla resembled the bivouac of an army.

The next morning, accompanied by Mateo, I revisited the square at sunrise. It was still strewed with groups of sleepers: some were reposing from the dance and revel of the evening; others, who had left their villages after work on the preceding day, having trudged on foot the greater part of the night, were taking a sound sleep to freshen themselves for the festivities of the day. Numbers from the mountains, and the remote villages of the plain, who had set out in the night, continued to arrive with their wives and children. All were in high spirits; greeting each other and exchanging jokes and pleasantries. The gay tumult thickened as the day advanced. Now came pouring in at the city gates, and parading through the streets, the deputations from the various villages, destined to swell the grand procession. These village deputations were headed by their priests, bearing their respective crosses and banners, and images of the blessed Virgin and of patron saints; all which were matters of great rivalship and jealousy among the peasantry. It was like the chivalrous gatherings of ancient days, when each town and village sent its chiefs, and warriors, and standards, to defend the capital, or grace its festivities.

At length all these various detachments congregated into one grand pageant, which slowly paraded round the Vivarrambla, and through the principal streets, where every window and balcony was hung with tapestry. In this procession were all the religious orders, the civil and military authorities, and the chief people of the parishes and villages : every church and convent had contributed its banners, its images, its relics, and poured forth its wealth for the occasion. In the centre of the procession walked the archbishop, under a damask canopy, and surrounded by inferior dignitaries and their dependants. The whole moved to the swell and cadence of numerous bands of music, and, passing through the midst of a countless yet silent multitude, proceeded onward to the cathedral.

I could not but be struck with the changes of times and customs, as I saw this monkish pageant passing through the Vivarrambla, the ancient seat of Moslem pomp and chivalry. The contrast was indeed forced upon the mind by the decorations of the square. The whole front of the wooden gallery erected for the procession, extending several hundred feet, was faced with canvas, on which some humble though patriotic artist had painted, by contract, a series of the principal scenes and exploits of the conquest, as recorded in chronicle and romance. It is thus the romantic legends of Granada mingle themselves with every thing, and are kept fresh in the public mind.

As we wended our way back to the Alhambra, Mateo was in high glee and garrulous vein. "Ah, Señor," exclaimed he, "there is no place in all the world like Granada for grand ceremonies, (*funciones grandes*), a man need spend nothing on pleasure here, it is all furnished him gratis." Pero, el dia de la Toma! Ah Señor! el dia de la Toma! "But the day of the Taking! ah, Señor, the day of the Taking;"—that was the great day which crowned Mateo's notions of perfect felicity. The Dia de la Toma, I found, was the anniversary of the capture or taking possession of Granada, by the army of Ferdinand and Isabella.

On that day, according to Mateo, the whole city is abandoned to revelry. The great alarm bell on the watchtower of the Alhambra (*la Torre de la vela*), sends forth its clanging peals from morn till night; the sound pervades the whole Vega, and echoes along the mountains, summoning the peasantry from far and near to the festivities of the metropolis. "Happy the damsel," says Mateo, "who can get a chance to ring that bell; it is a charm to insure a husband within the year."

Throughout the day the Alhambra is thrown open to the public. Its halls and courts, where the Moorish monarchs once held sway, resound with the guitar and castanet, and gay groups, in the fanciful dresses of Andalusia, perform their traditional dances inherited from the Moors.

A grand procession, emblematic of the taking possession of the city, moves through the principal streets. The banner of

Ferdinand and Isabella, that precious relic of the Conquest, is
brought forth from its depository, and borne in triumph by the
Alferez mayor, or grand standard-bearer.   The portable camp-
altar, carried about with the sovereigns in all their campaigns, is
transported into the chapel royal of the cathedral, and placed before their sepulchre, where their effigies lie in monumental marble.   High mass is then performed in memory of the Conquest;
and'at a certain part of the ceremony the Alferez mayor puts
on his hat, and waves the standard above the tomb of the conquerors.

A more whimsical memorial of the Conquest is exhibited in
the evening at the theatre.   A popular drama is performed, entitled AVE MARIA, turning on a famous achievement of Hernando
del Pulgar, surnamed "el de las Hazañas" (he of the exploits),
a madcap warrior, the favorite hero of the populace of Granada.
During the time of the siege, the young Moorish and Spanish
cavaliers vied with each other in extravagant bravadoes.   On
one occasion this Hernando del Pulgar, at the head of a handful
of followers, made a dash into Granada in the dead of the night,
nailed the inscription of AVE MARIA with his dagger to the gate
of the principal mosque, a token of having consecrated it to the
Virgin, and effected his retreat in safety.*

While the Moorish cavaliers admired this daring exploit,
they felt bound to resent it.   On the following day, therefore,
Tarfe, one of the stoutest among them, paraded in front of the
Christian army, dragging the tablet bearing the sacred inscription AVE MARIA, at his horse's tail.   The cause of the Virgin
was eagerly vindicated by Garcilaso de la Vega, who slew the

---

* See a more detailed account of the exploit in the chronicle of the
Conquest of Granada.

Moor in single combat, and elevated the tablet in devotion and triumph at the end of his lance.

The drama founded on this exploit is prodigiously popular with the common people. Although it has been acted time out of mind, it never fails to draw crowds, who become completely lost in the delusions of the scene. When their favorite Pulgar strides about with many a mouthy speech, in the very midst of the Moorish capital, he is cheered with enthusiastic bravos; and when he nails the tablet to the door of the mosque, the theatre absolutely shakes with the thunders of applause. On the other hand, the unlucky actors who figure in the part of the Moors, have to bear the brunt of popular indignation; which at times equals that of the Hero of Lamanche, at the puppet-show of Gines de Passamonte; for, when the infidel Tarfé plucks down the tablet to tie it to his horse's tail, some of the audience rise in fury, and are ready to jump upon the stage to revenge this insult to the Virgin.

By the way, the actual lineal descendant of Hernando del Pulgar, was the Marquis de Salar. As the legitimate representative of that madcap hero, and in commemoration and reward of this hero's exploit, above mentioned, he inherited the right to enter the cathedral on certain occasions, on horseback; to sit within the choir, and to put on his hat at the elevation of the host, though these privileges were often and obstinately contested by the clergy. I met him occasionally in society; he was young, of agreeable appearance and manners, with bright black eyes, in which appeared to lurk some of the fire of his ancestors. Among the paintings in the Vivarrambla, on the fête of Corpus Christi, were some depicting, in vivid style, the exploits of the family hero. An old gray-headed servant of the Pulgars shed tears on beholding them, and hurried home to inform the marquis. The eager zeal and enthusiasm of the old domestic only provoked a light laugh from his young master; whereupon, turning to the brother of the marquis, with that freedom allowed in Spain to old family servants, " Come, Señor," cried he, " you are more considerate than your brother ; come and see your ancestor in all his glory !"

In emulation of this great *Dia de la Toma* of Granada, almost every village and petty town of the mountains has its own anniversary, commemorating, with rustic pomp and uncouth ceremonial, its deliverance from the Moorish yoke. On these occasions, according to Mateo, a kind of resurrection takes place of ancient armor and weapons ; great two-handed swords, ponderous arquebuses with matchlocks, and other warlike relics, treasured up from generation to generation, since the time of the Conquest; and happy the community that possesses some old piece of ordnance, peradventure one of the identical lombards used by the conquerors; it is kept thundering along the mountains all day long, provided the community can afford sufficient expenditure of powder.

In the course of the day, a kind of warlike drama is enacted. Some of the populace parade the streets, fitted out with the old armor, as champions of the faith. Others appear dressed up as Moorish warriors. A tent is pitched in the public square, inclosing an altar with an image of the Virgin. The Christian warriors approach to perform their devotions ; the infidels surround the tent to prevent their entrance ; a mock fight ensues ; the combatants sometimes forget that they are merely playing a part, and dry blows of grievous weight are apt to be exchanged. The contest, however, invariably terminates in favor of the good cause. The Moors are defeated and taken prisoners. The image of the Virgin, rescued from thraldom, is elevated in triumph; a grand procession succeeds, in which the conquerors figure with great applause and vainglory; while their captives are led in chains, to the evident delight and edification of the spectators.

These celebrations are heavy drains on the treasuries of these petty communities, and have sometimes to be suspended for want of funds; but, when times grow better, or sufficient money has been hoarded for the purpose, they are resumed with new zeal and prodigality.

Mateo informed me that he had occasionally assisted at these fêtes and taken a part in the combats; but always on the side of the true faith; *porque Señor*, added the ragged descendant of the cardinal Ximenes, tapping his breast with something of an air, "*porque Señor, soy Christiano viejo.*"

LOCAL TRADITIONS.

THE common people of Spain have an Oriental passion for story-telling, and are fond of the marvellous. They will gather round the doors of their cottages in summer evenings, or in the great cavernous chimney-corners of the ventas in the winter, and listen with insatiable delight to miraculous legends of saints, perilous adventures of travellers, and daring exploits of robbers and contrabandistas. The wild and solitary character of the country, the imperfect diffusion of knowledge, the scarceness of general topics of conversation, and the romantic adventurous life that every one leads in a land where travelling is yet in its primitive state, all contribute to cherish this love of oral narration, and to produce a strong infusion of the extravagant and incredible. There is no theme, however, more prevalent and popular than that of treasures buried by the Moors; it pervades the whole country. In traversing the wild sierras, the scenes of ancient foray and exploit, you cannot see a Moorish atalaya, or watchtower, perched among the cliffs, or beetling above its rock-built village, but your muleteer, on being closely questioned, will suspend the smoking of his cigarillo to tell some tale of Moslem gold buried beneath its foundations; nor is there a ruined alcazar in a city but has its golden tradition, handed down from generation to generation among the poor people of the neighborhood.

These, like most popular fictions, have sprung from some scanty groundwork of fact. During the wars between Moor and Christian which distracted this country for centuries, towns and castles were liable frequently and suddenly to change owners, and the inhabitants, during sieges and assaults, were fain to bury their money and jewels in the earth, or hide them in vaults and wells, as is often done at the present day in the despotic and belligerent countries of the East. At the time of the expulsion of the Moors also, many of them concealed their most precious effects, hoping that their exile would be but temporary, and that they would be enabled to return and retrieve their treasures at some future day. It is certain that from time to time hoards of gold and silver coin have been accidentally digged up, after a lapse of centuries, from among the ruins of Moorish fortresses and habitations; and it requires but a few facts of the kind to give birth to a thousand fictions.

The stories thus originating have generally something of an Oriental tinge, and are marked with that mixture of the Arabic and the Gothic which seems to me to characterize every thing in Spain, and especially in its southern provinces. The hidden wealth is always laid under magic spell, and secured by charm and talisman. Sometimes it is guarded by uncouth monsters or fiery dragons, sometimes by enchanted Moors, who sit by it in armor, with drawn swords, but motionless as statues, maintaining a sleepless watch for ages.

The Alhambra of course, from the peculiar circumstances of its history, is a strong-hold for popular fictions of the kind; and various relics, digged up from time to time, have contributed to strengthen them. At one time an earthen vessel was found containing Moorish coins and the skeleton of a cock, which, according to the opinion of certain shrewd inspectors, must have been buried alive. At another time a vessel was dug up containing a great scarabæus or beetle of baked clay, covered with Arabic inscriptions, which was pronounced a prodigious amulet of occult virtues. In this way the wits of the ragged brood who inhabit the Alhambra have been set wool-gathering, until there is not a hall, nor tower, nor vault, of the old fortress, that has not been made the scene of some marvellous tradition. Having, I trust, in the preceding papers made the reader in some degree familiar with the localities of the Alhambra, I shall now launch out more largely into the wonderful legends connected with it, and which I have diligently wrought into shape and form, from various legendary scraps and hints picked up in the course of my perambulations; in the same manner, that an antiquary works out a regular historical document from a few scattered letters of an almost defaced inscription.

If any thing in these legends should shock the faith of the over-scrupulous reader, he must remember the nature of the place, and make due allowances. He must not expect here the same laws of probability that govern commonplace scenes and every-day life; he must remember that he treads the halls of an enchanted palace, and that all is " haunted ground."

THE HOUSE OF THE WEATHERCOCK.

On the brow of the lofty hill of the Albaycin, the highest part of Granada, and which rises from the narrow valley of the Darro, directly opposite to the Alhambra, stands all that is left of what was once a royal palace of the Moors. It has, in fact, fallen into such obscurity, that it cost me much trouble to find it; though aided in my researches, by the sagacious and all-knowing Mateo Ximenes. This edifice has borne for centuries the name of "The House of the Weathercock" (La casa del Gallo de Viento), from a bronze figure on one of its turrets, in ancient times, of a warrior on horseback, and turning with every breeze. This weathercock was considered by the Moslems of Granada a portentous talisman. According to some traditions, it bore the following Arabic inscription:

> Calet el Bedici Aben Habuz,
> Quidat ehahet Lindabuz.

Which has been rendered into Spanish

> Dice el sabio Aben Habuz,
> Que asi se defiende el Anduluz.

And into English:

> In this way, says Aben Habus the wise,
> Andaluz guards against surprise.

This Aben Habuz, according to some of the old Moorish chronicles, was a captain in the invading army of Taric, one of the conquerors of Spain, who left him as Alcayde of Granada. He is supposed to have intended this effigy as a perpetual warning to the Moslems of Andaluz, that, surrounded by foes, their safety depended upon their being always on their guard and ready for the field.

Others, among whom is the Christian historian Marmol, affirms 'Badis Aben Habus' to have been a Moorish sultan of Granada, and that the weathercock was intended as a perpetual admonition of the instability of Moslem power, bearing the following words in Arabic:

" Thus Ibn Habus al badise predicts Andalus shall one day vanish and pass away."*

Another version of this portentous inscription is given by a Moslem historian, on the authority of Sidi Hasan, a faquir who flourished about the time of Ferdinand and Isabella, and who was present at the taking down of the weathercock, when the old Kassaba was undergoing repairs.

" I saw it," says the venerable faquir, "with my own eyes ; it was of a heptagonal shape, and had the following inscription in verse:

"The palace at fair Granada presents a talisman."

" The horseman, though a solid body, turns with every wind."

" This to a wise man reveals a mystery. In a little while comes a calamity to ruin both the palace and its owner."

In effect it was not long after this meddling with the portentous weathercock that the following event occurred. As old Muley Abul Hassan, the king of Granada, was seated under a sumptuous

* Marmol, *Hist. Rebellion of the Moors.*

pavilion, reviewing his troops who paraded before him in armor of polished steel, and gorgeous silken robes, mounted on fleet steeds, and equipped with swords, spears and shields, embossed with gold and silver; suddenly a tempest was seen hurrying from the south-west. In a little while, black clouds overshadowed the heavens and burst forth with a deluge of rain. Torrents came roaring down from the mountains, bringing with them rocks and trees; the Darro overflowed its banks; mills were swept away; bridges destroyed, gardens laid waste; the inundation rushed into the city, undermining houses, drowning their inhabitants, and overflowing even the square of the Great Mosque. The people rushed in affright to the mosques to implore the mercy of Allah, regarding this uproar of the elements as the harbinger of dreadful calamities; and, indeed, according to the Arabian historian, Al Makkari, it was but a type and prelude of the direful war which ended in the downfall of the Moslem kingdom of Granada.

I have thus given historic authorities, sufficient to show the portentous mysteries connected with the House of the Weathercock, and its talismanic horseman.

I now proceed to relate still more surprising things about Aben Habuz and his palace; for the truth of which, should any doubt be entertained, I refer the dubious reader to Mateo Ximenes and his fellow-historiographers of the Alhambra.

LEGEND OF THE ARABIAN ASTROLOGER.

IN old times, many hundred years ago, there was a Moorish king named Aben Habuz, who reigned over the kingdom of Granada. He was a retired conqueror, that is to say, one who having in his more youthful days led a life of constant foray and depredation, now that he was grown feeble and superannuated, "languished for repose," and desired nothing more than to live at peace with all the world, to husband his laurels, and to enjoy in quiet the possessions he had wrested from his neighbors.

It so happened, however, that this most reasonable and pacific old monarch had young rivals to deal with; princes full of his early passion for fame and fighting, and who were disposed to call him to account for the scores he had run up with their fathers. Certain distant districts of his own territories, also, which during the days of his vigor he had treated with a high hand, were prone, now that he languished for repose, to rise in rebellion and threaten to invest him in his capital. Thus he had foes on every side; and as Granada is surrounded by wild and craggy mountains, which hide the approach of an enemy, the unfortunate Aben Habuz was kept in a constant state of viligance and alarm, not knowing in what quarter hostilities might break out.

It was in vain that he built watchtowers on the mountains, and stationed guards at every pass with orders to make fires by night and smoke by day, on the approach of an enemy. His alert foes, baffling every precaution, would break out of some unthought-of defile, ravage his lands beneath his very nose, and then make off with prisoners and booty to the mountains. Was ever peaceable and retired conqueror in a more uncomfortable predicament?

While Aben Habuz was harassed by these perplexities and molestations, an ancient Arabian physician arrived at his court. His gray beard descended to his girdle, and he had every mark of extreme age, yet he had travelled almost the whole way from Egypt on foot, with no other aid than a staff, marked with hieroglyphics. His fame had preceded him. His name was Ibrahim Ebn Abu Ayub, he was said to have lived ever since the days of Mahomet, and to be son of Abu Ayub, the last of the companions of the Prophet. He had, when a child, followed the conquering army of Amru into Egypt, where he had remained many years studying the dark sciences, and particularly magic among the Egyptian priests.

It was, moreover, said that he had found out the secret of prolonging life, by means of which he had arrived to the great age of upwards of two centuries, though, as he did not discover the secret until well stricken in years, he could only perpetuate his gray hairs and wrinkles.

This wonderful old man was honorably entertained by the king; who, like most superannuated monarchs, began to take physicians into great favor. He would have assigned him an apartment in his palace, but the astrologer preferred a cave in the side of the hill which rises above the city of Granada, being the same on which the Alhambra has since been built. He caused the cave to be enlarged so as to form a spacious and lofty hall, with a circular hole at the top, through which, as through a well, he could see the heavens and behold the stars even at mid-day. The walls of this hall were covered with Egyptian hieroglyphics, with cabalistic symbols, and with the figures of the stars in their signs. This hall he furnished with many implements, fabricated under his directions by cunning artificers of Granada, but the occult properties of which were known only to himself.

In a little while the sage Ibrahim became the bosom counsellor of the king, who applied to him for advice in every emergency. Aben Habus was once inveighing against the injustice of his neighbors, and bewailing the restless vigilance he had to observe to guard himself against their invasions; when he had finished, the astrologer remained silent for a moment, and then replied, "Know, O King, that when I was in Egypt I beheld a great marvel devised by a pagan priestess of old. On a mountain, above the city of Borsa, and overlooking the great valley of the Nile, was a figure of a ram, and above it a figure of a cock, both of molten brass, and turning upon a pivot. Whenever the country was threatened with invasion, the ram would turn in the direction of the enemy, and the cock would crow; upon this the inhabitants of the city knew of the danger, and of the quarter from which it was approaching, and could take timely means to guard against it."

"God is great!" exclaimed the pacific Aben Habuz, "what a treasure would be such a ram to keep an eye upon these mountains around me; and then such a cock, to crow in time of danger! Allah Akbar! how securely I might sleep in my palace with such sentinels on the top!"

The astrologer waited until the ecstasies of the king had subsided, and then proceeded.

" After the victorious Amru (may he rest in peace !) had finished his conquest of Egypt, I remained among the priests of the
land, studying the rites and ceremonies of their idolatrous faith,
and seeking to make myself master of the hidden knowledge for
which they are renowned. I was one day seated on the banks of
the Nile, conversing with an ancient priest, when he pointed to
the mighty pyramids which rose like mountains out of the neighboring desert. 'All that we can teach thee,' said he, 'is nothing
to the knowledge locked up in those mighty piles. In the centre
of the central pyramid is a sepulchral chamber, in which is inclosed the mummy of the high-priest, who aided in rearing that
stupendous pile ; and with him is buried a wondrous book of
knowledge containing all the secrets of magic and art. This book
was given to Adam after his fall, and was handed down from generation to generation to King Solomon the wise, and by its aid
he built the temple of Jerusalem. How it came into the possession of the builder of the pyramids, is known to him alone who
knows all things.'

" When I heard these words of the Egyptian priest, my heart
burned to get possession of that book. I could command the
services of many of the soldiers of our conquering army, and of
a number of the native Egyptians : with these I set to work, and
pierced the solid mass of the pyramid, until, after great toil, I
came upon one of its interior and hidden passages. Following
this up, and threading a fearful labyrinth, I penetrated into the
very heart of the pyramid, even to the sepulchral chamber, where
the mummy of the high-priest had lain for ages. I broke through
the outer cases of the mummy, unfolded its many wrappers and

bandages, and at length found the precious volume on its bosom. I seized it with a trembling hand, and groped my way out of the pyramid, leaving the mummy in its dark and silent sepulchre, there to await the final day of resurrection and judgment."

"Son of Abu Ayub," exclaimed Aben Habuz, "thou hast been a great traveller, and seen marvellous things; but of what avail to me is the secret of the pyramid, and the volume of knowledge of the wise Solomon?"

"This it is, O king! By the study of that book I am instructed in all magic arts, and can command the assistance of genii to accomplish my plans. The mystery of the Talisman of Borsa is therefore familiar to me, and such a talisman can I make; nay, one of greater virtues."

"O wise son of Abu Ayub," cried Aben Habuz, "better were such a talisman, than all the watchtowers on the hills, and sentinels upon the borders. Give me such a safeguard, and the riches of my treasury are at thy command."

The astrologer immediately set to work to gratify the wishes of the monarch. He caused a great tower to be erected upon the top of the royal palace, which stood on the brow of the hill of the Albaycin. The tower was built of stones brought from Egypt, and taken, it is said, from one of the pyramids. In the upper part of the tower was a circular hall, with windows looking towards every point of the compass, and before each window was a table, on which was arranged, as on a chess-board, a mimic army of horse and foot, with the effigy of the potentate that ruled in that direction, all carved of wood. To each of these tables there was a small lance, no bigger than a bodkin, on which were engraved certain Chaldaic characters. This hall was kept constantly closed, by a gate of brass, with a great lock of steel, the key of which was in possession of the king.

On the top of the tower was a bronze figure of a Moorish horseman, fixed on a pivot, with a shield on one arm, and his lance elevated perpendicularly. The face of this horseman was towards the city, as if keeping guard over it; but if any foe were at hand, the figure would turn in that direction, and would level the lance as if for action.

When this talisman was finished, Aben Habuz was all impatient to try its virtues; and longed as ardently for an invasion as he had ever sighed after repose. His desire was soon gratified. Tidings were brought, early one morning, by the sentinel appointed to watch the tower, that the face of the bronze horseman was turned towards the mountains of Elvira, and that his lance pointed directly against the Pass of Lope.

"Let the drums and trumpets sound to arms, and all Granada be put on the alert," said Aben Habuz.

"O king," said the astrologer, "let not your city be disquieted, nor your warriors called to arms; we need no aid of force to deliver you from your enemies. Dismiss your attendants, and let us proceed alone to the secret hall of the tower."

The ancient Aben Habuz mounted the staircase of the tower, leaning on the arm of the still more ancient Ibrahim Ebn Abu Ayub. They unlocked the brazen door and entered. The window that looked towards the Pass of Lope was open. "In this direction," said the astrologer, "lies the danger; approach, O king, and behold the mystery of the table."

King Aben Habuz approached the seeming chess-board, on which were arranged the small wooden effigies, when, to his surprise, he perceived that they were all in motion. The horses pranced and curveted, the warriors brandished their weapons, and there was a faint sound of drums and trumpets, and the clang of

arms, and neighing of steeds; but all no louder, nor more distinct, than the hum of the bee, or the summer-fly, in the drowsy
ear of him who lies at noontide in the shade.

"Behold, O king," said the astrologer, "a proof that thy
enemies are even now in the field. They must be advancing
through yonder mountains, by the Pass of Lope. Would you produce a panic and confusion amongst them, and cause them to retreat without loss of life, strike these effigies with the but-end of
this magic lance; would you cause bloody feud and carnage, strike
with the point."

A livid streak passed across the countenance of Aben Habuz;
he seized the lance with trembling eagerness; his gray beard
wagged with exultation as he tottered toward the table: "Son of
Abu Ayub," exclaimed he, in chuckling tone, "I think we will
have a little blood!"

So saying, he thrust the magic lance into some of the pigmy
effigies, and belabored others with the but-end, upon which the
former fell as dead upon the board, and the rest turning upon
each other began, pell-mell, a chance-medley fight.

It was with difficulty the astrologer could stay the hand of the
most pacific of monarchs, and prevent him from absolutely ex-
terminating his foes; at length he prevailed upon him to leave
the tower, and to send out scouts to the mountains by the Pass
of Lope.

They returned with the intelligence, that a Christian army
had advanced through the heart of the Sierra, almost within sight
of Granada, where a dissension had broken out among them;
they had turned their weapons against each other, and after much
slaughter had retreated over the border.

Aben Habuz was transported with joy on thus proving the

efficacy of the talisman. " At length," said he, " I shall lead a life of tranquillity, and have all my enemies in my power. O wise son of Abu Ayub, what can I bestow on thee in reward for such a blessing?"

" The wants of an old man and a philosopher, O king, are few and simple; grant me but the means of fitting up my cave as a suitable hermitage, and I am content."

" How noble is the moderation of the truly wise!" exclaimed Aben Habuz, secretly pleased at the cheapness of the recompense. He summoned his treasurer, and bade him dispense whatever sums might be required by Ibrahim to complete and furnish his hermitage.

The astrologer now gave orders to have various chambers hewn out of the solid rock, so as to form ranges of apartments connected with his astrological hall; these he caused to be furnished with luxurious ottomans and divans, and the walls to be hung with the richest silks of Damascus. " I am an old man," said he, " and can no longer rest my bones on stone couches, and these damp walls require covering."

He had baths too constructed, and provided with all kinds of perfumes and aromatic oils: " For a bath," said he, " is necessary to counteract the rigidity of age, and to restore freshness and suppleness to the frame withered by study."

He caused the apartments to be hung with innumerable silver and crystal lamps, which he filled with a fragrant oil, prepared according to a receipt discovered by him in the tombs of Egypt. This oil was perpetual in its nature, and diffused a soft radiance like the tempered light of day. " The light of the sun," said he, " is too gairish and violent for the eyes of an old man, and the light of the lamp is more congenial to the studies of a philosopher."

The treasurer of king Aben Habuz groaned at the sums daily demanded to fit up this hermitage, and he carried his complaints to the king. The royal word, however, had been given; Aben Habuz shrugged his shoulders: " We must have patience," said he, " this old man has taken his idea of a philosophic retreat from the interior of the pyramids, and of the vast ruins of Egypt; but all things have an end, and so will the furnishing of his cavern."

The king was in the right; the hermitage was at length complete, and formed a sumptuous subterranean palace. The astrologer expressed himself perfectly content, and, shutting himself up, remained for three whole days buried in study. At the end of that time he appeared again before the treasurer. " One thing more is necessary," said he, " one trifling solace for the intervals of mental labor."

" O wise Ibrahim, I am bound to furnish every thing necessary for thy solitude; what more dost thou require?"

" I would fain have a few dancing women."

" Dancing women !" echoed the treasurer, with surprise.

" Dancing women," replied the sage, gravely; " and let them be young and fair to look upon; for the sight of youth and beauty is refreshing. A few will suffice, for I am a philosopher of simple habits and easily satisfied."

While the philosophic Ibrahim Ebn Abu Ayub passed his time thus sagely in his hermitage, the pacific Aben Habuz carried on furious campaigns in effigy in his tower. It was a glorious thing for an old man, like himself, of quiet habits, to have war made easy, and to be enabled to amuse himself in his chamber by brushing away whole armies like so many swarms of flies.

For a time he rioted in the indulgence of his humors, and even taunted and insulted his neighbors, to induce them to make in-

8*

cursions ; but by degrees they grew wary from repeated disasters, until no one ventured to invade his territories. For many months the bronze horseman remained on the peace establishment with his lance elevated in the air, and the worthy old monarch began to repine at the want of his accustomed sport, and to grow peevish at his monotonous tranquillity.

At length, one day, the talismanic horseman veered suddenly round, and lowering his lance, made a dead point towards the mountains of Guadix. Aben Habuz hastened to his tower, but the magic table in that direction remained quiet; not a single warrior was in motion. Perplexed at the circumstance, he sent forth a troop of horse to scour the mountains and reconnoitre. They returned after three days' absence.

" We have searched every mountain pass," said they, " but not a helm nor spear was stirring. All that we have found in the course of our foray, was a Christian damsel of surpassing beauty, sleeping at noontide beside a fountain, whom we have brought away captive."

" A damsel of surpassing beauty !" exclaimed Aben Habuz, his eyes gleaming with animation ; "let her be conducted into my presence."

The beautiful damsel was accordingly conducted into his presence. She was arrayed with all the luxury of ornament that had prevailed among the Gothic Spaniards at the time of the Arabian conquest. Pearls of dazzling whiteness were entwined with her raven tresses ; and jewels sparkled on her forehead, rivalling the lustre of her eyes. Around her neck was a golden chain, to which was suspended a silver lyre, which hung by her side.

The flashes of her dark refulgent eye were like sparks of fire on the withered, yet combustible, heart of Aben Habuz ; the swimming voluptuousness of her gait made his senses reel. "Fairest of women," cried he, with rapture, "who and what art thou?"

"The daughter of one of the Gothic princes, who but lately ruled over this land. The armies of my father have been destroyed, as if by magic, among these mountains; he has been driven into exile, and his daughter is a captive."

"Beware, O king!" whispered Ibrahim Ebn Abu Ayub, "this may be one of these northern sorceresses of whom we have heard, who assume the most seductive forms to beguile the unwary. Methinks I read witchcraft in her eye, and sorcery in every movement. Doubtless this is the enemy pointed out by the talisman."

"Son of Abu Ayub," replied the king, "thou art a wise man, I grant, a conjuror for aught I know; but thou art little versed in the ways of woman. In that knowledge will I yield to no man; no, not to the wise Solomon himself, notwithstanding the number of his wives and concubines. As to this damsel, I see no harm in her; she is fair to look upon, and finds favor in my eyes."

"Hearken, O king!" replied the astrologer. "I have given thee many victories by means of my talisman, but have never shared any of the spoil. Give me then this stray captive, to solace me in my solitude with her silver lyre. If she be indeed a sorceress, I have counter spells that set her charms at defiance."

"What! more women!" cried Aben Habuz. "Hast thou not already dancing women enough to solace thee?"

"Dancing women have I, it is true, but no singing women. I would fain have a little minstrelsy to refresh my mind when weary with the toils of study."

"A truce with thy hermit cravings," said the king, impatiently. " This damsel have I marked for my own. I see much comfort in her; even such comfort as David, the father of Solomon the wise, found in the society of Abishag the Shunamite."

Further solicitations and remonstrances of the astrologer only provoked a more peremptory reply from the monarch, and they parted in high displeasure. The sage shut himself up in his hermitage to brood over his disappointment; ere he departed, however, he gave the king one more warning to beware of his dangerous captive. But where is the old man in love that will listen to council? Aben Habuz resigned himself to the full sway of his passion. His only study was how to render himself amiable in the eyes of the Gothic beauty. He had not youth to recommend him, it is true, but then he had riches; and when a lover is old, he is generally generous. The Zacatin of Granada was ransacked for the most precious merchandise of the East; silks, jewels, precious gems, exquisite perfumes, all that Asia and Africa yielded of rich and rare, were lavished upon the princess. All kinds of spectacles and festivities were devised for her entertainment; minstrelsy, dancing, tournaments, bull-fights:—Granada for a time was a scene of perpetual pageant. The Gothic princess regarded all this splendor with the air of one accustomed to magnificence. She received every thing as a homage due to her rank, or rather to her beauty; for beauty is more lofty in its exactions even than rank. Nay, she seemed to take a secret pleasure in exciting the monarch to expenses that made his treasury shrink; and then treating his extravagant generosity as a mere matter of course. With all his assiduity and munificence, also, the venerable lover could not flatter himself that he had made any impression on her heart. She never frowned on him, it is true, but then she never smiled. Whenever he began to plead his passion, she struck her silver lyre. There was a mystic charm in the sound. In an instant the monarch began to nod; a drowsiness stole over him, and he gradually sank into a sleep, from which he awoke wonderfully refreshed, but perfectly cooled for the time of his passion. This was very baffling to his suit; but then these slumbers were accompanied by agreeable dreams, which completely inthralled the senses of the drowsy lover; so he continued to dream on, while all Granada scoffed at his infatuation, and groaned at the treasures lavished for a song.

At length a danger burst on the head of Aben Habuz, against which his talisman yielded him no warning. An insurrection broke out in his very capital: his palace was surrounded by an armed rabble, who menaced his life and the life of his Christian paramour. A spark of his ancient warlike spirit was awakened in the breast of the monarch. At the head of a handful of his guards he sallied forth, put the rebels to flight. and crushed the insurrection in the bud.

When quiet was again restored, he sought the astrologer, who still remained shut up in his hermitage, chewing the bitter cud of resentment.

Aben Habuz approached him with a conciliatory tone. " O wise son of Abu Ayub," said he, " well didst thou predict dangers to me from this captive beauty : tell me then, thou who art so quick at foreseeing peril, what I should do to avert it."

" Put from thee the infidel damsel who is the cause."

" Sooner would I part with my kingdom," cried Aben Habuz.

" Thou art in danger of losing both," replied the astrologer.

" Be not harsh and angry, O most profound of philosophers : consider the double distress of a monarch and a lover, and devise some means of protecting me from the evils by which I am men-

aced.   I care not for grandeur, I care not for power, I languish
only for repose ; would that I had some quiet retreat where I
might take refuge from the world, and all its cares, and pomps,
and troubles, and devote the remainder of my days to tranquillity
and love."

The astrologer regarded him for a moment, from under his
bushy eyebrows.

" And what wouldst thou give, if I could provide thee such
a retreat ?"

" Thou shouldst name thy own reward, and whatever it might
be, if within the scope of my power, as my soul liveth, it should
be thine."

" Thou hast heard, O king, of the garden of Irem, one of the
prodigies of Arabia the happy."

" I have heard of that garden ; it is recorded in the Koran,
even in the chapter entitled ' The Dawn of Day.'   I have moreover, heard marvellous things related of it by pilgrims who
had been to Mecca ; but I considered them wild fables, such as
travellers are wont to tell who have visited remote countries."

" Discredit not, O king, the tales of travellers," rejoined the
astrologer, gravely, "for they contain precious rarities of knowledge brought from the ends of the earth.   As to the palace and
garden of Irem, what is generally told of them is true ; I have
seen them with mine own eyes—listen to my adventure ; for it
has a bearing upon the object of your request.

" In my younger days, when a mere Arab of the desert, I
tended my father's camels.   In traversing the desert of Aden,
one of them strayed from the rest, and was lost.   I searched
after it for several days, but in vain, until, wearied and faint, I
laid myself down at noontide, and slept under a palm-tree by the

side of a scanty well. When I awoke, I found myself at the gate of a city. I entered, and beheld noble streets, and squares, and market-places; but all were silent and without an inhabitant. I wandered on until I came to a sumptuous palace with a garden adorned with fountains and fishponds, and groves and flowers, and orchards laden with delicious fruit; but still no one was to be seen. Upon which, appalled at this loneliness, I hastened to depart; and, after issuing forth at the gate of the city, I turned to look upon the place, but it was no longer to be seen; nothing but the silent desert extended before my eyes.

"In the neighborhood I met with an aged dervise, learned in the traditions and secrets of the land, and related to him what had befallen me. 'This,' said he, 'is the far-famed garden of Irem, one of the wonders of the desert. It only appears at times to some wanderer like thyself, gladdening him with the sight of towers and palaces and garden walls overhung with richly-laden fruit-trees, and then vanishes, leaving nothing but a lonely desert. And this is the story of it. In old times, when this country was inhabited by the Addites, King Sheddad, the son of Ad, the great grandson of Noah, founded here a splendid city. When it was finished, and he saw its grandeur, his heart was puffed up with pride and arrogance, and he determined to build a royal palace, with gardens which should rival all related in the Koran of the celestial paradise. But the curse of heaven fell upon him for his presumption. He and his subjects were swept from the earth, and his splendid city, and palace, and gardens, were laid under a perpetual spell, which hides them from human sight, excepting that they are seen at intervals, by way of keeping his sin in perpetual remembrance.

"This story, O king, and the wonders I had seen, ever dwelt

in my mind ; and in after years, when I had been in Egypt, and was possessed of the book of knowledge of Solomon the wise, I determined to return and revisit the garden of Irem. I did so, and found it revealed to my instructed sight. I took possession of the palace of Sheddad, and passed several days in his mock paradise. The genii who watch over the place, were obedient to my magic power, and revealed to me the spells by which the whole garden had been, as it were, conjured into existence, and by which it was rendered invisible. Such a palace and garden, O king, can I make for thee, even here, on the mountain above thy city. Do I not know all the secret spells? and am I not in possession of the book of knowledge of Solomon the wise?"

" O wise son of Abu Ayub!" exclaimed Aben Habuz, trembling with eagerness, " thou art a traveller indeed, and hast seen and learned marvellous things! Contrive me such a paradise, and ask any reward, even to the half of my kingdom."

" Alas !" replied the other, " thou knowest I am an old man, and a philosopher, and easily satisfied ; all the reward I ask is the first beast of burden, with its load, which shall enter the magic portal of the palace."

The monarch gladly agreed to so moderate a stipulation, and the astrologer began his work. On the summit of the hill, immediately above his subterranean hermitage, he caused a great gateway or barbican to be erected, opening through the centre of a strong tower.

There was an outer vestibule or porch, with a lofty arch, and within it a portal secured by massive gates. On the key-stone of the portal the astrologer, with his own hand, wrought the figure of a huge key ; and on the key-stone of the outer arch of the vestibule, which was loftier than that of the portal. he carved a gigantic hand. These were potent talismans, over which he repeated many sentences in an unknown tongue.

When this gateway was finished he shut himself up for two days in his astrological hall, engaged in secret incantations ; on the third he ascended the hill, and passed the whole day on its summit. At a late hour of the night he came down, and presented himself before Aben Habuz. " At length, O king," said he, " my labor is accomplished. On the summit of the hill stands one of the most delectable palaces that ever the head of man devised, or the heart of man desired. It contains sumptuous halls and galleries, delicious gardens, cool fountains, and fragrant baths ; in a word, the whole mountain is converted into a paradise. Like the garden of Irem, it is protected by a mighty charm, which hides it from the view and search of mortals, excepting such as possess the secret of its talismans."

" Enough !" cried Aben Habuz, joyfully, " to-morrow morning with the first light we will ascend and take possession." The happy monarch slept but little that night. Scarcely had the rays of the sun begun to play about the snowy summit of the Sierra Nevada, when he mounted his steed, and, accompanied only by a few chosen attendants, ascended a steep and narrow road leading up the hill. Beside him, on a white palfrey, rode the Gothic princess, her whole dress sparkling with jewels, while round her neck was suspended her silver lyre. The astrologer walked on the other side of the king, assisting his steps with his hieroglyphic staff, for he never mounted steed of any kind.

Aben Habuz looked to see the towers of the palace brightening above him, and the imbowered terraces of its gardens stretching along the heights ; but as yet nothing of the kind was to be descried. " That is the mystery and safeguard of the place,"

said the astrologer, " nothing can be discerned until you have
passed the spell-bound gateway, and been put in possession of
the place."

As they approached the gateway, the astrologer paused, and
pointed out to the king the mystic hand and key carved upon
the portal of the arch. " These," said he, " are the talismans
which guard the entrance to this paradise. Until yonder hand
shall reach down and seize that key, neither mortal power nor
magic artifice can prevail against the lord of this mountain."

While Aben Habuz was gazing, with open mouth and silent
wonder, at these mystic talismans, the palfrey of the princess
proceeded, and bore her in at the portal, to the very centre of the
barbican.

" Behold," cried the astrologer, " my promised reward; the
first animal with its burden which should enter the magic gateway."

Aben Habuz smiled at what he considered a pleasantry of
the ancient man; but when he found him to be in earnest, his
grey beard trembled with indignation.

" Son of Abu Ayub," said he, sternly, " what equivocation is
this ? Thou knowest the meaning of my promise : the first beast
of burden, with its load, that should enter this portal. Take the
strongest mule in my stables, load it with the most precious
things of my treasury, and it is thine; but dare not raise thy
thoughts to her who is the delight of my heart."

" What need I of wealth," cried the astrologer, scornfully;
" have I not the book of knowledge of Solomon the wise, and
through it the command of the secret treasures of the earth ?
The princess is mine by right; thy royal word is pledged: I
claim her as my own."

The princess looked down haughtily from her palfrey, and a light smile of scorn curled her rosy lip at this dispute between two gray-beards, for the possession of youth and beauty. The wrath of the monarch got the better of his discretion. " Base son of the desert," cried he, " thou may'st be master of many arts, but know me for thy master, and presume not to juggle with thy king."

" My master ! my king !" echoed the astrologer—" The mon arca of a mole-hill to claim sway over him who possesses the talismans of Solomon ! Farewell, Aben Habuz; reign over thy petty kingdom, and revel in thy paradise of fools ; for me, I will laugh at thee in my philosophic retirement."

So saying he seized the bridle of the palfrey, smote the earth with his staff, and sank with the Gothic princess through the centre of the barbican. The earth closed over them, and no trace remained of the opening by which they had descended.

Aben Habuz was struck dumb for a time with astonishment. Recovering himself, he ordered a thousand workmen to dig, with pickaxe and spade, into the ground where the astrologer had disappeared. They digged and digged, but in vain ; the flinty bosom of the hill resisted their implements ; or if they did penetrate a little way, the earth filled in again as fast as they threw it out. Aben Habuz sought the mouth of the cavern at the foot of the hill, leading to the subterranean palace of the astrologer ; but it was nowhere to be found. Where once had been an entrance, was now a solid surface of primeval rock. With the disappearance of Ibrahim Ebn Abu Ayub ceased the benefit of his talismans. The bronze horseman remained fixed, with his face turned toward the hill, and his spear pointed to the spot where the astrologer had descended, as if there still lurked the deadliest foe of Aben Habuz.

From time to time the sound of music, and the tones of a female voice, could be faintly heard from the bosom of the hill; and a peasant one day brought word to the king, that in the preceding night he had found a fissure in the rock, by which he had crept in, until he looked down into a subterranean hall, in which sat the astrologer, on a magnificent divan, slumbering and nodding to the silver lyre of the princess, which seemed to hold a magic sway over his senses.

Aben Habuz sought the fissure in the rock, but t was again closed. He renewed the attempt to unearth his rival, but all in vain. The spell of the hand and key was too potent to be counteracted by human power. As to the summit of the mountain, the site of the promised palace and garden, it remained a naked waste; either the boasted elysium was hidden from sight by enchantment, or was a mere fable of the astrologer. The world charitably supposed the latter, and some used to call the place "The King's Folly;" while others named it "The Fool's Paradise."

To add to the chagrin of Aben Habuz, the neighbors whom he had defied and taunted, and cut up at his leisure while master of the talismanic horseman, finding him no longer protected by magic spell, made inroads into his territories from all sides, and the remainder of the life of the most pacific of monarchs was a tissue of turmoils.

At length Aben Habuz died, and was buried. Ages have since rolled away. The Alhambra has been built on the eventful mountain, and in some measure realizes the fabled delights of the garden of Irem. The spell-bound gateway still exists entire, protected no doubt by the mystic hand and key, and now forms the Gate of Justice, the grand entrance to the fortress.

Under that gateway, it is said, the old astrologer remains in his subterranean hall, nodding on his divan, lulled by the silver lyre of the princess.

The old invalid sentinels who mount guard at the gate hear the strains occasionally in the summer nights; and, yielding to their soporific power, doze quietly at their posts. Nay, so drowsy an influence pervades the place, that even those who watch by day may generally be seen nodding on the stone benches of the barbican, or sleeping under the neighboring trees; so that in fact it is the drowsiest military post in all Christendom. All this, say the ancient legends, will endure from age to age. The princess will remain captive to the astrologer; and the astrologer, bound up in magic slumber by the princess, until the last day, unless the mystic hand shall grasp the fated key, and dispel the whole charm of this enchanted mountain.

NOTE TO THE ARABIAN ASTROLOGER.

Al Makkari, in his history of the Mahommedan Dynasties in Spain, cites from another Arabian writer an account of a talismanic effigy somewhat similar to the one in the foregoing legend.

In Cadiz, says he, there formerly stood a square tower upwards of one hundred cubits high, built of huge blocks of stone, fastened together with clamps of brass. On the top was the figure of a man, holding a staff in his right hand, his face turned to the Atlantic, and pointing with the forefinger of his left hand to the Straits of Gibraltar. It was said to have been set up in ancient times by the Gothic kings of Andalus, as a beacon or guide to navigators. The Moslems of Barbary and Andalus, considered it a talisman which exercised a spell over the seas. Under its guidance, swarms of piratical people of a nation called Majus, appeared on the coast in large vessels with a square sail in the bow, and another in the stern. They came every six or seven years; cap-

tured every thing they met with on the sea; guided by the statue, they passed
through the Straits into the Mediterranean, landed on the coasts of Andalus,
laid every thing waste with fire and sword; and sometimes carried their depre-
dations on the opposite coasts even as far as Syria.

At length, it came to pass in the time of the civil wars, a Moslem Admiral
who had taken possession of Cadiz, hearing that the statue on top of the tower
was of pure gold, had it lowered to the ground and broken to pieces; when it
proved to be of gilded brass. With the destruction of the idol, the spell over
the sea was at an end. From that time forward, nothing more was seen of the
piratical people of the ocean, excepting that two of their barks were wrecked
on the coast, one at Marsu-l-Majus (the port of the Majus), the other close to
the promontory of Al-Aghan.

The maritime invaders above mentioned by Al Makkari must have been
the Northmen.

VISITORS TO THE ALHAMBRA.

FOR nearly three months had I enjoyed undisturbed my dream of sovereignty in the Alhambra : a longer term of quiet than had been the lot of many of my predecessors. During this lapse of time the progress of the season had wrought the usual change. On my arrival I had found every thing in the freshness of May ; the foliage of the trees was still tender and transparent; the pomegranate had not yet shed its brilliant crimson blossoms; the orchards of the Xenil and the Darro were in full bloom; the rocks were hung with wild flowers, and Granada seemed completely surrounded by a wilderness of roses; among which innumerable nightingales sang, not merely in the night, but all day long.

Now the advance of summer had withered the rose and silenced the nightingale, and the distant country began to look parched and sunburnt; though a perennial verdure reigned immediately round the city and in the deep narrow valleys at the foot of the snow-capped mountains.

The Alhambra possesses retreats graduated to the heat of the weather, among which the most peculiar is the almost subterranean apartment of the baths. This still retains its ancient Oriental character, though stamped with the touching traces of decline. At the entrance, opening into a small court formerly adorned with flowers, is a hall, moderate in size, but light and graceful in architecture. It is overlooked by a small gallery supported by marble pillars and moresco arches. An alabaster fountain in the centre of the pavement still throws up a jet of water to cool the place. On each side are deep alcoves with raised platforms, where the bathers, after their ablutions, reclined on cushions, soothed to voluptuous repose by the fragrance of the perfumed air and the notes of soft music from the gallery. Beyond this hall are the interior chambers, still more retired; the sanctum sanctorum of female privacy : for here the beauties of the Harem indulged in the luxury of the baths. A soft mysterious light reigns through the place, admitted through small apertures (lumbreras) in the vaulted ceiling. The traces of ancient elegance are still to be seen; and the alabaster baths in which the sultanas once reclined. The prevailing obscurity and silence have made these vaults a favorite resort of bats, who nestle during the day in the dark nooks and corners, and on being disturbed, flit mysteriously about the twilight chambers, heightening, in an indescribable degree, their air of desertion and decay.

In this cool and elegant, though dilapidated retreat, which had the freshness and seclusion of a grotto, I passed the sultry hours of the day as summer advanced, emerging towards sunset; and bathing, or rather swimming, at night in the great reservoir of the main court. In this way I was enabled in a measure to counteract the relaxing and enervating influence of the climate.

My dream of absolute sovereignty, however, came at length to an end. I was roused one morning by the report of fire-arms, which reverberated among the towers as if the castle had been taken by surprise. On sallying forth, I found an old cavalier with a number of domestics, in possession of the Hall of Ambassadors. He was an ancient count who had come up from his palace in Granada to pass a short time in the Alhambra for the benefit of purer air; and who, being a veteran and inveterate sportsman, was endeavoring to get an appetite for his breakfast by shooting at swallows from the balconies. It was a harmless amusement; for though, by the alertness of his attendants in loading his pieces, he was enabled to keep up a brisk fire, I could not accuse him of the death of a single swallow. Nay, the birds themselves seemed to enjoy the sport, and to deride his want of skill, skimming in circles close to the balconies, and twittering as they darted by.

The arrival of this old gentleman changed essentially the aspect of affairs, but caused no jealousy nor collision. We tacitly shared the empire between us, like the last kings of Granada, excepting that we maintained a most amicable alliance. He reigned absolute over the court of the Lions and its adjacent halls while I maintained peaceful possession of the regions of the baths and the little garden of Lindaraxa. We took our meals together under the arcades of the court, where the fountains cooled the air, and bubbling rills ran along the channels of the marble pavement.

In the evenings a domestic circle would gather about the worthy old cavalier. The countess, his wife by a second marriage, would come up from the city accompanied by her step-daughter Carmen, an only child, a charming little being, still in her girlish years. Then there were always some of his official dependents, his chaplain, his lawyer, his secretary, his steward, and other officers and agents of his extensive possessions, who brought him up the news or gossip of the city, and formed his evening party of tresillo or ombre. Thus he held a kind of domestic court, where each one paid him deference, and

9

sought to contribute to his amusement, without, however, any
appearance of servility, or any sacrifice of self-respect. In
fact, nothing of the kind was exacted by the demeanor of the
Count; for whatever may be said of Spanish pride, it rarely
chills or constrains the intercourse of social or domestic life.
Among no people are the relations between kindred more unre-
served and cordial, or between superior and dependent more free
from haughtiness on the one side, and obsequiousness on the
other. In these respects there still remains in Spanish life,
especially in the provinces, much of the vaunted simplicity of the
olden time.

The most interesting member of this family group, in my
eyes, was the daughter of the count, the lovely little Carmen;
she was but about sixteen years of age, and appeared to be considered a mere child, though the idol of the family, going generally by the child-like, but endearing appellation of la Niña.
Her form had not yet attained full maturity and development,
but possessed already the exquisite symmetry and pliant grace
so prevalent in this country. Her blue eyes, fair complexion,
and light hair, were unusual in Andalusia, and gave a mildness
and gentleness to her demeanor in contrast to the usual fire of
Spanish beauty, but in unison with the guileless and confiding
innocence of her manners. She had at the same time the innate
aptness and versatility of her fascinating countrywomen. Whatever she undertook to do she did well and apparently without
effort. She sang, played the guitar and other instruments, and
danced the picturesque dances of her country to admiration, but
never seemed to seek admiration. Every thing was spontaneous,
prompted by her own gay spirits and happy temper.

The presence of this fascinating little being spread a new

charm about the Alhambra, and seemed to be in unison with the place. While the count and countess, with the chaplain or secretary, were playing their game of tresillo under the vestibule of the court of Lions, she, attended by Dolores, who acted as her maid of honor, would sit by one of the fountains, and accompanying herself on the guitar, would sing some of those popular romances which abound in Spain, or, what was still more to my taste, some traditional ballad about the Moors.

Never shall I think of the Alhambra without remembering this lovely little being, sporting in happy and innocent girlhood in its marble halls, dancing to the sound of the Moorish castanets, or mingling the silver warbling of her voice with the music of its fountains.

RELICS AND GENEALOGIES.

IF I had been pleased and interested by the count and his family, as furnishing a picture of a Spanish domestic life, I was still more so when apprised of historical circumstances which linked them with the heroic times of Granada. In fact, in this worthy old cavalier, so totally unwarlike, or whose deeds in arms extended, at most, to a war on swallows and martlets, I discovered a lineal descendant and actual representative of Gonsalvo of Cordova, "The Grand Captain," who won some of his brightest laurels before the walls of Granada, and was one of the cavaliers commissioned by Ferdinand and Isabella to negotiate the terms of surrender; nay, more, the count was entitled, did he choose it, to claim remote affinity with some of the ancient Moorish princes, through a scion of his house, Don Pedro Venegas, surnamed the Tornadizo; and by the same token, his daughter, the fascinating little Carmen, might claim to be rightful representative of the princess Cetimerien or the beautiful Lindaraxa.*

* Lest this should be deemed a mere stretch of fancy, the reader is referred to the following genealogy, derived by the historian Alcantara, from an Arabian manuscript, on parchment, in the archives of the marquis of Corvera. It is a specimen of the curious affinities between Christians and Moslems, produced by capture and intermarriages, during the Moorish wars. From Aben

Understanding from the count that he had some curious relics of the Conquest, preserved in his family archives, I accompanied him early one morning down to his palace in Granada to examine them. The most important of these relics was the sword of the Grand Captain; a weapon destitute of all ostentatious ornament, as the weapons of great generals are apt to be, with a plain hilt of ivory and a broad thin blade. It might furnish a comment on hereditary honors, to see the sword of the grand captain legitimately declined into such feeble hands.

The other relics of the Conquest were a number of espingardas or muskets of unwieldy size and ponderous weight, worthy to rank with those enormous two-edged swords preserved in old armories, which look like relics from the days of the giants.

Beside other hereditary honors, I found the old count was Alferez mayor, or grand standard-bearer, in which capacity he was entitled to bear the ancient standard of Ferdinand and Isabella, on certain high and solemn occasions, and to wave it over their tombs. I was shown also the caparisons of velvet, sumptuously embroidered with gold and silver, for six horses, with which he appeared in state when a new sovereign was to be proclaimed in Granada and Seville; the count mounting one of the horses, and the other five being led by lackeys in rich liveries.

Hud, the Moorish king, the conqueror of the Almohades, was descended in right line Cid Yahia Abraham Alnagar, prince of Almeria, who married a daughter of king Bermejo. They had three children, commonly called the Cetimerian Princes. 1st. *Jusef ben Alhamar*, who for a time usurped the throne of Granada. 2d. The *Prince Nasar;* who married the celebrated Lindaraxa. 3d. The *Princess Cetimerien,* who married Don Pedro Venegas, captured by the Moors in his boyhood, a younger son of the *House of Luque*, of which house the old count was the present head.

I had hoped to find among the relics and antiquities of the count's palace, some specimens of the armor and weapons of the Moors of Granada, such as I had heard were preserved as trophies by the descendants of the Conquerors ; but in this I was disappointed. I was the more curious in this particular, because an erroneous idea has been entertained by many, as to the costumes of the Moors of Spain ; supposing them to be of the usual oriental type. On the contrary, we have it on the authority of their own writers, that they adopted in many respects the fashions of the Christians. The turban, especially, so identified in idea with the Moslem, was generally abandoned, except in the western provinces, where it continued in use among people of rank and wealth, and those holding places under government. A woollen cap, red or green, was commonly worn as a substitute ; probably the same kind originating in Barbary, and known by the name of Tunis or Fez, which at the present day is worn throughout the east ; though generally under the turban. The Jews were obliged to wear them of a yellow color.

In Murcia, Valencia, and other eastern provinces, men of the highest rank might be seen in public bareheaded. The warrior king, Aben Hud, never wore a turban, neither did his rival and competitor Al Hamar, the founder of the Alhambra. A short cloak called Taylasan similar to that seen in Spain in the sixteenth and seventeenth centuries, was worn by all ranks. It had a hood or cape which people of condition sometimes drew over the head ; but the lower class never.

A Moslem cavalier in the thirteenth century, as described by Ibnu Said, was equipped for war very much in the Christian style. Over a complete suit of mail he wore a short scarlet tunic. His helmet was of polished steel ; a shield was slung at his back ; he wielded a huge spear with a broad point, sometimes a double point. His saddle was cumbrous, projecting very much in front and in rear, and he rode with a banner fluttering behind him.

In the time of Al Khattib of Granada, who wrote in the fourteenth century, the Moslems of Andalus had resumed the oriental costumes, and were again clad and armed in Arabic fashion : with light helmet, thin but well tempered cuirass, long slender lance, commonly of reed, Arabian saddle and leathern buckler, made of double folds of the skin of the antelope. A wonderful luxury prevailed at that time in the arms and equipments of the Granadian cavaliers. Their armor was inlaid with gold and silver. Their cimeters were of the keenest Damascus blades, with sheaths richly wrought and enamelled, and belts of golden filagree studded with gems. Their daggers of Fez had jewelled hilts, and their lances were set off with gay banderoles. Their horses were caparisoned in correspondent style, with velvet and embroidery.

All this minute description, given by a contemporary, and an author of distinction, verifies those gallant pictures in the old Morisco Spanish ballads which have sometimes been deemed apocryphal, and give a vivid idea of the brilliant appearance of the chivalry of Granada, when marshalled forth in warlike array, or when celebrating the chivalrous fêtes of the Vivarrambla.

THE GENERALIFE.

High above the Alhambra, on the breast of the mountain, amidst embowered gardens and stately terraces, rise the lofty towers and white walls of the Generalife; a fairy palace, full of storied recollections. Here is still to be seen the famous cypresses of enormous size which flourished in the time of the Moors, and which tradition has connected with the fabulous story of Boabdil and his sultana.

Here are preserved the portraits of many who figured in the romantic drama of the Conquest. Ferdinand and Isabella, Ponce de Leon, the gallant marquis of Cadiz, and Garcilaso de la Vega, who slew in desperate fight Tarfe the Moor, a champion of Herculean strength. Here too hangs a portrait which has long passed for that of the unfortunate Boabdil, but which is said to be that of Aben Hud, the Moorish king from whom descended the princes of Almeria. From one of these princes, who joined the standard of Ferdinand and Isabella towards the close of the Conquest, and was christianized by the name of Don Pedro de Granada Venegas, was descended the present proprietor of the palace, the marquis of Campotejar. The proprietor, however, dwells in a foreign land, and the palace has no longer a princely inhabitant.

Yet here is every thing to delight a southern voluptuary; fruits, flowers, fragrance, green arbors and myrtle hedges, delicate air and gushing waters. Here I had an opportunity of witnessing those scenes which painters are fond of depicting about southern palaces and gardens. It was the saint's day of the count's daughter, and she had brought up several of her youthful companions from Granada, to sport away a long summer's day among the breezy halls and bowers of the Moorish palaces. A visit to the Generalife was the morning's entertainment. Here some of the gay company dispersed itself in groups about the green walks, the bright fountains, the flights of Italian steps, the noble terraces and marble balustrades. Others, among whom I was one, took their seats in an open gallery or colonnade commanding a vast prospect; with the Alhambra, the city, and the Vega, far below, and the distant horizon of mountains—a dreamy world, all glimmering to the eye in summer sunshine. While thus seated, the all-pervading tinkling of the guitar and click of the castañets came stealing up from the valley of the Darro, and half way down the mountain we descried a festive party under the trees enjoying themselves in true Andalusian style; some lying on the grass, others dancing to the music.

All these sights and sounds, together with the princely seclusion of the place, the sweet quiet which prevailed around, and the delicious serenity of the weather had a witching effect upon the mind, and drew from some of the company, versed in local story, several of the popular fancies and traditions connected with this old Moorish palace; they were " such stuff as dreams are made of," but out of them I have shaped the following legend; which I hope may have the good fortune to prove acceptable to the reader.

9*

LEGEND OF PRINCE AHMED AL KAMEL;

OR,

THE PILGRIM OF LOVE.

THERE was once a Moorish king of Granada, who had but one
son, whom he named Ahmed, to which his courtiers added the
surname of al Kamel, or the perfect, from the indubitable signs
of superexcellence which they perceived in him in his very
infancy. The astrologers countenanced them in their foresight,
predicting every thing in his favor that could make a perfect
prince and a prosperous sovereign. One cloud only rested
upon his destiny, and even that was of a roseate hue; he would
be of an amorous temperament, and run great perils from the
tender passion. If, however, he could be kept from the allure-
ments of love until of mature age, these dangers would be
averted, and his life thereafter be one uninterrupted course of
felicity.

To prevent all danger of the kind, the king wisely determined
to rear the prince in a seclusion where he should never see a
female face, nor hear even the name of love. For this purpose
he built a beautiful palace on the brow of the hill above the Alhambra, in the midst of delightful gardens, but surrounded by

lofty walls, being, in fact, the same palace known at the present day by the name of the Generalife. In this palace the youthful prince was shut up, and intrusted to the guardianship and instruction of Eben Bonabben, one of the wisest and dryest of Arabian sages, who had passed the greatest part of his life in Egypt, studying hieroglyphics, and making researches among the tombs and pyramids, and who saw more charms in an Egyptian mummy than in the most tempting of living beauties. The sage was ordered to instruct the prince in all kinds of knowledge but one—he was to be kept utterly ignorant of love. "Use every precaution for the purpose you may think proper," said the king, "but remember, O Eben Bonabben, if my son learns aught of that forbidden knowledge while under your care, your head shall answer for it." A withered smile came over the dry visage of the wise Bonabben at the menace. "Let your majesty's heart be as easy about your son, as mine is about my head: am I a man likely to give lessons in the idle passion?"

Under the vigilant care of the philosopher, the prince grew up, in the seclusion of the palace and its gardens. He had black slaves to attend upon him — hideous mutes who knew nothing of love, or if they did, had not words to communicate it. His mental endowments were the peculiar care of Eben Bonabben, who sought to initiate him into the abstruse lore of Egypt; but in this the prince made little progress, and it was soon evident that he had no turn for philosophy.

He was, however, amazingly ductile for a youthful prince, ready to follow any advice, and always guided by the last counsellor. He suppressed his yawns, and listened patiently to the long and learned discourses of Eben Bonabben, from which he imbibed a smattering of various kinds of knowledge, and thus happily attained his twentieth year, a miracle of princely wisdom —but totally ignorant of love.

About this time, however, a change came over the conduct of the prince. He completely abandoned his studies, and took to strolling about the gardens, and musing by the side of the fountains. He had been taught a little music among his various accomplishments; it now engrossed a great part of his time, and a turn for poetry became apparent. The sage Eben Bonabben took the alarm, and endeavored to work these idle humors out of him by a severe course of algebra; but the prince turned from it with distaste. "I cannot endure algebra," said he; "it is an abomination to me. I want something that speaks more to the heart."

The sage Eben Bonabben shook his dry head at the words. "Here is an end to philosophy," thought he. "The prince has discovered he has a heart!" He now kept anxious watch upon his pupil, and saw that the latent tenderness of his nature was in activity, and only wanted an object. He wandered about the gardens of the Generalife in an intoxication of feelings of which he knew not the cause. Sometimes he would sit plunged in a delicious reverie; then he would seize his lute, and draw from it the most touching notes, and then throw it aside, and break forth into sighs and ejaculations.

By degrees this loving disposition began to extend to inanimate objects; he had his favorite flowers, which he cherished with tender assiduity; then he became attached to various trees, and there was one in particular, of a graceful form and drooping foliage, on which he lavished his amorous devotion, carving his name on its bark, hanging garlands on its branches, and singing couplets in its praise, to the accompaniment of his lute.

Eben Bonabben was alarmed at this excited state of his pupil. He saw him on the very brink of forbidden knowledge—the least hint might reveal to him the fatal secret. Trembling for the safety of the prince and the security of his own head, he hastened to draw him from the seductions of the garden, and shut him up in the highest tower of the Generalife. It contained beautiful apartments, and commanded an almost boundless prospect, but was elevated far above that atmosphere of sweets and those witching bowers so dangerous to the feelings of the too susceptible Ahmed.

What was to be done, however, to reconcile him to this restraint and to beguile the tedious hours? He had exhausted almost all kinds of agreeable knowledge ; and algebra was not to be mentioned. Fortunately Eben Bonabben had been instructed, when in Egypt, in the language of birds, by a Jewish Rabbin, who had received it in lineal transmission from Solomon the wise, who had been taught it by the queen of Sheba. At the very mention of such a study, the eyes of the prince sparkled with animation, and he applied himself to it with such avidity, that he soon became as great an adept as his master.

The tower of the Generalife was no longer a solitude ; he had companions at hand with whom he could converse. The first acquaintance he formed was with a hawk, who built his nest in a crevice of the lofty battlements, whence he soared far and wide in quest of prey. The prince, however, found little to like or esteem in him. He was a mere pirate of the air, swaggering and boastful, whose talk was all about rapine and carnage, and desperate exploits.

His next acquaintance was an owl, a mighty wise looking bird, with a huge head and staring eyes, who sat blinking and goggling all day in a hole in the wall, but roamed forth at night. He had great pretensions to wisdom, talked something of astrology and the moon, and hinted at the dark sciences; he was grievously given to metaphysics, and the prince found his prosings even more ponderous than those of the sage Eben Bonabben.

Then there was a bat, that hung all day by his heels in the dark corner of a vault, but sallied out in slipshod style at twilight. He, however, had but twilight ideas on all subjects, derided things of which he had taken but an imperfect view, and seemed to take delight in nothing.

Besides these there was a swallow, with whom the prince was at first much taken. He was a smart talker, but restless, bustling, and for ever on the wing; seldom remaining long enough for any continued conversation. He turned out in the end to be a mere smatterer, who did but skim over the surface of things, pretending to know every thing, but knowing nothing thoroughly.

These were the only feathered associates with whom the prince had any opportunity of exercising his newly acquired language; the tower was too high for any other birds to frequent it. He soon grew weary of his new acquaintances, whose conversation spoke so little to the head, and nothing to the heart; and gradually relapsed into his loneliness. A winter passed away, spring opened with all its bloom and verdure and breathing sweetness, and the happy time arrived for birds to pair and build their nests. Suddenly, as it were, a universal burst of song and melody broke forth from the groves and gardens of the Generalife, and reached the prince in the solitude of his tower. From every side he heard the same universal theme—love—love—love—chanted forth, and responded to it in every variety of note and tone. The prince listened in silence and perplexity. "What can be this love," thought he, "of which the world seems so full, and of which I know nothing?" He applied for information to his friend the hawk. The ruffian bird answered in a tone of scorn: "You must apply," said he, "to the vulgar peaceable birds of earth, who are made for the prey of us princes of the air. My trade is war, and fighting my delight. I am a warrior, and know nothing of this thing called love."

The prince turned from him with disgust, and sought the owl in his retreat. "This is a bird," said he, "of peaceful habits, and may be able to solve my question." So he asked the owl to tell him what was this love about which all the birds in the groves below were singing.

Upon this, the owl put on a look of offended dignity. "My nights," said he, "are taken up in study and research, and my days in ruminating in my cell upon all that I have learnt. As to these singing birds of whom you talk, I never listen to them—I despise them and their themes. Allah be praised, I cannot sing; I am a philosopher, and know nothing of this thing called love."

The prince now repaired to the vault, where his friend the bat was hanging by the heels, and propounded the same question. The bat wrinkled up his nose into a most snappish expression. "Why do you disturb me in my morning's nap with such an idle question?" said he, peevishly. "I only fly by twilight, when all birds are asleep, and never trouble myself with their concerns. I am neither bird nor beast, and I thank heaven for it. I have found out the villany of the whole of them, and hate them one and all. In a word, I am a misanthrope—and know nothing of this thing called love."

As a last resort, the prince now sought the swallow, and

stopped him just as he was circling about the summit of
the tower. The swallow, as usual, was in a prodigious hurry,
and had scarce time to make a reply. "Upon my word,"
said he, "I have so much public business to attend to, and so
many pursuits to follow, that I have had no time to think on the
subject. I have every day a thousand visits to pay ; a thousand
affairs of importance to examine into, that leave me not a moment
of leisure for these little sing-song matters. In a word, I am a
citizen of the world—I know nothing of this thing called love."
So saying, the swallow dived into the valley, and was out of sight
in a moment.

The prince remained disappointed and perplexed, but with
his curiosity still more piqued by the difficulty of gratifying it.
While in this mood, his ancient guardian entered the tower.
The prince advanced eagerly to meet him. "O, Eben Bonabben," cried he, "thou hast revealed to me much of the wisdom of
the earth ; but there is one thing of which I remain in utter
ignorance, and would fain be informed."

"My prince has but to make the inquiry, and every thing
within the limited range of his servant's intellect is at his command."

"Tell me then, O most profound of sages, what is the nature
of this thing called love ?"

Eben Bonabben was struck as with a thunderbolt. He
trembled and turned pale, and felt as if his head sat but loosely
on his shoulders.

"What could suggest such a question to my prince—where
could he have learnt so idle a word ?"

The prince led him to the window of the tower. "Listen,
O Eben Bonabben," said he. The sage listened. The nightin-

gales at in a thicket below the tower, singing to his paramour the rose; from every blossomed spray and tufted grove rose a strain of melody; and love — love — love — was still the unvarying strain.

"Allah Akbar! God is great!" exclaimed the wise Bonabben. "Who shall pretend to keep this secret from the heart of man, when even the birds of the air conspire to betray it?"

Then turning to Ahmed—" O my prince," cried he, " shut thine ears to these seductive strains. Close thy mind against this dangerous knowledge. Know that this love is the cause of half the ills of wretched mortality. It is this which produces bitterness and strife between brethren and friends; which causes treacherous murder and desolating war. Care and sorrow, weary days and sleepless nights, are its attendants. It withers the bloom and blights the joys of youth, and brings on the ills and griefs of premature old age. Allah preserve thee, my prince, in total ignorance of this thing called love!"

The sage Eben Bonabben hastily retired, leaving the prince plunged in still deeper perplexity. It was in vain he attempted to dismiss the subject from his mind; it still continued uppermost in his thoughts, and teased and exhausted him with vain conjectures. Surely, said he to himself, as he listened to the tuneful strains of the birds, there is no sorrow in those notes; every thing seems tenderness and joy. If love be a cause of such wretchedness and strife, why are not these birds drooping in solitude, or tearing each other in pieces, instead of fluttering cheerfully about the groves, or sporting with each other among flowers?

He lay one morning on his couch meditating on this inexplicable matter. The window of his chamber was open to admit the soft morning breeze, which came laden with the perfume of orange blossoms from the valley of the Darro. The voice of the nightingale was faintly heard, still chanting the wonted theme. As the prince was listening and sighing, there was a sudden rushing noise in the air; a beautiful dove, pursued by a hawk, darted in at the window, and fell panting on the floor; while the pursuer, balked of his prey, soared off to the mountains.

The prince took up the gasping bird, smoothed its feathers, and nestled it in his bosom. When he had soothed it by his caresses, he put it in a golden cage, and offered it, with his own hands, the whitest and finest of wheat and the purest of water. The bird, however, refused food, and sat drooping and pining, and uttering piteous moans.

"What aileth thee?" said Ahmed. "Hast thou not every thing thy heart can wish?"

"Alas, no!" replied the dove; "am I not separated from the partner of my heart, and that too in the happy spring-time, the very season of love!"

"Of love!" echoed Ahmed; "I pray thee, my pretty bird, canst thou then tell me what is love?"

"Too well can I, my prince. It is the torment of one, the felicity of two, the strife and enmity of three. It is a charm which draws two beings together, and unites them by delicious sympathies, making it happiness to be with each other, but misery to be apart. Is there no being to whom you are drawn by these ties of tender affection?"

"I like my old teacher Eben Bonabben better than any other being; but he is often tedious, and I occasionally feel myself happier without his society."

"That is not the sympathy I mean. I speak of love, the

great mystery and principle of life: the intoxicating revel of youth; the sober delight of age. Look forth, my prince, and behold how at this blest season all nature is full of love. Every created being has its mate; the most insignificant bird sings to its paramour; the very beetle wooes its lady-beetle in the dust, and yon butterflies which you see fluttering high above the tower, and toying in the air, are happy in each other's loves. Alas, my prince! hast thou spent so many of the precious days of youth without knowing any thing of love? Is there no gentle being of another sex—no beautiful princess nor lovely damsel who has ensnared your heart, and filled your bosom with a soft tumult of pleasing pains and tender wishes?"

"I begin to understand," said the prince, sighing; "such a tumult I have more than once experienced, without knowing the cause; and where should I seek for an object such as you describe, in this dismal solitude?"

A little further conversation ensued, and the first amatory lesson of the prince was complete.

"Alas!" said he, "if love be indeed such a delight, and its interruption such a misery, Allah forbid that I should mar the joy of any of its votaries." He opened the cage, took out the dove, and having fondly kissed it, carried it to the window. "Go, happy bird," said he, "rejoice with the partner of thy heart in the days of youth and spring-time. Why should I make thee a fellow-prisoner in this dreary tower, where love can never enter?"

The dove flapped its wings in rapture, gave one vault into the air, and then swooped downward on whistling wings to the blooming bowers of the Darro.

The prince followed him with his eyes, and then gave way

to bitter repining. The singing of the birds which once delighted him, now added to his bitterness. Love! love! love! Alas,
poor youth! he now understood the strain.

His eyes flashed fire when next he beheld the sage Bonabben. "Why hast thou kept me in this abject ignorance?" cried
he. "Why has the great mystery and principle of life been
withheld from me, in which I find the meanest insect is so learned? Behold all nature is in a revel of delight. Every created
being rejoices with its mate. This — this is the love about
which I have sought instruction. Why am I alone debarred its
enjoyment? Why has so much of my youth been wasted without
a knowledge of its raptures?"

The sage Bonabben saw that all further reserve was useless;
for the prince had acquired the dangerous and forbidden knowledge. He revealed to him, therefore, the predictions of the
astrologers, and the precautions that had been taken in his education to avert the threatened evils. "And now, my prince,"
added he, "my life is in your hands. Let the king your father
discover that you have learned the passion of love while under
my guardianship, and my head must answer for it."

The prince was as reasonable as most young men of his age,
and easily listened to the remonstrances of his tutor, since
nothing pleaded against them. Besides, he really was attached
to Eben Bonabben, and being as yet but theoretically acquainted
with the passion of love, he consented to confine the knowledge
of it to his own bosom, rather than endanger the head of the
philosopher.

His discretion was doomed, however, to be put to still further
proofs. A few mornings afterwards, as he was ruminating on the
battlements of the tower. the dove which had been released by

him came hovering in the air, and alighted fearlessly upon his shoulder.

The prince fondled it to his heart. " Happy bird,' said he, " who can fly, as it were, with the wings of the morning to the uttermost parts of the earth. Where hast thou been since we parted ?"

" In a far country, my prince, whence I bring you tidiːgs in reward for my liberty. In the wild compass of my flight, which extends over plain and mountain, as I was soaring in the air, I beheld below me a delightful garden with all kinds of fruits and flowers. It was in a green meadow, on the banks of a wandering stream ; and in the centre of the garden was a stately palace. I alighted in one of the bowers to repose after my weary flight. On the green bank below me was a youthful princess, in the very sweetness and bloom of her years. She was surrounded by female attendants, young like herself, who decked her with garlands and coronets of flowers ; but no flower of field or garden could compare with her for loveliness. Here, however, she bloomed in secret, for the garden was surrounded by high walls, and no mortal man was permitted to enter. When I beheld this beauteous maid, thus young and innocent and unspotted by the world, I thought, here is the being formed by heaven to inspire my prince with love."

The description was a spark of fire to the combustible heart of Ahmed; all the latent amorousness of his temperament had at once found an object, and he conceived an immeasurable passion for the princess. He wrote a letter, couched in the most impassioned language, breathing· his fervent devotion, but bewailing the unhappy thraldom of his person, which prevented him from seeking her out and throwing himself at her feet. He added couplets of the most tender and moving eloquence, for he was a poet by nature, and inspired by love. He addressed his letter — "To the unknown beauty, from the captive Prince Ahmed;" then perfuming it with musk and roses, he gave it to the dove.

"Away, trustiest of messengers!" said he. "Fly over mountain and valley, and river, and plain; rest not in bower, nor set foot on earth, until thou hast given this letter to the mistress of my heart."

The dove soared high in air, and taking his course darted away in one undeviating direction. The prince followed him with his eye until he was a mere speck on a cloud, and gradually disappeared behind a mountain.

Day after day he watched for the return of the messenger of love, but he watched in vain. He began to accuse him of forgetfulness, when towards sunset one evening the faithful bird fluttered into his apartment, and falling at his feet expired. The arrow of some wanton archer had pierced his breast, yet he had struggled with the lingerings of life to excute his mission. As the prince bent with grief over this gentle martyr to fidelity, he beheld a chain of pearls round his neck, attached to which, beneath his wing, was a small enamelled picture. It represented a lovely princess in the very flower of her years. It was doubtless the unknown beauty of the garden; but who and where was she—how had she received his letter, and was this picture sent as a token of her approval of his passion? Unfortunately the death of the faithful dove left every thing in mystery and doubt.

The prince gazed on the picture till his eyes swam with tears. He pressed it to his lips and to his heart; he sat for hours contemplating it almost in an agony of tenderness. "Beautiful image! said he, "alas, thou art but an image! Yet thy dewy eyes beam tenderly upon me; those rosy lips look as though they would speak encouragement: vain fancies! Have they not looked the same on some more happy rival? But where in this wide world shall I hope to find the original? Who knows what mountains, what realms may separate us; what adverse chances may intervene? Perhaps now, even now, lovers may be crowding around her, while I sit here a prisoner in a tower, wasting my time in adoration of a painted shadow."

The resolution of Prince Ahmed was taken. "I will fly from this palace," said he, "which has become an odious prison; and, a pilgrim of love, will seek this unknown princess throughout the world." To escape from the tower in the day, when every one was awake, might be a difficult matter; but at night the palace was slightly guarded; for no one apprehended any attempt of the kind from the prince, who had always been so passive in his captivity. How was he to guide himself, however, in his darkling flight, being ignorant of the country? He bethought him of the owl, who was accustomed to roam at night, and must know every by-lane and secret pass. Seeking him in his hermitage, he questioned him touching his knowledge of the land. Upon this the owl put on a mighty self-important look. "You must know, O prince," said he, "that we owls are of a very ancient and extensive family, though rather fallen to decay, and possess ruinous castles and palaces in all parts of Spain. There is scarcely a tower of the mountains, or a fortress of the plains, or an old citadel of a city, but has some brother or uncle, or cousin, quartered in it; and in going the rounds to visit this my numerous kindred, I have pryed into every nook and corner, and made myself acquainted with every secret of the land."

The prince was overjoyed to find the owl so deeply versed in topography, and now informed him, in confidence, of his tender passion and his intended elopement, urging him to be his companion and counsellor.

" Go to !" said the owl, with a look of displeasure; " am I a bird to engage in a love affair ?   I whose whole time is devoted to meditation and the moon ?"

" Be not offended, most solemn owl," replied the prince " abstract thyself for a time from meditation and the moon, and aid me in my flight, and thou shalt have whatever heart can wish."

" I have that already," said the owl : " a few mice are suffi cient for my frugal table, and this hole in the wall is spacious enough for my studies; and what more does a philosopher like myself desire ?"

" Bethink thee, most wise owl, that while moping in thy cell and gazing at the moon, all thy talents are lost to the world.   I shall one day be a sovereign prince, and may advance thee to some post of honor and dignity."

The owl, though a philosopher and above the ordinary wants of life, was not above ambition ; so he was finally prevailed on to elope with the prince, and be his guide and mentor in his pilgrimage.

The plans of a lover are promptly executed.   The prince collected all his jewels, and concealed them about his person as travelling funds.   That very night he lowered himself by his scarf from a balcony of the tower, clambered over the outer walls of the Generalife, and, guided by the owl, made good his escape before morning to the mountains.

He now held a council with his mentor as to his future course.

" Might I advise," said the owl, " I would recommend you to repair to Seville. You must know that many years since I was on a visit to an uncle, an owl of great dignity and power, who lived in a ruined wing of the Alcazar of that place. In my hoverings at night over the city I frequently remarked a light burning in a lonely tower. At length I alighted on the battlements, and found it to proceed from the lamp of an Arabian magician : he was surrounded by his magic books, and on his shoulder was perched his familiar, an ancient raven who had come with him from Egypt. I am acquainted with that raven, and owe to him a great part of the knowledge I possess. The magician is since dead, but the raven still inhabits the tower, for these birds are of wonderful long life. I would advise you, O prince, to seek that raven, for he is a soothsayer and a conjurer, and deals in the black art, for which all ravens, and especially those of Egypt, are renowned."

The prince was struck with the wisdom of this advice, and accordingly bent his course towards Seville. He travelled only in the night, to accommodate his companion, and lay by during the day in some dark cavern or mouldering watchtower, for the owl knew every hiding hole of the kind, and had a most antiquarian taste for ruins.

At length one morning at daybreak they reached the city of Seville, where the owl, who hated the glare and bustle of crowded streets, halted without the gate, and took up his quarters in a hollow tree.

The prince entered the gate, and readily found the magic tower, which rose above the houses of the city, as a palm-tree

10

rises above the shrubs of the desert; it was in fact the same tower standing at the present day, and known as the Giralda, the famous Moorish tower of Seville.

The prince ascended by a great winding staircase to the summit of the tower, where he found the cabalistic raven, an old, mysterious, gray-headed bird, ragged in feather, with a film over one eye that gave him the glare of a spectre. He was perched on one leg, with his head turned on one side, poring with his remaining eye on a diagram described on the pavement.

The prince approached him with the awe and reverence naturally inspired by his venerable appearance and supernatural wisdom. "Pardon me, most ancient and darkly wise raven," exclaimed he, "if for a moment I interrupt those studies which are the wonder of the world. You behold before you a votary of love, who would fain seek your counsel how to obtain the object of his passion."

"In other words," said the raven, with a significant look, "you seek to try my skill in palmistry. Come, show me your hand, and let me decipher the mysterious lines of fortune."

"Excuse me," said the prince, "I come not to pry into the decrees of fate, which are hidden by Allah from the eyes of mortals; I am a pilgrim of love, and seek but to find a clue to the object of my pilgrimage."

"And can you be at any loss for an object in amorous Andalusia?" said the old raven, leering upon him with his single eye; "above all, can you be at a loss in wanton Seville, where black-eyed damsels dance the zambra under every orange grove?"

The prince blushed, and was somewhat shocked at hearing an old bird with one foot in the grave talk thus loosely. "Believe me," said he, gravely, "I am on none such light and vagrant

ᴜrrand as thou dost insinuate. The black-eyed damsels of Anda·
lusia who dance among the orange groves of the Guadalquivir
are as naught to me. I seek one unknown but immaculate
beauty, the original of this picture; and I beseech thee, most
potent raven, if it be within the scope of thy knowledge or the
reach of thy art, inform me where she may be found."

The gray-headed raven was rebuked by the gravity of the
prince.

"What know I," replied he, dryly, "of youth and beauty?
my visits are to the old and withered, not the fresh and fair: the
harbinger of fate am I; who croak bodings of death from the
chimney top, and flap my wings at the sick man's window. You
must seek elsewhere for tidings of your unknown beauty."

"And where can I seek if not among the sons of wisdom,
versed in the book of destiny? Know that I am a royal prince,
fated by the stars, and sent on a mysterious enterprise on which
may hang the destiny of empires."

When the raven heard that it was a matter of vast moment,
in which the stars took interest, he changed his tone and manner,
and listened with profound attention to the story of the prince.
When it was concluded, he replied, "Touching this princess, I
can give thee no information of myself, for my flight is not among
gardens, or around ladies' bowers; but hie thee to Cordova, seek
the palm-tree of the great Abderahman, which stands in the court
of the principal mosque: at the foot of it thou wilt find a great
traveller who has visited all countries and courts, and been a
favorite with queens and princesses. He will give thee tidings
of the object of thy search."

"Many thanks for this precious information," said the prince.
"Farewell, most venerable conjurer."

" Farewell, pilgrim of love," said the raven, dryly, and again
fell to pondering on the diagram.

The prince sallied forth from Seville, sought his fellow-travel-
ler the owl, who was still dozing in the hollow tree, and set off
for Cordova.

He approached it along hanging gardens, and orange and citron groves, overlooking the fair valley of the Guadalquivir.
When arrived at its gates the owl flew up to a dark hole in the
wall, and the prince proceeded in quest of the palm-tree planted
in days of yore by the great Abderahman.   It stood in the midst
of the great court of the mosque, towering from amidst orange and
cypress trees.   Dervises and Faquirs were seated in groups under
the cloisters of the court, and many of the faithful were perform-
ing their ablutions at the fountains before entering the mosque.

At the foot of the palm-tree was a crowd listening to the
words of one who appeared to be talking with great volubility.
" This," said the prince to himself, " must be the great traveller
who is to give me tidings of the unknown princess."   He mingled
in the crowd, but was astonished to perceive that they were all
listening to a parrot, who with his bright green coat, pragmatical
eye, and consequential top-knot, had the air of a bird on excellent
terms with himself.

" How is this," said the prince to one of the bystanders, " that
so many grave persons can be delighted with the garrulity of a
chattering bird?"

" You know not whom you speak of," said the other ; " this
parrot is a descendant of the famous parrot of Persia, renowned
for his story-telling talent.   He has all the learning of the East
at the tip of his tongue, and and can quote poetry as fast as he
can talk.   He has visited various foreign courts, where he has

been considered an oracle of erudition. He has been a universal favorite also with the fair sex, who have a vast admiration for erudite parrots that can quote poetry."

"Enough," said the prince, "I will have some private talk with this distinguished traveller."

He sought a private interview, and expounded the nature of his errand. He had scarcely mentioned it when the parrot burst into a fit of dry rickety laughter that absolutely brought tears in his eyes. "Excuse my merriment," said he, "but the mere mention of love always sets me laughing."

The prince was shocked at this ill-timed mirth. "Is not love," said he, "the great mystery of nature, the secret principle of life, the universal bond of sympathy?"

"A fig's end!" cried the parrot, interrupting, him; "prithee where hast thou learned this sentimental jargon? trust me, love is quite out of vogue; one never hears of it in the company of wits and people of refinement."

The prince sighed as he recalled the different language of his friend the dove. But this parrot, thought he, has lived about the court, he affects the wit and the fine gentleman, he knows nothing of the thing called love. Unwilling to provoke any more ridicule of the sentiment which filled his heart, he now directed his inquiries to the immediate purport of his visit.

"Tell me," said he, "most accomplished parrot, thou who hast every where been admitted to the most secret bowers of beauty, hast thou in the course of thy travels met with the original of this portrait?"

The parrot took the picture in his claw, turned his head from side to side, and examined it curiously with either eye. "Upon my honor," said he, "a very pretty face; very pretty: but then one sees so many pretty women in one's travels that one can hardly—but hold—bless me! now I look at it again—sure enough this is the princess Aldegonda : how could I forget one that is so prodigious a favorite with me!"

" The princess Aldegonda !" echoed the prince; " and where is she to be found ?"

" Softly, softly," said the parrot, " easier to be found than gained. She is the only daughter of the Christian king who reigns at Toledo, and is shut up from the world until her seventeenth birth-day, on account of some prediction of those meddlesome fellows the astrologers. You'll not get a sight of her; no mortal man can see her. I was admitted to her presence to entertain her, and I assure you, on the word of a parrot, who has seen the world, I have conversed with much sillier princesses in my time."

" A word in confidence, my dear parrot," said the prince; " I am heir to a kingdom, and shall one day sit upon a throne. I see that you are a bird of parts, and understand the world. Help me to gain possession of this princess, and I will advance you to some distinguished place about court."

" With all my heart," said the parrot ; " but let it be a sinecure if possible, for we wits have a great dislike to labor."

Arrangements were promptly made ; the prince sallied forth from Cordova through the same gate by which he had entered ; called the owl down from the hole in the wall, introduced him to his new travelling companion as a brother savant, and away they set off on their journey.

They travelled much more slowly than accorded with the impatience of the prince, but the parrot was accustomed to high life, and did not like to be disturbed early in the morning. The owl,

on the other hand, was for sleeping at mid-day, and lost a great
deal of time by his long siestas.   His antiquarian taste also was
in the way ; for he insisted on pausing and inspecting every ruin,
and had long legendary tales to tell about every old tower and
castle in the country.   The prince had supposed that he and the
parrot, being both birds of learning, would delight in each other's
society, but never had he been more mistaken.   They were eter-
nally bickering. The one was a wit, the other a philosopher.   The
parrot quoted poetry, was critical on new readings and eloquent
on small points of erudition ; the owl treated all such knowledge
as trifling, and relished nothing but metaphysics.   Then the parrot would sing songs and repeat bon mots and crack jokes upon
his solemn neighbor, and laugh outrageously at his own wit; all
which proceedings the owl considered as a grievous invasion of
his dignity, and would scowl and sulk and swell, and be silent for
a whole day together.

The prince heeded not the wranglings of his companions,
being wrapped up in the dreams of his own fancy and the con-
templation of the portrait of the beautiful princess.   In this way
they journeyed through the stern passes of the Sierra Morena,
across the sunburnt plains of La Mancha and Castile, and along
the banks of the " Golden Tagus," which winds its wizard mazes
over one half of Spain and Portugal.   At length they came in
sight of a strong city with walls and towers built on a rocky promontory, round the foot of which the Tagus circled with brawling
violence.

" Behold," exclaimed the owl, " the ancient and renowned
city of Toledo ; a city famous for its antiquities.   Behold those
venerable domes and towers, hoary with time and clothed with
legendary grandeur, in which so many of my ancestors have
meditated."

"Pish!" cried the parrot, interrupting his solemn antiquarian rapture, "what have we to do with antiquities, and legends, and your ancestry? Behold what is more to the purpose—behold the abode of youth and beauty—behold at length, O prince, the abode of your long-sought princess."

The prince looked in the direction indicated by the parrot, and beheld, in a delightful green meadow on the banks of the Tagus, a stately palace rising from amidst the bowers of a delicious garden. It was just such a place as had been described by the dove as the residence of the original of the picture. He gazed at it with a throbbing heart; "perhaps at this moment," thought he, "the beautiful princess is sporting beneath those shady bowers, or pacing with delicate step those stately terraces, or reposing beneath those lofty roofs!" As he looked more narrowly he perceived that the walls of the garden were of great height, so as to defy access, while numbers of armed guards patrolled around them.

The prince turned to the parrot. "O most accomplished of birds," said he, "thou hast the gift of human speech. Hie thee to yon garden; seek the idol of my soul, and tell her that prince Ahmed, a pilgrim of love, and guided by the stars, has arrived in quest of her on the flowery banks of the Tagus."

The parrot, proud of his embassy, flew away to the garden mounted above its lofty walls, and after soaring for a time over the lawns and groves, alighted on the balcony of a pavilion that overhung the river. Here, looking in at the casement, he beheld the princess reclining on a couch, with her eyes fixed on a paper, while tears gently stole after each other down her pallid cheek.

Pluming his wings for a moment, adjusting his bright green coat, and elevating his top-knot, the parrot perched himself beside her with a gallant air: then assuming a tenderness of tone, "Dry thy tears, most beautiful of princesses," said he, "I come to bring solace to thy heart."

The princess was startled on hearing a voice, but turning and seeing nothing but a little green-coated bird bobbing and bowing before her; "Alas! what solace canst thou yield," said she, "seeing thou art but a parrot?"

The parrot was nettled at the question. "I have consoled many beautiful ladies in my time," said he; "but let that pass. At present I come ambassador from a royal prince. Know that Ahmed, the prince of Granada, has arrived in quest of thee, and is encamped even now on the flowery banks of the Tagus."

The eyes of the beautiful princess sparkled at these words even brighter than the diamonds in her coronet. "O sweetest of parrots," cried she, "joyful indeed are thy tidings, for I was faint and weary, and sick almost unto death with doubt of the constancy of Ahmed. Hie thee back, and tell him that the words of his letter are engraven in my heart, and his poetry has been the food of my soul. Tell him, however, that he must prepare to prove his love by force of arms; to-morrow is my seventeenth birth-day, when the king my father holds a great tournament; several princes are to enter the lists, and my hand is to be the prize of the victor."

The parrot again took wing, and rustling through the groves, flew back to where the prince awaited his return. The rapture of Ahmed on finding the original of his adored portrait, and finding her kind and true, can only be conceived by those favored mortals who have had the good fortune to realize day-dreams and turn a shadow into substance: still there was one thing that alloyed his transport—this impending tournament. In fact, the

10*

banks of the Tagus were already glittering with arms, and resounding with trumpts of the various knights, who, with proud
retinues, were prancing on towards Toledo to attend the ceremonial The same star that had controlled the destiny of the
prince had governed that of the princess, and until her seventeenth birth-day she had been shut up from the world, to guard
her from the tender passion. The fame of her charms, however,
had been enhanced rather than obscured by this seclusion.
Several powerful princes had contended for her hand; and her
father, who was a king of wondrous shrewdness, to avoid making
enemies by showing partiality, had referred them to the arbitra-
ment of arms. Among the rival candidates were several renowned
for strength and prowess. What a predicament for the unfortunate
Ahmed, unprovided as he was with weapons, and unskilled in the
exercise of chivalry ! " Luckless prince that I am !" said he,
" to have been brought up in seclusion under the eye of a philosopher ! Of what avail are algebra and philosophy in affairs
of love ? Alas, Eben Bonabben ! why hast thou neglected to
instruct me in the management of arms ?" Upon this the owl
broke silence, preluding his harangue with a pious ejaculation, for
he was a devout Mussulman.

"Allah Akbar ! God is great !" exclaimed he ; "in his hands
are all secret things—he alone governs the destiny of princes !
Know, O prince, that this land is full of mysteries, hidden from
all but those who, like myself, can grope after knowledge in the
dark. Know that in the neighboring mountains there is a cave,
and in that cave there is an iron table, and on that table there
lies a suit of magic armor, and beside that table there stands a
spell-bound steed, which have been shut up there for many gene
rations."

The prince stared with wonder, while the owl, blinking his huge round eyes, and erecting his horns, proceeded.

" Many years since, I accompanied my father to these parts on a tour of his estates, and we sojourned in that cave; and thus became I acquainted with the mystery. It is a tradition in our family which I have heard from my grandfather, when I was yet but a very little owlet, that this armor belonged to a Moorish magician, who took refuge in this cavern when Toledo was cap tured by the Christians, and died here, leaving his steed and weapons under a mystic spell, never to be used but by a Mos-lem, and by him only from sunrise to mid-day. In that interval, whoever uses them will overthrow every opponent."

" Enough : let us seek this cave !" exclaimed Ahmed.

Guided by his legendary mentor, the prince found the cavern, which was in one of the wildest recesses of those rocky cliffs which rise around Toledo ; none but the mousing eye of an owl or an antiquary could have discovered the entrance to it. A sepulchral lamp of everlasting oil shed a solemn light through the place. On an iron table in the centre of the cavern lay the magic armor, against it leaned the lance, and beside it stood an Arabian steed, caparisoned for the field, but motionless as a statue. The armor was bright and unsullied as it had gleamed in days of old ; the steed as in good condition as if just from the pasture ; and when Ahmed laid his hand upon his neck, he pawed the ground and gave a loud neigh of joy that shook the walls of the cavern. Thus amply provided with " horse and rider and weapon to wear," the prince determined to defy the field in the impending tourney.

The eventful morning arrived. The lists for the combat were prepared in the Vega, or plain, just below the cliff-built walls of Toledo, where stages and galleries were erected for the spectators, covered with rich tapestry, and sheltered from the sun by silken awnings. All the beauties of the land were assembled in those galleries, while below pranced plumed knights with their pages and esquires, among whom figured conspicuously the princes who were to contend in the tourney. All the beauties of the land, however, were eclipsed when the princess Aldegonda appeared in the royal pavilion, and for the first time broke forth upon the gaze of an admiring world. A murmur of wonder ran through the crowd at her transcendent loveliness; and the princes who were candidates for her hand, merely on the faith of her reported charms, now felt tenfold ardor for the conflict.

The princess, however, had a troubled look. The color came and went from her cheek, and her eye wandered with a restless and unsatisfied expression over the plumed throng of knights. The trumpets were about sounding for the encounter, when the herald announced the arrival of a strange knight; and Ahmed rode into the field. A steel helmet studded with gems rose above his turban; his cuirass was embossed with gold; his cimeter and dagger were of the workmanship of Fez, and flamed with precious stones. A round shield was at his shoulder, and in his hand he bore the lance of charmed virtue. The caparison of his Arabian steed was richly embroidered and swept the ground, and the proud animal pranced and snuffed the air, and neighed with joy at once more beholding the array of arms. The lofty and graceful demeanor of the prince struck every eye, and when his appellation was announced, " The Pilgrim of Love," a universal flutter and agitation prevailed among the fair dames in the galleries.

When Ahmed presented himself at the lists, however, they

were closed against him : none but princes, he was told, were admitted to the contest. He declared his name and rank. Still worse !—he was a Moslem, and could not engage in a tourney where the hand of a Christian princess was the prize.

The rival princes surrounded him with haughty and menacing aspects ; and one of insolent demeanor and herculean frame sneered at his light and youthful form, and scoffed at his amorous appellation. The ire of the prince was roused. He defied his rival to the encounter. They took distance, wheeled, and charged ; and at the first touch of the magic lance, the brawny scoffer was tilted from his saddle. Here the prince would have paused, but alas ! he had to deal with a demoniac horse and armor ; once in action nothing could control them. The Arabian steed charged into the thickest of the throng; the lance overturned every thing that presented ; the gentle prince was carried pell-mell about the field, strewing it with high and low. gentle and simple, and grieving at his own involuntary exploits. The king stormed and raged at this outrage on his subjects and his guests. He ordered out all his guards—they were unhorsed as fast as they came up. The king threw off his robes, grasped buckler and lance, and rode forth to awe the stranger with the presence of majesty itself. Alas ! majesty fared no better than the vulgar ; the steed and lance were no respecters of persons : to the dismay of Ahmed, he was borne full tilt against the king. and in a moment the royal heels were in the air, and the crown was rolling in the dust.

At this moment the sun reached the meridian; the magic spell resumed its power ; the Arabian steed scoured across the plain, leaped the barrier, plunged into the Tagus, swam its raging current, bore the prince breathless and amazed to the cavern, and resumed his station, like a statue, beside the iron table. The prince dismounted right gladly, and replaced the armor, to abide the further decrees of fate. Then seating himself in the cavern, he ruminated on the desperate state to which this demoniac steed and armor had reduced him. Never should he dare to show his face at Toledo after inflicting such disgrace upon its chivalry, and such an outrage on its king. What too would the princess think of so rude and riotous an achievement? Full of anxiety, he sent forth his winged messengers to gather tidings. The parrot resorted to all the public places and crowded resorts of the city, and soon returned with a world of gossip. All Toledo was in consternation. The princess had been borne off senseless to the palace; the tournament had ended in confusion; every one was talking of the sudden apparition, prodigious exploits, and strange disappearance of the Moslem knight. Some pronounced him a Moorish magician; others thought him a demon who had assumed a human shape, while others related traditions of enchanted warriors hidden in the caves of the mountains, and thought it might be one of these, who had made a sudden irruption from his den. All agreed that no mere ordinary mortal could have wrought such wonders, or unhorsed such accomplished and stalwart Christian warriors.

The owl flew forth at night and hovered about the dusky city, perching on the roofs and chimneys. He then wheeled his flight up to the royal palace, which stood on a rocky summit of Toledo, and went prowling about its terraces and battlements, eaves-dropping at every cranny, and glaring in with his big goggling eyes at every window where there was a light, so as to throw two or three maids of honor into fits. It was not until the gray dawn began to peer above the mountains that he returned from his mousing expedition, and related to the prince what he had seen.

"As I was prying about one of the loftiest towers of the palace," said he, "I beheld through a casement a beautiful princess. She was reclining on a couch with attendants and physicians around her, but she would none of their ministry and relief. When they retired I beheld her draw forth a letter from her bosom, and read and kiss it, and give way to loud lamentations; at which, philosopher as I am, I could but be greatly moved."

The tender heart of Ahmed was distressed at these tidings. "Too true were thy words, O sage Eben Bonabben," cried he; "care and sorrow and sleepless nights are the lot of lovers. Allah preserve the princess from the blighting influence of this thing called love!"

Further intelligence from Toledo corroborated the report of the owl. The city was a prey to uneasiness and alarm. The princess was conveyed to the highest tower of the palace, every avenue to which was strongly guarded. In the mean time a devouring melancholy had seized upon her, of which no one could divine the cause—she refused food and turned a deaf ear to every consolation. The most skilful physicians had essayed their art in vain; it was thought some magic spell had been practised upon her, and the king made proclamation, declaring that whoever should effect her cure should receive the richest jewel in the royal treasury.

When the owl, who was dozing in a corner, heard of this proclamation, he rolled his large eyes and looked more mysterious than ever.

"Allah Akbar!" exclaimed he, "happy the man that shall

effect that cure, should he but know what to choose from the royal treasury."

"What mean you, most reverend owl?" said Ahmed.

"Hearken, O prince, to what I shall relate. We owls, you must know, are a learned body, and much given to dark and dusty research. During my late prowling at night about the domes and turrets of Toledo, I disovered a college of antiquarian owls, who hold their meetings in a great vaulted tower where the royal treasury is deposited. Here they were discussing the forms and inscriptions and designs of ancient gems and jewels, and of golden and silver vessels, heaped up in the treasury, the fashion of every country and age ; but mostly they were interested about certain relics and talismans that have remained in the treasury since the time of Roderick the Goth. Among these was a box of sandal-wood secured by bands of steel of Oriental workmanship, and inscribed with mystic characters known only to the learned few. This box and its inscription had occupied the college for several sessions, and had caused much long and grave dispute. At the time of my visit a very ancient owl, who had recently arrived from Egypt, was seated on the lid of the box lecturing upon the inscription, and he proved from it that the coffer contained the silken carpet of the throne of Solomon the wise ; which doubtless had been brought to Toledo by the Jews who took refuge there after the downfall of Jerusalem."

When the owl had concluded his antiquarian harangue the prince remained for a time absorbed in thought. "I have heard," said he, "from the sage Eben Bonabben, of the wonderful properties of that talisman, which disappeared at the fall of Jerusalem, and was supposed to be lost to mankind. Doubtless it remains a sealed mystery to the Christians of Toledo. If I can get possession of that carpet, my fortune is secure."

The next day the prince laid aside his rich attire, and arrayed himself in the simple garb of an Arab of the desert. He dyed his complexion to a tawny hue, and no one could have recognized in him the splendid warrior who had caused such admiration and dismay at the tournament. With staff in hand, and scrip by his side, and a small pastoral reed, he repaired to Toledo, and presenting himself at the gate of the royal palace, announced himself as a candidate for the reward offered for the cure of the princess. The guards would have driven him away with blows. " What can a vagrant Arab like thyself pretend to do," said they, " in a case where the most learned of the land have failed ?" The king, however, overheard the tumult, and ordered the Arab to be brought into his presence.

" Most potent king," said Ahmed, " you behold before you a Bedouin Arab, the greater part of whose life has been passed in the solitudes of the desert. These solitudes, it is well known, are the haunts of demons and evil spirits, who beset us poor shepherds in our lonely watchings, enter into and possess our flocks and herds, and sometimes render even the patient camel furious ; against these our counter-charm is music ; and we have legendary airs handed down from generation to generation, that we chant and pipe, to cast forth these evil spirits. I am of a gifted line, and possess this power in its fullest force. If it be any evil influence of the kind that holds a spell over thy daughter, I pledge my head to free her from its sway."

The king, who was a man of understanding and knew the wonderful secrets possessed by the Arabs, was inspired with hope by the confident language of the prince. He conducted him immediately to the lofty tower, secured by several doors, in the summit of which was the chamber of the princess. The windows opened upon a terrace with balustrades, commanding a view over Toledo and all the surrounding country. The windows were darkened, for the princess lay within, a prey to a devouring grief that refused all alleviation.

The prince seated himself on the terrace, and performed several wild Arabian airs on his pastoral pipe, which he had learnt from his attendants in the Generalife at Granada. The princess continued insensible, and the doctors who were present shook their heads, and smiled with incredulity and contempt: at length the prince laid aside the reed, and, to a simple melody, chanted the amatory verses of the letter which had declared his passion.

The princess recognized the strain—a fluttering joy stole to her heart; she raised her head and listened; tears rushed to her eyes and streamed down her cheeks; her bosom rose and fell with a tumult of emotions. She would have asked for the minstrel to be brought into her presence, but maiden coyness held her silent. The king read her wishes, and at his command Ahmed was conducted into the chamber. The lovers were discreet: they but exchanged glances, yet those glances spoke volumes. Never was triumph of music more complete. The rose had returned to the soft cheek of the princess, the freshness to her lip, and the dewy light to her languishing eyes.

All the physicians present stared at each other with astonishment. The king regarded the Arab minstrel with admiration mixed with awe. "Wonderful youth!" exclaimed he, "thou shalt henceforth be the first physician of my court, and no other prescription will I take but thy melody. For the present receive thy reward, the most precious jewel in my treasury."

"O king," replied Ahmed, "I care not for silver or gold or

precious stones.   One relic hast thou in thy treasury, handed
down from the Moslems who once owned Toledo—a box of sandal-
wood containing a silken carpet: give me that box, and I am
content."

All present were surprised at the moderation of the Arab;
and still more when the box of sandal-wood was brought and the
carpet drawn forth.   It was of fine green silk, covered with He-
brew and Chaldaic characters.   The court physicians looked
at each other, shrugged their shoulders, and smiled at the sim
plicity of this new practitioner, who could be content with so pal-
try a fee.

"This carpet," said the prince, "once covered the throne of
Solomon the wise; it is worthy of being placed beneath the feet
of beauty."

So saying, he spread it on the terrace beneath an ottoman
that had been brought forth for the princess; then seating himself at her feet—

"Who," said he, "shall counteract what is written in the
book of fate?   Behold the prediction of the astrologers verified.
Know, O king, that your daughter and I have long loved each
other in secret.   Behold in me the Pilgrim of Love!"

These words were scarcely from his lips, when the carpet rose
in the air, bearing off the prince and princess.   The king and the
physicians gazed after it with open mouths and straining eyes
until it became a little speck on the white bosom of a cloud, and
then disappeared in the blue vault of heaven.

The king in a rage summoned his treasurer.   "How is this,"
said he, "that thou hast suffered an infidel to get possession of
such a talisman?"

"Alas, sir, we knew not its nature, nor could we decipher the inscription of the box. If it be indeed the carpet of the throne of the wise Solomon, it is possessed of magic power, and can transport its owner from place to place through the air."

The king assembled a mighty army, and set off for Granada in pursuit of the fugitives. His march was long and toilsome. Encamping in the Vega, he sent a herald to demand restitution of his daughter. The king himself came forth with all his court to meet him. In the king he beheld the real minstrel, for Ahmed had succeeded to the throne on the death of his father, and the beautiful Aldegonda was his sultana.

The Christian king was easily pacified when he found that his daughter was suffered to continue in her faith; not that he was particularly pious; but religion is always a point of pride and etiquette with princes. Instead of bloody battles, there was a succession of feasts and rejoicings, after which the king returned well pleased to Toledo, and the youthful couple continued to reign as happily as wisely, in the Alhambra.

It is proper to add, that the owl and the parrot had severally followed the prince by easy stages to Granada; the former travelling by night, and stopping at the various hereditary possessions of his family; the latter figuring in gay circles of every town and city on his route.

Ahmed gratefully requited the services which they had rendered on his pilgrimage. He appointed the owl his prime minister, the parrot his master of ceremonies. It is needless to say that never was a realm more sagely administered, nor a court conducted with more exact punctilio.

A RAMBLE AMONG THE HILLS.

I used freqently to amuse myself towards the close of the day, when the heat had subsided, with taking long rambles about the neighboring hills and the deep umbrageous valleys, accompanied by my historiographic squire, Mateo, to whose passion for gossiping I on such occasions gave the most unbounded license; and there was scarce a rock, or ruin, or broken fountain, or lonely glen, about which he had not some marvellous story; or, above all, some golden legend; for never was poor devil so munificent in dispensing hidden treasures.

In the course of one of these strolls Mateo was more than usually communicative. It was toward sunset that we sallied forth from the great Gate of Justice, and ascended an alley of trees until we came to a clump of figs and pomegranates at the foot of the Tower of the Seven Floors (de los siéte suelos), the identical tower whence Boabdil is said to have issued, when he surrendered his capital. Here, pointing to a low archway in the foundation, Mateo informed me of a monstrous sprite or hobgoblin, said to infest this tower, ever since the time of the Moors and to guard the treasures of a Moslem king. Sometimes it issues forth in the dead of the night, and scours the avenues of the Alhambra, and the streets of Granada, in the shape of a headless horse, pursued by six dogs with terrible yells and howlings.

"But have you ever met with it yourself, Mateo, in any of your rambles?" demanded I.

"No, Señor, God be thanked! but my grandfather, the tailor, knew several persons that had seen it, for it went about much oftener in his time than at present; sometimes in one shape, sometimes in another. Every body in Granada has heard of the Belludo, for the old women and the nurses frighten the children with it when they cry. Some say it is the spirit of a cruel Moorish king, who killed his six sons and buried them in these vaults, and that they hunt him at nights in revenge."

I forbear to dwell upon the marvellous details given by the simple-minded Mateo about this redoubtable phantom, which has, in fact, been time out of mind a favorite theme of nursery tales and popular tradition in Granada, and of which honorable mention is made by an ancient and learned historian and topographer of the place.

Leaving this eventful pile, we continued our course, skirting the fruitful orchards of the Generalife, in which two or three nightingales were pouring forth a rich strain of melody. Behind these orchards we passed a number of Moorish tanks, with a door cut into the rocky bosom of the hill, but closed up. These tanks, Mateo informed me, were favorite bathing-places of himself and his comrades in boyhood, until frightened away by a story of a hideous Moor, who used to issue forth from the door in the rock to entrap unwary bathers.

Leaving these haunted tanks behind us, we pursued our ramble up a solitary mule-path winding among the hills, and soon found ourselves amidst wild and melancholy mountains, destitute of trees, and here and there tinted with scanty verdure. Every thing within sight was severe and sterile, and it was scarcely possible to realize the idea that but a short distance behind us was the Generalife, with its blooming orchards and terraced gardens, and that we were in the vicinity of delicious Granada, that city of groves and fountains. But such is the nature of Spain; wild and stern the moment it escapes from cultivation; the desert and the garden are ever side by side.

The narrow defile up which we were passing is called, according to Mateo, *el Barranco de la tinaja*, or the ravine of the jar, because a jar full of Moorish gold was found here in old times. The brain of poor Mateo was continually running upon these golden legends.

"But what is the meaning of the cross I see yonder upon a heap of stones, in that narrow part of the ravine?"

"Oh, that's nothing—a muleteer was murdered there some years since."

"So then, Mateo, you have robbers and murderers even at the gates of the Alhambra?"

"Not at present, Señor; that was formerly, when there used to be many loose fellows about the fortress; but they've all been weeded out. Not but that the gipsies who live in caves in the hill-sides, just out of the fortress, are many of them fit for any thing; but we have had no murder about here for a long time past. The man who murdered the muleteer was hanged in the fortress."

Our path continued up the barranco, with a bold, rugged height to our left, called the "Silla del Moro," or, Chair of the Moor, from the tradition already alluded to, that the unfortunate Boabdil fled thither during a popular insurrection, and remained all day seated on the rocky summit, looking mournfully down on his factious city.

We at length arrived on the highest part of the promontory

above Granada, called the mountain of the sun. The evening
was approaching; the setting sun just gilded the loftiest heights.
Here and there a solitary shepherd might be descried driving
his flock down the declivities, to be folded for the night; or a
muleteer and his lagging animals, threading some mountain path,
to arrive at the city gates before nightfall.

Presently the deep tones of the cathedral bell came swelling
up the defiles, proclaiming the hour of " oration " or prayer.
The note was responded to from the belfry of every church, and
from the sweet bells of the convents among the mountains. The
shepherd paused on the fold of the hill, the muleteer in the midst
of the road, each took off his hat and remained motionless for a
time, murmuring his evening prayer. There is always something
pleasingly solemn in this custom, by which, at a melodious signal, every human being throughout the land unites at the same
moment in a tribute of thanks to God for the mercies of the day.
It spreads a transient sanctity over the land, and the sight of the
sun sinking in all his glory, adds not a little to the solemnity of
the scene.

In the present instance the effect was heightened by the wild
and lonely nature of the place. We were on the naked and broken summit of the haunted mountain of the sun, where ruined
tanks and cisterns, and the mouldering foundations of extensive
buildings, spoke of former populousness, but where all was now
silent and desolate.

As we were wandering about among these traces of old times,
we came to a circular pit, penetrating deep into the bosom of the
mountain ; which Mateo pointed out as one of the wonders and
mysteries of the place. I supposed it to be a well dug by the
indefatigable Moors, to obtain their favorite element in its great-

est purity. Mateo, however, had a different story, and one much more to his humor. According to a tradition, in which his father and grandfather firmly believed, this was an entrance to the subterranean caverns of the mountain, in which Boabdil and his court lay bound in magic spell; and whence they sallied forth at night, at allotted times, to revisit their ancient abodes.

'' Ah, Señor, this mountain is full of wonders of the kind. In another place there was a hole somewhat like this, and just within it hung an iron pot by a chain; nobody knew what was in that pot, for it was always covered up; but every body supposed it full of Moorish gold. Many tried to draw it forth, for it seemed just within reach; but the moment it was touched it would sink far, far down, and not come up again for some time. At last one who thought it must be enchanted touched it with the cross, by way of breaking the charm; and faith he did break it, for the pot sank out of sight and never was seen any more.''

" All this is fact, Señor; for my grandfather was an eye-witness."

" What! Mateo; did he see the pot ?"

" No, Señor, but he saw the hole where the pot had hung."

" It's the same thing, Mateo."

The deepening twilight, which, in this climate, is of short duration, admonished us to leave this haunted ground. As we descended the mountain defile, there was no longer herdsman nor muleteer to be seen, nor any thing to be heard but our own footsteps and the lonely chirping of the cricket. The shadows of the valley grew deeper and deeper, until all was dark around us. The lofty summit of the Sierra Nevada alone retained a lingering gleam of daylight; its snowy peaks glaring against the dark blue firmament, and seeming close to us, from the extreme purity of the atmosphere.

11

" How near the Sierra looks this evening !" said Mateo ; " it seems as if you could touch it with your hand ; and yet it is many long leagues off." While he was speaking, a star appeared over the snowy summit of the mountain, the only one yet visible in the heavens, and so pure, so large, so bright and beautiful, as to call forth ejaculations of delight from honest Mateo.

" Que estrella hermosa ! que clara y limpia es !—No pueda ser estrella mas brillante !"

(What a beautiful star ! how clear and lucid—a star could not be more brilliant !)

I have often remarked this sensibility of the common people of Spain to the charms of natural objects. The lustre of a star, the beauty or fragrance of a flower, the crystal purity of a fountain, will inspire them with a kind of poetical delight ; and then, what euphonious words their magnificent language affords, with which to give utterance to their transports !

" But what lights are those, Mateo, which I see twinkling along the Sierra Nevada, just below the snowy region, and which might be taken for stars, only that they are ruddy, and against the dark side of the mountain ?"

" Those, Señor, are fires, made by the men who gather snow and ice for the supply of Granada. They go up every afternoon with mules and asses, and take turns, some to rest and warm themselves by the fires, while others fill the panniers with ice. They then set off down the mountains, so as to reach the gates of Granada before sunrise. That Sierra Nevada, Señor, is a lump of ice in the middle of Andalusia, to keep it all cool in summer."

It was now completely dark ; we were passing through the barranco, where stood the cross of the murdered muleteer ; when I beheld a number of lights moving at a distance, and apparently advancing up the ravine. On nearer approach, they proved to be torches borne by a train of uncouth figures arrayed in black : it would have been a procession dreary enough at any time, but was peculiarly so in this wild and solitary place.

Mateo drew near, and told me, in a low voice, that it was a funeral train bearing a corpse to the burying-ground among the hills.

As the procession passed by, the lugubrious light of the torches, falling on the rugged features and funeral-weeds of the attendants, had the most fantastic effect, but was perfectly ghastly, as it revealed the countenance of the corpse, which, according to the Spanish custom, was borne uncovered on an open bier. I remained for some time gazing after the dreary train as it wound up the dark defile of the mountain. It put me in mind of the old story of a procession of demons bearing the body of a sinner up the crater of Stromboli.

"Ah! Señor," cried Mateo, "I could tell you a story of a procession once seen among these mountains, but then you'd laugh at me, and say it was one of the legacies of my grandfather the tailor."

"By no means, Mateo. There is nothing I relish more than a marvellous tale."

"Well, Señor, it is about one of those very men we have been talking of, who gather snow on the Sierra Nevada.

"You must know, that a great many years since, in my grandfather's time, there was an old fellow, Tio Nicolo (Uncle Nicholas) by name, who had filled the panniers of his mule with snow and ice, and was returning down the mountain. Being very drowsy, he mounted upon the mule, and soon falling asleep, went with his head nodding and bobbing about from side to side, while his surefooted old mule stepped along the edge of precipices, and down steep and broken barrancos, just as safe and steady as if it had been on plain ground. At length, Tio Nicolo awoke, and gazed about him, and rubbed his eyes—and, in good truth, he had reason. The moon shone almost as bright as day, and he saw the city below him, as plain as your hand, and shining with its white buildings, like a silver platter in the moonshine; but, Lord! Señor, it was nothing like the city he had left a few hours before! Instead of the cathedral, with its great dome and turrets, and the churches with their spires, and the convents with their pinnacles, all surmounted with the blessed cross, he saw nothing but Moorish mosques, and minarets, and cupolas, all topped off with glittering crescents, such as you see on the Barbary flags. Well, Señor, as you may suppose, Tio Nicolo was mightily puzzled at all this, but while he was gazing down upon the city, a great army came marching up the mountains, winding along the ravines, sometimes in the moonshine, sometimes in the shade. As it drew nigh, he saw that there were horse and foot all in Moorish armor. Tio Nicolo tried to scramble out of their way, but his old mule stood stock still, and refused to budge, trembling, at the same time, like a leaf—for dumb beasts, Señor, are just as much frightened at such things as human beings. Well, Señor, the hobgoblin army came marching by; there were men that seemed to blow trumpets, and others to beat drums and strike cymbals, yet never a sound did they make; they all moved on without the least noise, just as I have seen painted armies move across the stage in the theatre of Granada, and all looked as pale as death. At last, in the rear of the army, between two black Moorish horsemen, rode the Grand Inquisitor of Granada, on a mule as white as snow. Tio Nicolo wondered to see him in such company, for the Inquisitor was famous for his hatred of Moors, and indeed, of all kinds of Infidels, Jews, and Heretics, and used to hunt them out with fire and scourge. However, Tio Nicolo felt himself safe, now that there was a priest of such sanctity at hand. So making the sign of the cross, he called out for his benediction, when, hombre! he received a blow that sent him and his old mule over the edge of a steep bank, down which they rolled, head over heels, to the bottom! Tio Nicolo did not come to his senses until long after sunrise, when he found himself at the bottom of a deep ravine, his mule grazing beside him, and his panniers of snow completely melted. He crawled back to Granada sorely bruised and battered, but was glad to find the city looking as usual, with Christian churches and crosses. When he told the story of his night's adventure, every one laughed at him; some said he had dreamed it all, as he dozed on his mule; others thought it all a fabrication of his own—but what was strange, Señor, and made people afterwards think more seriously of the matter, was, that the Grand Inquisitor died within the year. I have often heard my grandfather, the tailor, say that there was more meant by that hobgoblin army bearing off the resemblance of the priest, than folks dared to surmise."

" Then you would insinuate, friend Mateo, that there is a kind of Moorish limbo, or purgatory, in the bowels of these mountains, to which the padre Inquisitor was borne off."

" God forbid, Señor! I know nothing of the matter. I only relate what I heard from my grandfather."

By the time Mateo had finished the tale which I have more succinctly related, and which was interlarded with many comments, and spun out with minute details, we reached the gate of the Alhambra.

The marvellous stories hinted at by Mateo, in the early part of our ramble about the Tower of the Seven Floors, set me as usual upon my goblin researches. I found that the redoubtable phantom, the Belludo, had been time out of mind a favorite theme of nursery tales and popular traditions in Granada, and that honorable mention had even been made of it by an ancient historian and topographer of the place. The scattered members of one of these popular traditions I have gathered together, collated them with infinite pains, and digested them into the following legend; which only wants a number of learned notes and references at bottom to take its rank among those concrete productions gravely passed upon the world for Historical Facts.

LEGEND OF THE MOOR'S LEGACY.

JUST within the fortress of the Alhambra, in front of the royal palace, is a broad open esplanade, called the Place or Square of the Cisterns, (la Plaza de los Algibes,) so called from being undermined by reservoirs of water, hidden from sight, and which have existed from the time of the Moors. At one corner of this esplanade is a Moorish well, cut through the living rock to a great depth, the water of which is cold as ice and clear as crystal. The wells made by the Moors are always in repute, for it is well known what pains they took to penetrate to the purest and sweetest springs and fountains. The one of which we now speak is famous throughout Granada, insomuch that water-carriers, some bearing great water-jars on their shoulders, others driving asses before them laden with earthen vessels, are ascending and descending the steep woody avenues of the Alhambra, from early dawn until a late hour of the night.

Fountains and wells, ever since the scriptural days, have been noted gossiping places in hot climates; and at the well in question there is a kind of perpetual club kept up during the livelong day, by the invalids, old women, and other curious donothing folk of the fortress, who sit here on the stone benches, under an awning spread over the well to shelter the toll-gatherer from the sun, and dawdle over the gossip of the fortress, and question every water-carrier that arrives about the news of the city, and make long comments on every thing they hear and see. Not an hour of the day but loitering housewives and idle maid-servants may be seen, lingering with pitcher on head or in hand, to hear the last of the endless tattle of these worthies.

Among the water-carriers who once resorted to this well, there was a sturdy, strong-backed, bandy-legged little fellow, named Pedro Gil, but called Peregil for shortness. Being a water-carrier, he was a Gallego, or native of Gallicia, of course. Nature seems to have formed races of men, as she has of animals, for different kinds of drudgery. In France the shoeblacks are all Savoyards, the porters of hotels all Swiss, and in the days of hoops and hair-powder in England, no man could give the regular swing to a sedan-chair but a bog-trotting Irishman. So in Spain, the carriers of water and bearers of burdens are all sturdy little natives of Gallicia. No man says, " Get me a porter," but, " Call a Gallego."

To return from this digression, Peregil the Gallego had begun business with merely a great earthen jar which he carried upon his shoulder; by degrees he rose in the world, and was enabled to purchase an assistant of a correspondent class of animals, being a stout shaggy-haired donkey. On each side of this his long-eared aid-de-camp, in a kind of pannier, were slung his water-jars, covered with fig-leaves to protect them from the sun. There was not a more industrious water-carrier in all Granada, nor one more merry withal. The streets rang with his cheerful voice as he trudged after his donkey, singing forth the usual summer note that resounds through the Spanish towns : " *Quien quiere agua—agua mas fria que la nieve ?*" — " Who wants water—water colder than snow ? Who wants water from the

well of the Alhambra, cold as ice and clear as crystal?" When
he served a customer with a sparkling glass, it was always with
a pleasant word that caused a smile; and if, perchance, it was a
comely dame or dimpling damsel, it was always with a sly leer
and a compliment to her beauty that was irresistible. Thus
Peregil the Gallego was noted throughout all Granada for being
one of the civilest, pleasantest, and happiest of mortals. Yet it is
not he who sings loudest and jokes most that has the lightest
heart. Under all this air of merriment, honest Peregil had his
cares and troubles. He had a large family of ragged children to
support, who were hungry and clamorous as a nest of young
swallows, and beset him with their outcries for food whenever he
came home of an evening. He had a helpmate, too, who was
any thing but a help to him. She had been a village beauty
before marriage, noted for her skill at dancing the bolero and
rattling the castanets; and she still retained her early propen-
sities, spending the hard earnings of honest Peregil in frippery,
and laying the very donkey under requisition for junketing
parties into the country on Sundays, and saints' days, and those
innumerable holidays which are rather more numerous in Spain
than the days of the week. With all this she was a little of a
slattern something more of a lie-abed, and, above all, a gossip
of the first water; neglecting house, household, and every thing
else, to loiter slipshod in the houses of her gossip neighbors.

He, however, who tempers the wind to the shorn lamb, ac-
commodates the yoke of matrimony to the submissive neck.
Peregil bore all the heavy dispensations of wife and children with
as meek a spirit as his donkey bore the water-jars; and, however
he might shake his ears in private, never ventured to question
the household virtues of his slattern spouse.

11*

He loved his children too even as an owl loves its owlets, seeing in them his own image multiplied and perpetuated; for they were a sturdy, long-backed, bandy-legged little brood. The great pleasure of honest Peregil was, whenever he could afford himself a scanty holiday, and had a handful of marevedis to spare, to take the whole litter forth with him, some in his arms, some tugging at his skirts, and some trudging at his heels, and to treat them to a gambol among the orchards of the Vega, while his wife was dancing with her holiday friends in the Angosturas of the Darro.

It was a late hour one summer night, and most of the water-carriers had desisted from their toils. The day had been uncommonly sultry; the night was one of those delicious moon-lights, which tempt the inhabitants of southern climes to indemnify themselves for the heat and inaction of the day, by lingering in the open air, and enjoying its tempered sweetness until after midnight. Customers for water were therefore still abroad. Peregil, like a considerate, painstaking father, thought of his hungry children. " One more journey to the well," said he to himself, " to earn a Sunday's puchero for the little ones." So saying, he trudged manfully up the steep avenue of the Al-hambra, singing as he went, and now and then bestowing a hearty thwack with a cudgel on the flanks of his donkey, either by way of cadence to the song, or refreshment to the animal; for dry blows serve in lieu of provender in Spain for all beasts of burden.

When arrived at the well, he found it deserted by every one except a solitary stranger in Moorish garb, seated on a stone bench in the moonlight. Peregil paused at first and regarded him with surprise, not unmixed with awe, but the Moor feebly beckoned him to approach. "I am faint and ill," said he, "aid me to return to the city, and I will pay thee double what thou couldst gain by thy jars of water."

The honest heart of the litle water-carrier was touched with compassion at the appeal of the stranger. "God forbid," said he, "that I should ask fee or reward for doing a common act of humanity." He accordingly helped the Moor on his donkey, and set off slowly for Granada, the poor Moslem being so weak that it was necessary to hold him on the animal to keep him from falling to the earth.

When they entered the city, the water-carrier demanded whither he should conduct him. "Alas!" said the Moor, faintly, "I have neither home nor habitation, I am a stranger in the land. Suffer me to lay my head this night beneath thy roof, and thou shalt be amply repaid."

Honest Peregil thus saw himself unexpectedly saddled with an infidel guest, but he was too humane to refuse a night's shelter to a fellow being in so forlorn a plight, so he conducted the Moor to his dwelling. The children, who had sallied forth open-mouthed as usual on hearing the tramp of the donkey, ran back with affright, when they beheld the turbaned stranger, and hid themselves behind their mother. The latter stepped forth intrepidly, like a ruffling hen before her brood when a vagrant dog approaches.

"What infidel companion," cried she, "is this you have brought home at this late hour, to draw upon us the eyes of the inquisition?"

"Be quiet, wife," replied the Gallego, "here is a poor sick stranger, without friend or home; wouldst thou turn him forth to perish in the streets?"

The wife would still have remonstrated, for although she lived in a hovel she was a furious stickler for the credit of her house; the little water-carrier, however, for once was stiffnecked, and refused to bend beneath the yoke. He assisted the poor Moslem to alight, and spread a mat and a sheep-skin for him, on the ground, in the coolest part of the house; being the only kind of bed that his poverty afforded.

In a little while the Moor was seized with violent convulsions, whice defied all the minstering skill of the simple water-carrier. The eye of the poor patient acknowledged his kindness. During an interval of his fits he called him to his side, and addressing him in a low voice, " My end," said he, " I fear is at hand. If I die, I bequeath you this box as a reward for your charity :" so saying, he opened his albornoz, or cloak, and showed a small box of sandal-wood, strapped round his body. " God grant, my friend," replied the worthy little Gallego, " that you may live many years to enjoy your treasure, whatever it may be." The Moor shook his head; he laid his hand upon the box, and would have said something more concerning it, but his convulsions returned with increasing violence, and in a little while he expired.

The water-carrier's wife was now as one distracted. " This comes," said she, " of your foolish good nature, always running into scrapes to oblige others. What will become of us when this corpse is found in our house? We shall be sent to prison as murderers; and if we escape with our lives, shall be ruined by notaries and alguazils."

Poor Peregil was in equal tribulation, and almost repented himself of having done a good deed. At length a thought struck him. " It is not yet day," said he; " I can convey the dead

body out of the city, and bury it in the sands on the banks of
the Xenil. No one saw the Moor enter our dwelling, and no one
will know any thing of his death."

So said, so done. The wife aided him; they rolled the body
of the unfortunate Moslem in the mat on which he had expired,
laid it across the ass, and Peregil set out with it for the banks
of the river.

As ill luck would have it, there lived opposite to the water-
carrier a barber named Pedrillo Pedrugo, one of the most prying, tattling, and mischief-making of his gossip tribe. He was a
weasel-faced, spider-legged varlet, supple and insinuating; the
famous barber of Seville could not surpass him for his universal
knowledge of the affairs of others, and he had no more power of
retention than a sieve. It was said that he slept but with one
eye at a time, and kept one ear uncovered, so that, even in his
sleep, he might see and hear all that was going on. Certain it is,
he was a sort of scandalous chronicle for the quid-nuncs of Granada, and had more customers than all the rest of his fraternity.

This meddlesome barber heard Peregil arrive at an unusual
hour at night, and the exclamations of his wife and children.
His head was instantly popped out of a little window which
served him as a look-out, and he saw his neighbor assist a man
in Moorish garb into his dwelling. This was so strange an occurrence, that Pedrillo Pedrugo slept not a wink that night.
Every five minutes he was at his loophole, watching the lights
that gleamed through the chinks of his neighbor's door, and before daylight he beheld Peregil sally forth with his donkey unusually laden.

The inquisitive barber was in a fidget; he slipped on his
clothes, and, stealing forth silently, followed the water-carrier at

a distance, until he saw him dig a hole in the sandy bank of the Xenil, and bury something that had the appearance of a dead body.

The barber hied him home, and fidgeted about his shop, setting every thing upside down, until sunrise. He then took a basin under his arm, and sallied forth to the house of his daily customer the alcalde.

The alcalde was just risen. Pedrillo Pedrugo seated him in a chair, threw a napkin round his neck, put a basin of hot water under his chin, and began to mollify his beard with his fingers.

" Strange doings!" said Pedrugo, who played barber and newsmonger at the same time—" Strange doings! Robbery, and murder, and burial all in one night!"

" Hey!—how!—what is that you say?" cried the alcalde.

" I say," replied the barber, rubbing a piece of soap over the nose and mouth of the dignitary, for a Spanish barber disdains to employ a brush—" I say that Peregil the Gallego has robbed and murdered a Moorish Mussulman, and buried him, this blessed night. *Maldita sea la noche*—accursed be the night for the same!"

" But how do you know all this?" demanded the alcalde.

" Be patient, Señor, and you shall hear all about it," replied Pedrillo, taking him by the nose and sliding a razor over his cheek. He then recounted all that he had seen, going through both operations at the same time, shaving his beard, washing his chin, and wiping him dry with a dirty napkin, while he was robbing, murdering, and burying the Moslem.

Now it so happened that this alcalde was one of the most overbearing, and at the same time most griping and corrupt curmudgeons in all Granada. It could not be denied, however, that he set a high value upon justice, for he sold it at its weight in gold. He presumed the case in point to be one of murder and robbery; doubtless there must be a rich spoil; how was it to be secured into the legitimate hands of the law? for as to merely entrapping the delinquent—that would be feeding the gallows; but entrapping the booty—that would be enriching the judge, and such, according to his creed, was the great end of justice. So thinking, he summoned to his presence his trustiest alguazil —a gaunt, hungry-looking varlet, clad, according to the custom of his order, in the ancient Spanish garb, a broad black beaver turned up at its sides; a quaint ruff; a small black cloak dangling from his shoulders; rusty black under-clothes that set off his spare wiry frame, while in his hand he bore a slender white wand, the dreaded insignia of his office. Such was the legal bloodhound of the ancient Spanish breed, that he put upon the traces of the unlucky water-carrier, and such was his speed and certainty, that he was upon the haunches of poor Peregil before he had returned to his dwelling, and brought both him and his donkey before the dispenser of justice.

The alcalde bent upon him one of the most terrific frowns. "Hark ye, culprit!" roared he, in a voice that made the knees of the little Gallego smite together—"hark ye, culprit! there is no need of denying thy guilt, every thing is known to me. A gallows is the proper reward for the crime thou hast committed, but I am merciful, and readily listen to reason. The man that has been murdered in thy house was a Moor, an infidel, the enemy of our faith. It was doubtless in a fit of religious zeal that thou hast slain him. I will be indulgent, therefore; render up the property of which thou hast robbed him, and we will hush the matter up."

The poor water-carrier called upon all the saints to witness his innocence ; alas! not one of them appeared ; and if they had, the alcalde would have disbelieved the whole calendar. The water-carrier related the whole story of the dying Moor with the straightforward simplicity of truth, but it was all in vain. " Wilt thou persist in saying," demanded the judge, " that this Moslem had neither gold nor jewels, which were the object of thy cupidity ?"

" As I hope to be saved, your worship," replied the water-carrier, " he had nothing but a small box of sandal-wood which he bequeathed to me in reward for my services."

" A box of sandal-wood ! a box of sandal-wood !" exclaimed the alcalde, his eyes sparkling at the idea of precious jewels. " And where is this box ? where have you concealed it ?"

" An' it please your grace," replied the water-carrier, " it is in one of the panniers of my mule, and heartily at the service of your worship."

He had hardly spoken the words, when the keen alguazil darted off, and reappeared in an instant with the mysterious box of sandal-wood. The alcalde opened it with an eager and trembling hand ; all pressed forward to gaze upon the treasure it was expected to contain ; when, to their disappointment, nothing appeared within, but a parchment scroll, covered with Arabic characters, and an end of a waxen taper.

When there is nothing to be gained by the conviction of a prisoner, justice, even in Spain, is apt to be impartial. The alcalde, having recovered from his disappointment, and found that there was really no booty in the case, now listened dispassionately to the explanation of the water-carrier, which was corroborated by the testimony of his wife. Being convinced, therefore, of his innocence, he discharged him from arrest ; nay more,

he permitted him to carry off the Moor's legacy, the box of sandal-wood and its contents, as the well-merited reward of his
humanity; but he retained his donkey in payment of costs and
charges.

Behold the unfortunate little Gallego reduced once more to
the necessity of being his own water-carrier, and trudging up to
the well of the Alhambra with a great earthen jar upon his
shoulder.

As he toiled up the hill in the heat of a summer noon, his
usual good humor forsook him. "Dog of an alcalde!" would
he cry, "to rob a poor man of the means of his subsistence, of
the best friend he had in the world!" And then at the remembrance of the beloved companion of his labors, all the kindness
of his nature would break forth. "Ah, donkey of my heart!"
would he exclaim, resting his burden on a stone, and wiping the
sweat from his brow—"Ah, donkey of my heart! I warrant me
thou thinkest of thy old master! I warrant me thou missest the
water-jars—poor beast."

To add to his afflictions, his wife received him, on his return home, with whimperings and repinings; she had clearly
the vantage-ground of him, having warned him not to commit the
egregious act of hospitality which had brought on him all these
misfortunes; and, like a knowing woman, she took every occasion to throw her superior sagacity in his teeth. If her children
lacked food, or needed a new garment, she could answer with a
sneer—"Go to your father—he is heir to king Chico of the Alhambra: ask him to help you out of the Moor's strong box."

Was ever poor mortal so soundly punished for having done
a good action? The unlucky Peregil was grieved in flesh and
spirit, but still he bore meekly with the railings of his spouse.

At length, one evening, when, after a hot day's toil, she taunted him in the usual manner, he lost all patience. He did not venture to retort upon her, but his eye rested upon the box of sandal-wood, which lay on a shelf with lid half open, as if laughing in mockery at his vexation. Seizing it up, he dashed it with indignation to the floor: " Unlucky was the day that I ever set eyes on thee," he cried, " or sheltered thy master beneath my roof !"

As the box struck the floor, the lid flew wide open, and the parchment scroll rolled forth.

Peregil sat regarding the scroll for some time in moody silence. At length rallying his ideas : " Who knows," thought he, " but this writing may be of some importance, as the Moor seems to have guarded it with such care ?" Picking it up therefore, he put it in his bosom, and the next morning, as he was crying water through the streets, he stopped at the shop of a Moor, a native of Tangiers, who sold trinkets and perfumery in the Zacatin, and asked him to explain the contents.

The Moor read the scroll attentively, then stroked his beard and smiled. " This manuscript," said he, " is a form of incantation for the recovery of hidden treasure, that is under the power of enchantment. It is said to have such virtue, that the strongest bolts and bars, nay the adamantine rock itself, will yield before it !"

" Bah !" cried the little Gallego, " what is all that to me ? I am no enchanter, and know nothing of buried treasure." So saying, he shouldered his water-jar, left the scroll in the hands of the Moor, and trudged forward on his daily rounds.

That evening, however, as he rested himself about twilight at the well of the Alhambra, he found a number of gossips assembled at the place, and their conversation, as is not unusual at that shadowy hour, turned upon old tales and traditions of a supernatural nature. Being all poor as rats, they dwelt with peculiar fondness upon the popular theme of enchanted riches left by the Moors in various parts of the Alhambra. Above all, they concurred in the belief that there were great treasures buried deep in the earth under the tower of the seven floors.

These stories made an unusual impression on the mind of the honest Peregil, and they sank deeper and deeper into his thoughts as he returned alone down the darkling avenues. " If. after all, there should be treasure hid beneath that tower: and if the scroll I left with the Moor should enable me to get at it !" In the sudden ecstasy of the thought he had well nigh let fall his water-jar.

That night he tumbled and tossed, and could scarcely get a wink of sleep for the thoughts that were bewildering his brain. Bright and early, he repaired to the shop of the Moor, and told him all that was passing in his mind. " You can read Arabic," said he; " suppose we go together to the tower, and try the effect of the charm; if it fails we are no worse off than before; but if it succeeds, we will share equally all the treasure we may discover."

" Hold," replied the Moslem ; " this writing is not sufficient of itself; it must be read at midnight, by the light of a taper singularly compounded and prepared, the ingredients of which are not within my reach. Without such a taper the scroll is of no avail."

" Say no more !" cried the little Gallego ; " I have such a taper at hand, and will bring it here in a moment." So saying he hastened home, and soon returned with the end of yellow wax taper that he had found in the box of sandal-wood.

The Moor felt it and smelt to it. " Here are rare and costly perfumes," said he, " combined with this yellow wax. This is the kind of taper specified in the scroll. While this burns, the strongest walls and most secret caverns will remain open. Woe to him, however, who lingers within until it be extinguished. He will remain enchanted with the treasure."

It was now agreed between them to try the charm that very night. At a late hour, therefore, when nothing was stirring but bats and owls, they ascended the woody hill of the Alhambra, and approached that awful tower, shrouded by trees and rendered formidable by so many traditionary tales. By the light of a lantern, they groped their way through bushes, and over fallen stones, to the door of a vault beneath the tower. With fear and trembling they descended a flight of steps cut into the rock. It led to an empty chamber damp and drear, from which another flight of steps led to a deeper vault. In this way they descended four several flights, leading into as many vaults one below the other, but the floor of the fourth was solid; and though, according to tradition, there remained three vaults still below, it was said to be impossible to penetrate further, the residue being shut up by strong enchantment. The air of this vault was damp and chilly, and had an earthy smell, and the light scarce cast forth any rays. They paused here for a time in breathless suspense, until they faintly heard the clock of the watchtower strike midnight; upon this they lit the waxen taper, which diffused an odor of myrrh and frankincense and storax.

The Moor began to read in a hurried voice. He had scarce finished when there was a noise as of subterraneous thunder. The earth shook, and the floor, yawning open, disclosed a flight of steps. Trembling with awe they descended, and by the light

of the lantern found themselves in another vault, covered with Arabic inscriptions. In the centre stood a great chest, secured with seven bands of steel, at each end of which sat an enchanted Moor in armor, but motionless as a statue, being controlled by the power of the incantation. Before the chest were several jars filled with gold and silver and precious stones. In the largest of these they thrust their arms up to the elbow, and at every dip hauled forth handfuls of broad yellow pieces of Moorish gold, or bracelets and ornaments of the same precious metal, while occasionally a necklace of oriental pearl would stick to their fingers. Still they trembled and breathed short while cramming their pockets with the spoils ; and cast many a fearful glance at the two enchanted Moors, who sat grim and motionless, glaring upon them with unwinking eyes. At length, struck with a sudden panic at some fancied noise, they both rushed up the staircase, tumbled over one another into the upper apartment, overturned and extinguished the waxen taper, and the pavement again closed with a thundering sound.

Filled with dismay, they did not pause until they had groped their way out of the tower, and beheld the stars shining through the trees. Then seating themselves upon the grass, they divided the spoil, determining to content themselves for the present with this mere skimming of the jars, but to return on some future night and drain them to the bottom. To make sure of each other's good faith, also, they divided the talismans between them, one retaining the scroll and the other the taper; this done, they set off with light hearts and well-lined pockets for Granada

As they wended their way down the hill, the shrewd Moor whispered a word of counsel in the ear of the simple little water-carrier.

"Friend Peregil," said he, "all this affair must be kept a pro-found secret until we have secured the treasure, and conveyed it out of harm's way. If a whisper of it gets to the ear of the alcalde, we are undone!"

"Certainly," replied the Gallego, "nothing can be more true."

"Friend Peregil," said the Moor, "you are a discreet man, and I make no doubt can keep a secret: but you have a wife.'

"She shall not know a word of it," replied the little water-carrier, sturdily.

"Enough," said the Moor, "I depend upon thy discretion and thy promise."

Never was promise more positive and sincere; but, alas! what man can keep a secret from his wife? Certainly not such a one as Peregil the water-carrier, who was one of the most loving and tractable of husbands. On his return home, he found his wife moping in a corner. "Mighty well," cried she as he entered, "you've come at last; after rambling about until this hour of the night. I wonder you have not brought home another Moor as a house-mate." Then bursting into tears, she began to wring her hands and smite her breast: "Unhappy woman that I am!" ex-claimed she, "what will become of me? My house stripped and plundered by lawyers and alguazils; my husband a do-no-good, that no longer brings home bread to his family, but goes ram-bling about day and night, with infidel Moors! O my children! my children! what will become of us? we shall all have to beg in the streets!"

Honest Peregil was so moved by the distress of his spouse, that he could not help whimpering also. His heart was as full as his pocket, and not to be restrained. Thrusting his hand into the latter he hauled forth three or four broad gold pieces, and slipped them into her bosom. The poor woman stared with astonishment, and could not understand the meaning of this golden shower. Before she could recover her surprise, the little Gallego drew forth a chain of gold and dangled it before her, capering with exultation, his mouth distended from ear to ear.

"Holy Virgin protect us!" exclaimed the wife. What hast thou been doing, Peregil? surely thou hast not been committing murder and robbery!"

The idea scarce entered the brain of the poor woman, than it became a certainty with her. She saw a prison and a gallows in the distance, and a little bandy-legged Gallego hanging pendant from it; and, overcome by the horrors conjured up by her imagination, fell into violent hysterics.

What could the poor man do? He had no other means of pacifying his wife, and dispelling the phantoms of her fancy, than by relating the whole story of his good fortune. This, however, he did not do until he had exacted from her the most solemn promise to keep it a profound secret from every living being.

To describe her joy would be impossible. She flung her arms round the neck of her husband, and almost strangled him with her caresses. "Now, wife," exclaimed the little man with honest exultation, "what say you now to the Moor's legacy? Henceforth never abuse me for helping a fellow-creature in distress."

The honest Gallego retired to his sheep-skin mat, and slept as soundly as if on a bed of down. Not so his wife; she emptied the whole contents of his pockets upon the mat, and sat counting gold pieces of Arabic coin, trying on necklaces and earrings, and fancying the figure she should one day make when permitted to enjoy her riches.

On the following morning the honest Gallego took a broad

golden coin, and repaired with it to a jeweller's shop in the Zacatin to offer it for sale, pretending to have found it among the ruins of the Alhambra. The jeweller saw that it had an Arabic inscription, and was of the purest gold; he offered, however, but a third of its value, with which the water-carrier was perfectly content. Peregil now bought new clothes for his little flock, and all kinds of toys, together with ample provisions for a hearty meal, and returning to his dwelling, sat all his children dancing around him, while he capered in the midst, the happiest of fathers.

The wife of the water-carrier kept her promise of secrecy with surprising strictness. For a whole day and a half she went about with a look of mystery and a heart swelling almost to bursting, yet she held her peace, though surrounded by her gossips. It is true, she could not help giving herself a few airs, apologized for her ragged dress, and talked of ordering a new basquina all trimmed with gold lace and bugles, and a new lace mantilla. She threw out hints of her husband's intention of leaving off his trade of water-carrying, as it did not altogether agree with his health. In fact she thought they should all retire to the country for the summer, that the children might have the benefit of the mountain air, for there was no living in the city in this sultry season.

The neighbors stared at each other, and thought the poor woman had lost her wits; and her airs and graces and elegant pretensions were the theme of universal scoffing and merriment among her friends, the moment her back was turned.

If she restrained herself abroad, however, she indemnified herself at home, and putting a string of rich oriental pearls round her neck, Moorish bracelets on her arms, and an aigrette of diamonds on her head, sailed backwards and forwards in her slattern rags about the room, now and then stopping to admire herself in a broken mirror. Nay, in the impulse of her simple vanity, she could not resist, on one occasion, showing herself at the window to enjoy the effect of her finery on the passers by.

As the fates would have it, Pedrillo Pedrugo, the meddle-some barber, was at this moment sitting idly in his shop on the opposite side of the street, when his ever-watchful eye caught the sparkle of a diamond. In an instant he was at his loophole re-connoitering the slattern spouse of the water-carrier, decorated with the splendor of an eastern bride. No sooner had he taken an accurate inventory of her ornaments, than he posted off with all speed to the alcalde. In a little while the hungry alguazil was again on the scent, and before the day was over the unfortunate Peregil was once more dragged into the presence of the judge.

"How is this, villain!" cried the alcalde, in a furious voice. "You told me that the infidel who died in your house left no-thing behind but an empty coffer, and now I hear of your wife flaunting in her rags decked out with pearls and diamonds. Wretch that thou art! prepare to render up the spoils of thy miserable victim, and to swing on the gallows that is already tired of waiting for thee."

The terrified water-carrier fell on his knees, and made a full relation of the marvellous manner in which he had gained his wealth. The alcalde, the alguazil, and the inquisitive barber, listened with greedy ears to this Arabian tale of enchanted treasure. The alguazil was dispatched to bring the Moor who had assisted in the incantation. The Moslem entered half frightened out of his wits at finding himself in the hands of the harpies of the law. When he beheld the water-carrier standing with sheep-

12

ish looks and downcast countenance, he comprehended the whole matter. " Miserable animal," said he, as he passed near him, " did I not warn thee against babbling to thy wife ?"

The story of the Moor coincided exactly with that of his colleague ; but the alcalde affected to be ..low of belief, and threw out menaces of imprisonment and rigorous investigation.

" Softly, good Señor Alcalde," said the Mussulman, who by this time had recovered his usual shrewdness and self-possession. " Let us not mar fortune's favors in the scramble for them. Nobody knows any thing of this matter but ourselves ; let us keep the secret. There is wealth enough in the cave to enrich us all. Promise a fair division, and all shall be produced ; refuse, and the cave shall remain for ever closed."

The alcalde consulted apart with the alguazil. The latter was an old fox in his profession. " Promise any thing," said he, " until you get possession of the treasure. You may then seize upon the whole, and if he and his accomplice dare to murmur, threaten them with the fagot and the stake as infidels and sorcerers."

The alcalde relished the advice. Smoothing his brow and turning to the Moor, " This is a strange story," said he, " and may be true, but I must have ocular proof of it. This very night you must repeat the incantation in my presence. If there be really such treasure, we will share it amicably between us, and say nothing further of the matter ; if ye have deceived me, expect no mercy at my hands. In the mean time you must remain in custody."

The Moor and the water-carrier cheerfully agreed to these conditions, satisfied that the event would prove the truth of their words.

Towards midnight the alcalde sallied forth secretly, attended by the alguazil and the meddlesome barber, all strongly armed. They conducted the Moor and the water-carrier as prisoners, and were provided with the stout donkey of the latter to bear off the expected treasure. They arrived at the tower without being observed, and tying the donkey to a fig-tree, descended into the fourth vault of the tower

The scroll was produced, the yellow waxen taper lighted, and the Moor read the form of incantation. The earth trembled as before, and the pavement opened with a thundering sound, disclosing the narrow flight of steps. The alcalde, the alguazil, and the barber were struck aghast, and could not summon courage to descend. The Moor and the water-carrier entered the lower vault, and found the two Moors seated as before, silent and motionless. They removed two of the great jars, filled with golden coin and precious stones. The water-carrier bore them up one by one upon his shoulders, but though a strong-backed little man, and accustomed to carry burdens, he staggered beneath their weight, and found, when slung on each side of his donkey, they were as much as the animal could bear.

"Let us be content for the present," said the Moor; "here is as much treasure as we can carry off without being perceived, and enough to make us all wealthy to our heart's desire."

"Is there more treasure remaining behind?" demanded the alcalde.

"The greatest prize of all," said the Moor, "a huge coffer bound with bands of steel, and filled with pearls and precious stones."

"Let us have up the coffer by all means," cried the grasping alcalde.

" I will descend for no more," said the Moor, doggedly ;
" enough is enough for a reasonable man—more is superfluous."

" And I," said the water-carrier, " will bring up no further
burden to break the back of my poor donkey."

Finding commands, threats and entreaties equally vain, the
alcalde turned to his two adherents. " Aid me," said he, " to
bring up the coffer, and its contents shall be divided between us."
So saying he descended the steps, followed with trembling reluc-
tance by the alguazil and the barber.

No sooner did the Moor behold them fairly earthed than he
extinguished the yellow taper ; the pavement closed with its
usual crash, and the three worthies remained buried in its
womb.

He then hastened up the different flights of steps, nor stop
ped until in the open air.   The little water-carrier followed him
as fast as his short legs would permit.

" What hast thou done ?" cried Peregil, as soon as he could
recover breath. " The alcalde and the other two are shut up in
the vault."

" It is the will of Allah !" said the Moor devoutly.

" And will you not release them ?" demanded the Gallego.

" Allah forbid !" replied the Moor, smoothing his beard. " It
is written in the book of fate that they shall remain enchanted
until some future adventurer arrive to break the charm.   The
will of God be done !" so saying, he hurled the end of the waxen
taper far among the gloomy thickets of the glen.

There was now no remedy, so the Moor and the water-carrier
proceeded with the richly laden donkey toward the city, nor
could honest Peregil refrain from hugging and kissing his long-
eared fellow-laborer, thus restored to him from the clutches of

the law ; and in fact, it is doubtful which gave the simple heart-
ed little man most joy at the moment, the gaining of the treasure,
or the recovery of the donkey.

The two partners in good luck divided their spoil amicably
and fairly, except that the Moor, who had a little taste for trin-
ketry, made out to get into his heap the most of the pearls and
precious stones and other baubles, but then he always gave the
water-carrier in lieu magnificent jewels of massy gold, of five
times the size, with which the latter was heartily content. They
took care not to linger within reach of accidents, but made off
to enjoy their wealth undisturbed in other countries. The Moor
returned to Africa, to his native city of Tangiers, and the Gallego,
with his wife, his children, and his donkey, made the best of his
way to Portugal. Here, under the admonition and tuition of his
wife, he became a personage of some consequence, for she made
the worthy little man array his long body and short legs in
doublet and hose, with a feather in his hat and a sword by his
side, and laying aside his familiar appellation of Peregil, assume
the more sonorous title of Don Pedro Gil: his progeny grew up
a thriving and merry-hearted, though short and bandy-legged
generation, while Señora Gil, befringed, belaced, and betasselled
from her head to her heels, with glittering rings on every finger,
became a model of slattern fashion and finery.

As to the alcalde and his adjuncts, they remained shut up under the great tower of the seven floors, and there they remain
spell-bound at the present day. Whenever there shall be a lack
in Spain of pimping barbers, sharking alguazils, and corrupt
alcaldes, they may be sought after ; but if they have to wait until
such time for their deliverance there is danger of their enchantment enduring until doomsday.

THE TOWER OF LAS INFANTAS.

In an evening's stroll up a narrow glen, overshadowed by fig trees, pomegranates, and myrtles, which divides the lands of the fortress from those of the Generalife, I was struck with the romantic appearance of a Moorish tower in the outer wall of the Alhambra, rising high above the tree-tops, and catching the ruddy rays of the setting sun. A solitary window at a great height commanded a view of the glen; and as I was regarding it, a young female looked out, with her head adorned with flowers. She was evidently superior to the usual class of people inhabiting the old towers of the fortress; and this sudden and picturesque glimpse of her reminded me of the descriptions of captive beauties in fairy tales. These fanciful associations were increased on being informed by my attendant Mateo, that this was the Tower of the Princesses (La Torre de las Infantas); so called, from having been, according to tradition, the residence of the daughters of the Moorish kings. I have since visited the tower. It is not generally shown to strangers, though well worthy attention, for the interior is equal, for beauty of architecture, and delicacy of ornament, to any part of the palace. The elegance of the central hall, with its marble fountain, its lofty arches, and richly fretted dome; the arabesques and stucco-work of the small but well-proportioned chambers, though injured by time and neglect, all accord with the story of its being anciently the abode of royal beauty.

The little old fairy queen who lives under the staircase of the Alhambra, and frequents the evening tertulias of Dame Antonia, tells some fanciful traditions about three Moorish princesses, who were once shut up in this tower by their father, a tyrant king of Granada, and were only permitted to ride out at night about the hills, when no one was permitted to come in their way under pain of death. They still, according to her account, may be seen occasionally when the moon is in the full, riding in lonely places along the mountain side, on palfreys richly caparisoned and sparkling with jewels, but they vanish on being spoken to.

But before I relate any thing further respecting these princesses, the reader may be anxious to know something about the fair inhabitant of the tower with her head dressed with flowers, who looked out from the lofty window. She proved to be the newly-married spouse of the worthy adjutant of invalids; who, though well stricken in years, had had the courage to take to his bosom a young and buxom Andalusian damsel. May the good old cavalier be happy in his choice, and find the Tower of the Princesses a more secure residence for female beauty than it seems to have proved in the time of the Moslems, if we may believe the following legend!

LEGEND OF THE THREE BEAUTIFUL PRINCESSES.

In old times there reigned a Moorish king in Granada, whose name was Mohamed, to which his subjects added the appellation of El Hayzari, or "The Left-handed." Some say he was so called on account of his being really more expert with his sinister than his dexter hand; others, because he was prone to take every thing by the wrong end; or in other words, to mar wherever he meddled. Certain it is, either through misfortune or mismanagement, he was continually in trouble: thrice was he driven from his throne, and, on one occasion, barely escaped to Africa with his life, in the disguise of a fisherman.* Still he was as brave as he was blundering; and though left-handed, wielded his cimeter to such purpose, that he each time re-established himself upon his throne by dint of hard fighting. Instead, however, of learning wisdom from adversity, he hardened his neck, and stiffened his left arm in wilfulness. The evils of a public nature which he thus brought upon himself and his kingdom may be learned by those who will delve into the Arabian annals of Granada; the present legend deals but with his domestic policy.

As this Mohamed was one day riding forth with a train of

* The reader will recognize the sovereign connected with the fortunes of the Abencerrages. His story appears to be a little fictionized in the legend.

his courtiers, by the foot of the mountain of Elvira, he met a band of horsemen returning from a foray into the land of the Christians. They were conducting a long string of mules laden with spoil, and many captives of both sexes, among whom the monarch was struck with the appearance of a beautiful damsel, richly attired, who sat weeping on a low palfrey, and heeded not the consoling words of a duenna who rode beside her.

The monarch was struck with her beauty, and, on inquiring of the captain of the troop, found that she was the daughter of the alcayde of a frontier fortress, that had been surprised and sacked in the course of the foray. Mohamed claimed her as his royal share of the booty, and had her conveyed to his harem in the Alhambra. There every thing was devised to soothe her melancholy ; and the monarch, more and more enamored, sought to make her his queen. The Spanish maid at first repulsed his addresses—he was an infidel—he was the open foe of her country —what was worse, he was stricken in years !

The monarch, finding his assiduities of no avail, determined to enlist in his favor the duenna, who had been captured with the lady. She was an Andalusian by birth, whose Christian name is forgotten, being mentioned in Moorish legends by no other appellation than that of the discreet Kadiga—and discreet in truth she was, as her whole history makes evident. No sooner had the Moorish king held a little private conversation with her, than she saw at once the cogency of his reasoning, and undertook his cause with her young mistress.

"Go to, now !" cried she ; "what is there in all this to weep and wail about ? Is it not better to be mistress of this beautiful palace, with all its gardens and fountains, than to be shut up within your father's old frontier tower ? As to this Mohamed

being an infidel, what is that to the purpose? You marry him,
not his religion: and if he is waxing a little old, the sooner will
you be a widow, and mistress of yourself; at any rate, you are in
his power, and must either be a queen or a slave. When in the
hands of a robber, it is better to sell one's merchandise for a fair
price, than to have it taken by main force."

The arguments of the discreet Kadiga prevailed. The Spanish lady dried her tears, and became the spouse of Mohamed the
Left-handed; she even conformed, in appearance, to the faith of
her royal husband; and her discreet duenna immediately became
a zealous convert to the Moslem doctrines: it was then the latter
received the Arabian name of Kadiga, and was permitted to remain in the confidential employ of her mistress.

In due process of time the Moorish king was made the proud
and happy father of three lovely daughters, all born at a birth:
he could have wished they had been sons, but consoled himself
with the idea that three daughters at a birth were pretty well for
a man somewhat stricken in years, and left-handed!

As usual with all Moslem monarchs, he summoned his astrologers on this happy event. They cast the nativities of the three
princesses, and shook their heads. "Daughters, O king!" said
they, "are always precarious property; but these will most need
your watchfulness when they arrive at a marriageable age; at
that time gather them under your wings, and trust them to no
other guardianship."

Mohamed the Left-handed was acknowledged to be a wise
king by his courtiers, and was certainly so considered by himself.
The prediction of the astrologers caused him but little disquiet,
trusting to his ingenuity to guard his daughters and outwit the
Fates.

The three-fold birth was the last matrimonial trophy of the monarch; his queen bore him no more children, and died within a few years, bequeathing her infant daughters to his love, and to the fidelity of the discreet Kadiga.

Many years had yet to elapse before the princesses would arrive at that period of danger—the marriageable age : " It is good, however, to be cautious in time," said the shrewd monarch; so he determined to have them reared in the royal castle of Salobreña. This was a sumptuous palace, incrusted, as it were, in a powerful Moorish fortress on the summit of a hill overlooking the Mediterranean sea. It was a royal retreat, in which the Moslem monarchs shut up such of their relatives, as might endanger their safety; allowing them all kinds of luxuries and amusements, in the midst of which they passed their lives in voluptuous indolence.

Here the princesses remained, immured from the world, but surrounded by enjoyment, and attended by female slaves who anticipated their wishes. They had delightful gardens for their recreation, filled with the rarest fruits and flowers, with aromatic groves and perfumed baths. On three sides the castle looked down upon a rich valley, enamelled with all kinds of culture, and bounded by the lofted Alpuxarra mountains; on the other side it overlooked the broad sunny sea.

In this delicious abode, in a propitious climate, and under a cloudless sky, the three princesses grew up into wondrous beauty; but, though all reared alike, they gave early tokens of diversity of character. Their names were Zayda, Zorayda, and Zorahayda; and such was their order of seniority, for there had been precisely three minutes between their births.

Zayda, the eldest, was of an intrepid spirit, and took the lead of her sisters in every thing, as she had done in entering into the

11

world.   She was curious and inquisitive, and fond of getting at
the bottom of things.

Zorayda had a great feeling for beauty, which was the reason,
no doubt, of her delighting to regard her own image in a mirror
or a fountain, and of her fondness for flowers, and jewels, and
other tasteful ornaments.

As to Zorahayda, the youngest, she was soft and timid, and
extremely sensitive, with a vast deal of disposable tenderness, as
was evident from her number of pet-flowers, and pet-birds, and
pet-animals, all of which she cherished with the fondest care.   Her
amusements, too, were of a gentle nature, and mixed up with
musing and reverie.   She would sit for hours in a balcony, gazing
on the sparkling stars of a summer's night; or on the sea when
lit up by the moon; and at such times, the song of a fisherman,
faintly heard from the beach, or the notes of a Moorish flute from
some gliding bark, sufficed to elevate her feelings into ecstasy.
The least uproar of the elements, however, filled her with dismay;
and a clap of thunder was enough to throw her into a swoon.

Years rolled on smoothly and serenely; the discreet Kadiga,
to whom the princesses were confided, was faithful to her trust,
and attended them with unremitting care.

The castle of Salobreña, as has been said, was built upon a
hill on the sea-coast.   One of the exterior walls straggled down
the profile of the hill, until it reached a jutting rock overhanging
the sea, with a narrow sandy beach at its foot, laved by the rip
pling billows.   A small watchtower on this rock had been fitted
up as a pavilion, with latticed windows to admit the sea-breeze.
Here the princesses used to pass the sultry hours of mid-day.

The curious Zayda was one day seated at a window of the
pavilion, as her sisters, reclining on ottomans, were taking the

siesta or noontide slumber. Her attention was attracted to a galley which came coasting along, with measured strokes of the oar. As it drew near, she observed that it was filled with armed men. The galley anchored at the foot of the tower: a number of Moorish soldiers landed on the narrow beach, conducting several Christian prisoners. The curious Zayda awakened her sisters, and all three peeped cautiously through the close jalousies of the lattice which screened them from sight. Among the prisoners were three Spanish cavaliers, richly dressed. They were in the flower of youth, and of noble presence; and the lofty manner in which they carried themselves, though loaded with chains and surrounded with enemies, bespoke the grandeur of their souls. The princesses gazed with intense and breathless interest. Cooped up as they had been in this castle among female attendants, seeing nothing of the male sex but black slaves, or the rude fishermen of the sea-coast, it is not to be wondered at that the appearance of three gallant cavaliers, in the pride of youth and manly beauty, should produce some commotion in their bosom.

"Did ever nobler being tread the earth than that cavalier in crimson?" cried Zayda, the eldest of the sisters. "See how proudly he bears himself, as though all around him were his slaves!"

"But notice that one in green!" exclaimed Zorayda. "What grace! what elegance! what spirit!"

The gentle Zorahayda said nothing, but she secretly gave preference to the cavalier in blue.

The princesses remained gazing until the prisoners were out of sight; then heaving long-drawn sighs, they turned round, looked at each other for a moment, and sat down, musing and pensive, on their ottomans.

The discreet Kadiga found them in this situation; they related what they had seen, and even the withered heart of the duenna was warmed. "Poor youths!" exclaimed she, "I'll warrant their captivity makes many a fair and high-born lady's heart ache in their native land! Ah! my children, you have little idea of the life these cavaliers lead in their own country. Such prankling at tournaments! such devotion to the ladies! such courting and serenading!"

The curiosity of Zayda was fully aroused; she was insatiable in her inquiries, and drew from the duenna the most animated pictures of the scenes of her youthful days and native land. The beautiful Zorayda bridled up, and slyly regarded herself in a mirror, when the theme turned upon the charms of the Spanish ladies; while Zorahayda suppressed a struggling sigh at the mention of moonlight serenades.

Every day the curious Zayda renewed her inquiries, and every day the sage duenna repeated her stories, which were listened to with profound interest, though with frequent sighs, by her gentle auditors. The discreet old woman awoke at length to the mischief she might be doing. She had been accustomed to think of the princesses only as children; but they had imperceptibly ripened beneath her eye, and now bloomed before her three lovely damsels of the marriageable age. It is time, thought the duenna, to give notice to the king.

Mohamed the Left-handed was seated one morning on a divan in a cool hall of the Alhambra, when a slave arrived from the fortress of Salobreña, with a message from the sage Kadiga, congratulating him on the anniversary of his daughters' birth-day. The slave at the same time presented a delicate little basket decorated with flowers, within which, on a couch of vine and fig-leaves, lay a peach, an apricot, and a nectarine, with their bloom and down and dewy sweetness upon them, and all in the early stage of tempting ripeness. The monarch was versed in the Oriental language of fruits and flowers, and rapidly divined the meaning of this emblematical offering.

" So," said he, " the critical period pointed out by the astrologers is arrived : my daughters are at a marriageable age. What is to be done? They are shut up from the eyes of men ; they are under the eyes of the discreet Kadiga—all very good,—but still they are not under my own eye, as was prescribed by the astrologers : I must gather them under my wing, and trust to no other guardianship."

So saying, he ordered that a tower of the Alhambra should be prepared for their reception, and departed at the head of his guards for the fortress of Salobreña, to conduct them home in person.

About three years had elapsed since Mohamed had beheld his daughters, and he could scarcely credit his eyes at the wonderful change which that small space of time had made in their appearance. During the interval, they had passed that wondrous boundary line in female life which separates the crude, unformed, and thoughtless girl from the blooming, blushing, meditative woman. It is like passing from the flat, bleak, uninteresting plains of La Mancha to the voluptuous valleys and swelling hills of Andalusia.

Zayda was tall and finely formed, with a lofty demeanor and a penetrating eye. She entered with a stately and decided step, and made a profound reverence to Mohamed, treating him more as her sovereign than her father. Zorayda was of the middle height, with an alluring look and swimming gait, and a sparkling beauty, heightened by the assistance of the toilette. She approached her father with a smile, kissed his hand, and saluted him with several stanzas from a popular Arabian poet with which the monarch was delighted. Zorahayda was shy and timid, smaller than her sisters, and with a beauty of that tender beseeching kind which looks for fondness and protection. She was little fitted to command, like her elder sister, or to dazzle like the second, but was rather formed to creep to the bosom of manly affection, to nestle within it, and be content. She drew near to her father, with a timid and almost faltering step, and would have taken his hand to kiss, but on looking up into his face, and seeing it beaming with a paternal smile, the tenderness of her nature broke forth, and she threw herself upon his neck.

Mohamed the Left-handed surveyed his blooming daughters with mingled pride and perplexity; for while he exulted in their charms, he bethought himself of the prediction of the astrologers. " Three daughters ! three daughters !" muttered he repeatedly to himself, " and all of a marriageable age ! Here's tempting Hesperian fruit, that requires a dragon watch !"

He prepared for his return to Granada, by sending heralds before him, commanding every one to keep out of the road by which he was to pass, and that all doors and windows should be closed at the approach of the princesses. This done, he set forth, escorted by a troop of black horsemen of hideous aspect, and clad in shining armor.

The princesses rode beside the king, closely veiled, on beautiful white palfreys, with velvet caparisons, embroidered with gold, and sweeping the ground; the bits and stirrups were of gold, and the silken bridles adorned with pearls and precious stones. The palfreys were covered with little silver bells, which made the most musical tinkling as they ambled gently along. Wo to the unlucky wight, however, who lingered in the way when he heard the tinkling of these bells!—the guards were ordered to cut him down without mercy.

The cavalcade was drawing near to Granada, when it overtook on the banks of the river Xenil, a small body of Moorish soldiers with a convoy of prisoners. It was too late for the soldiers to get out of the way, so·they threw themselves on their faces on the earth, ordering their captives to do the like. Among the prisoners were the three identical cavaliers whom the princesses had seen from the pavilion. They either did not understand, or were too haughty to obey the order, and remained standing and gazing upon the cavalcade as it approached.

The ire of the monarch was kindled at this flagrant defiance of his orders. Drawing his cimeter, and pressing forward, he was about to deal a left-handed blow that might have been fatal to, at least, one of the gazers, when the princesses crowded round him, and implored mercy for the prisoners; even the timid Zorahayda forgot her shyness, and became eloquent in their behalf. Mohamed paused, with uplifted cimeter, when the captain of the guard threw himself at his feet. " Let not your highness," said he, " do a deed that may cause great scandal throughout the kingdom. These are three brave and noble Spanish knights, who have been taken in battle, fighting like lions ; they are of high birth, and may bring great ransoms."—" Enough !" said the king. " I will spare their lives, but punish their audacity—let them be taken to the Vermilion Towers, and put to hard labor."

Mohamed was making one of his usual left-handed blunders. In the tumult and agitation of this blustering scene, the veils of the three princesses had been thrown back, and the radiance of their beauty revealed; and in prolonging the parley, the king had given that beauty time to have its full effect. In those days people fell in love much more suddenly than at present, as all ancient stories make manifest: it is not a matter of wonder, therefore, that the hearts of the three cavaliers were completely captured; especially as gratitude was added to their admiration: it is a little singular, however, though no less certain, that each of them was enraptured with a several beauty. As to the princesses, they were more than ever struck with the noble demeanor of the captives, and cherished in their breasts all that they had heard of their valor and noble lineage.

The cavalcade resumed its march; the three princesses rode pensively along on their tinkling palfreys, now and then stealing a glance behind in search of the Christian captives, and the latter were conducted to their alloted prison in the Vermilion Towers.

The residence provided for the princesses was one of the most dainty that fancy could devise. It was in a tower somewhat apart from the main palace of the Alhambra, though connected with it by the wall which encircled the whole summit of the hill. On one side it looked into the interior of the fortress, and had, at its foot, a small garden filled with the rarest flowers. On the other side it overlooked a deep embowered ravine separating the grounds of the Alhambra from those of the Generalife. The interior of the tower was divided into small fairy apartments, beautifully ornamented in the light Arabian style, surrounding a lofty hall, the vaulted roof of which rose almost to the summit of the tower. The walls and the ceilings of the hall were adorned with arabesque and fretwork, sparkling with gold and with brilliant pencilling. In the centre of the marble pavement was an alabaster fountain, set round with aromatic shrubs and flowers, and throwing up a jet of water that cooled the whole edifice and had a lulling sound. Round the hall were suspended cages of gold and silver wire, containing singing-birds of the finest plumage or sweetest note.

The princesses had been represented as always cheerful when in the castle of the Salobreña; the king had expected to see them enraptured with the Alhambra. To his surprise, however, they began to pine, and grow melancholy, and dissatisfied with every thing around them. The flowers yielded them no fragrance, the song of the nightingale disturbed their night's rest, and they were out of all patience with the alabaster fountain with its eternal drop-drop and splash-splash, from morning till night, and from night till morning.

The king, who was somewhat of a testy, tyrannical disposition, took this at first in high dudgeon; but he reflected that his daughters had arrived at an age when the female mind expands and its desires augment. "They are no longer children," said he to himself, "they are women grown, and require suitable objects to interest them." He put in requisition, therefore, all the dress-makers, and the jewellers, and the artificers in gold and silver throughout the Zacatin of Granada, and the princesses were overwhelmed with robes of silk, and tissue, and brocade, and cashmere shawls, and necklaces of pearls and diamonds, and rings, and bracelets, and anklets, and all manner of precious things.

All, however, was of no avail; the princesses continued pale and languid in the midst of their finery, and looked like three blighted rose-buds, drooping from one stalk. The king was at his wits' end. He had in general a laudable confidence in his own judgment, and never took advice. "The whims and caprices of three marriageable damsels, however, are sufficient," said he, "to puzzle the shrewdest head." So for once in his life he called in the aid of counsel.

The person to whom he applied was the experienced duenna.

"Kadiga," said the king, "I know you to be one of the most discreet women in the whole world, as well as one of the most trustworthy; for these reasons I have always continued you about the persons of my daughters. Fathers cannot be too wary in whom they repose such confidence; I now wish you to find out the secret malady that is preying upon the princesses, and to devise some means of restoring them to health and cheerfulness"

Kadiga promised implicit obedience. In fact she knew more of the malady of the princesses than they did themselves. Shutting herself up with them, however, she endeavored to insinuate herself into their confidence.

"My dear children, what is the reason you are so dismal and downcast in so beautiful a place, where you have every thing that heart can wish?"

The princesses looked vacantly round the apartment, and sighed.

"What more, then, would you have? Shall I get you the wonderful parrot that talks all languages, and is the delight of Granada?"

"Odious!" exclaimed the princess Zayda. "A horrid, screaming bird, that chatters words without ideas: one must be without brains to tolerate such a pest."

"Shall I send for a monkey from the rock of Gibraltar, to divert you with his antics?"

"A monkey! faugh!" cried Zorayda; "the detestable mimic of man. I hate the nauseous animal."

"What say you to the famous black singer Casem, from the royal harem, in Morocco? They say he has a voice as fine as a woman's."

"I am terrified at the sight of these black slaves," said the delicate Zorahayda; "besides, I have lost all relish for music."

"Ah! my child, you would not say so," replied the old woman, slyly, "had you heard the music I heard last evening, from the three Spanish cavaliers, whom we met on our journey. But, bless me, children! what is the matter that you blush so, and are in such a flutter?"

"Nothing, nothing, good mother; pray proceed."

"Well; as I was passing by the Vermilion Towers last evening, I saw the three cavaliers resting after their day's labor. One was playing on the guitar, so gracefully, and the others sang by turns; and they did it in such style, that the very guards seemed like statues, or men enchanted. Allah forgive me! I could not help being moved at hearing the songs of my native country. And then to see three such noble and handsome youths in chains and slavery!"

Here the kind-hearted old woman could not restrain her tears.

"Perhaps, mother, you could manage to procure us a sight of these cavaliers," said Zayda.

"I think," said Zorayda, "a little music would be quite reviving."

The timid Zorahayda said nothing, but threw her arms round the neck of Kadiga.

"Mercy on me!" exclaimed the discreet old woman; "what are you talking of, my children? Your father would be the death of us all if he heard of such a thing. To be sure, these cavaliers are evidently well-bred, and high-minded youths; but what of that? they are the enemies of our faith, and you must not even think of them but with abhorrence."

There is an admirable intrepidity in the female will, particu larly when about the marriageable age, which is not to be deter red by dangers and prohibitions. The princesses hung round their old duenna, and coaxed, and entreated, and declared that a refusal would break their hearts.

What could she do? She was certainly the most discreet old woman in the whole world, and one of the most faithful servants to the king; but was she to see three beautiful princesses break their hearts for the mere tinkling of a guitar? Besides, though she had been so long among the Moors, and changed her faith in imitation of her mistress, like a trusty follower, yet she was a Spaniard born, and had the lingerings of Christianity in her heart. So she set about to contrive how the wish of the prin cesses might be gratified.

The Christian captives, confined in the Vermilion Towers, were under the charge of a big-whiskered, broad-shouldered renegado, called Hussein Baba, who was reputed to have a most itching palm. She went to him privately, and slipping a broad piece of gold into his hand, "Hussein Baba," said she; "my mistresses, the three princesses, who are shut up in the tower, and in sad want of amusement, have heard of the musical talents of the three Spanish cavaliers, and are desirous of hearing a specimen of their skill. I am sure you are too kind-hearted to refuse them so innocent a gratification."

"What! and to have my head set grinning over the gate of my own tower! for that would be the reward, if the king should discover it."

"No danger of any thing of the kind; the affair may be managed so that the whim of the princesses may be gratified, and their father be never the wiser. You know the deep ravine outside of the walls which passes immediately below the tower. Put the three Christians to work there, and at the intervals of their labor, let them play and sing, as if for their own recreation. In this way the princesses will be able to hear them from the windows of the tower, and you may be sure of their paying well for your compliance."

As the good old woman concluded her harangue, she kindly pressed the rough hand of the renegado, and left within it another piece of gold.

Her eloquence was irresistible. The very next day the three cavaliers were put to work in the ravine. During the noontide heat, when their fellow-laborers were sleeping in the shade, and the guard nodding drowsily at his post, they seated themselves among the herbage at the foot of the tower, and sang a Spanish roundelay to the accompaniment of the guitar.

The glen was deep, the tower was high, but their voices rose distinctly in the stillness of the summer noon. The princesses listened from their balcony, they had been taught the Spanish language by their duenna, and were moved by the tenderness of the song. The discreet Kadiga, on the contrary, was terribly shocked. "Allah preserve us!" cried she, "they are singing a love-ditty, addressed to yourselves. Did ever mortal hear of such audacity? I will run to the slave-master, and have them soundly bastinadoed."

"What! bastinado such gallant cavaliers, and for singing so charmingly!" The three beautiful princesses were filled with horror at the idea. With all her virtuous indignation, the good

old woman was of a placable nature, and easily appeased.
Besides, the music seemed to have a beneficial effect upon her
young mistresses. A rosy bloom had already come to their
cheeks, and their eyes began to sparkle. She made no further
objection, therefore, to the amorous ditty of the cavaliers.

When it was finished, the princesses remained silent for a
time; at length Zorayda took up a lute, and with a sweet, though
faint and trembling voice, warbled a little Arabian air, the burden
of which was, " The rose is concealed among her leaves, but she
listens with delight to the song of the nightingale."

From this time forward the cavaliers worked almost daily in
the ravine. The considerate Hussein Baba became more and
more indulgent, and daily more prone to sleep at his post. For
some time a vague intercourse was kept up by popular songs and
romances, which, in some measure, responded to each other, and
breathed the feelings of the parties. By degrees the princesses
showed themselves at the balcony, when they could do so without
being perceived by the guards. They conversed with the cavaliers
also, by means of flowers, with the symbolical language of which
they were mutually acquainted : the difficulties of their intercourse added to its charms, and strengthened the passion they
had so singularly conceived; for love delights to struggle with
difficulties, and thrives the most hardily on the scantiest soil.

The change effected in the looks and spirits of the princesses
by this secret intercourse, surprised and gratified the Left-handed
king; but no one was more elated than the discreet Kadiga,
who considered it all owing to her able management.

At length there was an interruption in this telegraphic correspondence : for several days the cavaliers ceased to make their
appearance in the glen. The princesses looked out from the

tower in vain. In vain they stretched their swan-like necks from the balcony; in vain they sang like captive nightingales in their cage : nothing was to be seen of their Christian lovers; not a note responded from the groves. The discreet Kadiga sallied forth in quest of intelligence, and soon returned with a face full of trouble. " Ah, my children !" cried she, " I saw what all this would come to, but you would have your way ; you may now hang up your lutes on the willows. The Spanish cavaliers are ransomed by their families ; they are down in Granada, and preparing to return to their native country."

The three beautiful princesses were in despair at the tidings. Zayda was indignant at the slight put upon them, in thus being deserted without a parting word. Zorayda wrung her hands and cried, and looked in the glass, and wiped away her tears, and cried afresh. The gentle Zorahayda leaned over the balcony and wept in silence, and her tears fell drop by drop among the flowers of the bank where the faithless cavaliers had so often been seated.

The discreet Kadiga did all in her power to soothe their sorrow " Take comfort, my children," said she, " this is nothing when you are used to it. This is the way of the world. Ah! when you are as old as I am, you will know how to value these men. I'll warrant these cavaliers have their loves among the Spanish beauties of Cordova and Seville, and will soon be serenading under their balconies, and thinking no more of the Moorish beauties in the Alhambra. Take comfort, therefore, my children, and drive them from your hearts."

The comforting words of the discreet Kadiga only redoubled the distress of the three princesses, and for two days they con-

13

tinued inconsolable. On the morniug of the third, the good old woman entered their apartment, all ruffling with indignation.

"Who would have believed such insolence in mortal man!" exclaimed she, as soon as she could find words to express herself; "but I am rightly served for having connived at this deception of your worthy father. Never talk more to me of your Spanish cavaliers."

"Why, what has happened, good Kadiga?" exclaimed the princesses in breathless anxiety.

"What has happened?—treason has happened! or what is almost as bad, treason has been proposed; and to me, the most faithful of subjects, the trustiest of duennas! Yes, my children, the Spanish cavaliers have dared to tamper with me, that I should persuade you to fly with them to Cordova, and become their wives!"

Here the excellent old woman covered her face with her hands, and gave way to a violent burst of grief and indignation. The three beautiful princesses turned pale and red, pale and red, and trembled, and looked down, and cast shy looks at each other, but said nothing. Meantime, the old woman sat rocking backward and forward in violent agitation, and now and then breaking out into exclamations, "That ever I should live to be so insulted!—I, the most faithful of servants!"

At length, the eldest princess, who had most spirit and always took the lead, approached her, and laying her hand upon her shoulder, "Well, mother," said she, " supposing we were willing to fly with these Christian cavaliers—is such a thing possible?"

The good old woman paused suddenly in her grief, and looking up, "Possible," echoed she; "to be sure, it is possible. Have not the cavaliers already bribed Hussein Baba, the renegado captain of the guard, and arranged the whole plan? But, then, to think of deceiving your father! your father, who has placed such confidence in me!" Here the worthy woman gave way to a fresh burst of grief, and began again to rock backward and forward, and to wring her hands.

"But our father has never placed any confidence in us," said the eldest princess, "but has trusted to bolts and bars, and treated us as captives."

"Why, that is true enough," replied the old woman, again pausing in her grief; he has indeed treated you most unreasonably, keeping you shut up here, to waste your bloom in a moping old tower, like roses left to wither in a flower-jar. But, then, to fly from your native land!"

"And is not the land we fly to, the native land of our mother, where we shall live in freedom? And shall we not each have a youthful husband in exchange for a severe old father?"

"Why, that again is all very true; and your father, I must confess, is rather tyrannical: but what then," relapsing into her grief, "would you leave me behind to bear the brunt of his vengeance?"

"By no means, my good Kadiga; cannot you fly with us?"

"Very true, my child; and, to tell the truth, when I talked the matter over with Hussein Baba, he promised to take care of me, if I would accompany you in your flight: but then, bethink you, my children, are you willing to renounce the faith of your father?"

"The Christian faith was the original faith of our mother," said the eldest princess; "I am ready to embrace it, and so, I am sure, are my sisters."

"Right again," exclaimed the old woman, brightening up;

" it was the original faith of your mother, and bitterly did she lament, on her death-bed, that she had renounced it. I promised her then to take care of your souls, and I rejoice to see that they are now in a fair way to be saved. Yes, my children, I, too, was born a Christian, and have remained a Christian in my heart, and am resolved to return to the faith. I have talked on the subject with Hussein Baba, who is a Spaniard by birth, and comes from a place not far from my native town. He is equally anxious to see his own country, and to be reconciled to the church; and the cavaliers have promised, that, if we are disposed to become man and wife, on returning to our native land, they will provide for us handsomely."

In a word, it appeared that this extremely discreet and provident old woman had consulted with the cavaliers and the renegado, and had concerted the whole plan of escape. The eldest princess immediately assented to it; and her example, as usual, determined the conduct of her sisters. It is true, the youngest hesitated, for she was gentle and timid of soul, and there was a struggle in her bosom between filial feeling and youthful passion: the latter, however, as usual, gained the victory, and with silent tears, and stifled sighs, she prepared herself for flight.

The rugged hill, on which the Alhambra is built, was, in old times, perforated with subterranean passages, cut through the rock, and leading from the fortress to various parts of the city, and to distant sally-ports on the banks of the Darro and the Xenil. They had been constructed at different times by the Moorish kings, as means of escape from sudden insurrections, or of secretly issuing forth on private enterprises. Many of them are now entirely lost, while others remain, partly choked with rubbish, and partly walled up; monuments of the jealous precautions and warlike stratagems of the Moorish government. By one of these passages, Hussein Baba had undertaken to conduct the princesses to a sally-port beyond the walls of the city, where the cavaliers were to be ready with fleet steeds, to bear the whole party over the borders.

The appointed night arrived: the tower of the princesses had been locked up as usual, and the Alhambra was buried in deep sleep. Towards midnight, the discreet Kadiga listened from the balcony of a window that looked into the garden. Hussein Baba, the renegado, was already below, and gave the appointed signal. The duenna fastened the end of a ladder of ropes to the balcony, lowered it into the garden and descended. The two eldest princesses followed her with beating hearts; but when it came to the turn of the youngest princess, Zorahayda, she hesitated, and trembled. Several times she ventured a delicate little foot upon the ladder, and as often drew it back, while her poor little heart fluttered more and more the longer she delayed. She cast a wistful look back into the silken chamber; she had lived in it, to be sure, like a bird in a cage; but within it she was secure; who could tell what dangers might beset her, should she flutter forth into the wide world! Now she bethought her of her gallant Christian lover, and her little foot was instantly upon the ladder; and anon she thought of her father, and shrank back. But fruitless is the attempt to describe the conflict in the bosom of one so young and tender and loving; but so timid, and so ignorant of the world.

In vain her sisters implored, the duenna scolded, and the renegado blasphemed beneath the balcony; the gentle little Moorish maid stood doubting and wavering on the verge of elopement; tempted by the sweetness of the sin, but terrified at its perils

Every moment increased the danger of discovery.   A distant tramp was heard.   " The patrols are walking their rounds," cried the renegado; " if we linger, we perish.   Princess, descend instantly, or we leave you."

Zorahayda was for a moment in fearful agitation; then loosening the ladder of ropes, with desperate resolution, she flung it from the balcony.

" It is decided !" cried she; " flight is now out of my power ! Allah guide and bless ye, my dear sisters !"

The two eldest princesses were shocked at the thoughts of leaving her behind, and would fain have lingered, but the patrol was advancing; the renegado was furious, and they were hurried away to the subterraneous passage.   They groped their way through a fearful labyrinth, cut through the heart of the mountain, and succeeded in reaching, undiscovered, an iron gate that opened outside of the walls.   The Spanish cavaliers were waiting to receive them, disguised as Moorish soldiers of the guard, commanded by the renegado.

The lover of Zorahayda was frantic, when he learned that she had refused to leave the tower; but there was no time to waste in lamentations.   The two princesses were placed behind their lovers, the discreet Kadiga mounted behind the renegado, and they all set off at a round pace in the direction of the Pass of Lope, which leads through the mountains towards Cordova.

They had not proceeded far when they heard the noise of drums and trumpets from the battlements of the Alhambra.

" Our flight is discovered !" said the renegado.

" We have fleet steeds, the night is dark, and we may distance all pursuit," replied the cavaliers.

They put spurs to their horses, and scoured across the Vega

They attained the foot of the mountain of Elvira, which stretches like a promontory into the plain. The renegado paused and listened. "As yet," said he, "there is no one on our traces, we shall make good our escape to the mountains." While he spoke, a light blaze sprang up on the top of the watchtower of the Alhambra.

"Confusion!" cried the renegado, "that bale fire will put all the guards of the passes on the alert. Away! away! Spur like mad,—there is no time to be lost."

Away they dashed—the clattering of their horses' hoofs echoed from rock to rock, as they swept along the road that skirts the rocky mountain of Elvira. As they galloped on, the bale fire of the Alhambra was answered in every direction; light after light blazed on the Atalayas, or watchtowers of the mountains.

"Forward! forward!" cried the renegado, with many an oath, "to the bridge,—to the bridge, before the alarm has reached there!"

They doubled the promontory of the mountains, and arrived in sight of the famous Bridge of Pinos, that crosses a rushing stream often dyed with Christian and Moslem blood. To their confusion, the tower on the bridge blazed with lights and glittered with armed men. The renegado pulled up his steed, rose in his stirrups and looked about him for a moment; then beckoning to the cavaliers, he struck off from the road, skirted the river for some distance, and dashed into its waters. The cavaliers called upon the princesses to cling to them, and did the same. They were borne for some distance down the rapid current, the surges roared round them, but the beautiful princesses clung to their Christian knights, and never uttered a complaint. The cavaliers attained the opposite bank in safety, and were conducted by the renegado, by rude and unfrequented paths, and wild barrancos, through the heart of the mountains, so as to avoid all the regular passes. In a word, they succeeded in reaching the ancient city of Cordova; where their restoration to their country and friends was celebrated with great rejoicings, for they were of the noblest families. The beautiful princesses were forthwith received into the bosom of the Church, and, after being in all due form made regular Christians, were rendered happy wives.

In our hurry to make good the escape of the princesses across the river, and up the mountains, we forgot to mention the fate of the discreet Kadiga. She had clung like a cat to Hussein Baba in the scamper across the Vega, screaming at every bound, and drawing many an oath from the whiskered renegado ;. but when he prepared to plunge his steed into the river, her terror knew no bounds. "Grasp me not so tightly," cried Hussein Baba; "hold on by my belt and fear nothing." She held firmly with both hands by the leathern belt that girded the broad-backed renegado; but when he halted with the cavaliers to take breath on the mountain summit, the duenna was no longer to be seen.

"What has become of Kadiga?" cried the princesses in alarm.

"Allah alone knows!" replied the renegado; "my belt came loose when in the midst of the river, and Kadiga was swept with it down the stream. The will of Allah be done! but it was an embroidered belt, and of great price."

There was no time to waste in idle regrets; yet bitterly did the princesses bewail the loss of their discreet counsellor. That excellent old woman, however, did not lose more than half of her nine lives in the water : a fisherman, who was drawing his nets some distance down the stream, brought her to land, and was not a little astonished at his miraculous draught. What further became of the discreet Kadiga, the legend does not mention ; certain it is that she evinced her discretion in never venturing within the reach of Mohamed the Left-handed.

Almost as little is known of the conduct of that sagacious monarch when he discovered the escape of his daughters, and the deceit practised upon him by the most faithful of servants. It was the only instance in which he had called in the aid of counsel, and he was never afterwards known to be guilty of a similar weakness. He took good care, however, to guard his remaining daughter, who had no disposition to elope : it is thought, indeed, that she secretly repented having remained behind : now and then she was seen leaning on the battlements of the tower, and looking mournfully towards the mountains in the direction of Cordova, and sometimes the notes of her lute were heard accompanying plaintive ditties, in which she was said to lament the loss of her sisters and her lover, and to bewail her solitary life. She died young, and, according to popular rumor, was buried in a vault beneath the tower, and her untimely fate has given rise to more than one traditionary fable.

The following legend, which seems in some measure to spring out of the foregoing story, is too closely connected with high

13*

historic names to be entirely doubted. The Count's daughter,
and some of her young companions, to whom it was read in one
of the evening tertullias, thought certain parts of it had much
appearance of reality; and Dolores, who was much more versed
than they in the improbable truths of the Alhambra, believed
every word of it.

LEGEND OF THE ROSE OF THE ALHAMBRA.

For some time after the surrender of Granada by the Moors, that delightful city was a frequent and favorite residence of the Spanish sovereigns, until they were frightened away by successive shocks of earthquakes, which toppled down various houses, and made the old Moslem towers rock to their foundation.

Many, many years then rolled away, during which Granada was rarely honored by a royal guest. The palaces of the nobility remained silent and shut up; and the Alhambra, like a slighted beauty, sat in mournful desolation, among her neglected gardens. The tower of the Infantas, once the residence of the three beautiful Moorish princesses, partook of the general desolation; the spider spun her web athwart the gilded vault, and bats and owls nestled in those chambers that had been graced by the presence of Zayda, Zorayda, and Zorahayda. The neglect of this tower may partly have been owing to some superstitious notions of the neighbors. It was rumored that the spirit of the youthful Zorahayda, who had perished in that tower, was often seen by moonlight seated beside the fountain in the hall, or moaning about the battlements, and that the notes of her silver lute would be heard at midnight by wayfarers passing along the glen.

At length the city of Granada was once more welcomed by the royal presence. All the world knows that Philip V. was the first Bourbon that swayed the Spanish sceptre. All the world knows that he married, in second nuptials, Elizabetta or Isabella (for they are the same), the beautiful princess of Parma; and all the world knows that by this chain of contingencies a French prince and an Italian princess were seated together on the Spanish throne. For a visit of this illustrious pair, the Alhambra was repaired and fitted up with all possible expedition. The arrival of the court changed the whole aspect of the lately deserted palace. The clangor of drum and trumpet, the tramp of steed about the avenues and outer court, the glitter of arms and display of banners about barbican and battlement, recalled the ancient and warlike glories of the fortress. A softer spirit, however, reigned within the royal palace. There was the rustling of robes and the cautious tread and murmuring voice of reverential courtiers about the antechambers; a loitering of pages and maids of honor about the gardens, and the sound of music stealing from open casements.

Among those who attended in the train of the monarchs was a favorite page of the queen, named Ruyz de Alarcon. To say that he was a favorite page of the queen was at once to speak his eulogium, for every one in the suite of the stately Elizabetta was chosen for grace, and beauty, and accomplishments. He was just turned of eighteen, light and lithe of form, and graceful as a young Antinous. To the queen he was all deference and respect, yet he was at heart a roguish stripling, petted and spoiled by the ladies about the court, and experienced in the ways of women far beyond his years.

This loitering page was one morning rambling about the

groves of the Generalife, which overlook the grounds of the Alhambra. He had taken with him for his amusement a favorite
ger-falcon of the queen. In the course of his rambles, seeing a
bird rising from a thicket, he unhooded the hawk and let him
fly. The falcon towered high in the air, made a swoop at his
quarry, but missing it, soared away, regardless of the calls of the
page. The latter followed the truant bird with his eye, in its
capricious flight, until he saw it alight upon the battlements of
a remote and lonely tower, in the outer wall of the Alhambra,
built on the edge of a ravine that separated the royal fortress
from the grounds of the Generalife. It was in fact the " Tower
of the Princesses."

The page descended into the ravine and approached the tower,
but it had no entrance from the glen, and its lofty height rendered any attempt to scale it fruitless. Seeking one of the gates
of the fortress, therefore, he made a wide circuit to that side of
the tower facing within the walls.

A small garden, inclosed by a trellis-work of reeds overhung
with myrtle, lay before the tower. Opening a wicket, the page
passed between beds of flowers and thickets of roses to the door.
It was closed and bolted. A crevice in the door gave him a peep
into the interior. There was a small Moorish hall with fretted
walls, light marble columns, and an alabaster fountain surrounded with flowers. In the centre hung a gilt cage containing a
singing bird, beneath it, on a chair, lay a tortoise-shell cat among
reels of silk and other articles of female labor, and a guitar decorated with ribbons leaned against the fountain.

Ruyz de Alarcon was struck with these traces of female taste
and elegance in a lonely, and, as he had supposed, deserted tower.
They reminded him of the tales of enchanted halls current in the

Alhambra; and the tortoiseshell cat might be some spell-bound princess.

He knocked gently at the door. A beautiful face peeped out from a little window above, but was instantly withdrawn. He waited, expecting that the door would be opened, but he waited in vain ; no footstep was to be heard within—all was silent. Had his senses deceived him, or was this beautiful apparition the fairy of the tower ? He knocked again, and more loudly. After a little while the beaming face once more peeped forth ; it was that of a blooming damsel of fifteen.

The page immediately doffed his plumed bonnet, and entreated in the most courteous accents to be permitted to ascend the tower in pursuit of his falcon.

" I dare not open the door, Señor," replied the little damsel, blushing, " my aunt has forbidden it."

" I do beseech you, fair maid—it is the favorite falcon of the queen : I dare not return to the palace without it."

" Are you then one of the cavaliers of the court ?"

" I am, fair maid ; but I shall lose the queen's favor and my place, if I lose this hawk."

" Santa Maria ! It is against you cavaliers of the court my aunt has charged me especially to bar the door."

" Against wicked cavaliers doubtless, but I am none of these, but a simple harmless page, who will be ruined and undone if you deny me this small request."

The heart of the little damsel was touched by the distress of the page. It was a thousand pities he should be ruined for the want of so trifling a boon. Surely too he could not be one of those dangerous beings whom her aunt had described as a species of cannibal, ever on the prowl to make prey of thoughtless damsels ; he was gentle and modest, and stood so entreatingly with cap in hand, and looked so charming.

The sly page saw that the garrison began to waver, and re-doubled his entreaties in such moving terms that it was not in the nature of mortal maiden to deny him ; so the blushing little warden of the tower descended, and opened the door with a trembling hand, and if the page had been charmed by a mere glimpse of her countenance from the window, he was ravished by the full length portrait now revealed to him.

Her Andalusian bodice and trim basquiña set off the round but delicate symmetry of her form, which was as yet scarce verg-ing into womanhood. Her glossy hair was parted on her forehead with scrupulous exactness, and decorated with a fresh plucked rose, according to the universal custom of the country. It is true her complexion was tinged by the ardor of a southern sun, but it served to give richness to the mantling bloom of her cheek, and to heighten the lustre of her melting eyes.

Ruyz de Alarcon beheld all this with a single glance, for it became him not to tarry ; he merely murmured his acknowledg-ments, and then bounded lightly up the spiral staircase in quest of his falcon.

He soon returned with the truant bird upon his fist. The damsel, in the mean time, had seated herself by the fountain in the hall, and was winding silk ; but in her agitation she let fall the reel upon the pavement. The page sprang and picked it up, then dropping gracefully on one knee, presented it to her ; but, seizing the hand extended to receive it, imprinted on it a kiss more fervent and devout than he had ever imprinted on the fair hand of his sovereign.

"Ave Maria, Señor !" exclaimed the damsel, blushing still

deeper with confusion and surprise, for never before had she received such a salutation.

The modest page made a thousand apologies, assuring her it
was the way at court, of expressing the most profound homage
and respect

Her anger, if anger she felt, was easily pacified, but her agitation and embarrassment continued, and she sat blushing deeper
and deeper, with her eyes cast down upon her work, entangling
the silk which she attempted to wind.

The cunning page saw the confusion in the opposite camp, and
would fain have profited by it, but the fine speeches he would have
uttered died upon his lips ; his attempts at gallantry were awk-
ward and ineffectual; and to his surprise, the adroit page, who
had figured with such grace and effrontery among the most knowing and experienced ladies of the court, found himself awed and
abashed in the presence of a simple damsel of fifteen.

In fact, the artless maiden, in her own modesty and innocence,
had guardians more effectual than the bolts and bars prescribed
by her vigilant aunt. Still, where is the female bosom proof
against the first whisperings of love ? The little damsel, with all
her artlessness, instinctively comprehended all that the faltering
tongue of the page failed to express, and her heart was fluttered at
beholding, for the first time, a lover at her feet—and such a lover !

The diffidence of the page, though genuine, was short-lived,
and he was recovering his usual ease and confidence, when a shrill
voice was heard at a distance.

" My aunt is returning from mass !" cried the damsel in
affright: " I pray you, Señor, depart."

" Not until you grant me that rose from your hair as a remembrance."

She hastily untwisted the rose from her raven locks. "Take it," cried she, agitated and blushing, "but pray begone."

The page took the rose, and at the same time covered with kisses the fair hand that gave it. Then, placing the flower in his bonnet, and taking the falcon upon his fist, he bounded off through the garden, bearing away with him the heart of the gentle Jacinta

When the vigilant aunt arrived at the tower, she remarked the agitation of her niece, and an air of confusion in the hall; but a word of explanation sufficed. "A ger-falcon had pursued his prey into the hall."

"Mercy on us! to think of a falcon flying into the tower. Did ever one hear of so saucy a hawk? Why, the very bird in the cage is not safe!"

The vigilant Fredegonda was one of the most wary of ancient spinsters. She had a becoming terror and distrust of what she denominated "the opposite sex," which had gradually increased through a long life of celibacy. Not that the good lady had ever suffered from their wiles, nature having set up a safeguard in her face that forbade all trespass upon her premises; but ladies who have least cause to fear for themselves are most ready to keep a watch over their more tempting neighbors.

The niece was the orphan of an officer who had fallen in the wars. She had been educated in a convent, and had recently been transferred from her sacred asylum to the immediate guardianship of her aunt, under whose overshadowing care she vegetated in obscurity, like an opening rose blooming beneath a brier. Nor indeed is this comparison entirely accidental; for, to tell the truth, her fresh and dawning beauty had caught the public eye, even in her seclusion, and, with that poetical turn common to the people of Andalusia, the peasantry of the neighbor

hood had given her the appellation of " the Rose of the Alhambra."

The wary aunt continued to keep a faithful watch over her
tempting little niece as long as the court continued at Granada,
and flattered herself that her vigilance had been successful.   It
is true, the good lady was now and then discomposed by the
tinkling of guitars and chanting of love ditties from the moonlit
groves beneath the tower; but she would exhort her niece to shut
her ears against such idle minstrelsy, assuring her that it was one
of the arts of the opposite sex, by which simple maids were often
lured to their undoing.   Alas! what chance with a simple maid
has a dry lecture against a moonlight serenade?

At length king Philip cut short his sojourn at Granada, and
suddenly departed with all his train.   The vigilant Fredegonda
watched the royal pageant as it issued forth from the Gate of
Justice, and descended the great avenue leading to the city.
When the last banner disappeared from her sight, she returned
exulting to her tower, for all her cares were over.   To her surprise, a light Arabian steed pawed the ground at the wicket-gate
of the garden :—to her horror, she saw through the thickets of
roses a youth, in gayly-embroidered dress, at the feet of her
niece.   At the sound of her footsteps he gave a tender adieu,
bounded lightly over the barrier of reeds and myrtles, sprang
upon his horse, and was out of sight in an instant.

The tender Jacinta, in the agony of her grief, lost all thought
of her aunt's displeasure.   Throwing herself into her arms, she
broke forth into sobs and tears.

" Ay de mi !" cried she ; " he's gone !—he's gone!—he's gone !
and I shall never see him more !"

" Gone !—who is gone ?—what youth is that I saw at your
feet ?"

"A queen's page, aunt, who came to bid me farewell."

"A queen's page, child!" echoed the vigilant Fredegonda, faintly; "and when did you become acquainted with the queen's page?"

"The morning that the ger-falcon came into the tower. It was the queen's ger-falcon, and he came in pursuit of it."

"Ah silly, silly girl! know that there are no ger-falcons half so dangerous as these young prankling pages, and it is precisely such simple birds as thee that they pounce upon."

The aunt was at first indignant at learning that in despite of her boasted vigilance, a tender intercourse had been carried on by the youthful lovers, almost beneath her eye; but when she found that her simple-hearted niece, though thus exposed, without the protection of bolt or bar, to all the machinations of the opposite sex, had come forth unsinged from the fiery ordeal, she consoled herself with the persuasion that it was owing to the chaste and cautious maxims in which she had, as it were, steeped her to the very lips.

While the aunt laid this soothing unction to her pride, the niece treasured up the oft-repeated vows of fidelity of the page. But what is the love of restless, roving man? A vagrant stream that dallies for a time with each flower upon its bank, then passes on, and leaves them all in tears.

Days, weeks, months elapsed, and nothing more was heard of the page. The pomegranate ripened, the vine yielded up its fruit, the autumnal rains descended in torrents from the mountains; the Sierra Nevada became covered with a snowy mantle, and wintry blasts howled through the halls of the Alhambra—still he came not. The winter passed away. Again the genial spring burst forth with song and blossom and balmy zephyr; the snows melted from the mountains, until none remained but on the lofty summit of Nevada, glistening through the sultry summer air. Still nothing was heard of the forgetful page.

In the mean time, the poor little Jacinta grew pale and thoughtful. Her former occupations and amusements were abandoned, her silk lay entangled, her guitar unstrung, her flowers were neglected, the notes of her bird unheeded, and her eyes, once so bright, were dimmed with secret weeping. If any solitude could be devised to foster the passion of a love-lorn damsel, it would be such a place as the Alhambra, where every thing seems disposed to produce tender and romantic reveries. It is a very paradise for lovers: how hard then to be alone in such a paradise—and not merely alone, but forsaken !

" Alas, silly child !" would the staid and immaculate Frede-gonda say, when she found her niece in one of her desponding moods—" did I not warn thee against the wiles and deceptions of these men ? What couldst thou expect, too, from one of a haughty and aspiring family—thou an orphan, the descendant of a fallen and impoverished line ? Be assured, if the youth were true, his father, who is one of the proudest nobles about the court, would prohibit his union with one so humble and por tionless as thou. Pluck up thy resolution, therefore, and drive these idle notions from thy mind."

The words of the immaculate Fredegonda only served to in-crease the melancholy of her niece, but she sought to indulge it in private. At a late hour one midsummer night, after her aunt had retired to rest, she remained alone in the hall of the tower, seated beside the alabaster fountain. It was here that the faith-less page had first knelt and kissed her hand; it was here that he had often vowed eternal fidelity. The poor little damsel's heart was overladen with sad and tender recollections, her tears began to flow, and slowly fell drop by drop into the fountain. By degrees the crystal water became agitated, and—bubble—bubble —bubble—boiled up and was tossed about, until a female figure, richly clad in Moorish robes, slowly rose to view.

Jacinta was so frightened that she fled from the hall, and did not venture to return. The next morning she related what she had seen to her aunt, but the good lady treated it as a phantasy of her troubled mind, or supposed she had fallen asleep and dreamt beside the fountain. "Thou hast been thinking of the story of the three Moorish princesses that once inhabited this tower," continued she, "and it has entered into thy dreams."

"What story, aunt? I know nothing of it."

"Thou hast certainly heard of the three princesses, Zayda, Zorayda, and Zorahayda, who were confined in this tower by the king their father, and agreed to fly with three Christian cavaliers. The two first accomplished their escape, but the third failed in her resolution, and, it is said, died in this tower."

"I now recollect to have heard of it," said Jacinta, "and to have wept over the fate of the gentle Zorahayda."

"Thou mayest well weep over her fate," continued the aunt, "for the lover of Zorahayda was thy ancestor. He long bemoaned his Moorish love; but time cured him of his grief, and he married a Spanish lady, from whom thou art descended."

Jacinta ruminated upon these words. "That what I have seen is no phantasy of the brain," said she to herself, "I am confident. If indeed it be the spirit of the gentle Zorahayda, which I have heard lingers about this tower, of what should I be afraid? I'll watch by the fountain to-night—perhaps the visit will be repeated."

Towards midnight, when every thing was quiet, she again took her seat in the hall. As the bell in the distant watchtower of the Alhambra struck the midnight hour, the fountain was again agitated; and bubble—bubble—bubble—it tossed about the waters until the Moorish female again rose to view. She was young and beautiful; her dress was rich with jewels, and in her hand she held a silver lute. Jacinta trembled and was faint, but was reasured by the soft and plaintive voice of the apparition, and the sweet expression of her pale, melancholy countenance.

"Daughter of mortality," said she, "what aileth thee? Why do thy tears trouble my fountain, and thy sighs and plaints disturb the quiet watches of the night?"

"I weep because of the faithlessness of man, and I bemoan my solitary and forsaken state."

"Take comfort; thy sorrows may yet have an end. Thou beholdest a Moorish princess, who, like thee, was unhappy in her love. A Christian knight, thy ancestor, won my heart, and would have borne me to his native land and to the bosom of his church. I was a convert in my heart, but I lacked courage equal to my faith, and lingered till too late. For this the evil genii are permitted to have power over me, and I remain enchanted in this tower until some pure Christian will deign to break the magic spell. Wilt thou undertake the task?"

"I will," replied the damsel, trembling.

"Come hither then, and fear not; dip thy hand in the fountain, sprinkle the water over me, and baptize me after the manner of thy faith; so shall the enchantment be dispelled, and my troubled spirit have repose."

The damsel advanced with faltering steps, dipped her hand in the fountain, collected water in the palm, and sprinkled it over the pale face of the phantom.

The latter smiled with ineffable benignity. She dropped her silver lute at the feet of Jacinta, crossed her white arms upon her bosom, and melted from sight, so that it seemed merely as if a shower of dew-drops had fallen into the fountain.

Jacinta retired from the hall filled with awe and wonder. She scarcely closed her eyes that night; but when she awoke at daybreak out of a troubled slumber, the whole appeared to her like a distempered dream. On decending into the hall, however, the truth of the vision was established, for, beside the fountain, she beheld the silver lute glittering in the morning sunshine.

She hastened to her aunt, to relate all that had befallen her, and called her to behold the lute as a testimonial of the reality of her story. If the good lady had any lingering doubts, they were removed when Jacinta touched the instrument, for she drew forth such ravishing tones as to thaw even the frigid bosom of the immaculate Fredegonda, that region of eternal winter, into a genial flow. Nothing but supernatural melody could have produced such an effect.

The extraordinary power of the lute became every day more and more apparent. The wayfarer passing by the tower was detained, and, as it were, spell-bound, in breathless ecstasy. The very birds gathered in the neighboring trees, and hushing their own strains, listened in charmed silence.

Rumor soon spread the news abroad. The inhabitants of Granada thronged to the Alhambra to catch a few notes of the transcendent music that floated about the tower of Las Infantas.

The lovely little minstrel was at length drawn forth from her retreat. The rich and powerful of the land contended who should entertain and do honor to her; or rather, who should secure the charms of her lute to draw fashionable throngs to

their saloons. Wherever she went her vigilant aunt kept a
dragon watch at her elbow, awing the throngs of impassioned
admirers, who hung in raptures on her strains. The report of
her wonderful powers spread from city to city. Malaga, Seville,
Cordova, all became successively mad on the theme; nothing was
talked of throughout Andalusia but the beautiful minstrel of the
Alhambra. How could it be otherwise among a people so musical
and gallant as the Andalusians, when the lute was magical in its
powers, and the minstrel inspired by love !

While all Andalusia was thus music mad, a different mood
prevailed at the court of Spain. Philip V., as is well known,
was a miserable hypochondriac, and subject to all kinds of
fancies. Sometimes he would keep to his bed for weeks together,
groaning under imaginary complaints. At other times he would
insist upon abdicating his throne, to the great annoyance of his
royal spouse, who had a strong relish for the splendors of a court
and the glories of a crown, and guided the sceptre of her imbecile
lord with an expert and steady hand.

Nothing was found to be so efficacious in dispelling the royal
megrims as the power of music ; the queen took care, therefore,
to have the best performers, both vocal and instrumental, at
hand, and retained the famous Italian singer Farinelli about the
court as a kind of royal physician.

At the moment we treat of, however, a freak had come over
the mind of this sapient and illustrious Bourbon that surpassed
all former vagaries. After a long spell of imaginary illness,
which set all the strains of Farinelli and the consulations of a
whole orchestra of court fiddlers at defiance, the monarch fairly,
in idea, gave up the ghost, and considered himself absolutely
dead.

This would have been harmless enough, and even convenient both to his queen and courtiers, had he been content to remain in the quietude befitting a dead man ; but to their annoyance he insisted upon having the funeral ceremonies performed over him, ard, to their inexpressible perplexity, began to grow impatient, and to revile bitterly at them for negligence and disrespect, in leaving him unburied. What was to be done ? To disobey the king's positive commands was monstrous in the eyes of the obsequious courtiers of a punctilious court—but to obey him, and bury him alive would be downright regicide !

In the midst of this fearful dilemma a rumor reached the court, of the female minstrel who was turning the brains of all Andalusia. The queen dispatched missions in all haste to summon her to St. Ildefonso, where the court at that time resided.

Within a few days, as the queen with her maids of honor was walking in those stately gardens, intended, with their avenues and terraces and fountains, to eclipse the glories of Versailles, the far-famed minstrel was conducted into her presence. The imperial Elizabetta gazed with surprise at the youthful and unpretending appearance of the little being that had set the world madding. She was in her picturesque Andalusian dress, her silver lute in hand, and stood with modest and downcast eyes, but with a simplicity and freshness of beauty that still bespoke her " the Rose of the Alhambra."

As usual she was accompanied by the ever-vigilant Fredegonda, who gave the whole history of her parentage and descent to the inquiring queen. If the stately Elizabetta had been interested by the appearance of Jacinta, she was still more pleased when she learnt that she was of a meritorious though impoverished line, and that her father had bravely fallen in the service

14

of the crown. " If thy powers equal their renown," said she,
" and thou canst cast forth this evil spirit that possesses thy
sovereign, thy fortunes shall henceforth be my care, and honors
and wealth attend thee."

Impatient to make trial of her skill, she led the way at once
to the apartment of the moody monarch.

Jacinta followed with downcast eyes through files of guards
and crowds of courtiers. They arrived at length at a great
chamber hung with black. The windows were closed to exclude
the light of day : a number of yellow wax tapers in silver sconces
diffused a lugubrious light, and dimly revealed the figures of
mutes in mourning dresses, and courtiers who glided about with
noiseless step and woebegone visage. In the midst of a funeral
bed or bier, his hands folded on his breast, and the tip of his
nose just visible, lay extended this would-be-buried monarch.

The queen entered the chamber in silence, and pointing to a
footstool in an obscure corner, beckoned to Jacinta to sit down
and commence.

At first she touched her lute with a faltering hand, but gathering confidence and animation as she proceeded, drew forth such
soft aerial harmony, that all present could scarce believe it mortal. As to the monarch, who had already considered himself in
the world of spirits, he set it down for some angelic melody or
the music of the spheres. By degrees the theme was varied,
and the voice of the minstrel accompanied the instrument. She
poured forth one of the legendary ballads treating of the ancient
glories of the Alhambra and the achievements of the Moors.
Her whole soul entered into the theme, for with the recollections
of the Alhambra was associated the story of her love. The
funeral chamber resounded with the animating strain. It

entered into the gloomy heart of the monarch. He raised his head and gazed around : he sat up on his couch, his eye began to kindle—at length, leaping upon the floor, he called for sword and buckler.

The triumph of music, or rather of the enchanted lute, was complete ; the demon of melancholy was cast forth ; and, as it were, a dead man brought to life. The windows of the apartment were thrown open ; the glorious effulgence of Spanish sunshine burst into the late lugubrious chamber ; all eyes sought the lovely enchantress, but the lute had fallen from her hand, she had sunk upon the earth, and the next moment was clasped to the bosom of Ruyz de Alarcon.

The nuptials of the happy couple were celebrated soon afterwards with great splendor, and the Rose of the Alhambra became the ornament and delight of the court. " But hold—not so fast" —I hear the reader exclaim, " this is jumping to the end of a story at a furious rate ! First let us know how Ruyz de Alarcon managed to account to Jacinta for his long neglect ?" Nothing more easy ; the venerable, time-honored excuse, the opposition to his wishes by a proud, pragmatical old father : besides, young people, who really like one another, soon come to an amicable understanding, and bury all past grievances when once they meet.

But how was the proud pragmatical old father reconciled to the match ?

Oh ! as to that, his scruples were easily overcome by a word or two from the queen ; especially as dignities and rewards were showered upon the blooming favorite of royalty. Besides, the lute of Jacinta, you know, possessed a magic power, and could control the most stubborn head and hardest breast.

And what came of the enchanted lute ?

O that is the most curious matter of all, and plainly proves the truth of the whole story. That lute remained for some time in the family, but was purloined and carried off, as was supposed, by the great singer Farinelli, in pure jealousy. At his death it passed into other hands in Italy, who were ignorant of its mystic powers, and melting down the silver, transferred the strings to an old Cremona fiddle. The strings still retain something of their magic virtues. A word in the reader's ear, but let it go no further—that fiddle is now bewitching the whole world—it is the fiddle of Paganini!

THE VETERAN.

Among the curious acquaintances I made in my rambles about the fortress, was a brave and battered old colonel of Invalids, who was nestled like a hawk in one of the Moorish towers. His history, which he was fond of telling, was a tissue of those adventures, mishaps, and vicissitudes that render the life of almost every Spaniard of note as varied and whimsical as the pages of Gil Blas.

He was in America at twelve years of age, and reckoned among the most signal and fortunate events of his life, his having seen General Washington. Since then he had taken a part in all the wars of his country ; he could speak experimentally of most of the prisons and dungeons of the Peninsula ; had been lamed of one leg, crippled in his hands, and so cut up and carbonadoed that he was a kind of walking monument of the troubles of Spain, on which there was a scar for every battle and broil, as every year of captivity was notched upon the tree of Robinson Cousoe. The greatest misfortune of the brave old cavalier, however, appeared to have been his having commanded at Malaga during a time of peril and confusion, and been made a general by the inhabitants, to protect them from the invasion of the French. This had entailed upon him a number of just claims upon government, that I feared would employ him until his dying day in writing and printing petitions and memorials, to the great disquiet of his mind, exhaustion of his purse, and penance of his friends ; not one of whom could visit him without having to listen to a mortal document of half an hour in length, and to carry away half a dozen pamphlets in his pocket. This, however, is the case throughout Spain; every where you meet with some worthy wight brooding in a corner, and nursing up some pet grievance and cherished wrong. Besides, a Spaniard who has a lawsuit, or a claim upon government, may be considered as furnished with employment for the remainder of his life.

I visited the veteran in his quarters in the upper part of the Torre del Vino, or Wine Tower. His room was small but snug, and commanded a beautiful view of the Vega. It was arranged with a soldier's precision. Three muskets and a brace of pistols, all bright and shining, were suspended against the wall, with a sabre and a cane hanging side by side, and above them, two cocked hats, one for parade, and one for ordinary use. A small shelf, containing some half dozen books, formed his library, one of which, a little old mouldy volume of philosophical maxims, was his favorite reading. This he thumbed and pondered over day by day; applying every maxim to his own particular case, provided it had a little tinge of wholesome bitterness, and treated of the injustice of the world.

Yet he was social and kind-hearted, and provided he could be diverted from his wrongs and his philosophy, was an entertaining companion. I like these old weather-beaten sons of fortune, and enjoy their rough campaigning anecdotes. In the course of my visits to the one in question, I learnt some curious facts about an old military commander of the fortress, who seems to have resembled him in some respects, and to have had similar fortunes in the wars. These particulars have been augmented by inquiries among some of the old inhabitants of the place, particularly the father of Mateo Ximenes, of whose traditional stories the worthy I am about to introduce to the reader, was a favorite hero.

THE GOVERNOR AND THE NOTARY.

In former times there ruled, as governor of the Alhambra, a doughty old cavalier, who, from having lost one arm in the wars, was commonly known by the name of el Gobernador Manco, or "the one-armed governor." He in fact prided himself upon being an old soldier, wore his mustaches curled up to his eyes, a pair of campaigning boots, and a toledo as long as a spit, with his pocket handkerchief in the basket-hilt.

He was, moreover, exceedingly proud and punctilious, and tenacious of all his privileges and dignities. Under his sway the immunities of the Alhambra, as a royal residence and domain, were rigidly exacted. No one was permitted to enter the fortress with firearms, or even with a sword or staff, unless he were of a certain rank; and every horseman was obliged to dismount at the gate, and lead his horse by the bridle. Now as the hill of the Alhambra rises from the very midst of the city of Granada, being, as it were, an excrescence of the capital, it must at all times be somewhat irksome to the captain-general, who commands the province, to have thus an *imperium in imperio*, a petty independent post in the very centre of his domains. It was rendered the more galling, in the present instance, from the irritable jealousy of the old governor, that took fire on the least question of authority and jurisdiction; and from the loose vagrant character of the people who had gradually nestled themselves within the fortress, as in a sanctuary, and thence carried on a system of roguery and depredation at the expense of the honest inhabit· ants of the city.

Thus there was a perpetual feud and heart-burning between the captain-general and the governor, the more virulent on the part of the latter, inasmuch as the smallest of two neighboring potentates is always the most captious about his dignity. The stately palace of the captain-general stood in the Plaza Nueva, immediately at the foot of the hill of the Alhambra, and here was always a bustle and parade of guards, and domestics, and city functionaries. A beetling bastion of the fortress overlooked the palace and public square in front of it ; and on this bastion the old governor would occasionally strut backwards and for- wards, with his toledo girded by his side, keeping a wary eye down upon his rival, like a hawk reconnoitering his quarry from his nest in a dry tree.

Whenever he descended into the city it was in grand parade, on horseback, surrounded by his guards, or in his state coach, an ancient and unwieldy Spanish edifice of carved timber and gilt leather, drawn by eight mules, with running footmen, outriders, and lackeys; on which occasions he flattered himself he impress- ed every beholder with awe and admiration as vicegerent of the king; though the wits of Granada, particularly those who loitered about the palace of the captain-general, were apt to sneer at his petty parade, and in allusion to the vagrant character of his sub- jects, to greet him with the appellation of " the king of the beg- gars." One of the most fruitful sources of dispute between these two doughty rivals was the right claimed by the governor to

14*

have all things passed free of duty through the city, that were
intended for the use of himself or his garrison. By degrees
this privilege had given rise to extensive smuggling. A nest of
contrabandistas took up their abode in the hovels of the fortress,
and the numerous caves in its vicinity, and drove a thriving
business under the connivance of the soldiers of the garrison.

The vigilance of the captain-general was aroused. He consulted his legal adviser and factotum, a shrewd meddlesome
escribano, or notary, who rejoiced in an opportunity of perplex-
ing the old potentate of the Alhambra, and involving him in a
maze of legal subtilties. He advised the captain-general to insist upon the right of examining every convoy passing through
the gates of his city, and penned a long letter for him in vin-
dication of the right. Governor Manco was a straightforward
cut-and-thrust old soldier, who hated an escribano worse than
the devil, and this one in particular worse than all other escribanos.

"What !" said he, curling up his mustaches fiercely, "does
the captain-general set his man of the pen to practise confusions
upon me? I'll let him see an old soldier is not to be baffled by
schoolcraft."

He seized his pen and scrawled a short letter in a crabbed
hand, in which, without deigning to enter into argument, he insisted on the right of transit free of search, and denounced vengeance on any custom-house officer who should lay his unhallow-
ed hand on any convoy protected by the flag of the Alhambra.
While this question was agitated between the two pragmatical
potentates, it so happened that a mule laden with supplies for the
fortress arrived one day at the gate of Xenil, by which it was to
traverse a suburb of the city on its way to the Alhambra. The

convoy was headed by a testy old corporal, who had long served under the governor, and was a man after his own heart; as rusty and stanch as an old Toledo blade.

As they approached the gate of the city, the corporal placed the banner of the Alhambra on the pack-saddle of the mule, and drawing himself up to a perfect perpendicular, advanced with his head dressed to the front, but with the wary side-glance of a cur passing through hostile ground, and ready for a snap and a snarl.

"Who goes there?" said the sentinel at the gate.

"Soldier of the Alhambra!" said the corporal, without turning his head.

"What have you in charge?"

"Provisions for the garrison."

"Proceed."

The corporal marched straight forward, followed by the convoy, but had not advanced many paces before a posse of custom-house officers rushed out of a small toll-house.

"Hallo there!" cried the leader; "Muleteer, halt, and open those packages."

The corporal wheeled round, and drew himself up in battle array. "Respect the flag of the Alhambra," said he; "these things are for the governor."

"A figo for the governor, and a figo for his flag. Muleteer, halt, I say."

"Stop the convoy at your peril!" cried the corporal, cocking his musket; "Muleteer, proceed."

The muleteer gave his beast a hearty thwack; the custom-house officer sprang forward and seized the halter; whereupon the corporal levelled his piece, and shot him dead.

The street was immediately in an uproar.

The old corporal was seized, and after undergoing sundry kicks, and cuffs, and cudgellings, which are generally given impromptu by the mob in Spain, as a foretaste of the after penalties of the law, he was loaded with irons, and conducted to the city prison ; while his comrades were permitted to proceed with the convoy, after it had been well rummaged, to the Alhambra.

The old governor was in a towering passion when he heard of this insult to his flag and capture of his corporal. For a time he stormed about the Moorish halls, and vapored about the bastions, and looked down fire and sword upon the palace of the captain-general. Having vented the first ebullition of his wrath, he dispatched a message demanding the surrender of the corporal, as to him alone belonged the right of sitting in judgment on the offences of those under his command. The captain-general, aided by the pen of the delighted escribano, replied at great length, arguing that as the offence had been committed within the walls of his city, and against one of his civil officers, it was clearly within his proper jurisdiction. The governor rejoined by a repetition of his demand ; the captain-general gave a sur-rejoinder of still greater length and legal acumen ; the governor became hotter and more peremptory in his demands, and the captain-general cooler and more copious in his replies ; until the old lion-hearted soldier absolutely roared with fury at being thus entangled in the meshes of legal controversy.

While the subtle escribano was thus amusing himself at the expense of the governor, he was conducting the trial of the corporal, who, mewed up in a narrow dungeon of the prison, had merely a small grated window at which to show his iron-bound visage and receive the consolations of his friends.

A mountain of written testimony was diligently heaped up, according to Spanish form, by the indefatigable escribano ; the corporal was completely overwhelmed by it.   He was convicted of murder, and sentenced to be hanged.

It was in vain the governor sent down remonstrance and menace from the Alhambra.   The fatal day was at hand, and the corporal was put *in capilla*, that is to say, in the chapel of the prison, as is always done with culprits the day before execution, that they may meditate on their approaching end and repent them of their sins.

Seeing things drawing to extremity, the old governor de termined to attend to the affair in person.   For this purpose he ordered out his carriage of state, and, surrounded by his guards, rumbled down the avenue of the Alhambra into the city.   Driving to the house of the escribano, he summoned him to the portal.

The eye of the old governor gleamed like a coal at beholding the smirking man of the law advancing with an air of exultation.

" What is this I hear," cried he, " that you are about to put to death one of my soldiers ?"

" All according to law—all in strict form of justice," said the self-sufficient escribano, chuckling and rubbing his hands. " I can show your excellency the written testimony in the case."

" Fetch it hither," said the governor.   The escribano bustled into his office, delighted with having another opportunity of displaying his ingenuity at the expense of the hard-headed veteran.

He returned with a satchel full of papers, and began to read a long deposition with professional volubility.   By this time a crowd had collected, listening with outstretched necks and gaping mouths.

"Prithee, man, get into the carriage, out of this pestilent throng, that I may the better hear thee," said the governor.

The escribano entered the carriage, when, in a twinkling, the door was closed, the coachman smacked his whip—mules, carriage, guards and all dashed off at a thundering rate, leaving the crowd in gaping wonderment; nor did the governor pause until he had lodged his prey in one of the strongest dungeons of the Alhambra.

He then sent down a flag of truce in military style, proposing a cartel or exchange of prisoners—the corporal for the notary. The pride of the captain-general was piqued; he returned a contemptuous refusal, and forthwith caused a gallows, tall and strong, to be erected in the centre of the Plaza Nueva for the execution of the corporal.

"Oho! is that the game?" said Governor Manco. He gave orders, and immediately a gibbet was reared on the verge of the great beetling bastion that overlooked the Plaza. "Now," said he in a message to the captain-general, "hang my soldier when you please; but at the same time that he is swung off in the square, look up to see your escribano dangling against the sky."

The captain-general was inflexible; troops were paraded in the square; the drums beat, the bell tolled. An immense multitude of amateurs gathered together to behold the execution. On the other hand, the governor paraded his garrison on the bastion, and tolled the funeral dirge of the notary from the Torre de la Campana, or Tower of the Bell.

The notary's wife pressed through the crowd with a whole progeny of little embryo escribanos at her heels, and throwing herself at the feet of the captain-general, implored him not to sacrifice the life of her husband, and the welfare of herself and her numerous little ones, to a point of pride; "for you know the old governor too well," said she, "to doubt that he will put his threat in execution, if you hang the soldier."

The captain-general was overpowered by her tears and lamentations, and the clamors of her callow brood. The corporal was sent up to the Alhambra, under a guard, in his gallows garb, like a hooded friar, but with head erect and a face of iron. The escribano was demanded in exchange, according to the cartel. The once bustling and self-sufficient man of the law was drawn forth from his dungeon more dead than alive. All his flippancy and conceit had evaporated; his hair, it is said, had nearly turned gray with affright, and he had a downcast, dogged look, as if he still felt the halter round his neck.

The old governor stuck his one arm a-kimbo, and for a moment surveyed him with an iron smile. "Henceforth, my friend," said he, "moderate your zeal in hurrying others to the gallows; be not too certain of your safety, even though you should have the law on your side; and above all take care how you play off your schoolcraft another time upon an old soldier."

GOVERNOR MANCO AND THE SOLDIER.

WHILE Governor Manco, or " the one-armed," kept up a show of
military state in the Alhambra, he became nettled at the re-
proaches continually cast upon his fortress, of being a nestling
place of rogues and contrabandistas. On a sudden, the old potentate determined on reform, and setting vigorously to work, ejected
whole nests of vagabonds out of the fortress and the gipsy caves
with which 'the surrounding hills are honeycombed. He sent out
soldiers, also, to patrol the avenues and footpaths, with orders to
take up all suspicious persons.

One bright summer morning, a patrol, consisting of the testy
old corporal who had distinguished himself in the affair of the
notary, a trumpeter and two privates, was seated under the garden
wall of the Generalife, beside the road which leads down from the
mountain of the sun, when they heard the tramp of a horse, and
a male voice singing in rough, though not unmusical tones, an old
Castilian campaigning song.

Presently they beheld a sturdy, sunburnt fellow, clad in the
ragged garb of a foot-soldier, leading a powerful Arabian horse,
caparisoned in the ancient Moresco fashion.

Astonished at the sight of a strange soldier descending, steed
in hand, from that solitary mountain, the corporal stepped forth
and challenged him.

" Who goes there ?"

" A friend."

" Who and what are you ?"

" A poor soldier just from the wars, with a cracked crown and empty purse for a reward."

By this time they were enabled to view him more narrowly. He had a black patch across his forehead, which, with a grizzled beard, added to a certain dare-devil cast of countenance, while a slight squint threw into the whole an occasional gleam of roguish good humor.

Having answered the questions of the patrol, the soldier seemed to consider himself entitled to make others in return. " May I ask," said he, " what city is that which I see at the foot of the hill ?"

" What city !" cried the trumpeter ; " come, that's too bad. Here's a fellow lurking about the mountain of the sun, and demands the name of the great city of Granada !"

" Granada ! Madre di Dios ! can it be possible ?"

" Perhaps not !" rejoined the trumpeter ; " and perhaps you have no idea that yonder are the towers of the Alhambra."

" Son of a trumpet," replied the stranger, " do not trifle with me ; if this be indeed the Alhambra, I have some strange matters to reveal to the governor."

" You will have an opportunity," said the corporal, " for we mean to take you before him." By this time the trumpeter had seized the bridle of the steed, the two privates had each secured an arm of the soldier, the corporal put himself in front, gave the word, " Forward—march !" and away they marched for the Alhambra.

The sight of a ragged foot-soldier and a fine Arabian horse,

brought in captive by the patrol, attracted the attention of all
the idlers of the fortress, and of those gossip groups that generally assemble about wells and fountains at early dawn.   The
wheel of the cistern paused in its rotations, and the slipshod
servant-maid stood gaping, with pitcher in hand, as the corporal
passed by with his prize.   A motley train gradually gathered in
the rear of the escort.

Knowing nods and winks and conjectures passed from one to
another.   "It is a deserter," said one ; "A contrabandista," said
another; "A bandalero," said a third ;—until it was affirmed
that a captain of a desperate band of robbers had been captured
by the prowess of the corporal and his patrol.   "Well, well," said
the old crones, one to another, "captain or not, let him get out
of the grasp of old Governor Manco if he can, though he is but
one-handed."

Governor Manco was seated in one of the inner halls of the
Alhambra, taking his morning's cup of chocolate in company
with his confessor, a fat Franciscan friar, from the neighboring
convent.   A demure, dark-eyed damsel of Malaga, the daughter
of his housekeeper, was attending upon him.   The world hinted
that the damsel, who, with all her demureness, was a sly buxom
baggage, had found out a soft spot in the iron heart of the old
governor, and held complete control over him.   But let that pass
—the domestic affairs of these mighty potentates of the earth
should not be too narrowly scrutinized.

When word was brought that a suspicious stranger had been
taken lurking about the fortress, and was actually in the outer
court, in durance of the corporal, waiting the pleasure of his
excellency, the pride and stateliness of office swelled the bosom
of the governor.   Giving back his chocolate cup into the hands

of the demure damsel, he called for his basket-hilted sword, girded it to his side, twirled up his mustaches, took his seat in a large high-backed chair, assumed a bitter and forbidding aspect, and ordered the prisoner into his presence. The soldier was brought in, still closely pinioned by his captors, and guarded by the corporal. He maintained, however, a resolute self confident air, and returned the sharp, scrutinizing look of the governor with an easy squint, which by no means pleased the punctilious old potentate.

Well, culprit," said the governor, after he had regarded him for a moment in silence, " what have you to say for your-self—who are you?"

"A soldier, just from the wars, who has brought away no-thing but scars and bruises."

" A soldier—humph—a foot-soldier by your garb. I under-stand you have a fine Arabian horse. I presume you brought him too from the wars, besides your scars and bruises."

" May it please your excellency, I have something strange to tell about that horse. Indeed I have one of the most wonderful things to relate. Something too that concerns the security of this fortress, indeed of all Granada. But it is a matter to be imparted only to your private ear, or in presence of such only as are in your confidence."

The governor considered for a moment, and then directed the corporal and his men to withdraw, but to post themselves outside of the door, and be ready at a call. " This holy friar," said he, " is my confessor, you may say any thing in his presence —and this damsel," nodding towards the handmaid, who had loitered with an air of great curiosity, " this damsel is of great secrecy and discretion, and to be trusted with any thing."

The soldier gave a glance between a squint and a leer at the demure handmaid. " I am perfectly willing," said he, " that the damsel should remain."

When all the rest had withdrawn, the soldier commenced his story. He was a fluent, smooth-tongued varlet, and had a command of language above his apparent rank.

" May it please your excellency," said he, " I am, as I before observed, a soldier, and have seen some hard service, but my term of enlistment being expired, I was discharged, not long since, from the army at Valladolid, and set out on foot for my native village in Andalusia. Yesterday evening the sun went down as I was traversing a great dry plain of Old Castile."

" Hold," cried the governor, " what is this you say? Old Castile is some two or three hundred miles from this."

" Even so," replied the soldier, coolly; "I told your excellency I had strange things to relate ; but not more strange than true ; as your excellency will find, if you will deign me a patient hearing."

" Proceed, culprit," said the governor, twirling up his mustaches.

" As the sun went down," continued the soldier, " I cast my eyes about in search of quarters for the night, but as .far as my sight could reach, there were no signs of habitation. I saw that I should have to make my bed on the naked plain, with my knapsack for a pillow ; but your excellency is an old soldier, and knows that to one who has been in the wars, such a night's lodging is no great hardship."

The governor nodded assent, as he drew his pocket handkerchief out of the basket-hilt, to drive away a fly that buzzed about his nose.

"Well, to make a long story short," continued the soldier, "I trudged forward for several miles until I came to a bridge over a deep ravine, through which ran a little thread of water, almost dried up by the summer heat. At one end of the bridge was a Moorish tower, the upper end all in ruins, but a vault in the foundation quite entire. Here, thinks I, is a good place to make a halt; so I went down to the stream, took a hearty drink, for the water was pure and sweet, and I was parched with thirst; then, opening my wallet, I took out an onion and a few crusts, which were all my provisions, and seating myself on a stone on the margin of the stream, began to make my supper; intending afterwards to quarter myself for the night in the vault of the tower; and capital quarters they would have been for a campaigner just from the wars, as your excellency, who is an old soldier, may suppose."

"I have put up gladly with worse in my time," said the governor, returning his pocket-handkerchief into the hilt of his sword.

"While I was quietly crunching my crust," pursued the soldier, "I heard something stir within the vault; I listened—it was the tramp of a horse. By and by a man came forth from a door in the foundation of the tower, close by the water's edge, leading a powerful horse by the bridle. I could not well make out what he was by the starlight. It had a suspicious look to be lurking among the ruins of a tower, in that wild solitary place. He might be a mere wayfarer, like myself; he might be a contrabandista; he might be a bandalero! what of that? thank heaven and my poverty, I had nothing to lose; so I sat still and crunched my crust.

"He led his horse to the water, close by where I was sitting,

so that I had a fair opportunity of reconnoitering him. To my
surprise he was dressed in a Moorish garb, with a cuirass of
steel, and a polished skull-cap that I distinguished by the reflec-
tion of the stars upon it. His horse, too, was harnessed in the
Moresco fashion, with great shovel stirrups. He led him, as I
said, to the side of the stream, into which the animal plunged
his head almost to the eyes, and drank until I thought he would
have burst.

"'Comrade,' said I, 'your steed drinks well; it's a good
sign when a horse plunges his muzzle bravely into the water.'

"'He may well drink,' said the stranger, speaking with
a Moorish accent; 'it is a good year since he had his last
draught.'

"'By Santiago,' said I, 'that beats even the camels I have
seen in Africa. But come, you seem to be something of a soldier, will you sit down and take part of a soldier's fare?' In
fact, I felt the want of a companion in this lonely place, and was
willing to put up with an infidel. Besides, as your excellency
well knows, a soldier is never very particular about the faith of
his company, and soldiers of all countries are comrades on peaceable ground."

The governor again nodded assent.

" Well, as I was saying, I invited him to share my supper,
such as it was, for I could not do less in common hospitality.
'I have no time to pause for meat or drink,' said he, 'I have a
long journey to make before morning.'

"'In which direction?' said I.

"'Andalusia,' said he.

"'Exactly my route,' said I, 'so, as you won't stop and eat
with me, perhaps you will let me mount and ride with you. I

see your horse is of a powerful frame, I'll warrant he'll carry double.'

" 'Agreed,' said the trooper ; and it would not have been civil and soldierlike to refuse, especially as I had offered to share my supper with him. So up he mounted, and up I mount‑ ed behind him.

" ' Hold fast,' said he, ' my steed goes like the wind.'

" ' Never fear me,' said I, and so off we set.

" From a walk the horse soon passed to a trot, from a trot to a gallop, and from a gallop to a harum-scarum scamper. It seemed as if rocks, trees, houses, every thing, flew hurry-scurry behind us.

" ' What town is this ?' said I.

" 'Segovia,' said he ; and before the word was out of his mouth, the towers of Segovia were out of sight. We swept up the Guadarama mountains, and down by the Escurial ; and we skirted the walls of Madrid, and we scoured away across the plains of La Mancha. In this way we went up hill and down dale, by towers and cities, all buried in deep sleep, and across mountains, and plains, and rivers, just glimmering in the starlight.

" To make a long story short, and not to fatigue your excellency, the trooper suddenly pulled up on the side of a mountain. ' Here we are,' said he, ' at the end of our journey.' I looked about, but could see no signs of habitation ; nothing but the mouth of a cavern. While I looked I saw multitudes of people in Moorish dresses. some on horseback, some on foot, arriving as if borne by the wind from all points of the compass, and hurrying into the mouth of the cavern like bees into a hive. Before I could ask a question the trooper struck his long Moorish spurs into the horse's flanks, and dashed in with the throng. We

passed along a steep winding way, that descended into the very
bowels of the mountain. As we pushed on, a light began to
glimmer up, by little and little, like the first glimmerings of day,
but what caused it I could not discern. It grew stronger and
stronger, and enabled me to see every thing around. I now
noticed, as we passed along, great caverns, opening to the right
and left, like halls in an arsenal. In some there were shields,
and helmets, and cuirasses, and lances, and cimeters, hanging
against the walls; in others there were great heaps of warlike
munitions, and camp equipage lying upon the ground.

"It would have done your excellency's heart good, being an
old soldier, to have seen such grand provision for war. Then, in
other caverns, there were long rows of horsemen armed to the
teeth, with lances raised and banners unfurled, all ready for the
field; but they all sat motionless in their saddles like so many
statues. In other halls were warriors sleeping on the ground
beside their horses, and foot-soldiers in groups ready to fall into
the ranks. All were in old-fashioned Moorish dresses and armor.

"Well, your excellency, to cut a long story short, we at
length entered an immense cavern, or I may say palace, of grotto
work, the walls of which seemed to be veined with gold and
silver, and to sparkle with diamonds and sapphires and all kinds
of precious stones. At the upper end sat a Moorish king on a
golden throne, with his nobles on each side, and a guard of African blacks with drawn cimeters. All the crowd that continued
to flock in, and amounted to thousands and thousands, passed
one by one before his throne, each paying homage as he passed.
Some of the multitude were dressed in magnificent robes, without
stain or blemish and sparkling with jewels; others in burnished
and enamelled armor; while others were in mouldered and

mildewed garments, and in armor all battered and dented and covered with rust.

"I had hitherto held my tongue, for your excellency well knows it is not for a soldier to ask many questions when on duty, but I could keep silent no longer.

"'Prithee, comrade,' said I, 'what is the meaning of all this?'

"'This,' said the trooper, 'is a great and fearful mystery. Know, O Christian, that you see before you the court and army of Boabdil the last king of Granada.'

"'What is this you tell me?' cried I. 'Boabdil and his court were exiled from the land hundreds of years agone, and all died in Africa.'

"'So it is recorded in your lying chronicles,' replied the Moor, 'but know that Boabdil and the warriors who made the last struggle for Granada were all shut up in the mountain by powerful enchantment. As for the king and army that marched forth from Granada at the time of the surrender, they were a mere phantom train of spirits and demons, permitted to assume those shapes to deceive the Christian sovereigns. And furthermore let me tell you, friend, that all Spain is a country under the power of enchantment. There is not a mountain cave, not a lonely watchtower in the plains, nor ruined castle on the hills, but has some spell-bound warriors sleeping from age to age within its vaults, until the sins are expiated for which Allah permitted the dominion to pass for a time out of the hands of the faithful. Once every year, on the eve of St. John, they are released from enchantment, from sunset to sunrise, and permitted to repair here to pay homage to their sovereign! and the crowds which you beheld swarming into the cavern are Moslem warriors

15

from their haunts in all parts of Spain. For my own part,
you saw the ruined tower of the bridge in Old Castile, where
I have now wintered and summered for many hundred years, and
where I must be back again by daybreak. As to the battalions of
horse and foot which you beheld drawn up in array in the neighboring caverns, they are the spell-bound warriors of Granada. It
is written in the book of fate, that when the enchantment is
broken, Boabdil will descend from the mountain at the head of
this army, resume his throne in the Alhambra and his sway of
Granada, and gathering together the enchanted warriors, from
all parts of Spain, will reconquer the Peninsula and restore it to
Moslem rule.'

"'And when shall this happen?' said I.

"'Allah alone knows: we had hoped the day of deliverance
was at hand; but there reigns at present a vigilant governor in
the Alhambra, a stanch old soldier, well known as Governor
Manco. While such a warrior holds command of the very out-
post, and stands ready to check the first irruption from the
mountain, I fear Boabdil and his soldiery must be content to
rest upon their arms.'"

Here the governor raised himself somewhat perpendicularly,
adjusted his sword, and twirled up his mustaches.

"To make a long story short, and not to fatigue your excellency, the trooper, having given me this account, dismounted
from his steed.

"'Tarry here,' said he, 'and guard my steed while I go and
bow the knee to Boabdil.' So saying, he strode away among the
throng that pressed forward to the throne.

"'What's to be done?' thought I, when thus left to myself;
'shall I wait here until this infidel returns to whisk me off on his

goblin steed, the Lord knows where; or shall I make the most of
my time and beat a retreat from this hobgoblin community?' A
soldier's mind is soon made up, as your excellency well knows.
As to the horse, he belonged to an avowed enemy of the faith
and the realm, and was a fair prize according to the rules of
war. So hoisting myself from the crupper into the saddle, I
turned the reins, struck the Moorish stirrups into the sides of
the steed, and put him to make the best of his way out of the
passage by which he had entered. As we scoured by the halls
where the Moslem horsemen sat in motionless battalions, I
thought I heard the clang of armor and a hollow murmur of
voices. I gave the steed another taste of the stirrups and
doubled my speed. There was now a sound behind me like a
rushing blast; I heard the clatter of a thousand hoofs; a countless
throng overtook me. I was borne along in the press, and hurled
forth from the mouth of the cavern, while thousands of shadowy
forms were swept off in every direction by the four winds of
heaven.

"In the whirl and confusion of the scene I was thrown senseless to the earth. When I came to myself I was lying on the
brow of a hill, with the Arabian steed standing beside me; for in
falling, my arm had slipped within the bridle, which, I presume,
prevented his whisking off to Old Castile.

"Your excellency may easily judge of my surprise, on looking
round, to behold hedges of aloes and Indian figs and other proofs
of a southern climate, and to see a great city below me, with
towers, and palaces, and a grand cathedral.

"I descended the hill cautiously, leading my steed, for I was
afraid to mount him again, lest he should play me some slippery
trick. As I descended I met with your patrol, who let me into

the secret that it was Granada that lay before me; and that I was actually under the walls of the Alhambra, the fortress of the redoubted Governor Manco, the terror of all enchanted Moslems. When I heard this, I determined at once to seek your excellency, to inform you of all that I had seen, and to warn you of the perils that surround and undermine you, that you may take measures in time to guard your fortress, and the kingdom itself, from this intestine army that lurks in the very bowels of the land."

"And prithee, friend, you who are a veteran campaigner, and have seen so much service," said the governor, "how would you advise me to proceed, in order to prevent this evil?"

"It is not for a humble private of the ranks," said the soldier, modestly, "to pretend to instruct a commander of your excellency's sagacity, but it appears to me that your excellency might cause all the caves and entrances into the mountains to be walled up with solid mason work, so that Boabdil and his army might be completely corked up in their subterranean habitation. If the good father, too," added the soldier, reverently bowing to the friar, and devoutly crossing himself, "would consecrate the barricadoes with his blessing, and put up a few crosses and relics and images of saints, I think they might withstand all the power of infidel enchantments."

"They doubtless would be of great avail," said the friar.

The governor now placed his arm a-kimbo, with his hand resting on the hilt of his Toledo, fixed his eye upon the soldier, and gently wagging his head from one side to the other,

"So, friend," said he, "then you really suppose I am to be gulled with this cock-and-bull story about enchanted mountains and enchanted Moors? Hark ye, culprit!—not another word. An old soldier you may be, but you'll find you have an older

soldier to deal with, and one not easily outgeneralled. Ho!
guards there! put this fellow in irons."

The demure handmaid would have put in a word in favor of
the prisoner, but the governor silenced her with a look.

As they were pinioning the soldier, one of the guards felt
something of bulk in his pocket, and drawing it forth, found a
long leathern purse that appeared to be well filled. Holding it
by one corner, he turned out the contents upon the table before
the governor, and never did freebooter's bag make more gorgeous
delivery. Out tumbled rings, and jewels, and rosaries of pearls,
and sparkling diamond crosses, and a profusion of ancient golden
coin, some of which fell jingling to the floor, and rolled away to
the uttermost parts of the chamber.

For a time the functions of justice were suspended; there
was a universal scramble after the glittering fugitives. The governor alone, who was imbued with true Spanish pride, maintained
his stately decorum, though his eye betrayed a little anxiety
until the last coin and jewel was restored to the sack.

The friar was not so calm ; his whole face glowed like a fur-
nace, and his eyes twinkled and flashed at sight of the rosaries
and crosses.

"Sacrilegious wretch that thou art!" exclaimed he ; "what
church or sanctuary hast thou been plundering of these sacred
relics?"

"Neither one nor the other, holy father. If they be sacrilegious spoils, they must have been taken, in times long past, by the
infidel trooper I have mentioned. I was just going to tell his
excellency when he interrupted me, that on taking possession of
the trooper's horse, I unhooked a leathern sack which hung at
the saddle-bow, and which I presume contained the plunder of

his campaignings in days of old, when the Moors overran the country."

"Mighty well; at present you will make up your mind to take up your quarters in a chamber of the vermilion tower, which, though not under a magic spell, will hold you as safe as any cave of your enchanted Moors."

"Your excellency will do as you think proper," said the prisoner, coolly. "I shall be thankful to your excellency for any accommodation in the fortress. A soldier who has been in the wars, as your excellency well knows, is not particular about his lodgings: provided I have a snug dungeon and regular rations, I shall manage to make myself comfortable. I would only entreat that while your excellency is so careful about me, you would have an eye to your fortress, and think on the hint I dropped about stopping up the entrances to the mountain."

Here ended the scene. The prisoner was conducted to a strong dungeon in the vermilion tower, the Arabian steed was led to his excellency's stable, and the trooper's sack was deposited in his excellency's strong box. To the latter, it is true, the friar made some demur, questioning whether the sacred relics, which were evidently sacrilegious spoils, should not be placed in custody of the church; but as the governor was peremptory on the subject, and was absolute lord in the Alhambra, the friar discreetly dropped the discussion, but determined to convey intelligence of the fact to the church dignitaries in Granada.

To explain these prompt and rigid measures on the part of old Governor Manco, it is proper to observe, that about this time the Alpuxarra mountains in the neighborhood of Granada were terribly infested by a gang of robbers, under the command of a daring chief named Manuel Borasco, who were accustomed to prowl about the country, and even to enter the city in various disguises, to gain intelligence of the departure of convoys of merchandise, or travellers with well-lined purses, whom they took care to waylay in distant and solitary passes of the road. These repeated and daring outrages had awakened the attention of government, and the commanders of the various posts had received instructions to be on the alert, and to take up all suspicious stragglers. Governor Manco was particularly zealous in consequence of the various stigmas that had been cast upon his fortress, and he now doubted not he had entrapped some formidable desperado of this gang.

In the mean time the story took wind, and became the talk, not merely of the fortress, but of the whole city of Granada. It was said that the noted robber Manuel Borasco, the terror of the Alpuxarras, had fallen into the clutches of old Governor Manco, and been cooped up by him in a dungeon of the vermilion towers; and every one who had been robbed by him flocked to recognize the marauder. The vermilion towers, as is well known, stand apart from the Alhambra on a sister hill, separated from the main fortress by the ravine down which passes the main avenue. There were no outer walls, but a sentinel patrolled before the tower. The window of the chamber in which the soldier was confined was strongly grated, and looked upon a small esplanade. Here the good folks of Granada repaired to gaze at him, as they would at a laughing hyena, grinning through the cage of a menagerie. Nobody, however, recognized him for Manuel Borasco, for that terrible robber was noted for a ferocious physiognomy, and had by no means the good-humored squint of the prisoner. Visitors came not merely from the city, but from all parts of the country; but nobody knew him, and there began to be doubts in the minds of the common people whether there might not be some truth in his story. That Boabdil and his army were shut up in the mountain, was an old tradition which many of the ancient inhabitants had heard from their fathers. Numbers went up to the mountain of the sun, or rather of St. Elena, in search of the cave mentioned by the soldier; and saw and peeped into the deep dark pit, descending, no one knows how far, into the mountain, and which remains there to this day—the fabled entrance to the subterranean abode of Boabdil.

By degrees the soldier became popular with the common people. A freebooter of the mountains is by no means the opprobrious character in Spain that a robber is in any other country: on the contrary, he is a kind of chivalrous personage in the eyes of the lower classes. There is always a disposition, also, to cavil at the conduct of those in command, and many began to murmur at the high-handed measures of old Governor Manco, and to look upon the prisoner in the light of a martyr.

The soldier, moreover, was a merry, waggish fellow, that had a joke for every one who came near his window, and a soft speech for every female. He had procured an old guitar also, and would sit by his window and sing ballads and love-ditties to the delight of the women of the neighborhood, who would assemble on the esplanade in the evening and dance boleros to his music. Having trimmed off his rough beard, his sunburnt face found favor in the eyes of the fair, and the demure handmaid of the governor declared that his squint was perfectly irresistible. This kind-hearted damsel had from the first evinced a deep sympathy in his fortunes, and having in vain tried to mollify the governor, had set to work privately to mitigate the rigor of his dispensations. Every day she brought the prisoner some crumbs of comfort which had fallen from the governor's table, or been abstracted from his larder, together with, now and then, a consoling bottle of choice Val de Peñas, or rich Malaga.

While this petty treason was going on, in the very centre of the old governor's citadel, a storm of open war was brewing up among his external foes. The circumstance of a bag of gold and jewels having been found upon the person of the supposed robber, had been reported, with many exaggerations, in Granada. A question of territorial jurisdiction was immediately started by the governor's inveterate rival, the captain-general. He insisted that the prisoner had been captured without the precincts of the Alhambra, and within the rules of his authority. He demanded his body therefore, and the *spolia opima* taken with him. Due information having been carried likewise by the friar to the grand inquisitor of the crosses and rosaries, and other relics contained in the bag, he claimed the culprit as having been guilty of sacrilege, and insisted that his plunder was due to the church, and his body to the next auto da fe. The feuds ran high; the governor was furious, and swore, rather than surrender his captive, he would hang him up within the Alhambra, as a spy caught within the purlieus of the fortress.

The captain-general threatened to send a body of soldiers to transfer the prisoner from the vermilion tower to the city. The grand inquisitor was equally bent upon dispatching a number of the familiars of the Holy Office. Word was brought late at night to the governor of these machinations. "Let them come," said he, "they'll find me beforehand with them; he must rise bright and early who would take in an old soldier." He accordingly issued orders to have the prisoner removed, at daybreak, to the donjon keep within the walls of the Alhambra. "And

15*

d'ye hear, child," said he to his demure handmaid, "tap **at** my door, and wake me before cock-crowing, that I may see to the matter myself."

The day dawned, the cock crowed, but nobody tapped at the door of the governor. The sun rose high above the mountain-tops, and glittered in at his casement, ere the governor was awakened from his morning dreams by his veteran corporal, who stood before him with terror stamped upon his iron visage.

"He's off! he's gone!" cried the corporal, gasping for breath.

"Who's off—who's gone?"

"The soldier—the robber—the devil, for aught I know; his dungeon is empty, but the door locked: no one knows how he has escaped out of it."

"Who saw him last?"

"Your handmaid, she brought him his supper."

"Let her be called instantly."

Here was new matter of confusion. The chamber of the demure damsel was likewise empty, her bed had not been slept in: she had doubtless gone off with the culprit, as she had appeared, for some days past, to have frequent conversations with him.

This was wounding the old governor in a tender part, but he had scarce time to wince at it, when new misfortunes broke upon his view. On going into his cabinet he found his strong box open, the leather purse of the trooper abstracted, and with it, a couple of corpulent bags of doubloons.

But how, and which way had the fugitives escaped? An old peasant who lived in a cottage by the road-side, leading up into the Sierra, declared that he had heard the tramp of a powerful steed just before daybreak, passing up into the mountains. He had looked out at his casement, and could just distinguish a horseman, with a female seated before him.

"Search the stables!" cried Governor Manco. The stables were searched; all the horses were in their stalls, excepting the Arabian steed. In his place was a stout cudgel tied to the manger, and on it a label bearing these words, "A gift to Governor Manco, from an Old Soldier."

A FETE IN THE ALHAMBRA.

THE Saints' day of my neighbor and rival potentate, the count, took place during his sojourn in the Alhambra, on which occasion he gave a domestic fête; assembling round him the members of his family and household, while the stewards and old servants from his distant possessions came to pay him reverence and partake of the good cheer, which was sure to be provided. It presented a type, though doubtless a faint one, of the establishment of a Spanish noble in the olden time.

The Spaniards were always grandiose in their notions of style. Huge palaces; lumbering equipages, laden with footmen and lackeys; pompous retinues, and useless dependents of all kinds; the dignity of a noble seemed commensurate with the legions who loitered about his halls, fed at his expense, and seemed ready to devour him alive. This, doubtless, originated in the necessity of keeping up hosts of armed retainers during the wars with the Moors; wars of inroads and surprises; when a noble was liable to be suddenly assailed in his castle by a foray of the enemy, or summoned to the field by his sovereign.

The custom remained after the wars were at an end; and what originated in necessity was kept up through ostentation. The wealth which flowed into the country from conquests and discoveries fostered the passion for princely establishments. According to magnificent old Spanish usage, in which pride and generosity bore equal parts, a superannuated servant was never turned off, but became a charge for the rest of his days; nay, his children, and his children's children, and often their relatives, to the right and left, became gradually entailed upon the family. Hence the huge palaces of the Spanish nobility, which have such an air of empty ostentation from the greatness of their size compared with the mediocrity and scantiness of their furniture, were absolutely required in the golden days of Spain, by the patriarchal habits of their possessors. They were little better than vast barracks for the hereditary generations of hangers on, that battened at the expense of a Spanish noble.

These patriarchal habits of the Spanish nobility have declined with their revenues; though the spirit which prompted them remains, and wars sadly with their altered fortunes. The poorest among them have always some hereditary hangers on, who live at their expense, and make them poorer. Some who, like my neighbor the count, retain a modicum of their once princely possessions, keep up a shadow of the ancient system, and their estates are overrun and the produce consumed by generations of idle retainers.

The count held estates in various parts of the kingdom, some including whole villages; yet the revenues collected from them were comparatively small; some of them, he assured me, barely fed the hordes of dependents nestled upon them, who seemed to consider themselves entitled to live rent free and be maintained into the bargain, because their forefathers had been so since time immemorial.

The saint's day of the old count gave me a glimpse into a

Spanish interior. For two or three days previous preparations were made for the fête. Viands of all kinds were brought up from town, greeting the olfactory nerves of the old invalid guards, as they were borne past them through the Gate of Justice. Servants hurried officiously about the courts; the ancient kitchen of the palace was again alive with the tread of cooks and scullions, and blazed with unwonted fires.

When the day arrived I beheld the old count in patriarchal state, his family and household around him, with functionaries who mismanaged his estates at a distance and consumed the proceeds; while numerous old worn-out servants and pensioners were loitering about the courts and keeping within smell of the kitchen.

It was a joyous day in the Alhambra. The guests dispersed themselves about the palace before the hour of dinner, enjoying the luxuries of its courts and fountains, and embosomed gardens, and music and laughter resounded through its late silent halls.

The feast, for a set dinner in Spain is literally a feast, was served in the beautiful Moresco Hall of " Las dos Hermanas." The table was loaded with all the luxuries of the season; there was an almost interminable succession of dishes; showing how truly the feast at the rich Camachos' wedding in Don Quixote was a picture of a Spanish banquet. A joyous conviviality prevailed round the board; for though Spaniards are generally abstemious, they are complete revellers on occasions like the present, and none more so than the Andalusians. For my part, there was something peculiarly exciting in thus sitting at a feast in the royal halls of the Alhambra, given by one who might claim remote affinity with its Moorish kings, and who was a lineal representative of Gonsalvo of Cordova, one of the most distinguished of the Christian conquerors.

The banquet ended, the company adjourned to the Hall of Ambassadors. Here every one endeavored to contribute to the general amusement, singing, improvising, telling wonderful tales, or dancing popular dances to that all pervading talisman of Spanish pleasure, the guitar.

The count's gifted little daughter was as usual the life and delight of the assemblage, and I was more than ever struck with her aptness and wonderful versatility. She took a part in two or three scenes of elegant comedy with some of her companions, and performed them with exquisite point and finished grace ; she gave imitations of the popular Italian singers, some serious, some comic, with a rare quality of voice, and, I was assured, with singular fidelity ; she imitated the dialects, dances, ballads, and movements and manners of the gipsies, and the peasants of the Vega, with equal felicity, but every thing was done with an all-pervading grace and a lady-like tact perfectly fascinating.

The great charm of every thing she did was its freedom from pretension or ambitious display, its happy spontaneity. Every thing sprang from the impulse of the moment ; or was in prompt compliance with a request. She seemed unconscious of the rarity and extent of her own talent, and was like a child at home revelling in the buoyancy of its own gay and innocent spirits. Indeed I was told she had never exerted her talents in general society, but only, as at present, in the domestic circle.

Her faculty of observation and her perception of character must have been remarkably quick, for she could have had only casual and transient glances at the scenes, manners and customs, depicted with such truth and spirit. " Indeed it is a continual wonder to us," said the countess, "where the child (la Niña) has picked up these things; her life being passed almost entirely at home, in the bosom of the family."

Evening approached; twilight began to throw its shadows about the halls, and the bats to steal forth from their lurking-place and flit about. A notion seized the little damsel and some of her youthful companions, to set out, under the guidance of Dolores, and explore the less frequented parts of the palace in quest of mysteries and enchantments. Thus conducted, they peeped fearfully into the gloomy old mosque, but quick drew back on being told that a Moorish king had been murdered there; they ventured into the mysterious regions of the bath, frightening themselves with the sounds and murmurs of hidden aqueducts, and flying with mock panic at the alarm of phantom Moors. They then undertook the adventure of the Iron Gate, a place of baleful note in the Alhambra. It is a postern gate, opening into a dark ravine; a narrow covered way leads down to it, which used to be the terror of Dolores and her playmates in childhood, as it was said a hand without a body would sometimes be stretched out from the wall and seize hold of the passers by.

The little party of enchantment hunters ventured to the entrance of the covered way, but nothing would tempt them to enter, in this hour of gathering gloom; they dreaded the grasp of the phantom arm.

At length they came running back into the Hall of Ambassadors in a mock paroxysm of terror; they had positively seen two spectral figures all in white. They had not stopped to examine them; but could not be mistaken, for they glared distinctly through the surrounding gloom. Dolores soon arrived and explained the mystery. The spectres proved to be two statues of nymphs in white marble, placed at the entrance of a vaulted passage. Upon this a grave, but, as I thought, somewhat sly old gentleman present, who, I believe, was the count's advocate or legal adviser, assured them that these statues were connected with one of the greatest mysteries of the Albambra; that there was a curious history concerning them, and moreover, that they stood a living monument in marble of female secrecy and discretion. All present entreated him to tell the history of the statues. He took a little time to recollect the details, and then gave them in substance the following legend.

LEGEND OF THE TWO DISCREET STATUES.

THERE lived once in a waste apartment of the Alhambra, a merry little fellow, named Lope Sanchez, who worked in the gardens, and was as brisk and blithe as a grasshopper, singing all day long. He was the life and soul of the fortress; when his work was over, he would sit on one of the stone benches of the esplanade, strum his guitar, and sing long ditties about the Cid, and Bernardo del Carpio, and Fernando del Pulgar, and other Spanish heroes, for the amusement of the old soldiers of the fortress, or would strike up a merrier tune, and set the girls dancing boleros and fandangos.

Like most little men, Lope Sanchez had a strapping buxom dame for a wife, who could almost have put him in her pocket; but he lacked the usual poor man's lot—instead of ten children he had but one. This was a little black-eyed girl about twelve years of age, named Sanchica, who was as merry as himself, and the delight of his heart. She played about him as he worked in the gardens, danced to his guitar as he sat in the shade, and ran as wild as a young fawn about the groves and alleys and ruined halls of the Alhambra.

It was now the eve of the blessed St. John, and the holiday-loving gossips of the Alhambra, men, women, and children, went up at night to the mountain of the sun, which rises above the Generalife, to keep their midsummer vigil on its level summit. It was a bright moonlight night, and all the mountains were gray and silvery, and the city, with its domes and spires, lay in shadows below, and the Vega was like a fairy land, with haunted streams gleaming among its dusky groves. On the highest part of the mountain they lit up a bonfire, according to an old custom of the country handed down from the Moors. The inhabitants of the surrounding country were keeping a similar vigil, and bonfires, here and there in the Vega, and along the folds of the mountains, blazed up palely in the moonlight.

The evening was gayly passed in dancing to the guitar of Lope Sanchez, who was never so joyous as when on a holiday revel of the kind. While the dance was going on, the little Sanchica with some of her playmates sported among the ruins of an old Moorish fort that crowns the mountain, when, in gathering pebbles in the fosse, she found a small hand curiously carved of jet, the fingers closed, and the thumb firmly clasped upon them. Overjoyed with her good fortune, she ran to her mother with her prize. It immediately became a subject of sage speculation, and was eyed by some with superstitious distrust. "Throw it away," said one; "it's Moorish—depend upon it there's mischief and witchcraft in it." "By no means," said another; "you may sell it for something to the jewellers of the Zacatin." In the midst of this discussion an old tawny soldier drew near, who had served in Africa, and was as swarthy as a Moor. He examined the hand with a knowing look. "I have seen things of this kind," said he, "among the Moors of Barbary. It is a great virtue to guard against the evil eye, and all kinds of spells and enchantments. I give you joy, friend Lope, this bodes good luck to your child."

Upon hearing this, the wife of Lope Sanchez tied the little hand of jet to a ribbon, and hung it round the neck of her daughter.

The sight of this talisman called up all the favorite superstitions about the Moors. The dance was neglected, and they sat in groups on the ground, telling old legendary tales handed down from their ancestors. Some of their stories turned upon the wonders of the very mountain upon which they were seated, which is a famous hobgoblin region. One ancient crone gave a long account of the subterranean palace in the bowels of that mountain where Boabdil and all his Moslem court are said to remain enchanted. "Among yonder ruins," said she, pointing to some crumbling walls and mounds of earth on a distant part of the mountain, "there is a deep black pit that goes down, down into the very heart of the mountain. For all the money in Granada I would not look down into it. Once upon a time a poor man of the Alhambra, who tended goats upon this mountain, scrambled down into that pit after a kid that had fallen in. He came out again all wild and staring, and told such things of what he had seen, that every one thought his brain was turned. He raved for a day or two about the hobgoblin Moors that had pursued him in the cavern, and could hardly be persuaded to drive his goats up again to the mountain. He did so at last, but, poor man, he never came down again. The neighbors found his goats browsing about the Moorish ruins, and his hat and mantle lying near the mouth of the pit, but he was never more heard of."

The little Sanchica listened with breathless attention to this story. She was of a curious nature, and felt immediately a great hankering to peep into this dangerous pit. Stealing away from her companions she sought the distant ruins, and after groping for some time among them came to a small hollow, or basin, near the brow of the mountain, where it swept steeply down into the valley of the Darro. In the centre of this basin yawned the mouth of the pit. Sanchica ventured to the verge, and peeped in. All was as black as pitch, and gave an idea of immeasurable depth. Her blood ran cold; she drew back, then peeped in again, then would have run away, then took another peep—the very horror of the thing was delightful to her. At length she rolled a large stone, and pushed it over the brink. For some time it fell in silence; then struck some rocky projection with a violent crash, then rebounded from side to side, rumbling and tumbling, with a noise like thunder, then made a final splash into water, far, far below—and all was again silent.

The silence, however, did not long continue. It seemed as if something had been awakened within this dreary abyss. A murmuring sound gradually rose out of the pit like the hum and buzz of a beehive. It grew louder and louder; there was the confusion of voices as of a distant multitude, together with the faint din of arms, clash of cymbals and clangor of trumpets, as if some army were marshalling for battle in the very bowels of the mountain.

The child drew off with silent awe, and hastened back to the place where she had left her parents and their companions. All were gone. The bonfire was expiring, and its last wreath of smoke curling up in the moonshine. The distant fires that had blazed along the mountains and in the Vega were all extinguished, and every thing seemed to have sunk to repose. Sanchica called her parents and some of her companions by name, but received no reply. She ran down the side of the mountain, and by the gardens of the Generalife, until she arrived in the alley of trees leading to the Alhambra, when she seated herself on a bench of a woody recess to recover breath. The bell from the watchtower of the Alhambra tolled midnight. There was a deep tranquillity as if all nature slept; excepting the low tinkling sound of an unseen stream that ran under the covert of the bushes. The breathing sweetness of the atmosphere was lulling her to sleep, when her eye was caught by something glittering at a distance, and to her surprise she beheld a long cavalcade of Moorish warriors pouring down the mountain side and along the leafy avenues. Some were armed with lances and shields; others with cimeters and battle-axes, and with polished cuirasses that flashed in the moonbeams. Their horses pranced proudly and champed upon their bits, but their tramp caused no more sound than if they had been shod with felt, and the riders were all as pale as death. Among them rode a beautiful lady, with a crowned head and long golden locks entwined with pearls. The housings of her palfry were of crimson velvet embroidered with gold, and swept the earth; but she rode all disconsolate, with eyes ever fixed upon the ground.

Then succeeded a train of courtiers magnificently arrayed in robes and turbans of divers colors, and amidst them, on a cream-colored charger, rode king Boabdil el Chico, in a royal mantle covered with jewels, and a crown sparkling with diamonds. The little Sanchica knew him by his yellow beard, and his resemblance to his portrait, which she had often seen in the picture gallery of the Generalife. She gazed in wonder and admiration at this royal pageant, as it passed glistening among the trees; but though she knew these monarchs and courtiers and warriors, so pale and silent, were out of the common course of nature, and things of magic and enchantment, yet she looked on with a bold heart, such courage did she derive from the mystic talisman of the hand, which was suspended about her neck.

The cavalcade having passed by, she rose and followed. It continued on to the great Gate of Justice, which stood wide open; the old invalid sentinels on duty lay on the stone benches of the barbican, buried in profound and apparently charmed sleep, and the phantom pageant swept noiselessly by them with flaunting banner and triumphant state. Sanchica would have followed; but to her surprise she beheld an opening in the earth, within the barbican, leading down beneath the foundations of the tower. She entered for a little distance, and was encouraged to proceed by finding steps rudely hewn in the rock, and a vaulted passage here and there lit up by a silver lamp, which, while it gave light, diffused likewise a grateful fragrance. Venturing on, she came at last to a great hall, wrought out of the heart of the mountain, magnificently furnished in the Moorish style, and lighted up by silver and crystal lamps. Here, on an ottoman, sat an old man in Moorish dress, with a long white beard, nodding and dozing, with a staff in his hand, which seemed ever to be slipping from his grasp; while at a little distance sat a beautiful lady, in ancient Spanish dress, with a coronet all sparkling with diamonds, and her hair entwined with pearls, who was softly playing on a silver lyre. The little Sanchica now recollected a story she had heard among the old people of the Alhambra, concerning a Gothic princess confined in the centre of the mountain by an old Arabian magician, whom she kept bound up in magic sleep by the power of music.

The lady paused with surprise at seeing a mortal in that enchanted hall. "Is it the eve of the blessed St. John?" said she.

"It is," replied Sanchica.

"Then for one night the magic charm is suspended. Come hither, child, and fear not. I am a Christian like thyself, though bound here by enchantment. Touch my fetters with the. talisman that hangs about thy neck, and for this night I shall be free."

So saying, she opened her robes and displayed a broad golden band round her waist, and a golden chain that fastened her to the ground. The child hesitated not to apply the little hand of jet to the golden band, and immediately the chain fell to the earth. At the sound the old man woke and began to rub his eyes; but the lady ran her fingers over the chords of the lyre, and again he fell into a slumber and began to nod, and his staff to falter in his hand. "Now," said the lady, "touch his staff with the talismanic hand of jet." The child did so, and it fell from his grasp, and he sank in a deep sleep on the ottoman. The lady gently laid the silver lyre on the ottoman, leaning it against the head of the sleeping magician; then touching the chords until they vibrated in his ear—"O potent spirit of harmony," said she, "continue thus to hold his senses in thraldom till the return of day. Now follow me, my child," continued she, "and thou shalt behold the Alhambra as it was in the days of its glory, for thou hast a magic talisman that reveals all enchantments." Sanchica followed the lady in silence. They passed up through the entrance of the cavern into the barbican of the Gate of Justice, and thence to the Plaza de los Algibes, or esplanade within the fortress.

This was all filled with Moorish soldiery, horse and foot, marshalled in squadrons, with banners displayed. There were royal guards also at the portal, and rows of African blacks with drawn cimeters. No one spoke a word, and Sanchica passed on fearlessly after her conductor. Her astonishment increased on entering the royal palace, in which she had been reared. The broad moonshine lit up all the halls and courts and gardens almost as brightly as if it were day, but revealed a far different scene from that to which she was accustomed. The walls of the apartments were no longer stained and rent by time. Instead of cobwebs, they were now hung with rich silks of Damascus, and the gildings and arabesque paintings were restored to their original brilliancy and freshness. The halls, no longer naked and unfurnished, were set out with divans and ottomans of the rarest stuffs, embroidered with pearls and studded with precious gems, and all the fountains in the courts and gardens were playing.

The kitchens were again in full operation; cooks were busy preparing shadowy dishes, and roasting and boiling the phantoms of pullets and partridges: servants were hurrying to and fro with silver dishes heaped up with dainties, and arranging a delicious banquet. The Court of Lions was thronged with guards, and courtiers, and alfaquis, as in the old times of the Moors; and at the upper end, in the saloon of judgment, sat Boabdil on his throne, surrounded by his court, and swaying a shadowy sceptre for the night. Notwithstanding all this throng and seeming bustle, not a voice nor a footstep was to be heard; nothing interrupted the midnight silence but the splashing of the fountains. The little Sanchica followed her conductress in mute amazement about the palace, until they came to a portal opening to the vaulted passages beneath the great tower of Comares. On each side of the portal sat the figure of a nymph, wrought out of alabaster. Their heads were turned aside, and their regards fixed upon the same spot within the vault. The enchanted lady

16

paused, and beckoned the child to her. " Here," said she, " is a great secret, which I will reveal to thee in reward for thy faith and courage. These discreet statues watch over a treasure hidden in old times by a Moorish king. Tell thy father to search the spot on which their eyes are fixed, and he will find what will make him richer than any man in Granada. Thy innocent hands alone, however, gifted as thou art also with the talisman, can remove the treasure. Bid thy father use it discreetly, and devote a part of it to the performance of daily masses for my deliverance from this unholy enchantment."

When the lady had spoken these words, she led the child onward to the little garden of Lindaraxa, which is hard by the vault of the statues. The moon trembled upon the waters of the solitary fountain in the centre of the garden, and shed a tender light upon the orange and citron trees. The beautiful lady plucked a branch of myrtle and wreathed it round the head of the child. " Let this be a memento," said she, " of what I have revealed to thee, and a testimonial of its truth. My hour is come ; I must return to the enchanted hall ; follow me not, lest evil befall thee—farewell. Remember what I have said, and have masses performed for my deliverance." So saying, the lady entered a dark passage leading beneath the tower of Comares, and was no longer seen.

The faint crowing of a cock was now heard from the cottages below the Alhambra, in the valley of the Darro, and a pale streak of light began to appear above the eastern mountains. A slight wind arose, there was a sound like the rustling of dry leaves through the courts and corridors, and door after door shut to with a jarring sound.

Sanchica returned to the scenes she had so lately beheld

thronged with the shadowy multitude, but Boabdil and his phantom court were gone. The moon shone into empty halls and galleries stripped of their transient splendor, stained and dilapidated by time, and hung with cobwebs. The bat flitted about in the uncertain light, and the frog croaked from the fish-pond.

Sanchica now made the best of her way to a remote staircase that led up to the humble apartment occupied by her family. The door as usual was open, for Lope Sanchez was too poor to need bolt or bar; she crept quietly to her pallet, and, putting the myrtle wreath beneath her pillow, soon fell asleep.

In the morning she related all that had befallen her to her father. Lope Sanchez, however, treated the whole as a mere dream, and laughed at the child for her credulity. He went forth to his customary labors in the garden, but had not been there long when his little daughter came running to him almost breathless. "Father! father!" cried she, "behold the myrtle wreath which the Moorish lady bound round my head."

Lope Sanchez gazed with astonishment, for the stalk of the myrtle was of pure gold, and every leaf was a sparkling emerald! Being not much accustomed to precious stones, he was ignorant of the real value of the wreath, but he saw enough to convince him that it was something more substantial than the stuff of which dreams are generally made, and that at any rate the child had dreamt to some purpose. His first care was to enjoin the most absolute secrecy upon his daughter; in this respect, however, he was secure, for she had discretion far beyond her years or sex. He then repaired to the vault, where stood the statues of the two alabaster nymphs. He remarked that their heads were turned from the portal, and that the regards of each were fixed upon the same point in the interior of the building. Lope Sanchez could not but admire this most discreet contrivance for guarding a secret. He drew a line from the eyes of the statues to the point of regard, made a private mark on the wall, and then re- tired.

All day, however, the mind of Lope Sanchez was distracted with a thousand cares. He could not help hovering within dis- tant view of the two statues, and became nervous from the dread that the golden secret might be discovered. Every footstep that approached the place made him tremble. He would have given any thing could he but have turned the heads of the statues, forgetting that they had looked precisely in the same direction for some hundreds of years, without any person being the wiser.

"A plague upon them," he would say to himself, "they'll betray all; did ever mortal hear of such a mode of guarding a secret?" Then on hearing any one advance, he would steal off, as though his very lurking near the place would awaken suspi- cion. Then he would return cautiously, and peep from a dis- tance to see if every thing was secure, but the sight of the statues would again call forth his indignation. " Ay, there they stand," would he say, " always looking, and looking, and looking, just where they should not. Confound them ! they are just like all their sex; if they have not tongues to tattle with, they'll be sure to do it with their eyes."

At length, to his relief, the long anxious day drew to a close. The sound of footsteps was no longer heard in the echoing halls of the Alhambra; the last stranger passed the threshold, the great portal was barred and bolted, and the bat and the frog and the hooting owl gradually resumed their nightly vocations in the deserted palace.

Lope Sanchez waited, however, until the night was far ad-

vanced before he ventured with his little daughter to the hall of
the two nymphs. He found them looking as knowingly and
mysteriously as ever at the secret place of deposit. "By your
leaves, gentle ladies," thought Lope Sanchez, as he passed between them, "I will relieve you from this charge that must have
set so heavy in your minds for the last two or three centuries."
He accordingly went to work at the part of the wall which he
had marked, and in a little while laid open a concealed recess,
in which stood two great jars of porcelain. He attempted to
draw them forth, but they were immovable, until touched by
the innocent hand of his little daughter. With her aid he dislodged them from their niche, and found, to his great joy, that
they were filled with pieces of Moorish gold, mingled with jewels
and precious stones. Before daylight he managed to convey
them to his chamber, and left the two guardian statues with
their eyes still fixed on the vacant wall.

Lope Sanchez had thus on a sudden become a rich man ; but
riches, as usual, brought a world of cares to which he had hitherto been a stranger. How was he to convey away his wealth with
safety ? How was he even to enter upon the enjoyment of it
without awakening suspicion ? Now, too, for the first time in
his life the dread of robbers entered into his mind. He looked
with terror at the insecurity of his habitation, and went to work
to barricade the doors and windows ; yet after all his precautions
he could not sleep soundly. His usual gayety was at an end, he
had no longer a joke or a song for his neighbors, and, in short,
became the most miserable animal in the Alhambra. His old
comrades remarked this alteration, pitied him heartily, and began
to desert him ; thinking he must be falling into want, and in
danger of looking to them for assistance. Little did they suspect that his only calamity was riches.

The wife of Lope Sanchez shared his anxiety, but then she had ghostly comfort. We ought before this to have mentioned that Lope, being rather a light inconsiderate little man, his wife was accustomed, in all grave matters, to seek the counsel and ministry of her confessor Fray Simon, a sturdy, broad-shouldered, blue-bearded, bullet-headed friar of the neighboring convent of San Francisco, who was in fact the spiritual comforter of half the good wives of the neighborhood. He was moreover in great esteem among divers sisterhoods of nuns; who requited him for his ghostly services by frequent presents of those little dainties and knick-knacks manufactured in convents, such as delicate confections, sweet biscuits, and bottles of spiced cordials, found to be marvellous restoratives after fasts and vigils.

Fray Simon thrived in the exercise of his functions. His oily skin glistened in the sunshine as he toiled up the hill of the Alhambra on a sultry day. Yet notwithstanding his sleek condition, the knotted rope round his waist showed the austerity of his self-discipline; the multitude doffed their caps to him as a mirror of piety, and even the dogs scented the odor of sanctity that exhaled from his garments, and howled from their kennels as he passed.

Such was Fray Simon, the spiritual counsellor of the comely wife of Lope Sanchez; and as the father confessor is the domestic confidant of women in humble life in Spain, he was soon acquainted, in great secrecy, with the story of the hidden treasure.

The friar opened his eyes and mouth and crossed himself a dozen times at the news. After a moment's pause, " Daughter of my soul !" said he, " know that thy husband has committed a double sin—a sin against both state and church ! The treasure he hath thus seized upon for himself, being found in the royal domains, belongs of course to the crown; but being infidel wealth, rescued as it were from the very fangs of Satan, should be devoted to the church. Still, however, the matter my be accommodated. Bring hither thy myrtle wreath."

When the good father beheld it, his eyes twinkled more than ever with admiration of the size and beauty of the emeralds. "This," said he, "being the first-fruits of this discovery, should be dedicated to pious purposes. I will hang it up as a votive offering before the image of San Francisco in our chapel and will earnestly pray to him, this very night, that your husband be permitted to remain in quiet possession of your wealth."

The good dame was delighted to make her peace with heaven at so cheap a rate, and the friar putting the wreath under his mantle, departed with saintly steps toward his convent.

When Lope Sanchez came home, his wife told him what had passed. He was excessively provoked, for he lacked his wife's devotion, and had for some time groaned in secret at the domestic visitations of the friar. "Woman," said he, "what hast thou done? thou hast put every thing at hazard by thy tattling."

"What!" cried the good woman, "would you forbid my disburdening my conscience to my confessor?"

"No, wife! confess as many of your own sins as you please; but as to this money-digging, it is a sin of my own, and my conscience is very easy under the weight of it."

There was no use, however, in complaining; the secret was told, and, like water spilled on the sand, was not again to be gathered. Their only chance was, that the friar would be discreet.

The next day, while Lope Sanchez was abroad there was a humble knocking at the door, and Fray Simon entered with meek and demure countenance.

"Daughter," said he, "I have earnestly prayed to San Fran cisco, and he has heard my prayer. In the dead of the night the saint appeared to me in a dream, but with a frowning aspect 'Why,' said he, 'dost thou pray to me to dispense with this treasure of the Gentiles, when thou seest the poverty of my chapel? Go to the house of Lope Sanchez, crave in my name a portion of the Moorish gold, to furnish two candlesticks for the main altar, and let him possess the residue in peace.'"

When the good woman heard of this vision, she crossed herself with awe, and going to the secret place where Lope had hid the treasure, she filled a great leathern purse with pieces of Moorish gold, and gave it to the friar. The pious monk bestowed upon her, in return, benedictions enough, if paid by Heaven, to enrich her race to the latest posterity; then slipping the purse into the sleeve of his habit, he folded his hands upon his breast, and departed with an air of humble thankfulness.

When Lope Sanchez heard of this second donation to the church, he had well nigh lost his senses. "Unfortunate man," cried he, "what will become of me? I shall be robbed by peace-meal; I shall be ruined and brought to beggary!"

It was with the utmost difficulty that his wife could pacify him, by reminding him of the countless wealth that yet remained, and how considerate it was for San Francisco to rest contented with so small a portion.

Unluckily, Fray Simon had a number of poor relations to be provided for, not to mention some half-dozen sturdy bullet-headed orphan children, and destitute foundlings that he had taken under his care. He repeated his visits, therefore, from day to day, with solicitations on behalf of Saint Dominick, Saint Andrew, Saint James, until poor Lope was driven to despair, and found that unless he got out of the reach of this holy friar, he should have to make peace-offerings to every saint in the calendar. He determined, therefore, to pack up his remaining wealth, beat a secret retreat in the night, and make off to another part of the kingdom.

Full of his project, he bought a stout mule for the purpose, and tethered it in a gloomy vault underneath the tower of the seven floors; the very place whence the Belludo. or goblin horse, is said to issue forth at midnight, and scour the streets of Granada, pursued by a pack of hell-hounds. Lope Sanchez had little faith in the story, but availed himself of the dread occasioned by it, knowing that no one would be likely to pry into the subterranean stable of the phantom steed. He sent off his family in the course of the day with orders to wait for him at a distant village. of the Vega. As the night advanced, he conveyed his treasure to the vault under the tower, and having loaded his mule, he led it forth, and cautiously descended the dusky avenue.

Honest Lope had taken his measures with the utmost secrecy, imparting them to no one but the faithful wife of his bosom. By some miraculous revelation, however, they became known to Fray Simon. The zealous friar beheld these infidel treasures on the point of slipping for ever out of his grasp, and determined to have one more dash at them for the benefit of the church and San Francisco. Accordingly, when the bells had rung for animas, and all the Alhambra was quiet, he stole out of his convent, and descending through the Gate of Justice, concealed himself among the thickets of roses and laurels that border the great avenue. Here he remained, counting the quarters of hours as they were sounded on the bell of the watchtower, and listening to the dreary hootings of owls, and the distant barking of dogs from the gipsy caverns.

16*

At length he heard the tramp of hoofs, and, through the gloom of the overshadowing trees, imperfectly beheld a steed descending the avenue. The sturdy friar chuckled at the idea of the knowing turn he was about to serve honest Lope.

Tucking up the skirts of his habit, and wriggling like a cat watching a mouse, he waited until his prey was directly before him, when darting forth from his leafy covert, and putting one hand on the shoulder and the other on the crupper, he made a vault that would not have disgraced the most experienced master of equitation, and alighted well-forked astride the steed. "Ah ha!" said the sturdy friar, "we shall now see who best understands the game." He had scarce uttered the words when the mule began to kick, and rear, and plunge and then set off full speed down the hill. The friar attempted to check him, but in vain. He bounded from rock to rock, and bush to bush; the friar's habit was torn to ribbons and fluttered in the wind, his shaven poll received many a hard knock from the branches of the trees, and many a scratch from the brambles. To add to his terror and distress, he found a pack of seven hounds in full cry at his heels, and perceived, too late, that he was actually mounted upon the terrible Belludo!

Away then they went, according to the ancient phrase, "pull devil, pull friar," down the great avenue, across the Plaza Nueva, along the Zacatin, around the Vivarrambla—never did huntsman and hound make a more furious run, or more infernal uproar. In vain did the friar invoke every saint in the calendar, and the holy Virgin into the bargain; every time he mentioned a name of the kind it was like a fresh application of the spur, and made the Belludo bound as high as a house. Through the remainder of the night was the unlucky Fray Simon carried hither and thither, and whither he would not, until every bone in his body ached, and he suffered a loss of leather too grievous to be mentioned. At length the crowing of a cock gave the signal of returning day. At the sound the goblin steed wheeled about, and galloped back for his tower. Again he scoured the Vivarrambla, the Zacatin, the Plaza Nueva, and the avenue of fountains, the seven dogs yelling, and barking, and leaping up, and snapping at the heels of the terrified friar. The first streak of day had just appeared as they reached the tower; here the goblin steed kicked up his heels, sent the friar a somerset through the air, plunged into the dark vault followed by the infernal pack, and a profound silence succeeded to the late deafening clamor.

Was ever so diabolical a trick played off upon a holy friar? A peasant going to his labors at early dawn found the unfortunate Fray Simon lying under a fig-tree at the foot of the tower, but so bruised and bedevilled that he could neither speak nor move. He was conveyed with all care and tenderness to his cell, and the story went that he had been waylaid and maltreated by robbers. A day or two elapsed before he recovered the use of his limbs; he consoled himself, in the meantime, with the thoughts that though the mule with the treasure had escaped him, he had previously had some rare pickings at the infidel spoils. His first care on being able to use his limbs, was to search beneath his pallet, where he had secreted the myrtle wreath and the leathern pouches of gold extracted from the piety of dame Sanchez. What was his dismay at finding the wreath, in effect, but a withered branch of myrtle, and the leathern pouches filled with sand and gravel!

Fray Simon, with all his chagrin, had the discretion to hold his tongue, for to betray the secret might draw on him the ridicule of the public, and the punishment of his superior: it was not until many years afterwards, on his death-bed, that he revealed to his confessor his nocturnal ride on the Belludo.

Nothing was heard of Lope Sanchez for a long time after his disappearance from the Alhambra. His memory was always cherished as that of a merry companion, though it was feared, from the care and melancholy observed in his conduct shortly before his mysterious departure, that poverty and distress had driven him to some extremity. Some years afterwards one of his old companions, an invalid soldier, being at Malaga, was knocked down and nearly run over by a coach and six. The carriage stopped; an old gentleman magnificently dressed, with a bag-wig and sword, stepped out to assist the poor invalid. What was the astonishment of the latter to behold in this grand cavalier his old friend Lope Sanchez, who was actually celebrating the marriage of his daughter Sanchica with one of the first grandees in the land.

The carriage contained the bridal party. There was dame Sanchez, now grown as round as a barrel, and dressed out with feathers and jewels, and necklaces of pearls, and necklaces of diamonds, and rings on every finger, altogether a finery of apparel that had not been seen since the days of Queen Sheba. The little Sanchica had now grown to be a woman, and for grace and beauty might have been mistaken for a duchess, if not a princess outright. The bridegroom sat beside her—rather a withered spindle-shanked little man, but this only proved him to be of the true-blue blood; a legitimate Spanish grandee being rarely above three cubits in stature. The match had been of the mother's making.

Riches had not spoiled the heart of honest Lope. He kept

his old comrade with him for several days; feasted him like a
king, took him to plays and bull-fights, and at length sent him
away rejoicing, with a big bag of money for himself, and another
to be distributed among his ancient messmates of the Alhambra.

Lope always gave out that a rich brother had died in America and left him heir to a copper mine; but the shrewd gossips
of the Alhambra insist that his wealth was all derived from his
having discovered the secret guarded by the two marble nymphs
of the Alhambra. It is remarked that these very discreet statues continue, even unto the present day, with their eyes fixed
most significantly on the same part of the wall; which leads
many to suppose there is still some hidden treasure remaining
there well worthy the attention of the enterprising traveller.
Though others, and particularly all female visitors, regard them
with great complacency as lasting monuments of the fact that
women can keep a secret.

THE CRUSADE OF THE GRAND MASTER OF ALCANTARA.

In the course of a morning's research among the old chronicles in the Library of the University, I came upon a little episode in the history of Granada, so strongly characteristic of the bigot zeal, which sometimes inflamed the Christian enterprises against this splendid but devoted city, that I was tempted to draw it forth from the parchment-bound volume in which it lay entombed and submit it to the reader.

In the year of redemption, 1394, there was a valiant and devout grand master of Alcántara, named Martin Yañez de Barbudo, who was inflamed with a vehement desire to serve God and fight the Moors. Unfortunately for this brave and pious cavalier, a profound peace existed between the Christian and Moslem powers. Henry III. had just ascended the throne of Castile, and Yusef ben Mohammed had succeeded to the throne of Granada, and both were disposed to continue the peace which had prevailed between their fathers. The grand master looked with repining at Moorish banners and weapons, which decorated his castle hall, trophies of the exploits of his predecessors; and repined at his fate to exist in a period of such inglorious tranquillity.

At length his impatience broke through all bounds, and seeing that he could find no public war in which to engage, he resolved to carve out a little war for himself. Such at least is the account given by some ancient chronicles, though others give the following as the motive for this sudden resolution to go campaigning.

As the grand master was one day seated at table with several of his cavaliers, a man suddenly entered the hall; tall, meagre and bony, with haggard countenance and fiery eye. All recognized him for a hermit, who had been a soldier in his youth, but now led a life of penitence in a cave. He advanced to the table and struck upon it with a fist that seemed of iron. " Cavaliers," said he, "why sit ye here idly, with your weapons resting against the wall, while the enemies of the faith lord it over the fairest portion of the land ?"

"Holy father, what wouldst thou have us do," asked the grand master, "seeing the wars are over and our swords bound up by treaties of peace ?"

"Listen to my words," replied the hermit. " As I was seated late at night at the entrance of my cave, contemplating the heavens, I fell into a reverie, and a wonderful vision was presented to me. I beheld the moon, a mere crescent, yet luminous as the brightest silver, and it hung in the heavens over the kingdom of Granada. While I was looking at it, behold there shot forth from the firmament a blazing star, which, as it went, drew after it all the stars of heaven ; and they assailed the moon and drove it from the skies ; and the whole firmament was filled with the glory of that blazing star. While mine eyes were yet dazzled by this wondrous sight, some one stood by me with snowy wings and a shining countenance. 'Oh man of prayer,' said he, ' get thee to the grand master of Alcántara and tell him of the vision thou hast beheld. He is the blazing star, destined to drive the crescent, the Moslem emblem, from the land. Let him boldly draw the sword and continue the good work begun by Pelazo of old, and victory will assuredly attend his banner.' "

The grand master listened to the hermit as to a messenger from heaven, and followed his counsel in all things. By his advice he dispatched two of his stoutest warriors, armed cap-a-pie, on an embassy to the Moorish king. They entered the gates of Granada without molestation, as the nations were at peace; and made their way to the Alhambra, where they were promptly admitted to the king, who received them in the Hall of Ambassadors. They delivered their message roundly and hardily. "We come, oh king, from Don Martin Tañez de Barbudo, grand master of Alcántara; who affirms the faith of Jesus Christ to be true and holy, and that of Mahomet false and detestable, and he challenges thee to maintain the contrary, hand to hand, in single combat. Shouldst thou refuse, he offers to combat with one hundred cavaliers against two hundred; or, in like proportion, to the number of one thousand, always allowing thy faith a double number of champions. Remember, oh king, that thou canst not refuse this challenge; since thy prophet, knowing the impossibility of maintaining his doctrines by argument, has commanded his followers to enforce them with the sword."

The beard of king Jusef trembled with indignation. "The master of Alcántara," said he, "is a madman to send such a message, and ye are saucy knaves to bring it."

So saying, he ordered the ambassadors to be thrown into a dungeon, by way of giving them a lesson in diplomacy; and they were roughly treated on their way thither by the populace, who were exasperated at this insult to their sovereign and their faith.

The grand master of Alcántara could scarcely credit the tidings of the maltreatment of his messengers; but the hermit rejoiced when they were repeated to him. " God," said he, " has blinded this infidel king for his downfall. Since he has sent no reply to thy defiance, consider it accepted. Marshal thy forces, therefore; march forward to Granada; pause not until thou seest the gate of Elvira. A miracle will be wrought in thy favor. There will be a great battle; the enemy will be overthrown; but not one of thy soldiers will be slain."

The grand master called upon every warrior zealous in the Christian cause to aid him in this crusade. In a little while three hundred horsemen and a thousand foot-soldiers rallied under his standard. The horsemen were veterans; seasoned to battle and well armed; but the infantry were raw and undisciplined. The victory, however, was to be miraculous; the grand master was a man of surpassing faith, and knew that the weaker the means the greater the miracle. He sallied forth confidently, therefore, with his little army, and the hermit strode ahead bearing a cross on the end of a long pole, and beneath it the pennon of the order of Alcántara.

As they approached the city of Cordova they were overtaken by messengers, spurring in all haste, bearing missives from the Castilian monarch, forbidding the enterprise. The grand master was a man of a single mind and a single will; in other words, a man of one idea. " Were I on any other errand," said he, " I should obey these letters as coming from my lord the king; but I am sent by a higher power than the king. In compliance with its commands I have advanced the cross thus far against the infidels; and it would be treason to the standard of Christ to turn back without achieving my errand."

So the trumpets were sounded; the cross was again reared aloft, and the band of zealots resumed their march. As they passed through the streets of Cordova the people were amazed at beholding a hermit bearing a cross at the head of a warlike multitude; but when they learnt that a miraculous victory was to be effected and Granada destroyed, laborers and artisans threw by the implements of their handicrafts and joined in the crusade; while a mercenary rabble followed on with a view of plunder.

A number of cavaliers of rank who lacked faith in the promised miracle, and dreaded the consequences of this unprovoked irruption into the country of the Moor, assembled at the bridge of the Guadalquivir and endeavored to dissuade the grand master from crossing. He was deaf to prayers, expostulations or menaces; his followers were enraged at this opposition to the cause of the faith; they put an end to the parley by their clamors; the cross was again reared and borne triumphantly across the bridge.

The multitude increased as it proceeded; by the time the grand master had reached Alcala la Real, which stands on a mountain overlooking the Vega of Granada, upwards of five thousand men on foot had joined his standard.

At Alcala came forth Alonzo Fernandez de Cordova, Lord of Aguilar, his brother Diego Fernandez, Marshal of Castile, and other cavaliers of valor and experience. Placing themselves in the way of the grand master, "What madness is this, Don Martin?" said they; "the Moorish king has two hundred thousand foot-soldiers and five thousand horse within his walls; what can you and your handful of cavaliers and your noisy rabble do against such force? Bethink you of the disasters which have befallen other Christian commanders, who have crossed these rocky borders with ten times your force. Think, too, of the mischief that will be brought upon this kingdom by an outrage of the kind committed by a man of your rank and importance, a grand master of Alcántara. Pause, we entreat you, while the truce is yet unbroken. Await within the borders the reply of the king of Granada to your challenge. If he agree to meet you singly, or with champions two or three, it will be your individual contest, and fight it out in God's name; if he refuse, you may return home with great honor and the disgrace will fall upon the Moors."

Several cavaliers, who had hitherto followed the grand master with devoted zeal, were moved by these expostulations, and suggested to him the policy of listening to this advice.

" Cavaliers," said he, addressing himself to Alonzo Fernandez de Cordova and his companions ; " I thank you for the counsel you have so kindly bestowed upon me, and if I were merely in pursuit of individual glory I might be swayed by it. But I am engaged to achieve a great triumph of the faith, which God is to effect by miracle through my means. As to you, cavaliers," turning to those of his followers who had wavered, "if your hearts fail you, or you repent of having put your hands to this good work ; return in God's name, and my blessing go with you. For myself, though I have none to stand by me but this holy hermit, yet will I assuredly proceed ; until I have planted this sacred standard on the walls of Granada, or perished in the attempt."

" Don Martin Yañez de Barbudo," replied the cavaliers, "we. are not men to turn our backs upon our commander, however rash his enterprise. We spoke but in caution. Lead on, therefore, and if it be to the death, be assured to the death we will follow thee "

By this time the common soldiers became impatient. "Forward! forward!" shouted they. "Forward in the cause of faith." So the grand master gave signal, the hermit again reared the cross aloft, and they poured down a defile of the mountain, with solemn chants of triumph.

That night they encamped at the river of Azores, and the next morning, which was Sunday, crossed the borders. Their first pause was at an atalaya or solitary tower, built upon a rock; a frontier post to keep a watch upon the border, and give notice of invasion. It was thence called el Torre del Exea (the tower of the spy). The grand master halted before it and summoned its petty garrison to surrender. He was answered by a shower of stones and arrows, which wounded him in the hand and killed three of his men.

"How is this, father?" said he to the hermit, "you assured me that not one of my followers would be slain!"

"True, my son; but I meant in the great battle of the infidel king; what need is there of miracle to aid in the capture of a petty tower?"

The grand master was satisfied. He ordered wood to be piled against the door of the tower to burn it down. In the mean time provisions were unloaded from the sumpter-mules, and the crusaders, withdrawing beyond bow-shot, sat down on the grass to a repast to strengthen them for the arduous day's work before them. While thus engaged, they were startled by the sudden appearance of a great Moorish host. The atalayas had given the alarm by fire and smoke from the mountain tops of "an enemy across the border," and the king of Granada had sallied forth with a great force to the encounter.

The crusaders, nearly taken by surprise, flew to arms and

prepared for battle. The grand master ordered his three hundred horsemen to dismount and fight on foot in support of the infantry. The Moors, however, charged so suddenly that they separated the cavaliers from the foot-soldiers and prevented their uniting. The grand master gave the old war cry, "Santiago! Santiago! and close Spain!" He and his knights breasted the fury of the battle, but were surrounded by a countless host and assailed with arrows, stones, darts, and arquebuses. Still they fought fearlessly, and made prodigious slaughter. The hermit mingled in the hottest of the fight. In one hand he bore the cross, in the other he brandished a sword, with which he dealt about him like a maniac, slaying several of the enemy, until he sank to the ground covered with wounds. The grand master saw him fall, and saw too late the fallacy of his prophecies. Despair, however, only made him fight the more fiercely, until he also fell overpowered by numbers. His devoted cavaliers emulated his holy zeal. Not one turned his back nor asked for mercy; all fought until they fell. As to the foot-soldiers, many were killed, many taken prisoners; the residue escaped to Alcala la Real. When the Moors came to strip the slain, the wounds of the cavaliers were all found to be in front.

Such was the catastrophe of this fanatic enterprise. The Moors vaunted it as a decisive proof of the superior sanctity of their faith, and extolled their king to the skies when he returned in triumph to Granada.

As it was satisfactorily shown that this crusade was the enterprise of an individual and contrary to the express orders of the king of Castile, the peace of the two kingdoms was not interrupted. Nay, the Moors evinced a feeling of respect for the valor of the unfortunate grand master, and readily gave up his body to Don Alonzo Fernandez de Cordova, who came from Alcala to seek it. The Christians of the frontier united in paying the last sad honors to his memory. His body was placed upon a bier, covered with the pennon of the order of Alcántara; and the broken cross, the emblem of his confident hopes and fatal disappointment, was borne before it. In this way his remains were carried back in funeral procession, through the mountain tract which he had traversed so resolutely. Wherever it passed, through a town or village, the populace followed, with tears and lamentations, bewailing him as a valiant knight and a martyr to the faith. His body was interred in the chapel of the convent of Santa Maria de Almocovara, and on his sepulchre may still be seen engraven in quaint and antique Spanish the following testimonial to his bravery:

" HERE LIES ONE WHOSE HEART NEVER KNEW FEAR."

(Aqui yaz aquel que par neua cosa nunca eve pavor en seu corazon.)*

* Torres. Hist. Ord. Alcántara. Cron. Enrique III., por Pedro Lopez de Ayala.

SPANISH ROMANCE.

In the latter part of my sojourn in the Alhambra, I made frequent descents into the Jesuit's Library of the University; and relished more and more the old Spanish chronicles, which I found there bound in parchment. I delight in those quaint histories which treat of the times when the Moslems maintained a foothold in the Peninsula. With all their bigotry and occasional intolerance, they are full of noble acts and generous sentiments, and have a high, spicy, oriental flavor, not to be found in other records of the times, which were merely European. In fact, Spain, even at the present day, is a country apart; severed in history, habits, manners, and modes of thinking, from all the rest of Europe. It is a romantic country; but its romance has none of the sentimentality of modern European romance; it is chiefly derived from the brilliant regions of the East, and from the high-minded school of Saracenic chivalry.

The Arab invasion and conquest brought a higher civilization and a nobler style of thinking, into Gothic Spain. The Arabs were a quick-witted, sagacious, proud-spirited, and poetical people and were imbued with oriental science and literature. Wherever they established a seat of power, it became a rallying place for the learned and ingenious; and they softened and refined the people whom they conquered. By degrees, occupancy seemed to give them an hereditary right to their foothold in the land; they ceased to be looked upon as invaders, and were regarded as rival neighbors. The peninsula, broken up into a variety of states, both Christian and Moslem, became, for centuries, a great campaigning ground, where the art of war seemed to be the principal business of man, and was carried to the highest pitch of romantic chivalry. The original ground of hostility, a difference of faith, gradually lost its rancor. Neighboring states, of opposite creeds, were occasionally linked together in alliances, offensive and defensive; so that the cross and crescent were to be seen side by side, fighting against some common enemy. In times of peace, too, the noble youth of either faith resorted to the same cities, Christian or Moslem, to school themselves in military science. Even in the temporary truces of sanguinary wars, the warriors who had recently striven together in the deadly conflicts of the field, laid aside their animosity, met at tournaments, jousts, and other military festivities, and exchanged the courtesies of gentle and generous spirits. Thus the opposite races became frequently mingled together in peaceful intercourse, or if any rivalry took place, it was in those high courtesies and nobler acts, which bespeak the accomplished cavalier. Warriors, of opposite creeds, became ambitious of transcending each other in magnanimity as well as valor. Indeed, the chivalric virtues were refined upon to a degree sometimes fastidious and constrained; but at other times, inexpressibly noble and affecting. The annals of the times teem with illustrious instances of high-wrought courtesy, romantic generosity, lofty disinterestedness, and punctilious honor, that warm the very soul to read them. These have furnished themes for national plays and poems, or have been cele-

brated in those all-pervading ballads, which are as the life-breath
of the people, and thus have continued to exercise an influence
on the national character, which centuries of vicissitude and decline have not been able to destroy; so that, with all their faults,
and they are many, the Spaniards, even at the present day, are,
on many points, the most high-minded and proud-spirited people
of Europe. It is true, the romance of feeling derived from the
sources I have mentioned, has, like all other romance, its affecta-
tions and extremes. It renders the Spaniard at times pompous
and grandiloquent; prone to carry the 'pundonor,' or point of
honor, beyond the bounds of sober sense and sound morality,
disposed, in the midst of poverty, to affect the 'grande caballero,'
and to look down with sovereign disdain upon 'arts mechanical,'
and all the gainful pursuits of plebeian life; but this very infla-
tion of spirit, while it fills his brain with vapors, lifts him above
a thousand meannesses; and though it often keeps him in indi-
gence, ever protects him from vulgarity.

In the present day, when popular literature is running into
the low levels of life, and luxuriating on the vices and follies of
mankind; and when the universal pursuit of gain is trampling
down the early growth of poetic feeling, and wearing out the verdure of the soul, I question whether it would not be of service
for the reader occasionally to turn to these records of prouder
times and loftier modes of thinking; and to steep himself to the
very lips in old Spanish romance.

With these preliminary suggestions, the fruit of a morning's
reading and rumination, in the old Jesuit's Library of the University, I will give him a legend in point, drawn forth from one
of the venerable chronicles alluded to.

17

LEGEND OF DON MUNIO SANCHO DE HINOJOSA.

In the cloisters of the ancient Benedictine convent of San Domingo, at Silos, in Castile, are the mouldering yet magnificent monuments of the once powerful and chivalrous family of Hinojosa. Among these reclines the marble figure of a knight, in complete armor, with the hands pressed together, as if in prayer. On one side of his tomb is sculptured in relief a band of Christian cavaliers, capturing a cavalcade of male and female Moors ; on the other side, the same cavaliers are represented kneeling before an altar. The tomb, like most of the neighboring monuments, is almost in ruins, and the sculpture is nearly unintelligible, excepting to the keen eye of the antiquary. The story connected with the sepulchre, however, is still preserved in the old Spanish chronicles, and is to the following purport.

In old times, several hundred years ago, there was a noble Castilian cavalier, named Don Munio Sancho de Hinojosa, lord of a border castle, which had stood the brunt of many a Moorish foray. He had seventy horsemen as his household troops. all of the ancient Castilian proof; stark warriors, hard riders, and men of iron; with these he scoured the Moorish lands, and made his name terrible throughout the borders. His castle hall was covered with banners, cimeters, and Moslem helms, the trophies of his prowess. Don Munio was, moreover, a keen huntsman; and rejoiced in hounds of all kinds, steeds for the chase, and hawks for the towering sport of falconry. When not engaged in warfare, his delight was to beat up the neighboring forests; and scarcely ever did he ride forth, without hound and horn, a boarspear in his hand, or a hawk upon his fist, and an attendant train of huntsmen.

His wife, Doña Maria Palacin, was of a gentle and timid nature, little fitted to be the spouse of so hardy and adventurous a knight; and many a tear did the poor lady shed, when he sallied forth upon his daring enterprises, and many a prayer did she offer up for his safety.

As this doughty cavalier was one day hunting, he stationed himself in a thicket, on the borders of a green glade of the forest, and dispersed his followers to rouse the game, and drive it toward his stand. He had not been here long, when a cavalcade of Moors, of both sexes, came prankling over the forest lawn. They were unarmed, and magnificently dressed in robes of tissue and embroidery, rich shawls of India, bracelets and anklets of gold, and jewels that sparkled in the sun.

At the head of this gay cavalcade rode a youthful cavalier, superior to the rest in dignity and loftiness of demeanor, and in splendor of attire: beside him was a damsel, whose veil, blown aside by the breeze, displayed a face of surpassing beauty, and eyes cast down in maiden modesty, yet beaming with tenderness and joy.

Don Munio thanked his stars for sending him such a prize, and exulted at the thought of bearing home to his wife the glittering spoils of these infidels. Putting his hunting horn to his lips, he gave a blast that rung through the forest. His huntsmen came running from all quarters, and the astonished Moors were surrounded and made captives

The beautiful Moor wrung her hands in despair, and her female attendants uttered the most piercing cries. The young Moorish cavalier alone retained self-possession. He inquired the name of the Christian knight, who commanded this troop of horsemen. When told that it was Don Munio Sancho de Hinojosa, his countenance lighted up. Approaching that cavalier, and kissing his hand, " Don Munio Sancho," said he, " I have heard of your fame as a true and valiant knight, terrible in arms, but schooled in the noble virtues of chivalry. Such do I trust to find you. In me you behold Abadil, son of a Moorish alcayde. I am on the way to celebrate my nuptials with this lady; chance has thrown us in your power, but I confide in your magnanimity. Take all our treasure and jewels; demand what ransom you think proper for our persons, but suffer us not to be insulted nor dishonored."

When the good knight heard this appeal, and beheld the beauty of the youthful pair, his heart was touched with tenderness and courtesy. " God forbid," said he, " that I should disturb such happy nuptials. My prisoners in troth shall ye be, for fifteen days, and immured within my castle, where I claim, as conqueror, the right of celebrating your espousals."

So saying, he dispatched one of his fleetest horsemen in advance, to notify Doña Maria Palacin of the coming of this bridal party; while he and his huntsmen escorted the cavalcade,

not as captors, but as a guard of honor. As they drew near
to the castle, the banners were hung out, and the trumpets sounded from the battlements ; and on their nearer approach, the draw-bridge was lowered, and Doña Maria came
forth to meet them, attended. by her ladies and knights, her
pages and her minstrels. She took the young bride, Allifra, in
her arms, kissed her with the tenderness of a sister, and conducted her into the castle. In the mean time, Don Munio sent forth
missives in every direction, and had viands and dainties of all
kinds collected from the country round ; and the wedding of the
Moorish lovers was celebrated with all possible state and festi-
vity. For fifteen days, the castle was given up to joy and revelry.
There were tiltings and jousts at the ring, and bull-fights, and
banquets, and dances to the sound of minstrelsy. When the
fifteen days were at an end, he made the bride and bridegroom
magnificent presents, and conducted them and their attendants
safely beyond the borders. Such, in old times, were the courtesy
and generosity of a Spanish cavalier.

Several years after this event, the king of Castile summoned
his nobles to assist him in a campaign against the Moors. Don
Munio Sancho was among the first to answer to the call, with
seventy horsemen, all stanch and well-tried warriors. His wife,
Doña Maria, hung about his neck. " Alas, my lord !" exclaimed she, " how often wilt thou tempt thy fate, and when will thy
thirst for glory be appeased !"

" One battle more," replied Don Munio, " one battle more,
for the honor of Castile, and I here make a vow, that when this
is over, I will lay by my sword, and repair with my cavaliers in
pilgrimage to the sepulchre of our Lord at Jerusalem." The
cavaliers all joined with him in the vow, and Doña Maria felt

ın some degree soothed in spirit; still, she saw with a heavy heart the departure of her husband, and watched his banner with wistful eyes, until it disappeared among the trees of the forest.

The king of Castile led his army to the plains of Almanara, where they encountered the Moorish host, near to Ucles. The battle was long and bloody; the Christians repeatedly wavered, and were as often rallied by the energy of their commanders. Don Munio was covered with wounds, but refused to leave the field. The Christians at length gave way, and the king was hardly pressed, and in danger of being captured.

Don Munio called upon his cavaliers to follow him to the rescue. "Now is the time," cried he, " to prove your loyalty. Fall to, like brave men! We fight for the true faith, and if we lose our lives here, we gain a better life hereafter."

Rushing with his men between the king and his pursuers, they checked the latter in their career, and gave time for their monarch to escape; but they fell victims to their loyalty. They all fought to the last gasp. Don Munio was singled out by a powerful Moorish knight, but having been wounded in the right arm, he fought to disadvantage, and was slain. The battle being over, the Moor paused to possess himself of the spoils of this redoubtable Christian warrior. When he unlaced the helmet, however, and beheld the countenance of Don Munio, he gave a great cry, and smote his breast. "Woe is me!" cried he, "I have slain my benefactor! The flower of knightly virtue! the most magnanimous of cavaliers!"

While the battle had been raging on the plain of Salmanara, Doña Maria Palacin remained in her castle, a prey to the keenest anxiety. Her eyes were ever fixed on the road that led from the country of the Moors, and often she asked the watchman of the tower, " What seest thou ?"

One evening, at the shadowy hour of twilight, the warden sounded his horn. " I see," cried he, " a numerous train winding up the valley. There are mingled Moors and Christians. The banner of my lord is in the advance. Joyful tidings !' exclaimed the old seneschal: " my lord returns in triumph, and brings captives !" Then the castle courts rang with shouts of joy ; and the standard was displayed, and the trumpets were sounded, and the draw-bridge was lowered, and Doña Maria went forth with her ladies, and her knights, and her pages, and her minstrels, to welcome her lord from the wars. But as the train drew nigh, she beheld a sumptuous bier, covered with black velvet, and on it lay a warrior, as if taking his repose : he lay in his armor, with his helmet on his head, and his sword in his hand, as one who had never been conquered, and around the bier were the escutcheons of the house of Hinojosa.

A number of Moorish cavaliers attended the bier, with emblems of mourning, and with dejected countenances ; and their leader cast himself at the feet of Doña Maria, and hid his face in his hands. She beheld in him the gallant Abadil, whom she had once welcomed with his bride to her castle ; but who now came with the body of her lord, whom he had unknowingly slain in battle !

The sepulchre erected in the cloisters of the convent of San Domingo, was achieved at the expense of the Moor Abadil, as a feeble testimony of his grief for the death of the good knight Don Munio, and his reverence for his memory. The tender and faithful Doña Maria soon followed her lord to the tomb. On one of the stones of a small arch, beside his sepulchre, is the following simple inscription: " *Hic jacet Maria Palacin, uxor Munonis Sancij De Finojosa :*" Here lies Maria Palacin, wife of Munio Sancho de Hinojosa.

The legend of Don Munio Sancho does not conclude with his death. On the same day on which the battle took place on the plain of Salmanara, a chaplain of the Holy Temple at Jerusalem, while standing at the outer gate, beheld a train of Christian cavaliers advancing, as if in pilgrimage. The chaplain was a native of Spain, and as the pilgrims approached, he knew the foremost to be Don Munio Sancho de Hinojosa, with whom he had been well acquainted in former times. Hastening to the patriarch, he told him of the honorable rank of the.pilgrims at the gate. The patriarch, therefore, went forth with a grand procession of priests and monks, and received the pilgrims with all due honor. There were seventy cavaliers, beside their leader, all stark and lofty warriors. They carried their helmets in their hands, and their faces were deadly pale. They greeted no one, nor looked either to the right or to the left, but entered the chapel, and kneeling before the sepulchre of our Saviour, performed their orisons in silence. When they had concluded, they rose as if to depart, and the patriarch and his attendants advanced to speak to them, but they were no more to be seen. Every one marvelled what could be the meaning of this prodigy. The patriarch carefully noted down the day, and sent to Castile to learn tidings of Don Munio Sancho de Hinojosa. He received for reply, that on the very day specified, that worthy knight, with seventy of his followers, had been slain in battle. These, therefore, must have been the blessed spirits of those Christian warriors, come to fulfil their vow of pilgrimage to the Holy Sepulchrc at Jerusalem. Such was Castilian faith, in the olden time, which kept its word, even beyond the grave.

If any one should doubt of the miraculous apparition of these phantom knights, let him consult the History of the Kings of Castile and Leon, by the learned and pious Fray Prudencio de Sandoval, bishop of Pamplona, where he will find it recorded in the History of king Don Alonzo VI., on the hundred and second page. It is too precious a legend, to be lightly abandoned to the doubter.

POETS AND POETRY OF MOSLEM ANDALUS.

DURING the latter part of my sojourn in the Alhambra I was more than once visited by the Moor of Tetuan, with whom I took great pleasure in rambling through the halls and courts, and getting him to explain to me the Arabic inscriptions. He endeavored to do so faithfully; but, though he succeeded in giving me the thought, he despaired of imparting an idea of the grace and beauty of the language. The aroma of the poetry, said he, is all lost in translation. Enough was imparted, however, to increase the stock of my delightful associations with this extraordinary pile. Perhaps there never was a monument more characteristic of an age and people than the Alhambra; a rugged fortress without, a voluptuous palace within; war frowning from its battlements; poetry breathing throughout the fairy architecture of its halls. One is irresistibly transported in imagination to those times when Moslem Spain was a region of light amid Christian, yet benighted Europe; externally a warrior power fighting for existence; internally a realm devoted to literature, science, and the arts; where philosophy was cultivated with passion, though wrought up into subtleties and refinements; and where the luxuries of sense were transcended by those of thought and imagination.

Arab poetry, we are told, arrived at its highest splendor under the Ommiades of Spain, who for a long time centred the power and splendor of the western Caliphat at Cordova. Most of the sovereigns of that brilliant line were themselves poets. One of the last of them was Mahomed ben Abderahman. He led the life of a sybarite in the famous palace and gardens of Azahara, surrounding himself with all that could excite the imagination and delight the senses. His palace was the resort of poets. His vizier, Ibn Zeydun, was called the Horace of Moslem Spain, from his exquisite verses, which were recited with enthusiasm even in the saloons of the Eastern Caliphs. The vizier became passionately enamored of the princess Walada, daughter of Mahomed. She was the idol of her father's court, a poetess of the highest order, and renowned for beauty as well as talent. If Ibn Zeydun was the Horace of Moslem Spain, she was its Sappho. The princess became the subject of the vizier's most impassioned verses; especially of a famous risáleh or epistle addressed to her, which the historian Ash-Shakandi declares has never been equalled for tenderness and melancholy. Whether the poet was happy in his love, the authors I have consulted do not say; but one intimates that the princess was discreet as she was beautiful, and caused many a lover to sigh in vain. In fact, the reign of love and poetry in the delicious abode of Zahara, was soon brought to a close by a popular insurrection. Mahomed with his family took refuge in the fortress of Ucles, near Toledo, where he was treacherously poisoned by the Alcayde; and thus perished one of the last of the Ommiades.

The downfall of that brilliant dynasty, which had concentrated every thing at Cordova, was favorable to the general literature of Morisco Spain.

"After the breaking of the necklace and the scattering of its pearls," says Ash-Shakandi, "the kings of small states divided among themselves the patrimony of the Beni Ommiah."

They vied with each other in filling their capitals with poets and learned men, and rewarded them with boundless prodigality. Such were the Moorish kings of Seville of the illustrious line of the Beni Abbad, "with whom," says the same writer, "resided fruit and palm-trees and pomegranates; who became the centre of eloquence in prose and verse; every day of whose reign was a solemn festivity; whose history abounds in generous actions and heroic deeds, that will last through surrounding ages and live for ever in the memory of man!"

No place, however, profited more in point of civilization and refinement by the downfall of the Western Caliphat than Granada. It succeeded to Cordova in splendor, while it surpassed it in romantic beauty of situation. The amenity of its climate, where the ardent heats of a southern summer were tempered by breezes from snow-clad mountains; the voluptuous repose of its valleys and the bosky luxuriance of its groves and gardens all awakened sensations of delight, and disposed the mind to love and poetry. Hence the great number of amatory poets that flourished in Granada. Hence those amorous canticles breathing of love and war, and wreathing chivalrous grace round the stern exercise of arms. Those ballads which still form the pride and delight of Spanish literature are but the echoes of amatory and chivalric lays, which once delighted the Moslem courts of Andalus; and in which a modern historian of Granada pretends to find the origin of the *rima Castellana* and the type of the "gay science" of the troubadours.*

* Miguel Lafuente Alcántara.

Poetry was cultivated in Granada by both sexes. "Had Allah," says Ash-Shakandi, "bestowed no other boon on Granada than that of making it the birth-place of so many poetesses; that alone would be sufficient for its glory."

Among the most famous of these was Hafsah; renowned, says the old chronicler, for beauty, talents, nobility, and wealth. We have a mere relic of her poetry in some verses, addressed to her lover, Ahmed, recalling an evening passed together in the garden of Maumal.

"Allah has given us a happy night, such as he never vouchafes to the wicked and the ignoble. We have beheld the cypresses of Maumal gently bowing their heads before the mountain breeze,— the sweet perfumed breeze that smelt of gillyflowers: the dove murmured her love among the trees; the sweet basil inclined its boughs to the limpid brook."

The garden of Maumal was famous among the Moors for its rivulets, its fountains, its flowers, and above all, its cypresses. It had its name from a vizier of Abdallah, grandson of Aben Habuz, and Sultan of Granada. Under the administration of this vizier many of the noblest public works were executed. He constructed an aqueduct by which water was brought from the mountains of Alfacar to irrigate the hills and orchards north of the city. He planted a public walk with cypress-trees, and "made delicious gardens for the solace of the melancholy Moors." "The name of Maumal," says Alcántara, "ought to be preserved in Granada in letters of gold." Perhaps it is as well preserved by being associated with the garden he planted; and by being mentioned in the verses of Hafsah. How often does a casual word from a poet confer immortality!

Perhaps the reader may be curious to learn something of the

story of Hafsah and her lover, thus connected with one of the beautiful localities of Granada. The following are all the particulars I have been able to rescue out of the darkness and oblivion which have settled upon the brightest names and geniuses of Moslem Spain.

Ahmed and Hafsah flourished in the sixth century of the Hegira; the twelfth of the Christian Era. Ahmed was the son of the Alcayde of Alcala la Real. His father designed him for public and military life and would have made him his lieutenant, but the youth was of a poetical temperament, and preferred a life of lettered ease in the delightful abodes of Granada. Here he surrounded himself by objects of taste in the arts, and by the works of the learned; he divided his time between study and social enjoyment. He was fond of the sports of the field, and kept horses, hawks, and hounds. He devoted himself to literature, became renowned for erudition, and his compositions in prose and verse were extolled for their beauty, and in the mouths of every one.

Of a tender, susceptible heart, and extremely sensible to female charms, he became the devoted lover of Hafsah. The passion was mutual, and for once the course of true love appeared to run smooth. The lovers were both young, equal in merit, fame, rank, and fortune, enamored of each other's genius as well as person, and inhabiting a region formed to be a realm of love and poetry. A poetical intercourse was carried on between them that formed the delight of Granada. They were continually interchanging verses and epistles; "the poetry of which," says the Arabian writer, Al Makkari, "was like the language of doves."

In the height of their happiness a change took place in the government of Granada. It was the time when the Almohades,

a Berber tribe of Mount Atlas, had acquired the control of
Moslem Spain, and removed the seat of government from Cordova
to Morocco. The Sultan Abdelmuman governed Spain through
his Walis and Alcaydes; and his son, Sidi Abu Said, was made
Wali of Granada. He governed in his father's name with royal
state and splendor, and with despotic sway. Being a stranger in
the country, and a Moor by birth, he sought to strengthen himself by drawing round him popular persons of the Arab race;
and to this effect made Ahmed, who was then in the zenith of his
fame and popularity, his vizier. Ahmed would have declined the
post, but the Wali was peremptory. Its duties were irksome to
him, and he spurned at its restraint. On a hawking party, with
some of his gay companions, he gave way to his poetic vein,
exulting in his breaking away from the thraldom of a despotic
master like a hawk from the jesses of the falconer, to follow the
soaring impulses of his soul.

His words were repeated to Sidi Abu Said. " Ahmed," said
the informant, " spurns at restraint and scoffs at thy authority."
The poet was instantly dismissed from office. The loss of an
irksome post was no grievance to one of his joyous temperament;
but he soon discovered the real cause of his removal. The Wali
was his rival. He had seen and become enamored of Hafsah.
What was worse, Hafsah was dazzled with the conquest she had
made.

For a time Ahmed treated the matter with ridicule; and
appealed to the prejudice existing between the Arab and Moorish
races. Sidi Abu Said was of a dark olive complexion. " How
canst thou endure that black man?" said he, scornfully. " By
Allah, for twenty dinars I can buy thee a better than he in the
slave market."

The scoff reached the ears of Sidi Abu Said and rankled in his heart.

At other times, Ahmed gave way to grief and tenderness, recalling past scenes of happiness, reproaching Hafsah with her inconstancy, and warning her in despairing accents that she would be the cause of his death. His words were unheeded. The idea of having the son of the Sultan for a lover had captivated the imagination of the poetess.

Maddened by jealousy and despair, Ahmed joined in a conspiracy against the ruling dynasty. It was discovered, and the conspirators fled from Granada. Some escaped to a castle on the mountains, Ahmed took refuge in Malaga, where he concealed himself, intending to embark for Valencia. He was discovered, loaded with chains and thrown into a dungeon, to abide the decision of Sidi Abu Said.

He was visited in prison by a nephew, who has left on record an account of the interview. The youth was moved to tears at seeing his illustrious relative, late so prosperous and honored, fettered like a malefactor.

"Why dost thou weep?" said Ahmed. "Are these tears shed for me? For me, who have enjoyed all that the world could give? Weep not for me. I have had my share of happiness; banqueted on the daintiest fare; quaffed out of crystal cups; slept on beds of down; been arrayed in the richest silks and brocades; ridden the fleetest steeds; enjoyed the loves of the fairest maidens. Weep not for me. My present reverse is but the inevitable course of fate. I have committed acts which render pardon hopeless. I must await my punishment."

His presentiment was correct. The vengeance of Sidi Abu Said was only to be satisfied by the blood of his rival, and the unfortunate Ahmed was beheaded at Malaga, in the month Jumadi, in the year 559 of the Hegira (April, 1164). When the news was brought to the fickle-hearted Hafsah, she was struck with sorrow and remorse, and put on mourning; recalling his warning words, and reproaching herself with being the cause of his death.

Of the after fortunes of Hafsah I have no further trace than that she died in Morocco, in 1184, outliving both her lovers, for Sidi Abu Said died in Morocco of the plague in 1175. A memorial of his residence in Granada remained in a palace which he built on the banks of the Xenil. The garden of Maumal, the scene of the early lives of Ahmed and Hafsah, is no longer in existence. Its site may be found by the antiquary in poetical research.

The authorities for the foregoing, Alcantara, Hist. Granada. Al Makkari, Hist. Mohamed. Dynasties in Spain, B. ii., c. 3. Notes and illustrations of the same, by Gayangos, v. 1., P. 440. Ibnu Al Kahttib, Biograph. Dic., cited by Gayangos. Conde Hist. Dom. Arab.

AN EXPEDITION IN QUEST OF A DIPLOMA.

ONE of the most important occurrences in the domestic life of the Alhambra, was the departure of Manuel, the nephew of Doña Antonia, for Malaga, to stand examination as a physician. I have already informed the reader that, on his success in obtaining a degree depended in a great measure the union and future fortunes of himself and his cousin Dolores ; at least so I was privately informed by Mateo Ximenes, and various circumstances concurred to corroborate his information. Their courtship, however, was carried on very quietly and discreetly, and I scarce think I should have discovered it, if I had not been put on the alert by the all-observant Mateo.

In the present instance, Dolores was less on the reserve, and had busied herself for several days in fitting out honest Manuel for his expedition. All his clothes had been arranged and packed in the neatest order, and above all she had worked a smart Andalusian travelling jacket for him with her own hands. On the morning appointed for his departure, a stout mule on which he was to perform the journey was paraded at the portal of the Alhambra, and Tio Polo (Uncle Polo), an old invalid soldier, attended to caparison him. This veteran was one of the curiosities of the place. He had a leathern lantern visage, tanned in the tropics, a long Roman nose, and a black beetle eye. I had frequently observed him reading, apparently with intense interest, an old parchment-bound volume; sometimes he would be surrounded by a group of his brother invalids; some seated on the parapets, some lying on the grass, listening with fixed attention, while he read slowly and deliberately out of his favorite work, sometimes pausing to explain or expound for the benefit of his less enlightened auditors.

I took occasion one day to inform myself of this ancient book, which appeared to be his *vade mecum*, and found it to be an odd volume of the works of Padre Benito Geronymo Feyjoo; and that one which treats about the Magic of Spain, the mysterious caves of Salamanca and Toledo, the Purgatory of San Patricio (St. Patrick), and other mystic subjects of the kind. From that time I kept my eye upon the veteran.

On the present occasion, I amused myself with watching him fit out the steed of Manuel with all the forecast of an old campaigner. First, he took a considerable time in adjusting to the back of the mule a cumbrous saddle of antique fashion, high in front and behind, with Moorish stirrups like shovels; the whole looking like a relic of the old armory of the Alhambra; then a fleecy sheep-skin was accommodated to the deep seat of the saddle; then a maleta, neatly packed by the hand of Dolores, was buckled behind; then a manta was thrown over it to serve either as cloak or couch; then the all-important alforjas, carefully stocked with provant, were hung in front, together with the bota, or leathern bottle for either wine or water, and lastly the trabucho, which the old soldier slung behind, giving it his benediction. It was like the fitting out in old times of a Moorish cavalier for a foray or a joust in the Vivarrambla. A number of the lazzaroni of the fortress had gathered round, with some of the invalids, all looking on, all offering their aid, and all giving advice, to the great annoyance of Tio Polo.

When all was ready Manuel took leave of the household; Tio Polo held his stirrup while he mounted; adjusted the girths and saddle, and cheered him off in military style; then turning to Dolores, who stood admiring her cavalier as he trotted off; " Ah Dolorocita," exclaimed he, with a nod and a wink, " *es muy guapo Manuelito in su Xaqueta*," (Ah Dolores, Manuel is mighty fine in his jacket.)   The little damsel blushed and laughed, and ran into the house.

Days elapsed without tidings from Manuel, though he had promised to write.   The heart of Dolores began to misgive her. Had any thing happened to him on the road?   Had he failed in his examination?   A circumstance occurred in her little household to add to her uneasiness and fill her mind with foreboding.   It was almost equal to the escapado of her pigeon. Her tortoise-shell cat eloped at night and clambered to the tiled roof of the Alhambra.   In the dead of the night there was a fearful caterwauling; some grimalkin was uncivil to her; then there was a scramble; then a clapper-clawing; then both parties rolled off the roof and tumbled from a great height among the trees on the hill side.   Nothing more was seen or heard of the fugitive, and poor Dolores considered it but the prelude to greater calamities.

At the end of ten days, however, Manuel returned in triumph, duly authorized to kill or cure; and all Dolores' cares were over. There was a general gathering in the evening, of the humble friends and hangers-on of Dame Antonio to congratulate her, and to pay their respects to *el Señor Medico*, who, peradventure, at some future day, might have all their lives in his hands. One of the most important of these guests was old Tio Polo; and I gladly seized the occasion to prosecute my acquaintance with him. " Oh Señor," cried Dolores, " you who are so eager to learn all the old histories of the Alhambra. Tio Polo knows more about them than any one else about the place. More than Mateo Ximenes and his whole family put together. *Vaya*— *Vaya*—Tio Polo, tell the Señor all those stories you told us one evening, about enchanted Moors, and the haunted bridge over the Darro, and the old stone pomegranates, that have been there since the days of King Chico.

It was some time before the old invalid could be brought into a narrative vein. He shook his head—they were all idle tales; not worthy of being told to a cavallero like myself. It was only by telling some stories of the kind myself I at last got him to open his budget. It was a whimsical farrago, partly made up of what he had heard in the Alhambra, partly of what he had read in Padre Feyjoo. I will endeavor to give the reader the substance of it, but I will not promise to give it in the very words of Tio Polo.

THE LEGEND OF THE ENCHANTED SOLDIER.

Every body has heard of the Cave of St. Cyprian at Salamanca, where in old times judicial astronomy, necromancy, chiromancy, and other dark and damnable arts were secretly taught by an ancient sacristan; or, as some will have it, by the devil himself, in that disguise. The cave has long been shut up and the very site of it forgotten; though, according to tradition, the entrance was somewhere about where the stone cross stands in the small square of the seminary of Carvajal; and this tradition appears in some degree corroborated by the circumstances of the following story.

There was at one time a student of Salamanca, Don Vicente by name, of that merry but mendicant class, who set out on the road to learning without a penny in pouch for the journey, and who, during college vacations, beg from town to town and village to village to raise funds to enable them to pursue their studies through the ensuing term. He was now about to set forth on his wanderings; and being somewhat musical, slung on his back a guitar with which to amuse the villagers, and pay for a meal or a night's lodgings.

As he passed by the stone cross in the seminary square, he pulled off his hat and made a short invocation to St. Cyprian, for good luck; when casting his eyes upon the earth, he perceived something glitter at the foot of the cross. On picking it up, it proved to be a seal ring of mixed metal, in which gold and silver appeared to be blended. The seal bore as a device two triangles crossing each other, so as to form a star. This device is said to be a cabalistic sign, invented by king Solomon the wise, and of mighty power in all cases of enchantment; but the honest student, being neither sage nor conjurer, knew nothing of the matter. He took the ring as a present from St. Cyprian in reward of his prayer; slipped it on his finger, made a bow to the cross, and strumming his guitar, set off merrily on his wandering.

The life of a mendicant student in Spain is not the most miserable in the world; especially if he has any talent at making himself agreeable. He rambles at large from village to village, and city to city, wherever curiosity or caprice may conduct him. The country curates, who, for the most part, have been mendicant students in their time, give him shelter for the night, and a comfortable meal, and often enrich him with several quartos, or half-pence in the morning. As he presents himself from door to door in the streets of the cities, he meets with no harsh rebuff, no chilling contempt, for there is no disgrace attending his mendicity, many of the most learned men in Spain having commenced their career in this manner; but if, like the student in question, he is a good looking varlet and a merry companion; and, above all, if he can play the guitar, he is sure of a hearty welcome among the peasants, and smiles and favors from their wives and daughters.

In this way, then, did our ragged and musical son of learning make his way over half the kingdom; with the fixed determination to visit the famous city of Granada before his

return. Sometimes he was gathered for the night into the fold
of some village pastor; sometimes he was sheltered under the
humble but hospitable roof of the peasant. Seated at the cottage door with his guitar, he delighted the simple folk with his
ditties; or striking up a fandango or bolero, set the brown
country lads and lasses dancing in the mellow twilight. In the
morning he departed with kind words from host and hostess,
and kind looks and, peradventure, a squeeze of the hand from
the daughter.

At length he arrived at the great object of his musical vaga-
bondizing, the far-famed city of Granada, and hailed with wonder
and delight its Moorish towers, its lovely vega and its snowy
mountains glistering through a summer atmosphere. It is needless to say with what eager curiosity he entered its gates and
wandered through its streets, and gazed upon its oriental monuments. Every female face peering through a window or beaming
from a balcony was to him a Zorayda or a Zelinda, nor could he
meet a stately dame on the Alameda but he was ready to fancy
her a Moorish princess, and to spread his student's robe beneath
her feet.

His musical talent, his happy humor, his youth and his good
looks, won him a universal welcome in spite of his ragged robes,
and for several days he led a gay life in the old Moorish capital
and its environs. One of his occasional haunts was the fountain
of Avellanos, in the valley of the Darro. It is one of the popular
resorts of Granada, and has been so since the days of the Moors;
and here the student had an opportunity of pursuing his studies
of female beauty; a branch of study to which he was a little
prone.

Here he would take his seat with his guitar, improvise love-ditties to admiring groups of majos and majas, or prompt with his music the ever ready dance. He was thus engaged one evening, when he beheld a padre of the church advancing at whose approach every one touched the hat. He was evidently a man of consequence; he certainly was a mirror of good if not of holy living; robust and rosy-faced, and breathing at every pore, with the warmth of the weather and the exercise of the walk. As he passed along he would every now and then draw a maravedi out of his pocket and bestow it on a beggar, with an air of signal beneficence. "Ah, the blessed father!" would be the cry; "long life to him, and may he soon be a bishop!"

To aid his steps in ascending the hill he leaned gently now and then on the arm of a handmaid, evidently the pet-lamb of this kindest of pastors. Ah, such a damsel! Andalus from head to foot: from the rose in her hair, to the fairy shoe and lacework stocking; Andalus in every movement; in every undulation of the body:—ripe, melting Andalus!—But then so modest!—so shy!—ever, with downcast eyes, listening to the words of the padre; or, if by chance she let flash a side glance, it was suddenly checked and her eyes once more cast to the ground.

The good padre looked benignantly on the company about the fountain, and took his seat with some emphasis on a stone bench, while the handmaid hastened to bring him a glass of sparkling water. He sipped it deliberately and with a relish, tempering it with one of those spongy pieces of frosted eggs and sugar so dear to Spanish epicures, and on returning the glass to the hand of the damsel pinched her cheek with infinite loving-kindness.

"Ah, the good pastor!" whispered the student to himself; "what a happiness would it be to be gathered into his fold with such a pet-lamb for a companion!"

18

But no such good fare was likely to befall him. In vain he essayed those powers of pleasing which he had found so irresistible with country curates and country lasses. Never had he touched his guitar with such skill; never had he poured forth more soul-moving ditties, but he had no longer a country curate or country lass to deal with. The worthy priest evidently did not relish music, and the modest damsel never raised her eyes from the ground. They remained but a short time at the fountain; the good padre hastened their return to Granada. The damsel gave the student one shy glance in retiring; but it plucked the heart out of his bosom!

He inquired about them after they had gone. Padre Tomás was one of the saints of Granada, a model of regularity; punctual in his hour of rising; his hour of taking a paseo for an appetite; his hours of eating; his hour of taking his siesta; his hour of playing his game of tresillo, of an evening, with some of the dames of the Cathedral circle; his hour of supping, and his hour of retiring to rest, to gather fresh strength for another day's round of similar duties. He had an easy sleek mule for his riding; a matronly housekeeper skilled in preparing tit-bits for his table; and the pet lamb, to smooth his pillow at night and bring him his chocolate in the morning.

Adieu now to the gay, thoughtless life of the student; the side glance of a bright eye had been the undoing of him. Day and night he could not get the image of this most modest damsel out of his mind. He sought the mansion of the padre. Alas! it was above the class of houses accessible to a strolling student like himself. The worthy padre had no sympathy with him; he had never been *Estudiante sopista,* obliged to sing for his supper. He blockaded the house by day, catching a glance of the damsel now and then as she appeared at a casement ; but these glances only fed his flame without encouraging his hope.   He serenaded her balcony at night, and at one time was flattered by the appearance of something white at a window.   Alas, it was only the nightcap of the padre.

Never was lover more devoted ; never damsel more shy : the poor student was reduced to despair.   At length arrived the eve of St. John, when the lower classes of Granada swarm into the country, dance away the afternoon, and pass midsummer's night on the banks of the Darro and the Xenil.   Happy are they who on this eventful night can wash their faces in those waters just as the Cathedral bell tells midnight ; for at that precise moment they have a beautifying power.   The student, having nothing to do, suffered himself to be carried away by the holiday-seeking throng until he found himself in the narrow valley of the Darro, below the lofty hill and ruddy towers of the Alhambra. The dry bed of the river ; the rocks which border it ; the terraced gardens which overhang it were alive with variegated groups, dancing under the vines and fig-trees to the sound of the guitar and castanets.

The student remained for some time in doleful dumps, leaning against one of the huge misshapen stone pomegranates which adorn the ends of the little bridge over the Darro.   He cast a wistful glance upon the merry scene, where every cavalier had his dame ; or, to speak more appropriately, every Jack his Jill ; sighed at his own solitary state, a victim to the black eye of the most unapproachable of damsels, and repined at his ragged garb, which seemed to shut the gate of hope against him.

By degrees his attention was attracted to a neighbor equally solitary with himself.   This was a tall soldier, of a stern aspect and grizzled beard, who seemed posted as a sentry at the opposite pomegranate. His face was bronzed by time; he was arrayed in ancient Spanish armor, with buckler and lance, and stood immovable as a statue. What surprised the student was, that though thus strangely equipped, he was totally unnoticed by the passing throng, albeit that many almost brushed against him.

"This is a city of old-time peculiarities," thought the student, "and doubtless this is one of them with which the inhabitants are too familiar to be surprised." His own curiosity, however, was awakened, and being of a social disposition, he accosted the soldier.

"A rare old suit of armor that which you wear, comrade. May I ask what corps you belong to?"

The soldier gasped out a reply from a pair of jaws which seemed to have rusted on their hinges.

"The royal guard of Ferdinand and Isabella."

"Santa Maria! Why, it is three centuries since that corps was in service."

"And for three centuries have I been mounting guard. Now I trust my tour of duty draws to a close. Dost thou desire fortune?"

The student held up his tattered cloak in reply.

"I understand thee. If thou hast faith and courage, follow me, and thy fortune is made."

"Softly, comrade, to follow thee would require small courage in one who has nothing to lose but life and an old guitar, neither of much value; but my faith is of a different matter, and not to be put in temptation. If it be any criminal act by which I am to mend my fortune, think not my ragged cloak will make me undertake it."

The soldier turned on him a look of high displeasure. "My sword," said he, "has never been drawn but in the cause of the faith and the throne. I am a *Cristiano viejo*, trust in me and fear no evil."

The student followed him wondering. He observed that no one heeded their conversation, and that the soldier made his way through the various groups of idlers unnoticed, as if invisible.

Crossing the bridge, the soldier led the way by a narrow and steep path past a Moorish mill and aqueduct, and up the ravine which separates the domains of the Generalife from those of the Alhambra. The last ray of the sun shone upon the red battlements of the latter, which beetled far above ; and the convert bells were proclaiming the festival of the ensuing day. The ravine was overshadowed by fig-trees, vines, and myrtles, and the outer towers and walls of the fortress. It was dark and lonely, and the twilight-loving bats began to flit about. At length the soldier halted at a remote and ruined tower, apparently intended to guard a Moorish aqueduct. He struck the foundation with the but-end of his spear. A rumbling sound was heard, and the solid stones yawned apart, leaving an opening as wide as a door.

"Enter in the name of the Holy Trinity," said the soldier, "and fear nothing." The student's heart quaked, but he made the sign of the cross, muttered his Ave Maria, and followed his mysterious guide into a deep vault cut out of the solid rock under the tower, and covered with Arabic inscriptions. The soldier pointed to a stone seat hewn along one side of the vault. "Behold," said he, "my couch for three hundred ye rs." The bewildered student tried to force a joke. "By the blessed St. Anthony," said he, "but you must have slept soundly, considering the hardness of your couch."

" On the contrary, sleep has been a stranger to these eyes; incessant watchfulness has been my doom. Listen to my lot. I was one of the royal guards of Ferdinand and Isabella; but was taken prisoner by the Moors in one of their sorties, and confined a captive in this tower. When preparations were made to surrender the fortress to the Christian sovereigns, I was prevailed upon by an Alfaqui, a Moorish priest, to aid him in secreting some of the treasures of Boabdil in this vault. I was justly punished for my fault. The Alfaqui was an African necromancer, and by his infernal arts cast a spell upon me—to guard his treasures. Something must have happened to him, for he never returned, and here have I remained ever since, buried alive. Years and years have rolled away; earthquakes have shaken this hill; I have heard stone by stone of the tower above tumbling to the ground, in the natural operation of time; but the spell-bound walls of this vault set both time and earthquakes at defiance.

" Once every hundred years, on the vestival of St. John, the enchantment ceases to have thorough sway ; I am permitted to go forth and post myself upon the bridge of the Darro, where you met me, waiting until some one shall arrive who may have power to break this magic spell. I have hitherto mounted guard there in vain. I walk as in a cloud, concealed from mortal sight. You are the first to accost me for now three hundred years. I behold the reason. I see on your finger the seal-ring of Solomon the wise, which is proof against all enchantment. With you it remains to deliver me from this awful dungeon, or to leave me to keep guard here for another hundred years."

The student listened to this tale in mute wonderment. He had heard many tales of treasure shut up under strong enchantment in the vaults of the Alhambra, but had treated them as fables. He now felt the value of the seal-ring, which had, in a manner, been given to him by St. Cyprian. Still, though armed by so potent a talisman, it was an awful thing to find himself tête-a-tête in such a place with an enchanted soldier, who, according to the laws of nature, ought to have been quietly in his grave for nearly three centuries.

A personage of this kind, however, was quite out of the ordinary run, and not to be trifled with, and he assured him he might rely upon his friendship and good will to do every thing in his power for his deliverance.

"I trust to a motive more powerful than friendship," said the soldier.

He pointed to a ponderous iron coffer, secured by locks inscribed with Arabic characters. "That coffer," said he, "contains countless treasure in gold and jewels, and precious stones. Break the magic spell by which I am enthralled, and one half of this treasure shall be thine."

"But how am I to do it?"

"The aid of a Christian priest, and a Christian maid is necessary. The priest to exorcise the powers of darkness; the damsel to touch this chest with the seal of Solomon. This must be done at night. But have a care. This is solemn work, and not to be effected by the carnal-minded. The priest must be a *Cristiano viejo*, a model of sanctity; and must mortify the flesh before he comes here, by a rigorous fast of four-and-twenty hours: and as to the maiden, she must be above reproach, and proof against temptation. Linger not in finding such aid. In three days my furlough is at an end; if not delivered before midnight of the third, I shall have to mount guard for another century.

"Fear not," said the student, "I have in my eye the very

priest and damsel you describe ; but how am I to regain admis-
sion to this tower ?"

" The seal of Solomon will open the way for thee."

The student issued forth from the tower much more gayly
than he had entered. The wall closed behind him, and remained
solid as before.

The next morning he repaired boldly to the mansion of the
priest, no longer a poor strolling student, thrumming his way
with a guitar ; but an ambassador from the shadowy world, with
enchanted treasures to bestow. No particulars are told of his
negotiation, excepting that the zeal of the worthy priest was
easily kindled at the idea of rescuing an old soldier of the faith
and a strong box of King Chico from the very clutches of Satan ;
and then what alms might be dispensed, what churches built,
and how many poor relatives enriched with the Moorish treasure !

As to the immaculate handmaid, she was ready to lend her
hand, which was all that was required, to the pious work ; and
if a shy glance now and then might be believed, the ambassador
began to find favor in her modest eyes.

The greatest difficulty, however, was the fast to which the good
Padre had to subject himself. Twice he attempted it, and twice
the flesh was too strong for the spirit. It was only on the third
day that he was enabled to withstand the temptations of the
cupboard ; but it was still a question whether he would hold out
until the spell was broken.

At a late hour of the night the party groped their way up
the ravine by the light of a lantern, and bearing a basket with
provisions for exorcising the demon of hunger so soon as the
other demons should be laid in the Red Sea.

The seal of Solomon opened their way into the tower. They found the soldier seated on the enchanted strong-box, awaiting their arrival. The exorcism was performed in due style. The damsel advanced and touched the locks of the coffer with the seal of Solomon. The lid flew open; and such treasures of gold and jewels and precious stones as flashed upon the eye!

" Here's cut and come again!" cried the student, exultingly, as he proceeded to cram his pockets.

" Fairly and softly," exclaimed the soldier. " Let us get the coffer out entire, and then divide."

They accordingly went to work with might and main; but it was a difficult task; the chest was enormously heavy, and had been imbedded there for centuries. While they were thus employed the good dominie drew on one side and made a vigorous onslaught on the basket, by way of exorcising the demon of hunger which was raging in his entrails. In a little while a fat capon was devoured, and washed down by a deep potation of Val de peñas; and, by way of grace after meat, he gave a kind-hearted kiss to the pet lamb who waited on him. It was quietly done in a corner, but the tell-tale walls babbled it forth as if in triumph. Never was chaste salute more awful in its effects. At the sound the soldier gave a great cry of despair; the coffer, which was half raised, fell back in its place and was locked once more. Priest, student, and damsel, found themselves outside of the tower, the wall of which closed with a thundering jar. Alas! the good Padre had broken his fast too soon!

When recovered from his surprise, the student would have re-entered the tower, but learnt to his dismay that the damsel, in her fright, had let fall the seal of Solomon; it remained within the vault.

18*

In a word, the cathedral bell tolled midnight; the spell was renewed; the soldier was doomed to mount guard for another hundred years, and there he and the treasure remain to this day —and all because the kind-hearted Padre kissed his handmaid. "Ah father! father!" said the student, shaking his head rucfully, as they returned down the ravine, "I fear there was less of the saint than the sinner in that kiss!"

Thus ends the legend as far as it has been authenticated. There is a tradition, however, that the student had brought off treasure enough in his pocket to set him up in the world; that he prospered in his affairs, that the worthy Padre gave him the pet lamb in marriage, by way of amends for the blunder in the vault; that the immaculate damsel proved a pattern for wives as she had been for handmaids, and bore her husband a numerous progeny; that the first was a wonder; it was born seven months after her marriage, and though a seven months boy, was the sturdiest of the flock. The rest were all born in the ordinary course of time.

The story of the enchanted soldier remains one of the popular traditions of Granada, though told in a variety of ways; the common people affirm that he still mounts guard on mid-summer eve, beside the gigantic stone pomegranate on the Bridge of the Darro; but remains invisible excepting to such lucky mortal as may possess the seal of Solomon.

NOTES TO THE ENCHANTED SOLDIER.

Among the ancient superstitions of Spain, were those of the existence of profound caverns in which the magic arts were taught, either by the devil in person, or some sage devoted to his service. One of the most famous of these caves, was at Salamanca. Don Francisco de Torreblanca makes mention of it in the first book of his work on Magic, C. 2, No. 4. The devil was said to play the part of Oracle there; giving replies to those who repaired thither to propoun· fateful questions, as in the celebrated cave of Trophonius. Don Francisco, though he records this story, does not put faith in it: he gives it however as certain, that a Sacristan, named Clement Potosi, taught secretly the magic arts in that cave. Padre Feyjoo, who inquired into the matter, reports it as a vulgar belief, that the devil himself taught those arts there; admitting only seven disciples at a time, one of whom, to be determined by lot, was to be devoted to him body and soul for ever. Among one of these sets of students, was a young man, son of the Marquis de Villena, on whom, after having accomplished his studies, the lot fell. He succeeded, however, in cheating the devil; leaving him his shadow instead of his body.

Don Juan de Dios, Professor of Humanities in the University, in the early part of the last century, gives the following version of the story, extracted, as he says, from an ancient manuscript. It will be perceived he has marred the supernatural part of the tale, and ejected the devil from it altogether.

As to the fable of the Cave of San Cyprian, says he, all that we have been able to verify is, that where the stone cross stands, in the small square or place called by the name of the Seminary of Carvajal, there was the parochial church of San Cyprian. A descent of twenty steps led down to a subterranean Sacristy, spacious and vaulted like a cave. Here a Sacristan once taught magic, judicial astrology, geomancy, hydromancy, pyromancy, acromancy, chiromancy, necromancy, &c.

The extract goes on to state that seven students engaged at a time with the Sacristan, at a fixed stipend. Lots were cast among them which one of their number should pay for the whole, with the understanding that he on whom the lot fell, if he did not pay promptly, should be detained in a chamber of the Sacristy, until the funds were forthcoming. This became thenceforth the usual practice.

On one occasion the lot fell on Henry de Villena, son of the marquis of the same name. He having perceived that there had been trick and shuffling in the casting of the lot, and suspecting the Sacristan to be cognizar{ thereof refused to pay. He was forthwith left in limbo. It so happened, that in a dark corner of the Sacristy was a huge jar or earthen reservoir for water, which was cracked and empty. In this the youth contrived to conceal himself. The Sacristan returned at night with a servant, bringing lights and a supper. Unlocking the door, they found no one in the vault, and a book of magic lying open on the table. They retreated in dismay, leaving the door open, by which Villena made his escape. The story went about that through magic he had made himself invisible.—The reader has now both versions of the story, and may make his choice. I will only observe that the sages of the Alhambra incline to the diabolical one.

This Henry de Villena flourished in the time of Juan II, King of Castile, of whom he was uncle. He became famous for his knowledge of the Natural Sciences; and hence, in that ignorant age was stigmatized as a necromancer. Fernan Perez de Guzman, in his account of distinguished men, gives him credit for great learning, but says he devoted himself to the arts of divination, the interpretation of dreams, of signs, and portents.

At the death of Villena, his library fell into the hands of the King, who was warned that it contained books treating of magic, and not proper to be read. King Juan ordered that they should be transported in carts to the residence of a reverend prelate to be examined. The prelate was less learned than devout. Some of the books treated of mathematics, others of astronomy, with figures and diagrams, and planetary signs; others of chemistry or alchemy, with foreign and mystic words. All these were necromancy in the eyes of the pious prelate, and the books were consigned to the flames, like the library of Don Quixote.

THE SEAL OF SOLOMON.—The device consists of two equilateral triangles, interlaced so as to form a star, and surrounded by a circle. According to Arab tradition, when the Most High gave Solomon the choice of blessings, and he chose wisdom, there came from heaven a ring, on which this device was engraven. This mystic talisman was the arcanum of his wisdom, felicity, and grandeur; by this he governed and prospered. In consequence of a temporary lapse from virtue, he lost the ring in the sea, and was at once reduced to the level of ordinary men. By penitence and prayer he made his peace with the Deity, was permitted to find his ring again in the belly of a fish, and thus recovered his celestial gifts. That he might not utterly lose them again, he communicated to others the secret of the marvellous ring.

This symbolical seal we are told was sacrilegiously used by the Mahometan infidels; and before them by the Arabian idolaters, and before them by the Hebrews, for "diabolical enterprises and abominable superstitions." Those who wish to be more thoroughly informed on the subject, will do well to consult the learned Father Athanasius Kirker's treatise on the *Cabala Sarracenica.*

A word more to the curious reader. There are many persons in these skeptical times, who affect to deride every thing connected with the occult sciences, or black art; who have no faith in the efficacy of conjurations, incantations or divinations; and who stoutly contend that such things never had existence. To such determined unbelievers the testimony of past ages is as nothing; they require the evidence of their own senses, and deny that such arts and practices have prevailed in days of yore, simply because they meet with no instance of them in the present day. They cannot perceive that, as the world became versed in the natural sciences, the supernatural became superfluous and fell into disuse; and that the hardy inventions of art superseded the mysteries of magic. Still, say the enlightened few, those mystic powers exist, though in a latent state, and untasked by the ingenuity of man. A talisman is still a talisman, possessing all its indwelling and awful properties; though it may have lain dormant for ages at the bottom of the sea, or in the dusty cabinet of the antiquary.

The signet of Solomon the Wise, for instance, is well known to have held potent control over genii, demons, and enchantments; now who will positively assert that the same mystic signet, wherever it may exist, does not at the present moment possess the same marvellous virtues which distinguished it in the olden time? Let those who doubt repair to Salamanca, delve into the cave of San Cyprian, explore its hidden secrets, and decide. As to those who will not be at the pains of such investigation, let them substitute faith for incredulity, and receive with honest credence the foregoing legend.

THE AUTHOR'S FAREWELL TO GRANADA.

My serene and happy reign in the Alhambra, was suddenly brought to a close by letters which reached me, while indulging in oriental luxury in the cool hall of the baths, summoning me away from my Moslem elysium to mingle once more in the bustle and business of the dusty world. How was I to encounter its toils and turmoils, after such a life of repose and reverie! How was I to endure its common-place, after the poetry of the Alhambra!

But little preparation was necessary for my departure. A two-wheeled vehicle, called a tartana, very much resembling a covered cart, was to be the travelling equipage of a young Englishman and myself through Murcia, to Alicant and Valencia, on our way to France; and a long-limbed varlet, who had been a contrabandista, and, for aught I knew, a robber, was to be our guide and guard. The preparations were soon made, but the departure was the difficulty. Day after day was it postponed; day after day was spent in lingering about my favorite haunts, and day after day they appeared more delightful in my eyes.

The social and domestic little world also, in which I had been moving, had become singularly endeared to me; and the concern evinced by them at my intended departure, convinced me that my kind feelings were reciprocated. Indeed, when at length the day arrived, I did not dare venture upon a leave-taking at the good dame Antonia's; I saw the soft heart of little Dolores, at least, was brim full and ready for an overflow. So I bade a silent adieu to the palace and its inmates, and descended into the city, as if intending to return. There, however, the tartana and the guide were ready; so, after taking a noonday's repast with my fellow traveller at the Posada, I set out with him on our journey.

Humble was the cortege and melancholy the departure of El Rey Chico the second ! Manuel, the nephew of Tia Antonia, Mateo, my officious but now disconsolate squire, and two or three old invalids of the Alhambra with whom I had grown into gossiping companionship, had come down to see me off; for it is one of the good old customs of Spain, to sally forth several miles to meet a coming friend, and to accompany him as far on his departure. Thus then we set out, our long-legged guard striding ahead, with his escopeta on his shoulder; Manuel and Mateo on each side of the tartana, and the old invalids behind.

At some little distance to the north of Granada, the road gradually ascends the hills; here I alighted and walked up slowly with Manuel, who took this occasion to confide to me the secret of his heart and of all those tender concerns between himself and Dolores, with which I had been already informed by the all knowing and all revealing Mateo Ximenes. His doctor's diploma had prepared the way for their union, and nothing more was wanting but the dispensation of the Pope, on account of their consanguinity. Then, if he could get the post of Medico of the fortress, his happiness would be complete ! I congratulated him on the judgment and good taste he had shown in his choice of a helpmate; invoked all possible felicity on their union, and trusted that the abundant affections of the kind-hearted little Dolores would in time have more stable objects to occupy them than recreant cats and truant pigeons

It was indeed a sorrowful parting when I took leave of these good people and saw them slowly descend the hills ; now and then turning round to wave me a last adieu. Manuel, it is true, had cheerful prospects to console him, but poor Mateo seemed perfectly cast down. It was to him a grievous fall from the station of prime minister and historiographer, to his old brown cloak and his starveling mystery of ribbon-weaving ; and the poor devil, notwithstanding his occasional officiousness, had, somehow or other, acquired a stronger hold on my sympathies than I was aware of. It would have really been a consolation in parting, could I have anticipated the good fortune in store for him, and to which I had contributed ; for the importance I had appeared to give to his tales and gossip and local knowledge, and the frequent companionship in which I had indulged him in the course of my strolls, had elevated his idea of his own qualifications and opened a new career to him ; and the son of the Alhambra has since become its regular and well-paid cicerone ; insomuch that I am told he has never been obliged to resume the ragged old brown cloak in which I first found him.

Towards sunset I came to where the road wound into the mountains, and here I paused to take a last look at Granada. The hill on which I stood commanded a glorious view of the city, the Vega, and the surrounding mountains. It was at an opposite point of the compass from *La cuesta de las lagrimas* (the hill of tears) noted for the " last sigh of the Moor." I now could realize something of the feelings of poor Boabdil when he bade adieu to the paradise he was leaving behind, and beheld before him a rugged and sterile road conducting him to exile.

The setting sun as usual shed a melancholy effulgence on the ruddy towers of the Alhambra. I could faintly discern the balconied window of the tower of Comares, where I had indulged in so many delightful reveries. The bosky groves and gardens about the city were richly gilded with the sunshine, the purple haze of a summer evening was gathering over the Vega; every thing was lovely, but tenderly and sadly so, to my parting gaze.

" I will hasten from this prospect," thought I, " before the sun is set. I will carry away a recollection of it clothed in all its beauty."

With these thoughts I pursued my way among the mountains A little further and Granada, the Vega, and the Alhambra, were shut from my view; and thus ended one of the pleasantest dreams of a life, which the reader perhaps may think has been but too much made up of dreams.

THE END